THE RUSSIAN HERO IN MODERN CHINESE FICTION

SUNY Series in Chinese Philosophy and Culture
David L. Hall and Roger T. Ames, Editors

The Russian Hero
in Modern Chinese Fiction

Mau-sang Ng

THE CHINESE UNIVERSITY PRESS
HONG KONG

STATE UNIVERSITY OF NEW YORK PRESS
NEW YORK

Jointly published by

State University of New York Press
State University Plaza
Albany, New York 12246
U.S.A.

The Chinese University Press
The Chinese University of Hong Kong
Shatin, New Territories
Hong Kong

Printed in the United States of America

For information, address State University of New York Press,
State University Plaza, Albany, N.Y. 12246

Library of Congress Cataloging-in-Publication Data

Ng, Mau-sang.
  The Russian hero in modern Chinese fiction.

  Bibliography: p.
  Includes index.
  1. Chinese fiction—20th century—History and criticism.
2. Russians in literature. I. Title.
PL2443.N45 1988   895.1'35'09352039171   88-2165
ISBN 0-88706-880-4
ISBN 0-88706-881-2 (pbk.)

10 9 8 7 6 5 4 3 2 1

To
Kwong Chung

Contents

Foreword

One of the most difficult, but also one of the most important, things to assess in literary history is the way in which the literature of one culture comes to affect that of another. Such influences are often associated with rapid historical change, or with a sudden renaissance in the arts of the language, culture and society which then acts as an inspiration upon another. In the European Middle Ages the great repository of cultural inspiration were the city states of Italy, principally Florence and Rome. Every cultivated European at that time aspired to speak Italian, and every painter or writer or musician founded his work automatically on Italian models. Often, as in the case of England, these models were received through France, and acquired an added vigour and variety through French interpretation. Chaucer is the greatest English beneficiary of this rich outgoing of literary culture.

With the rise of the novel the picture becomes rather different. Famous and much copied novels suddenly appear in one or another of half a dozen countries—*Don Quixote* in Spain, *La Princesse de Clèves* in France; and then, in the eighteenth century, a series of English novels—Goldsmith's *The Vicar of Wakefield*, Richardson's *Clarissa*, Sterne's *Tristram Shandy*—which became international best sellers and models all over the continent. In the next century the English novel greatly influenced the Russian literary renaissance—sometimes spoken of as the Golden Age of Russian literature—and at every stage of his life the great Tolstoy was always asking his friends to send him new English novels. Goldsmith, Dickens and Sterne had all been formative writers in the development of his own genius, but he was addicted to the English novel, good or bad, as a form of amusement and recreation. That, after all, was the traditional role of the novel in a literate bourgeois society. And it was only with Tolstoy and Dostoevsky themselves (and they both denied that the works they wrote were novels as such: they were what the Russians call *poema*—a long imaginative work, or, as Tolstoy said, a work in its own form which expressed what the writer wished to express) that the novel became fully and for the first time a "serious" and influential force in society, a force making for change, progress and enlightenment.

Dickens and, even more, George Eliot, had already shown the way in England; while in France Balzac and Zola had mapped and analysed society in such a way that its shortcomings were clearly visible, helping to pave the way for Marxist diagnosis and Marxist remedies. By the time of the Russian revolution the novel was firmly established as a prime instrument of propaganda and social change: Stalin was to say that writers were the engineers who would make a new Soviet man, and he and his henchmen had very positive ideas about the kind of novel—the "socialist realist" kind—that was needed to do the job. It was natural that when the Chinese communists turned to Russia for their chief inspiration they should also accept the Soviet version of the novel's form and function in society.

But they did not accept it uncritically. Chinese society is, after all, a very much older affair than anything Russia can show; Chinese understanding of, and distinction in, the arts goes back for thousands of years. So Chinese intellectuals were always critical, and brought their own kinds of tradition and intelligence to these new arts and new political solutions. Lu Xun and the May Fourth writers were of course a primary inspiration, and their works a kind of guideline. As Dr. Mau-sang Ng points out in his lucid and admirably revealing study, Lu Xun used to tell how May Fourth writers in search of guidance "found Russian literature". Lu Xun himself was greatly influenced by it, by Chekhov above all, but his marvellous stories fly clean away from the sources that influenced them, just as Chaucer's did in England from their Italian models, becoming original works of art and specifically Chinese in their own right.

The Russian hero, particularly the downtrodden hero, "the insulted and injured", was of course soon acclimatized to the Chinese literary scene; but again the influence was by no means a simple one, and no models were adopted uncritically. As Dr. Mau-sang Ng shows, the variety of contemporary Chinese heroes is probably richer than in the original Russian sources, and reflects a more rapidly growing and intellectually self-conscious attitude on the part of Chinese novelists and writers. Indeed, as he points out, the time came, at the period of the Cultural Revolution, when the Chinese authors were chiding their Russian colleagues for excessive humanization and individualization of the new hero, who had begun to be shown in the Russian novel of the Khruschev era, with all his personal and non-ideological faults and aspirations. Oddly enough this seems a good sign rather than a bad one; for it shows how independent Chinese reactions had become, and that they would soon be diversifying and humanizing on their own account, and enlarging—as we now see them doing—the potentialities of their own cultural and literary scene.

Dr. Mau-sang Ng's study not only has very great interest for the scholar of comparative literature but it will be absorbing reading for anyone who has a general desire to know more about the cultural background and literary history of contemporary China, and about the literary relation between the two large communist empires. I worked with Dr. Mau-sang Ng for some years in Oxford, and I have the greatest respect for his knowledge and understanding of literature, particularly the novel, his originality as a critic and his liveliness of mind. Such a mind is typical of the Far Eastern Renaissance which we can see coming, and it is a mind to welcome and interpret the new literature such a renaissance will bring.

JOHN BAYLEY
Warton Professor of English,
University of Oxford

Acknowledgements

Part of Chapter Six appeared in an earlier version as "Ba Jin and Russian Literature" in *Chinese Literature: Essays, Articles, Reviews*, and Chapter Seven is an expanded version of an earlier article, "Lu Xun and Russian Literature", published in *Journal of the Institute of Chinese Studies, The Chinese University of Hong Kong*. I wish to thank the editors of both journals for permission to use the published materials.

I am grateful to Professor John Bayley for his tutelage and for honouring this book with his Foreword, to Leo Ou-fan Lee and David E. Pollard for reading the drafts of the manuscript and making many insightful comments, and to many friends and scholars for giving me help and advice at various stages of the writing. Notable among these are the late Sir John Addis, Roger Ames, Peter Brady, Chan Man-hung, John Dent-Young, Glen Dudbridge, Mark Elvin, David Faure, Ge Baoquan, Donald A. Gibbs, David Hawkes, Alan Hirvela, Hu Congjing, Ke Ling, D. C. Lau, Lim Chee Then, Cyril Lin, Donald C. Price, Phillip S. Y. Sun, Tam Yue-him, Tang Tao, Tsim Tak-lung and Wong Kai-chee.

A scholarship from the Commonwealth Scholarship Commission of the United Kingdom and the British Council enabled me to do research at Oxford University and to finish the first draft of the manuscript, and a grant from the United Board for Christian Higher Education in Asia made possible a trip to Shanghai in 1982 to interview Ba Jin. I wish to record my joy at meeting this veteran writer and my gratitude for his advice and encouragement.

Finally, to my wife, Kwong Chung, I wish to acknowledge a very special debt of gratitude.

Abbreviations

AAS	*Asian and African Studies*
AO	*Archiv Orientalni*
BJZJ	*Ba Jin zhuanji* 巴金專集
DFZZ	*Dongfang zazhi* 東方雜誌
HJAS	*Harvard Journal of Asiatic Studies*
LXQJ	*Lu Xun quanji* (1981) 魯迅全集 (1981)
MCL	*Modern Chinese Literature in the May Fourth Era*
MWZJ	*Mao Dun wenyi zalunji* 茅盾文藝雜論集
MY	*Mangyuan* 莽原
QQWJ	*Qu Qiubai wenji* 瞿秋白文集
SW	*Selected Works of Lu Xun*
WXPL	*Wenxue pinglun* 文學評論
WXYJ	*Wenxue yanjiu* 文學研究
WYB	*Wenyi bao* 文藝報
WYFX	*Wenyi fuxing* 文藝復興
WYWX	*Woyu wenxue* 我與文學
XQN	*Xinqingnian* 新青年
XSYB	*Xiaoshuo yuebao* 小說月報
YDWJ	*Yu Dafu wenji* 郁達夫文集
YS	*Yusi* 語絲
ZWCZ	*Zhongguo xiandai wenxueshi cangkao ziliao* 中國現代文學史參考資料
ZXCS	*Zhongguo xiandai chuban shiliao* 中國現代出版史料
ZXD	*Zhongguo xinwenxue daxi* 中國新文學大系

INTRODUCTION
The May Fourth Intellectual Background

Nineteen-forty-two is an important year in modern Chinese literary development. In May of that year Chairman Mao delivered his famous "Talks at the Yan'an Forum on Literature and Art". His speech not only became the guiding light for works to be produced in the years to come, it also heralded the demise of the Westernized intellectual tradition which had evolved since the Literary Revolution of 1917. The Chairman declared that literature must serve the worker, peasant and soldier masses. The future of the intellectuals—people of whom he had always been suspicious—lay in their moulding themselves to a proper mass outlook. What resulted was a highly uniform literature under the banner of communism. The Chairman's scepticism about the intellectuals was not without foundation. In the years since the May Fourth Movement in 1919, the urban intelligentsia took a high profile in national affairs. They were vocal against the Warlords and later against the Nationalist Government, active in the many patriotic movements which marked the turbulent years of the 1920s and 1930s, and intensely concerned with their intellectual autonomy. Many of them saw their critical and patriotic activities as performing the function of an alternative government when the official channels were closed to them.

The rapid rise and concentration in modern China of the new

intellectual class is remarkable. Chinese literati in traditional society worked within the Confucian hierarchy. They owed their advancement in the state bureaucracy to the following factors: their professed loyalty to the Emperor, their ability to succeed in the civil examination, and their exploitation of such connexions as lineage, clan, birthplace and mentor. Social outcasts like Shen Fu, the author of *Fusheng liuji* (Six Records of a Floating Life), were few and far between. As Yu Dafu, himself a product of Confucian teaching who later embraced the tenets of the May Fourth Movement, eloquently remarked: traditional intellectuals lived for the Emperor, the Confucian ethic, and their parents.[1] To sensitive intellectuals like Yu Dafu, such a situation was intolerable. One of the greatest innovations of the May Fourth Movement is precisely the breakdown of this Confucian system. These intellectuals chose to dissociate themselves from the family, which they perceived as rotten; the government, which they criticized as corrupt and oppressive; and traditional ties, which they objected to as an improper method for advancement. In the wake of their enlightenment, many found that they did not belong to any class in society, but were simply "men of letters" without a proper profession, a situation which left them adrift in isolation. Lacking a corporate identity, many of them tended to fall back upon themselves, or relate only to people with similar experiences. Their exposure to Western thinking, especially the body of ideas current in nineteenth-century European thought, helped to inculcate in them a craving for freedom and individuality.[2] Many conceived of themselves as a band of self-conscious protagonists, standing alone in a bleak world, holding high the banner of science, democracy, compassion and a better life. In attempting to uproot what they considered the evil of Confucianism, many modern intellectuals, whether they attained adulthood with the May Fourth Movement or grew up with it, eagerly opened themselves to the influence of Western scientific and universalist thought.

Generally speaking, a Western-orientated tradition, commonly

[1] Introduction to *Zhongguo xinwenxue daxi, sanwen erji*, in *YDMJ*, Vol. 6, p. 261.

[2] See Bonnie McDougall's perceptive study, "The Impact of Western Literary Trends", in Merle Goldman (ed.), *MCL*, pp. 37–61.

known as the May Fourth tradition, evolved in the 1920s.[3] This tradition continued to prevail right up to the outbreak of the Sino-Japanese War in 1937, when intellectual as well as political allegiances were increasingly leaning towards communism. Among the important ingredients of this tradition are the aspirants' cosmopolitan outlook, utopian ideals and romantic notions of revolution. Many were awakened from the Sino-centrism of their imperial past and recognized that China is but a member of the family of nations, and that human beings all over the world share a common destiny. In order to liberate their suffering brethren from the yoke of Confucianism, and to ensure equal and humane treatment for all humanity, they sought a fundamental change in the foundation of Chinese national life. Many held the view that they could only bring about a loving and fraternal China by rejecting the present social order. They believed that it was their mission to expedite the advent of this new society and to help their less fortunate countrymen towards the light. The espousal of such romantic and utopian ideas became the hallmark of May Fourth intellectuals.

Essentially, what distinguished these intellectuals from their fellow revolutionaries was the former's belief in the importance of ideas. They held that by injecting the spirit of democracy, liberalism, scientism and humanitarianism into the national consciousness, by making people aware of the deficiencies of their national character and by working together towards the common good, they could revitalize China. Their problem was that their ideas about intellectual regeneration were vague, and they lacked a programme of action (as, in fact, did their fellow revolutionaries). Many intellectuals of the twenties and thirties remained essentially "men of ideas".

The honouring of "ideas", however, brought about the pre-eminence of the men of letters in May Fourth China. In a society where education was still limited to a fortunate few, the more articulate and outspoken among the educated soon assumed the role of "spokesmen" for their fellow intellectuals, and wielded enormous influence as a result. Leaders of opinion like Lu Xun, Hu Shi, Mao

---

[3] I have followed Goldman's interpretation of the "May Fourth Era" as spanning the period from the Republican Revolution in 1911 to Mao Zedong's "Yan'an Talk" in 1942, and her view of "May Fourth literature" as referring to the works written in that period, particularly in the 1920s and 1930s. Ibid., p. vii.

Dun and Guo Moruo combined the roles of thinker, reformer, critic, litterateur, and even of prophet. It is not surprising that many of these leaders of opinion were regarded by their readers and followers as "the conscience of the age". Just as they idealized the western writers and thinkers who inspired them, their readers also idealized or even idolized them and their works. This trend towards hero-worship, prevalent in the May Fourth intellectual tradition, was later fully exploited by the communist leadership.

The craving for intellectual regeneration also led to the widespread influence of literature, particularly of fictional works. Since the late Qing, fiction had been considered by such leading writers as Liang Qichao to be the most effective instrument of social reform. This inspired a body of "social novels" which formed an important part of the late Qing reform culture. Fiction was elevated to even greater heights by May Fourth writers. They saw fiction as capable of reflecting the moral fabric of society as well as transforming collective human consciousness. But at the same time it was a vehicle for the expression of their own ideas and feelings, and they produced a corpus of fictional works which is, in the words of Průšek, most subjective and individualistic.[4] These works are hero-centred and the drama is often enacted by the writer himself wearing different masks. Social materials serve only as elements to highlight the hero's inner life. The protagonist is invariably an intellectual—individualistic, idealistic, and sensitive, yet also diffident, sentimental and half-hearted. He may embrace the ideal of transforming society and bringing happiness to his fellow men, but he either lacks the will to carry out his purpose, or resorts to nihilistic measures to achieve it. The image of an inadequate, unheroic character vacillating between feeling and intellect, and circumscribed by his consciousness of impending tragedy, figures prominently in May Fourth fiction. This faltering hero-type only begins to lose ground in the mid-1930s. At this point, the worsening conditions in China are felt to require the invention of more heroic figures to inflame the national sensibility in the battle against the Japanese. It is the central argument of the present study that the divided intellectual hero, who is mark-

[4]Průšek, "Subjectivism and Individualism in Modern Chinese Literature", *AO*, 25.2 (1957), pp. 261–286.

edly different from his intellectual predecessors in classical Chinese fiction—the "profligate litterateur" (*caizi*) and the scholar official, owes much of his make-up to the celebrated nineteenth-century Russian superfluous hero and revolutionary Hamlet tradition.

The transcultural May Fourth intellectual climate provided the ideal environment for the growth of Western literary influence in Chinese soil. However, one particular influence, that of the youthful nineteenth-century Russian literature, outshone all others in modern Chinese fiction. As prominent May Fourth writer Zheng Zhenduo wrote unashamedly, Russian literature had first to be introduced before a modern Chinese literature could be created.[5] The works of the great Russian masters like Tolstoy, Dostoevsky, Turgenev, Chekhov and Gorky, as well as a host of less well known or even obscure writers rapidly gained currency in the 1920s and 1930s. While this Russian presence is generally acknowledged, complications arise when one goes a step further to ask how the May Fourth writers' reading and perception of the Russian works shaped their own. It is one thing to say that Gogol's social criticism or Tolstoy's humanitarianism affected someone's conception of life, but quite another to define how such an "influence" cross-fertilizes other elements in the recipients' works. Even if a writer professed a humanitarian outlook and reflected it in his work, such an outlook might have been formed by a variety of influences. The resemblance might be due to similar causes. What looks like an influence may be a parallel or a coincidence. A writer's testimony of his indebtedness to another writer, therefore, can only serve as a starting point for the study of literary influence, otherwise one is liable to fall into the trap of generalization, or even of triviality.

In the twenties when all values in China were being re-assessed, when idealism, liberalism, rationalism, utilitarianism, realism and agnosticism filled the minds of young intellectuals, the literary works which rose to popularity were those that provided the relevant social message or ideological guidance. This explains the immense following of Tolstoy, Dostoevsky, Turgenev, Andreyev, Artzybashev and Ropshin. While the image of the insulted and contrite heroes of

---

[5] Zheng Zhenduo, "Eguo wenxue fada de yuanyin yu yingxiang", *Gaizao*, 3.4 (1920.12), p. 94.

Tolstoy and Dostoevsky gripped the imagination of the Chinese audience, (though the polyphonic nature of Dostoevsky's work, or the multifarious content of Tolstoy's, went largely unappreciated), the impact of the superfluous man or revolutionary Hamlet prototypes in the works of Turgenev, Andreyev, Artzybashev and Ropshin was even greater. It gave rise to a generation of "Russian flavoured" intellectual heroes in May Fourth fiction. The extent of the influence can be revealed by a careful study of the works of four of the most prominent writers of the time—Lu Xun, Yu Dafu, Mao Dun and Ba Jin—all of them enthusiastic advocates of Russian literature. Indeed, the joint efforts by May Fourth writers to depict the real man of their day, and to translate their primary experiences into fictional works brought about a most exciting period of Russian literary influence.

The situation changed considerably after the establishment of the People's Republic. While the pre-revolutionary Russian works sanctioned by the Chinese Communist Party remained in print in the 1950s, it was Soviet literature which enjoyed unrivalled popularity. The works of Stalinist model writers like Fadeyev, Serafimovich, Gladkov, Semonov and Sholokov were fervently promoted by the Chinese Party, which adopted a literary policy more Stalinist than Stalin's own. The urban intelligentsia who had been in the centre of Chinese fiction for half a century had come to the end of the road. Instead, the literary stage was monopolized by the proletarian positive hero who faithfully acts out current Party policy. The call for heroism in literary works reached mythical proportions during the Cultural Revolution. It was only with the eclipse of the Cultural Revolution that the positive hero began to decline. The intellectual hero, suppressed since 1949, has begun to re-surface in recent works of fiction. One can cite the example of the protagonists of two widely read works, Dai Houying's *Man ah, Man!* and Zhao Zhenkai's *Waves*, who represent a change and a continuation of the May Fourth tradition.

A few words must be said concerning the rationale behind this work. Far reaching though the Russian influence was, there is, however, a surprising lack of research on the topic. Several studies have indeed looked into how literary attitudes of individual writers like Lu Xun, Qu Qiubai or Ba Jin were affected by their reading of Russian literature (for example, Fokkema, Pickowicz and Lang). But the larger, more complicated question of how the works of these and other Russian-inspired writers were transformed as a result has until now not been answered. It is to this end that the present book is written. My chief concern is with the rise and fall of the intellectual hero in modern Chinese fiction, and his interaction with his counterpart in nineteenth-century Russian fiction, as it is in this particular area that the Russian presence is most keenly felt. Attention is also paid to the circumstances leading to the rise of nineteenth-century Russian literature in China, the writers' response to it, and the evolution amidst Soviet influences of the intellectual hero in the People's Republic of China. It is hoped that as a pioneering study of its kind, covering the literatures of two countries, extending over a period of more than a century, this work will plough up "virgin soil" and kindle interest in this enormously rich field. Indeed, it is largely the cross-fertilization of ideas and techniques with the West which made the May Fourth one of the most stimulating periods in modern Chinese literary history.

A further word of explanation should be given concerning the concept of literary influence employed in this book. As very few May Fourth writers knew Russian, and none of the four writers in this study read Russian in the period under discussion (Ba Jin managed to learn it afterwards), they relied mostly on English, German or Japanese translations. In their anxiety to play the role of the Chinese "Prothemeus", they were predominantly attracted by the ideas in the Russian works, seldom by the style or the language. In any case, many of the stylistic or linguistic qualities of the originals are lost in translation. Literary influence in this study is therefore primarily concerned with the crossing of cultural frontiers of certain literary ideas, motifs and devices, and the manner and circumstances in which they crossed them. For these reasons, little attempt has been made to engage in textual analysis, although modern structuralist theory has opened new horizons in reception studies. In the final analysis, it is the total involvement of the author in his society, and his view of his works as a kind of moral as well as social criticism, that linked the May Fourth writer to his Russian predecessors. May Fourth fiction may indeed be criticized as naïve and sentimental by readers of today. But the writer's sincerity and his efforts to reflect and sensitize the moral consciousness of his society are unprecedented in the history of Chinese fiction. Signs are not lacking that some writers in today's China are again courageously bearing the torch as champions of just causes. In this they can be seen as the heirs of the May Fourth tradition. The continued toleration of their works and of their efforts to turn up new soil will be one test of the quality of life in China in the coming years.

Part I: The Response to Russian Literature

1 Translations and the Reading Public

I. From Nihilist Tales to Works of Fiction

In 1908, the Polish writer-cum-terrorist Leopold Kampf wrote in a preface to the Chinese translation of his *On the Eve*: ". . . Freedom can only be bought with the spilling of an endless amount of blood—blood of the most righteous kind. . . . In this play is described the struggle of our Russian comrades in the past few decades. . . . Comrades in China, don't you feel their sorrow, don't you see that their ordeal will one day also be passed down to you?"[1] Kampf's play won immediate recognition in China. It was translated more than once, avidly read, and received enthusiastically on stage.[2] Contemporary readers may ask: What was the source of its appeal since the play was of little literary merit and the author was virtually unknown. The most obvious answer is

[1] "*Ye weiyang* xuyan", translated by Yiming (Anonymous). Included in A Ying (ed.), *Wan Qing wenxue congchao, xiaoshuo xiqu yanjiu juan*, p. 306.
[2] *On the Eve* was written in 1905 in German by Kampf. It was translated into French, English and Russian, and performed with considerable success in France in 1907–1908. Li Shizeng, a Chinese student with anarchist aspirations then studying in Paris translated it into *wenyan* (classical) Chinese. It was published in Canton in 1908. Ba Jin later translated this play into *baihua* (modern Chinese), and included it in his *Menkan* (The Threshold), pp. 109–140.

its political content, which depicts the endeavours of the nihilistic heroes in the wake of the 1905 Revolution. Its introduction into China came amidst the growing tide of interest in Russian nihilism amongst the anti-Manchu intellectuals. Many began to imitate the ways and manner of the Russian nihilists. Wu Yue, a key figure who in 1905 risked death by throwing a bomb in an attempt to kill a group of ministers, wrote vehemently:

> At present nothing in the world attracts so much awe and attention as the fame of the Nihilist Party. In what period is the Russian Nihilist Party today? If I dared to be arbitrary I should say that the last half of the nineteenth century was the nihilist's period of assassination and the first half of the twentieth century is their period of revolution. Without the former how could you obtain today's results? Where are the Han people? Where are we, comrades? We, comrades, are in a period of assassination and future years will bring the Han people's period of revolution.[3]

Wu's passionate call not only kindled the enthusiasm of revolutionaries like himself, it also reflected the general temper of many who were intent on liberating themselves from the yoke of Manchu despotism. The apotheosis of the Russian revolutionary Sophia Perovskaya by Chinese men of letters is a case in point. The story of her terrorist activities and eventual execution after an abortive attempt to assassinate Czar Alexandar II was adapted and serialized in Liang Qichao's influential *Xin xiaoshuo* (New Fiction).[4] Her fictionalized biography excited late Qing sensibilities to an overwhelming degree. As the story was unravelled, accolades by leading litterateurs extolling her heroism and self-sacrificing spirit began to pour into the pages of the major magazines.[5] Many saw

---

[3] "Wu Yue yishu", *Tian Tao*, 7–8 and 10, translated by Martin Bernal in *Chinese Socialism to 1907*, p. 201. For a discussion of the influence of the Russian revolutionary tradition on Chinese intellectuals, see Bernal's study, pp. 198–226; Price, *Russian and the Roots of the Chinese Revolution, 1896–1911*, especially Chapter Seven.

[4] The story, which was serialized in *Xinxiaoshuo huipian*, was based on Kemuyama Sentarō's work *Kinsei museifushugi* published in Tokyo, 1902. The author Lingnan yuyi nüshi is the pseudonym of Luo Pu, a follower of Kang Youwei. See Price, ibid., p. 250.

[5] A Ying, as n. 1, pp. 570–572. The appeal of Sophia Perovskaya persisted throughout the May Fourth period. Zhou Zuoren, for example, lamented in 1929 that the courage and unselfish actions of the heroine are something that the Chinese

the Russian nihilists as models of revolutionary virtue; in their vengeful action to restore justice and their courage in dying for the cause they were more valiant than the knights-errant of the Warring States Period.[6] So enchanted was the editor of the popular *Yueyue xiaoshuo* (Fiction Monthly) by the exploits of the Russian activists that he dedicated a special section of his magazine to what he called "nihilist stories". The well-known novelist Zeng Pu devoted a long and important episode of his novel *Nie hai hua* (Flower on a Sea of Evil) to the Russian nihilists, and the novel became one of the most influential bestsellers of the time.[7] As Russian nihilism in China has been the subject of detailed documentation, it suffices to mention here that Chinese readers looked upon the Russian hero or heroine with awe and admiration. The dedication and asceticism of the nihilists served as their guide to revolutionary conduct, and captivated their imagination with the romanticism of revolutionary life.

In view of this background, it is not surprising that during the initial phase of Russo-Chinese literary contact, it was the Russian revolutionary tales which caught the imagination of Chinese readers. Russian literature proper, which was well known and had already made an impact in Europe and Japan, had hardly been heard of in China at this time. Neither did the first Chinese translation of one of these works, Pushkin's *The Captain's Daughter* in 1903, nor those which ensued, Lermontov's *A Hero of Our Time*, Chekhov's *The Black Monk*, or Gorky's *Cain and Artyom*—all of which came out in 1907—arouse any attention.[8] Tolstoy's

---

cannot understand. *YS*, 149 (1929.9.17), p. 451. She is also "the girl on the threshold" of whom Ba Jin wrote with "tears of enthusiasm" in Paris in 1927. See *Menkan*, as n. 2.

[6] Leng, afterword to "Sharen gongsi", *Yueyue xiaoshuo*, No. 17 (1908), p. 5.

[7] A Ying mentioned that within two years of its publication, *Nie hai hua* was reprinted fifteen times, and sold up to 50,000 copies, *Wan Qing xiaoshuo shi*, p. 22. This is a sizable figure, as publishers were using three thousand copies as a break-even target for an initial printing. See Bao Tianxiao, *Chuanyinglou huiyilu*, p. 377; also see Link, *Mandarin Ducks and Butterflies*, p. 149.

[8] Pushkin's story was translated by Ji Yihun under the title of *Eguo qingshi*, Lermontov's, Chekhov's and Gorky's works were all translated by Wu Shou, under the titles of *Yin niukou*, *Heiyi jiaoshi* and *Youhuan yusheng* respectively. See also A Ying, *Xiaoshuo sitan*, pp. 229–246.

Tales of Revolution might have fared slightly better. But what little interest it might have stirred was strictly confined to Christian circles.[9] The first attempt to introduce Russian literature systematically was that by Lu Xun and his brother Zhou Zuoren. Working closely together, the brothers translated and in 1909 published the *Yuwai xiaoshuo ji* (Collection of Short Stories from Abroad) in two volumes, almost entirely at their own expense. Their labour, however, went largely unrewarded at the time. As Zhou Zuoren recalled years later, only twenty-one copies of Volume One were sold, and only twenty of Volume Two. This cold reception deterred them from publishing a third volume, as they had originally intended.[10] It was not until a few years after the founding of the Republic (1911) that more Russian works appeared in Chinese translation. The number, however, remained small. Nor did any of those published ignite the enthusiasm of the reading public. The rise to popularity of Russian literature came only with the advent of the Literary Revolution in 1917. During the next two decades, it became common practice for literary magazines to carry not only translations but also studies of Russian works. In fact, so spontaneous and intense was the interest in Russian literature that even writers of divergent allegiances put aside their differences and promoted with vigour what they believed to be a literature of universal appeal, making it the most widely-read foreign literature in China.[11]

[9] *Tuosi zhongjiao xiaoshuo*, published by the Rhenish Missionary Society of Hong Kong in 1907, was a joint translation by German priest I. Genähr (Ye Daosheng in Chinese) and Mai Meisheng. According to Ge Baoquan, Tolstoy's works may have appeared in Chinese magazines as early as 1905, or even earlier. See his article "Tuoersitai he Zhongguo" in *Tuoersitai yanjiu lunwenji*, pp. 19–21.

[10] Zhou Zuoren, "Guanyu Lu Xun zhier", in *Yuzhou feng*, 30 (1936.12.1), pp. 304–305.

[11] For example, fervent advocates include Shen Yanbing, Zheng Zhenduo of the Association of Literary Studies, and Guo Moruo and Yu Dafu from the rival camp, the Creation Society. And Xu Zhimo, known as the gentleman poet at the time for his leaning towards English literature, says of a conversation with his mentor Katherine Mansfield: "I had the chance to inform her of the recent literary trends in China, ... [and] the influence of Russian writers was most deeply felt in our new fiction." *XSYB*, 14.5 (1923.5), p. 3.

II. Translations I: 1903–1929

It may be difficult to assess the extent of the Russian impact, but this does not prevent our drawing a picture of the popularity of Russian literature in China. One way of doing so is to examine the number of works translated into Chinese in a given period. The earliest list of Western literary works in Chinese translation published in book-form was the one prepared in 1907 by the editor of *Xiaoshuo lin* (Fiction Forest).[12] A total of 123 titles were listed, of which sixty were translations. (We cannot assume that the rest were works by Chinese authors. For example, *The Detective Stories of Sherlock Holmes* appeared twelve times under the section author-translator.) What is interesting from our point of view is that of the sixty-odd translations, thirty-one were by British authors, eight by American, eight by French, two by Russian, and one each by German, Greek and Indian writers, with two unspecified titles. The two Russian works were Chekhov's *The Black Monk* and Lermontov's *A Hero of Our Time.* Judging from the prevalence of the English titles, it hardly needs arguing that in 1907, Russian works were no match in popularity for those by Conan Doyle or H. Rider Haggard.[13]

While the works of Doyle and Haggard were made famous by Lin Shu, and Lin remained till his death a fervent advocate of English literature, we can detect a slight shift of emphasis in his choice of works around 1917. Of the twenty-three works of Haggard that he translated, most were done between 1905–1906, and only six in or after 1917, and he did not translate any Conan Doyle after 1909. In fact, Lin widened his net at this time to include more works from other countries. One remarkable addition was Tolstoy's fiction. A total of ten of the Russian master's works, including *Childhood*

---

[12] *Fiction Forest*, No. 9 (1907.1), pp. 1–10.

[13] *Joan Haste, Jiayin xiaozhuan* in Chinese, was translated in part by Bao Tianxiao in 1898. A complete translation done by Lin Shu appeared in 1905. See *Chuanyinglou huiyilu*, p. 172. Leo Lee points out succinctly that Lin Shu's fascination with the "world of heroism" left him open to the influence of Haggard's adventure stories. Guo Moruo, as Lee points out, also had a high regard for this work. Lee, *The Romantic Generation*, pp. 44–56, 181–182.

Boyhood Youth, The Death of Ivan Ilyich, The Kreutzer Sonata, Domestic Happiness, A Prisoner of the Caucasus, Three Deaths, The Two Hussars, and a number of his parables were translated by him and his partner between 1914–1923.[14] Lin's choice of Russian literature was remarkable in that it reflected a trend which was then beginning to gather momentum in China. In 1913, Ma Junwu's translation of *Resurrection* was published, and in 1917, *Anna Karenina* made its Chinese debut.[15] Two years later, Geng Jizhi, a young student from the Russian School in Beijing began his life-long association with Russian literature. With his classmate Qu Qiubai, he published a translation of Tolstoy's short stories in 1921—some of which first appeared in 1920 in the magazines *Shuguang* (Dawn) and *Xinshehui* (New Society) which they edited.[16] Students of the Russian School played a pioneering role in introducing Russian literature. Apart from Geng and Qu, their colleagues like Shen Ying, An Shouyi and He Qiming formed the core group of translators who worked directly from the original Russian. Together they translated works by Tolstoy, Turgenev, Gogol and others.[17] According to Zheng Zhenduo, a student from the Railway School and a close associate of both Geng and Qu, it was because of their influence that "he wanted to find some Russian novels and plays to read".[18] Later, a fruitful partnership was formed between himself and Geng. Besides translating Chekhov's plays together, each later wrote prefaces to works translated by the

[14] For a list of Lin's translations, see Yu Jiuhong, "Lin Shu fanyi zuopin kaosuo", in *Lin Shu yanjiu zhiliao*, pp. 403–427.

[15] Ma Junwu's translation is called *Xinyu* in Chinese, published by Zhonghua shuju in 1913. According to Ge Baoquan, another translation by Daming *et al.* was serialized in the monthly *Jinbu* in the same year. This translation was however incomplete, as n. 9, p. 22. *Anna Karenina* was translated by Chen Jialun and Chen Dadeng, and published by Zhonghua shuju in 1917.

[16] See *Wusi shiqi qikan jieshao*, Vol. 1(ii), pp. 796–805.

[17] Little is known of these students. The most detailed information to date is to be found in the reminiscences of Zheng Zhenduo about Geng and Qu. See *Zheng Zhenduo wenji*, Vol. 3; Shen Ying's and Wang Tongzhao's reminiscences about Qu Qiubai in *Yi Qiubai*, pp. 105–106, 114–123 respectively, also provide some useful information. An Shouyi translated Pushkin's *The Captain's Daughter*, and He Qiming, Gogol's *The Inspector*. Each translated only one book. Shen Ying was more productive, and his translations include Turgenev's *On the Eve, Faust* and Tolstoy's *The Fruits of Culture*.

[18] *Zheng Zhenduo wenji*, Vol. 3, p. 300.

other. Both were founding members in 1921 of the Association of Literary Studies, which had as one of its main objects the promotion of Russian literature. As to Qu Qiubai, he became in 1920 the first Russia correspondent of *Chen Bao* (Morning Post). His two years' assignment in the Soviet Union brought him first-hand knowledge of the country. Apart from recounting his thoughts and experiences in *Exiang jicheng* (A Journey to the Land of Hunger) and *Chi du xinshi* (Impressions of the Red Capital Seen Through the Mind), he completed in 1922 *Eguo wenxue shi* (A History of Russian Literature). Russian literature was to remain one of his major preoccupations throughout his short life.[19]

Another writer who did much to promote Russian writings is Shen Yanbing (alias Mao Dun), then editor of the influential *Short Story Monthly*. In 1920, Shen drew up a list of foreign works for translation, hoping that Chinese fiction would one day be modernized by adopting Western models. The list, covering a total of forty-four items by nineteen writers from eight countries, shows an unmistakable leaning towards classical Russian literature.[20] In all, twenty-one Russian works by seven of the most important writers were named. Others on the list included three French writers, eight items; one Swedish, three items; one German, two items; two Poles, two items. While the list contained such well-known works as Zola's *La Débâcle*, Ibsen's *The Wild Duck*, Maupassant's "Une Vie", and Shaw's *Three Plays for Puritans*, there can be no doubt that it was the Russian writings, representing as they did some of the most important works in Russian literature, which formed its backbone: Gogol's *Dead Souls*, "The Overcoat", and *The Terrible Cossack*; Turgenev's *A Hunter's Album*, *Fathers and Sons* and *Virgin Soil*; Herzen's *Whose Crime*; Tolstoy's *War and Peace*; Dostoevsky's *Notes from the Underground*, *Crime and Punishment* and *The Idiot*; Chekhov's *The Seagull*, *The Three Sisters*, *Ivanov* and *The Cherry Orchard*, and Gorky's *The Lower Depths* and "Creatures That Once Were Men". Shen excluded from his list such works as Tolstoy's *Resurrection* and *Anna Karenina* or Pushkin's *The Captain's*

[19] See Zheng's introduction to the second volume of *ZXD*, pp. 8–12. For a study of Qu Qiubai, see Pickowicz, *Marxist Literary Thought in China*.

[20] Shen Yanbing, "Xiaoshuo xinchaolan xuanyan", *XSYB*, 11.2 (1920.2), pp. 3–4

Daughter, as they had already been translated. It was his wish that these works and a score of others, such as Goethe's *Faust* and Pushkin's *The Queen of Spades,* would be rendered into Chinese within the year, so that by the end of that period the "foundation of our new literature" would have been established.[21]

Shen's wish, at least as regards translating Russian works, was not a vain one. Although masterpieces such as *War and Peace* and *The Idiot* went untranslated for many years, Chinese intellectuals made strenuous efforts to translate and promote Russian literature at this time, especially the works of Turgenev, Tolstoy, Chekhov and Andreyev. A list of foreign works in Chinese translation published in book form between 1919–1923 shows clearly the predominance of Russian works.[22] A total of 89 titles under the headings of fiction, drama and poetry were included in the list. The number of titles can be tabulated as follows:

	Fiction	Drama	Poetry	Total
Russia	15	18	2	35
France	8	4	—	12
India	4	5	3	12
England	3	8	—	11
Germany	4	1	—	5
Norway	—	4	—	4
Japan	1	2	—	3
Belgium	—	3	—	3
Poland	1	—	—	1
Sweden	—	1	—	1
Austria	—	1	—	1
South Africa	1	—	—	1
Total:	37	47	5	89

[21] Ibid., p. 4. In an article entitled "Ziranzhuyi de Zhongguo wenxue lun" included in Sun Nanggong (ed.), *Xin wenyi pinglun,* the author Li Zhichang mentioned the following works as models for Chinese writers: Ibsen's *Pillars of Society,* Strindberg's *Marriage,* Hauptmann's *Before Sunrise, The Weavers,* Turgenev's *The Hunter's Album,* Goncharov's *Oblomov,* Dostoevsky's *Poor Folks, Crime and Punishment,* and Tolstoy's *War and Peace.*

[22] See Pu Shao (Xu Diaofu), "Chuqi xinwenyi chubanwu bianmu", in ZXCS, Vol. 1, pp. 107–121.

It should be emphasized that the Russian list is more comprehensive and varied than the others. While England is represented on the list primarily by the works of Shakespeare, Oscar Wilde and Bernard Shaw, India by Tagore, Norway by Ibsen and Japan by Moshakoji Saneatsu, Russia provided a number of its most important authors. The list, for example, included Pushkin's *The Captain's Daughter*, Gogol's *The Inspector*, Tolstoy's *Resurrection*, *The Power of Darkness*, *The Man Who Was Dead*, *The Fruits of Culture* and four collections of short stories and parables; Ostrovsky's *Thunderstorm*, *Poverty Is No Crime*, and *Sin and Sorrow Are Common to All*; Chekhov's *Seagull*, *Ivanov*, *Uncle Vanya*, *Cherry Orchard*, and two collections of short stories; Andreyev's *The Confession of a Little Man during Great Days*, and his plays: *The Sorrow of Belgium*, *The Life of Man* and *Anathema*. The interest in Russian literature is dominant.

This claim can be further supported by a survey of the fictional works in translation which appeared from February 1919 to the end of 1922 in the feature page of the popular *Chen Bao*, one of the three major dailies in China at the time.[23] During this period, the paper published altogether 155 items of translation from well-known authors. Of this number, more than one-third (65) are by Russian writers. This number is followed by France, represented chiefly by the short stories of one man, Guy de Maupassant. The "most popular" Russian authors are, in descending order, Chekhov (16 pieces), Tolstoy (12), Pushkin (6) and Turgenev (5).

From then until the outbreak of the Sino-Japanese War, which concluded one chapter in the history of modern China, Russian literature enjoyed unrivalled popularity. This is shown clearly by yet another survey of translated works published in March 1929.[24] More than ten per cent (118 to be exact) of the works on the list, representing twenty-six countries, were by Russian authors. The figure is even more striking if the Soviet works rendered into Chinese before 1930 are included. A 1930 list in fact shows that there were then 133 works by 47 Soviet writers in Chinese translation.[25] As the fortunes of Soviet literature will be the topic of study of a later

[23] See *Wusi shiqi qikan jieshao*, Vol. 1(ii), pp. 475–518.
[24] Pu Shao, "Han yi dongxiyang wenxue zuopin bianmu", ZXCS, Vol. 1, pp. 271–323.
[25] Pu Shao, "Zhongyi SuE xiaoshuo bianmu", ZXCS, Vol. 2, pp. 280–289.

chapter, I shall confine myself here to one aspect of the Russian impact by taking a closer look at the 1929 survey. The list can be said to be most comprehensive, featuring the works of great masters like Pushkin, Gogol, Turgenev, Tolstoy, Dostoevsky, and Gorky; less well known ones like Andreyev, Korolenko, Garshin, Kuprin, Sologub and Bunin, and also such minor writers as Artzybashev and Ropshin.

If the number of translations can serve as a pointer to the popularity of an author in a foreign land, then Turgenev, Tolstoy, Chekhov and Andreyev can be said to have acquired popular appeal in China by the end of the 1920s. Not only were most of their major works available in Chinese translation by then; some of them were to be found in two or more versions. Turgenev's *Smoke, Spring Tide* and *First Love*, Tolstoy's *Resurrection* and *The Man Who Was Dead*, and Artzybashev's *Sanin* each had two translations; Andreyev's *Red Laugh* and *The Seven Who Were Hanged* had three, while Chekhov's short stories were translated over and over again. This, however, does not mean that less translated authors were necessarily less popular. In some instances a single translation or two secured the fame of a writer. Gogol's *The Inspector* is one such example. It was enthusiastically received by Lu Xun and other writers, even though his other major works, notably *Dead Souls* and "The Nose" were not available in Chinese translation until 1934. The same can be said of Ropshin's *The Pale Horse*, and Artzybashev's *Sanin*, which inflamed the revolutionary sentiment of many writers in the 1920s and 1930s. Equally remarkable is the absence of many of Dostoevsky's and Gorky's works. Only two relatively minor works of the former, *Poor Folks* and *Landlady*, appeared in the list, and the latter was represented by two meagre volumes of short stories and a novelette, *Malva*.

III. Translation II: 1930–1949

With Marxism rapidly gaining ground in China in the late 1920s, many writers began to turn their attention in that direction. Lu Xun, for example, translated the works on art and politics of Lunacharsky and Plekhanov in 1929 and 1930 respectively. Likewise, many translators saw what they considered to be a pressing need to introduce Soviet literature to the Chinese public. As a result, Soviet works, mostly novels, began to appear in Chinese in abundance. However, this does not mean that classical Russian literature had lost its appeal. In fact, the work of translating Russian literature hardly halted, even during the difficult years of the Sino-Japanese War between 1937-45. Judging from the books translated in this period, it is clear that the translators were more discriminating than their predecessors. Greater emphasis was given to recognized works, although some minor ones by obscure writers were translated. As more translators turned their attention to well-known writings, many of them, especially those by Turgenev, Tolstoy and Chekhov, were translated many times over. Here are some data on the major works of these three authors translated into Chinese during this period:[26]

Turgenev: *Rudin*—1936
                  Home of the Gentry—1931, 1933, 1937, 1940
                  Fathers and Sons—1931, 1939, 1943
                  Virgin Soil—1930, 1934
                  On the Eve—1943 (1947 reissue)
                  Smoke—1940
                  First Love—1936, 1943
                  Spring Tide—1937, 1945
                  Prose Poems—1930, 1931, 1933, 1936, 1945

Tolstoy: *Child Boyhood Youth*—1944, 1949
                  The Cossacks—1942, 1948, 1949
                  Prisoner of the Caucasus—1930, 1945, 1950
                  Kreutzer Sonata—1936, 1944
                  Resurrection—1942 (two editions)
                  Anna Karenina—1943, 1944, 1947
                  War and Peace—1931, 1942, 1949

[26] For Turgenev's popularity in China, see Ge Baoquan, "Tugeniefu he Zhongguo wenxue", *Shijie wenxue*, 1983.3, pp. 282–303; see also *Tuoersitai yanjiu lunwenji*, pp. 709–726 for a list of Tolstoy's works in Chinese translation.

Chekhov: *Ivanov*—1946
         Seagull—1946
         Uncle Vanya—1946
         Cherry Orchard—1946
         Three Sisters—1935, 1948
         One Act Plays—1946

Apart from adding more titles to the already very full list, this period also witnessed the large-scale translation of Dostoevsky's and Gorky's works, especially the latter's. Wei Congwu, the translator of *Poor Folks*, added *Crime and Punishment* in 1931. In the same year, *The Insulted and Injured* came out in Chinese, followed three years later by *Notes from the Underground* and *The Gamblers*.[27] The fame of Dostoevsky in China was greatly enhanced by the publications of Geng Jizhi. While lying low in Shanghai during the years of the Japanese Occupation, he began to carry out his plan to translate the entire works of the great Russian author. Though his labour was cut short by his untimely death in 1947, he succeeded in bringing out *The Brothers Karamazov* (1940), *The Possessed* (1946), *Memoirs of the House of Death* (1947), and *The Adolescent* (published posthumously in 1948). His manuscript of *Crime and Punishment* was destroyed when the Japanese set the office of the Commercial Press ablaze in 1932.[28] Other translations of Dostoevsky included *A Nasty Story*, and *Landlady*, while some, like *Poor Folks, Crime and Punishment, Memoirs of the House of Death* and *The Possessed* appeared in more than one translation.[29]

While the work of translating Dostoevsky was largely due to a few enthusiastic admirers, that of translating Gorky represented a

[27] The Chinese translation of *Crime and Punishment* was published by Kai Ming shudian in 1931, and went into its third impression in 1937. Both *Notes from the Underground* and *The Gamblers* were translated by Hong Lingfei and published by Chun Guang shudian in Shanghai.

[28] For Geng Jizhi's efforts to introduce Russian literature, see *Zheng Zhenduo wenji*, Vol. 3, pp. 248–257; see also the series of essays lamenting his death in *WYFX*, 2.3 (1947.5), pp. 265–282.

[29] *Poor Folks* was also translated by Wenying, and published in 1948; *Memoirs of the House of Death* by Liu Man in 1933; *The Gentle Maiden* by He Daosheng and Wang Weigao in 1933 and 1947 respectively. *A Nasty Story* by Li Wai in 1947. *The Insulted and Injured*, translated by Quanlun, and *The Possessed* by Gao Tao, and also by Yixian.

corporate effort by almost all of the important translators of Russian literature: Lu Xun, Qu Qiubai, Cao Jinghua, Geng Jizhi, Ba Jin, Shen Duanxian (alias Xia Yan), Zhou Yang and others. A list which appeared in 1948 showed that 55 of his works were available in Chinese translation. The number rises to 84 if titles in more than one version are included.[30] Figured in the list were all his major works, from his first short story "Makar Chuldra" to his final unfinished piece, *Klim Samghim*, which is an exaltation of "socialist" realism. Some of these writings, like his collection of short stories *In the Steppe*, his autobiographical novels, *Childhood, Out in the World*, and *My Universities* and his ever popular novel *Mother*, have all secured more than one translation. His important play, according to some his finest, *The Lower Depths*, exists in no less than eight different Chinese versions. It became popular when it was adapted for the stage in 1946 by Ke Ling and Shi Tuo and set in contemporary Shanghai. In addition, his several volumes of reminiscences and critical essays were also available in Chinese.

Thus, by the end of the 1940s, Russian literature was represented in China not only by its most important works and authors, but also by a host of those which were less important or even obscure. The effort to translate Russian classics continued into the 1950s with increasing momentum. Much of the work was undertaken by the Ping Ming Publishing House formed in 1949 with Ba Jin as chief editor. Of the many Russian titles it had published, one of the most important was the twenty-seven volume *Fictional Works of Chekhov* between 1950–1955, and a new translation of his major plays. Other publishing houses which took a lively interest in bringing out Russian literature included Renmin wenxue chubanshe (The People's Publishing House), Zuojia chubanshe (The Writer's Publishing House), Shanghai wenyi chubanshe (Shanghai Literary Publishing House), Xin wenyi chubanshe (New Literature Publishing House). Between them more than 350 titles of Russian works were published, most of which were commissioned after the founding of the People's Republic.[31] All this budding activity was brought

---

[30] Ge Baoquan, "Gaoerji zuopin Zhongyi bianmu", in ZXCS, Vol. 4(ii), pp. 463–493.

[31] See *Fanyi chuban waiguo gudian wenxue zhuzuo mulu, 1949–1979*, pp. 38–114.

to an abrupt halt towards the late 1950s when the Sino-Soviet conflict became serious. The thaw did not come until the mid-1970s after the Cultural Revolution, the death of Chairman Mao, and the downfall of the so-called "Gang of Four".

Commenting in the late 1940s on the popularity of Russian literature in China, Guo Moruo said that most of the major works of Czarist Russia had been translated into Chinese. The names of Gogol, Turgenev, Andreyev, Dostoevsky, Tolstoy and Chekhov were as familiar as or even more familiar than Shi Naian, Luo Guanzhong, Wu Jingzi, and Pu Songling to Chinese writers. Guo went on to assert without qualification that "Russian literature had an unrivalled impact on modern Chinese fiction."[32] Guo's remark, personal as it is, does reflect the enormous interest which Chinese readers had shown in Russian literature. As formal studies of reading patterns during the May Fourth period are scarce, it is virtually impossible to chart exactly the extent of interest in one literature or another. I can only attempt to put the rising attraction of Russian literature in China into some kind of perspective with the few data which are available.

IV. Reading Habits and Testimonies

In 1934, the National University of Beijing did a survey of the most frequently demanded works of literature in Chinese translation.[33] The result is as follows: Artzybashev's *Sanin*, Chekhov's *Collection of Short Stories*, Gorky's *Bystander*, Tolstoy's *Resurrection*, and Turgenev's *First Love*. Other works cited in the survey include Alexander Dumas' *La Dame aux Camelias*, Goethe's *Faust* and *Die Leiden des Jungen Werther*, Ibsen's *Plays*, Defoe's *Robinson Crusoe*, Oscar Wilde's *Lady Windermere's Fan*, and Bernard Shaw's *Mrs Warren's Profession*. The interest in Russian works is unmistakable. In yet another survey conducted about the same time,[34] the students of twenty-two colleges and eight

[32] Guo Moruo, "ZhongSu wenhua zhi jiaoliu", in *Moruo wenji*, Vol. 12, p. 22.
[33] See D. W. Lyon, "The Past Decade in Chinese Literature", *Journal of the North China Branch of the Royal Asiatic Society*, Vol. LXV (1934), pp. 62–72.
[34] Cited by Olga Lang in *Pa Chin and His Writings*, pp. 222–223.

secondary schools were asked about their favourite authors and works. English language and literature was taught in all these schools, whereas Russian was taught in only one of them. Nevertheless, the students were familiar with almost all of the Russian foreign classics and outstanding authors. As their favourite foreign books, they named English and American works 217 times, Russian works 162 times, and all other nationalities 186 times. Asked about their favourite authors, they named Russian writers 307 times, English and American writers 287 times, and authors of other nationalities 95 times. Russian literature again has the edge over other literatures.

In March 1934, the influential literary magazine *Wenxue* (Literature) published a special issue on works in translation. A total of twenty-one pieces from eleven countries were included. The number of works according to country is as follows: France (5), Russia (2), Great Britian (2), The United States (2), Scandinavia (2), Japan (2), The Netherlands (1), Belgium (1), Spain (1), Italy (1) and Germany (1). A questionnaire was attached to the back page in which nine questions were asked:

1. Do you feel that there are enough creative works for you to read?
2. Apart from works by modern Chinese authors, what sort of works do you like to read? Chinese classics or foreign works?
3. Can you read foreign works in their original languages?
4. What translated works have you read and which do you like best?
5. Which do you like better, original or translated works? Why?
6. Which translations in the present issue do you like best and why?
7. Which do you dislike most and why?
8. What do you think of the essays on translation published in the *Forum Column* of this issue?
9. What works do you think ought to be urgently translated into Chinese?[35]

These are all pertinent questions, which, had the readers responded well, would, no doubt, have helped to determine the reading habits

[35] *Wenxue*, 2.3 (1934.3).

of at least a section of the reading public. Unfortunately, *Literature* never published its findings. It was not until recently, in the second volume of Mao Dun's *Autobiography*, that certain data of the survey were revealed.[36] According to Mao Dun, altogether 630 replies were received. The majority of respondents said that there were too few creative works of quality; that they preferred foreign literature to Chinese classics; that most of them could not read the foreign originals; that more than half liked to read translations instead of works by Chinese writers; that of the translated works, they liked the Russian most; and that of the translations which appeared in the Special Issue, Gorky's *Twenty-six and One* was liked by most (341 replies), and "Symbolist Poetry in France" by the fewest (25 replies). The above finding further indicates the hold Russian literature had on the readers.

In a later issue, *Literature* published essays by fifty-nine writers on how they came into contact with literature.[37] Forty of them acknowledged their indebtedness to foreign literature, and twenty-nine out of these forty specified that they were affected by the literature of a particular country or countries. Fifteen named Russian literature, ten named European and American literature, and four named both Russian and European literature. Again, Russian literature was preeminent.

If the above facts about translation and reading habits delineate the general profile of the Russian influence, what gives this influence depth is the acclamation that the works received from Chinese readers. Reminiscing on the time when they first came into contact with Russian literature, Zheng Zhenduo wrote that Qu Qiubai, Geng Jizhi, Xu Dishan, Qu Shiying and he were "strongly attracted to Russian literature, admired it, and were filled with the desire to introduce it to Chinese readers".[38] Zheng stated further that while Qu and Geng were taught Tolstoy and Chekhov in the Russian School, he had to find his own way and came across the collection of the Home Library in the small reading room of the YMCA in Beijing, which contained a good number of Russian books in English

---

[36] Mao Dun, *Wo zhouguode daolu*, Vol. 2, p. 201.

[37] I obtained these figures from the essays commemorating the first anniversary of *Wenxue* (1934), later compiled in book-form under the title *Wo yu wenxue*.

[38] *Zheng Zhenduo wenji*, Vol. 3, p. 295.

translation. Zheng's experience is worth quoting here: "Apart from translating Russian works, we also read Russian literary history either written in English or translated into English. The small *An Outline of Russian Literature* with green jacket from the Home Library series became a treasured item. Qiubai and others translated the fictional works of Tolstoy, Turgenev, Gorky, the poems of Pushkin and Lermontov, and the parables of Krylov. I copied and translated from *An Outline* to present Russian authors [to the Chinese]. I also wrote to Tian Han in Japan, hoping that he would introduce some studies of Russian literary history to us".[39] With this single-minded purpose and a lot of hard work Zheng and other enthusiasts like him carved out important territory for Russian literature in China in the 1920s and 1930s. He compiled *The Concise History of Russian Literature* in 1924,[40] translated Turgenev, Tolstoy, Chekhov, Andreyev, and also Artzybashev's *Sanin* and Ropshin's *The Pale Horse*, and wrote a good number of studies on the subject.

Zheng's enthusiasm was shared by many. Yu Dafu acknowledged that he grew to maturity via the Russian writers, especially Turgenev. He recounted that during his first year in junior college in Japan (1913), he managed to read Turgenev's *First Love* and *Spring Tide* despite his heavy school work. Once he had come in contact with Western literature, his interest became all-absorbing, he even went to the extent of leaving his school work aside, and lying all day long in his hotel room reading novels. From Turgenev he proceeded to read Tolstoy, then Dostoevsky, Gorky, Chekhov, and from the Russian authors went to the German.[41] For Ba Jin, it was the Russian authors, in particular Tolstoy, Dostoevsky and

---

[39] Ibid., p. 302.

[40] Zheng's work, the first Chinese systematic study of Russian literary history published in 1924, was serialized in *Xiaoshuo yuebao* in 1923. The last chapter, "On the Recent Peasant Writers of Russia", was the work of Qu Qiubai. Zheng admitted that his work was based largely on *An Outline of Russian Literature* by Maurice Baring. A translation of Baring's book appeared in 1931. This work, together with Qu Qiubai's *A History* and *The Study of Russian Literature* edited by Shen Yanbing, were the most comprehensive guides for May Fourth readers interested in the subject.

[41] Yu Dafu, "Wuliu nian lai chuangzuo shenghuo de huigu", *YDWJ*, Vol. 7, p. 178.

Artzybashev who helped him to "become a real human being".[42] Russian literature also inspired the young writer Tonghua with hope and emboldened him to face untold sufferings. In order to study Russian literature, he enrolled in the Russian Department in a Japanese University, where he was persistently taunted and held in contempt. But "for the sake of the great Russian literature I am here to learn, I am prepared at the moment to drink my tears and bear all the human insults which are hurled at me. Our Russian brothers have experienced such sufferings before. Their strength to bear such hardships, which culminated in their final victory, is now pressing at my fragile heart. To brothers far far away, I send them my blessing. . . ."[43] Also in Japan, the young writer Yang Zao came across the works of Russian writers like Turgenev, which brought him into touch with literature.[44] The works of Turgenev, Gorky and others fired the enthusiasm of another young writer. After reading *Fathers and Sons* in particular, he "admitted wholeheartedly for the first time the greatness of art".[45] To Hu Yuzhi, Shen Yanbing and Shen Zemin, it was through the merits of Turgenev and Tolstoy that Russian literature captured the crown of world literature. Tolstoy was to them "the greatest humanitarian writer", and Turgenev, "a humanitarian writer as well as the greatest artistic genius".[46]

The works of Gogol, Korolenko, Garshin, Chekhov, Sologub, Andreyev and Artzybashev were also warmly received by Chinese readers. Lu Xun, for example, held Gogol's broad grasp of life and the deep hidden sadness in his bitter laughter in great esteem. He remarked as early as 1908 that "Gogol appeared, and with his invisible tears and melancholy revitalized his fellow men".[47] This view was shared by Qu Qiubai, who asserted that "Gogol succeeds in a natural but subtle manner in evoking the moral awareness in his readers".[48] Likewise, the works of Garshin, Sologub and Chekhov heightened the sensitivity of a young writer towards

---

[42] Ba Jin, *Yi*, pp. 172–173.
[43] Tonghua, "Zhongguoren de daiyu you yize", *YS*, 5.12 (1929.5.27), p. 668.
[44] *WYWX*, as n. 37, p. 141.
[45] Ibid., p. 46.
[46] "Dujieniefu", in *Jindai Eguo wenxuejia lun*, p. 2.
[47] Lu Xun, "Moluo shili shuo", *LXQJ*, Vol. 1, p. 64.
[48] Qu Qiubai, "Guogeli: Puyushi", *QQWJ*, Vol. 5, pp. 1304–1305.

human suffering, enabling him to feel more acutely the remorse, despondency and misery surrounding him.[49] According to Zhou Zuoren, his spirit was uplifted after translating Korolenko's *Makar's Dream*, because in it "the conflict between the beauty of nature and its cruelty, the sinfulness of humanity and its nobility . . . merge".[50]

Andreyev's works, on the other hand, heightened the responsiveness of many writers to the conflicts of thought and action in life, and they admired his ability to dissolve "the difference between the inner world and its outward manifestations". [51] As to Artzybashev, his *Sanin* was introduced by the editor of *Short Story Monthly* as an "unfading masterpiece", a "Bible of individual anarchism".[52] A reader of the same magazine was so moved by his "Shevyrev" that he urged all hot-blooded Chinese to follow the steps of this great Russian revolutionary forerunner.[53]

It is sufficient to say at this juncture that the works of the abovementioned authors acquired popular acclaim in China during the first phase of Russo-Chinese literary contact. One is left with the obvious questions here: why such a lively response? Why these writers? What did they mean to the Chinese readers? What sort of images, or mirages, did the Chinese writers have of Russian literature? These are the questions that I shall endeavour to answer in the following chapters.

[49] Shi Chenhai, "Youren Ma Jun de yishu", *YS*, 5.12 (1929.5.27), p. 631.
[50] Zhou Zuoren, "Majiaer de meng", *XQN*, 8.2 (1920.10), p. 30.
[51] Lu Xun, "Andande yanaili", translator's note, *LXQJ* (1938), Vol. 11, p. 23 . See also Zheng Zhenduo's preface to Geng Jizhi's translation of *The Life of Man* (Ren zhi yisheng), 1923.
[52] "Zuihou yiye", *XSYB*, 15.6 (1924.6), p. 2.
[53] Chen Zhejun, "Tongxin", *XSYB*, 13.12 (1922.12), pp. 2–3.

2 Chinese Consciousness and the Russian Impact

In 1926, Yu Dafu remarked on the enormous influence of Russian literature in these words: "Of all the fictional works the world over, the Russian novel influenced China most. Apart from the works of past authors such as Gogol (1808–1895), Turgenev (1818–1910), Dostoevsky (1821–1881) and Goncharev, recent ones like Chekhov, Andreyev and Artzybashev also exerted an overriding influence on many Chinese writers." At the end of his article he entreated "Chinese fiction to develop in the near future along the lines of the Russians".[1] No less fervent was the appreciation of the novelist-essayist Zhang Yiping, who wrote in a preface to the Russian translation of his *A Lian* (1928): "Modern Chinese literature has received abundant gifts from the great Russian literary works. The translations of your Tolstoy, Pushkin, Chekhov and Blok have been welcomed by many of our readers, have filled us with fervour, and moved us."[2] Lu Xun recounted with enthusiasm in 1932 that when May Fourth writers were looking for practical advice and guidance, they "found Russian literature".[3] Why did Chinese

[1] Yu Dafu, "Xiandai xiaoshuo de yuanyuan" in "Xiaoshuo lun", *YDWJ*, Vol. 5, p. 14.
[2] Zhang Yiping, *YS*, 4.14 (1928.4), p. 127.
[3] Lu Xun, "Zhu ZhongE wenzi zhi jiao", *LXQJ*, Vol. 4, p. 460.

writers "find", of all literatures, the Russian? What sort of inspiration
did they draw from it? Whose work did they respond to most? And
why did they accord the highest homage to this foreign literature?
These are questions which merit detailed examination. However,
one thing is clear from the outset: the large-scale transplantation
of Russian works onto Chinese soil is no accident or coincidence.
It represents a conscious effort on the part of Chinese intellectuals
to propagate a literature which they think is most suitable to China's
"national proclivities" (*guoqing*), a term frequently employed by
intellectuals in their claim for Russian literature.

I. Disintegration of the Imperial Order

The keeness of May Fourth intellectuals to learn from Russian
examples should first and foremost be approached from a broader
perspective—as a reaction to the Chinese anxiety to modernize their
country at a particular moment in history. The first decades of the
twentieth century saw immense social and political changes in China.
With the crumbling of the Manchu dynasty, the rapid rise of
capitalism and the city middle class, gradual industrialization, and
increased modernization, coupled with China's continuing defeats
by foreign powers, especially by Japan, many men of letters sought
to re-define their role as intellectuals. Many saw that the burning
problem of the day was the backwardness of the country in the
wake of foreign aggression—backwardness in the material sense:
pernicious poverty, outdated modes of government and institutions,
widespread corruption, deep-rooted inequality; backwardness in
the spiritual sense: the inhumanity and stifling effects of Confucianism, the suppression of the individual in Chinese tradition,
the narrowness in intellectual thinking, and the lack of a culture
that could reflect or represent national life. Conscience-ridden
intellectuals felt it their foremost responsibility to shake the country
out of its backwardness. Among many other things, they sought
a radical change in the philosophical foundation of national life,
a critical evaluation of China's cultural heritage, a pledge to care
for the plight of the common people and the liberation of the
individual from the stranglehold of social relationships.

How did this impulse for change affect the rise of Russian literature in China? This question should be approached in the light of the characteristic thought of the May Fourth writers. This was a time when different trends of thought—democracy, liberalism, anarchism, nihilism, socialism, social Darwinism—gained currency in China, a phenomenon which highlights the vitality as much as the chaos in the thinking processes of the May Fourth intellectuals. This "chaos" in fact represented something more profound: it arose as a consequence of the collapse of the Manchu monarchical order. As Benjamin Schwartz put it succinctly, the "cosmic order within which the kingship occupied a well-established, permanent, and pivotal locus"[4] was fundamentally undermined by 1911. What ensued was a period of unbridled thinking, of rigorous soul-searching. In daring to disown their past and brave the new world, they made possible the emergence of one of the most fertile periods of intellectual thought in Chinese history, a period which witnessed the "transformation of all values".[5] We may indeed take issue with the May Fourth intellectuals for their excessive idealism, and the naïvety or even shallowness of their way of thinking. But we should also bear in mind that intellectuals at this juncture in Chinese history had the most intense craving for knowledge and truth, and were unprecedentedly "cosmopolitan" in their outlook, identifying with mankind as a whole. China, they perceived, is but a member in the family of nations—a perception which was in stark contrast to that of many of their immediate predecessors, who saw the Middle Kingdom as the centre of the globe. In the realm of culture, this "cosmopolitanism" predisposed them to see issues and conflicts in transcultural terms; and in literature, gave them a predilection for world literature.[6]

---

[4] Benjamin Schwartz, "The Chinese Perception of World Order, Past and Present", in *The Chinese World Order*, p. 283.

[5] Chow Tse-tsung, *The May Fourth Movement*, pp. 289–313.

[6] One concrete example of the "world consciousness" of May Fourth writers is their espousal of "Esperanto", hoping that writings in this "internationalist language" will help to break national frontiers. Bonnie McDougall points out that the general trend in Europe and America at the close of the nineteenth century to regard cultural as well as biological phenomena as universal exerted a strong influence in May Fourth thinking. See her article, "The Impact of Western Literary Trends", in *MCL*, pp. 45–46.

As Luo Jialun, the editor of *Xinchao* (Renaissance), the influential student magazine of Beijing University, remarked in 1919: "Civilization is common to all. We should take from the strength of other nations to make good our shortcomings. Our Literary Revolution is a result of China's making contact with world literature, a result of literary evolution. . . ."[7] Sharing the same viewpoint, the noted commentator Hu Yuzhi wrote in the influential *Dongfang zazhi* in favour of a comparative study of literature, in the hope that Chinese literature would attain homogeneity with its foreign counterparts, and that indigenous literature would one day spread far and wide.[8] In the same spirit, Lu Xun advocated his own "take-whatever-ism" (*nalai zhuyi*) from the West, and Hu Shi pushed it to the extreme in recommending "wholesale Westernization". This desire for Western learning opened the way for the germination of Western literature in Chinese soil, and Russian literature was its fastest growing and most vigorous representative.

The collapse of the former universal order also brought to the fore an impulse towards an intellectual solution to social and political problems, an assumption that modernization could be precipitated through intellectual awakening and transformation, through the complete reformation and revolutionizing of the thinking and morality of the people. Or, as one historian summed it up: the "wholesale transformation of human consciousness".[9] The rationale behind this mode of thinking was that cultural change is fundamental to all other changes. For the May Fourth writers, cultural change was a change in the system of symbols, values and beliefs, which could be attained through changing man's conception of, and his relations to both cosmic and human reality, in short, as Lin Yü-sheng writes, a belief in the change of basic ideas qua ideas.[10] This is the central thesis of Zhou Zuoren's essay entitled,

[7] Luo Jialun, "Bo Hu Xianxiao jun de Zhongguo wenxue gailiang lun", *Xinchao*, 1.5 (1919.5), p. 782.

[8] Yuzhi, "Afterword to 'Bulanduisi' by Chen Xia", *DFZZ*, 17.5 (1920.3), p. 85.

[9] Maurice Meisner, "Cultural Iconoclasm, Nationalism, and Internationalism in the May Fourth Movement", in Benjamin Schwartz (ed.), *Reflections on the May Fourth Movement: A Symposium*, p. 15.

[10] This aspect of the May Fourth intellectuals is most forcefully delineated by Lin Yü-sheng in his recent study, *The Crisis of Chinese Consciousness*. He used the term "cultural-intellectualistic" to describe their approach to thinking. See his book, especially Chapters 1 and 2.

appropriately, "Thought Revolution".[11] Leading men of letters like Lu Xun, Chen Duxiu, Hu Shi, Qu Qiubai, Yu Dafu and many others remained at heart "men of ideas" throughout their lives.

Such eagerness to "transform human consciousness" results in the elevation of the importance of literature, which was regarded, perhaps somewhat too exclusively at the time, as the most effective weapon in the battle to change the human heart, and subsequently, collective human consciousness. Lu Xun, for example, revered literature as the spark of national spirit, and a torchlight leading this spirit forward.[12] This was also Qu Qiubai's notion when he campaigned for a literature which could break down social conventions. In their anguished cry for "life", "spontaneity" and "experience", and in their yearning for a genuinely human literature, they set their eyes firmly on the youthful yet enormously invigorating Russian literature.

II. The Changing Conception of Literature

While the Chinese literati have always viewed literature as functional, as a means of "propagating the Way" (*wen yi zai dao*), the perception by intellectuals of the "way" had changed substantially by the time Liang Qichao published his celebrated article, "The Relationship between Fiction and People's Sovereignty" (Lun xiaoshuo yu qunzhi de guanxi) in 1902. Liang's article opened up new vistas concerning the function of literature, especially that of fiction, in society.[13] For him, fiction was the most effective means to social and political reform, and the means to any kind of reform, he believed, lay in transforming the mind, and infusing the people with a spirit of duty and responsibility. This concept was not only echoed by his contemporaries, but further developed by the May Fourth writers a decade or more later. Lu Xun's choice of literature as a lifelong career to "change people's temperament and reform society" is a much quoted example.[14] While no less

[11] See his essay "Sixiang geming" in *ZXD*, Vol. 1, pp. 226–227.
[12] Lu Xun, "Lun zhengleyan kan", *LXQJ*, Vol. 1, p. 241.
[13] For a study of the social novel in the late Qing, see A Ying, *Wan Qing xiaoshuo shi*, especially pp. 1–7, 180–189. See also Link, *Mandarin Ducks and Butterflies*.
[14] Lu Xun, "Preface to *Yuwai xiaoshuo ji*", *LXQJ*, Vol. 10, p. 161.

utilitarian, many May Fourth writers were even more determinist
in their outlook on literature than their late Qing predecessors. This
came, somewhat ironically, as a result of their espousal of the theory
of evolution. Many fervently applied the same concept in the realm
of the social sciences and humanities. In literature, leading advocates
such as Chen Duxiu, Hu Shi, Lu Xun, Mao Dun and others held
the view that there are various stages, or periods of development
in literary history—from the classical age to that of romanticism,
realism/naturalism and then neo-romanticism. European literature,
they believed, had passed through the classical, romantic and realist
eras, and was in the period of neo-romanticism.[15] As to Chinese
literature, many considered that until the late Qing, it had remained
in the classical and romantic age. Just as industrialization and
modernization sparked off the age of "realism" in European
literature, many hoped and believed that it would do the same for
China. This hope provided them with the theoretical basis for
promoting "realist" literature. The view of a critic that, in order
to become modernized, Chinese literature "must first experience the
realist writing of the naturalist school, stressing scientific method,
before it can pass into the realm of neo-romanticism"[16] was shared
by many. "Realism", a popular though somewhat confused concept
to them,[17] generally meant that literature should reflect its epoch,
no matter how dark it was, so as to arouse people's awareness of
the human situation. They championed the so-called "blood and
tears" literature, believing that writers should be sensitive to the
sufferings of the people and the country, and should echo their "woes
and cries".

[15] See Bonnie McDougall's *The Introduction of Literary Theories into Modern
China*, Chapters 2–4.

[16] Zhu Xizu, "Wenyi de jinhua", *XQN*, 6.6 (1919.11), p. 584. This is a translation of a section of Kuriyagawa Hakuson's *Ten Lectures*. The summing up, as
it is quoted here, is however written by Zhu himself.

[17] Chinese writers and critics were somewhat confused as to the distinction
between realism and naturalism. Marián Gálik, for example, claims that Mao Dun's
literary criticism from 1921–1922 was one of "realistic criticism", and from 1922
onwards, he found agreeable the use of various methods by individual writers
—Ibsen, Maeterlinck, Hauptmann to name a few. See his work, *Mao Dun and
Literary Criticism*, p. 82. Gálik's article, "Naturalism: A Changing Concept", *East
and West*, 16:3–4 (1966), pp. 301–328, remains to date one of the best on the
topic.

This attitude was formally endorsed by the group of writers who rallied round the Association of Literary Studies. A loosely organized society, the literary beliefs of its diverse membership are most patently revealed in the foreword to the "Literary Association Series": "We believe that . . . the greatness and influence of literature has no rival. It holds up a mirror to life. With its benevolent light, it merges the different classes of society, different frontiers, and the differences in mankind. With its profound humanitarian concern, it swiftly casts away human barriers. Only literature can spread the gospel of brotherliness amidst the chaos and massacres in this world, inspiring oppressors to feel deeply for the plight of the oppressed. It makes visible the highest form of human feeling and emotion, and relieves human suffering through its quick and lively smile. . . ."[18] This predilection for a humanitarian and utilitarian conception of literature, and the emphasis on the moral responsibility of the writer, exerted a dominant influence over the literary circle of the May Fourth intellectuals. Admitting that life is valuable, and that art exists because of life, not vice versa, a noted critic put this question to his readers: "Why is it that in modern literature, the Russian is acclaimed as the greatest and best? Precisely because Russian masters like Turgenev, Tolstoy, Andreyev and Gorky all hold the view [that literature is for life]."[19] In their search for the "greatest and best", many May Fourth leaders took Russian literature as their guide.

It is clear even to the common reader that a strong moral thrust and deep sense of compassion pulsate through nineteenth-century Russian literature. Writing towards the end of the eighteenth century, Alexander Radishchev comments in the opening of his celebrated *A Journey from St. Petersburg to Moscow*: "I looked around—and my soul was wounded by the sufferings of man. I turned my gaze inward—and saw that the disasters of man proceed from man, and often because of the single fact that he does not look directly at the objects which surround him."[20] In gazing at the society in which he lived, Radishchev's work set the tone for the

---

[18] "Wenxue yanjiu hui congshu yuanqi" in *ZXCS*, Vol. 1, p. 179.

[19] Luo Jialun, as n. 7, p. 783.

[20] Quoted from Joe Andrews, *Russian Writers and Society in the Second Half of the Nineteenth Century*, p. x.

great nineteenth-century Russian novels. Indeed, the impression one gets from reading the works of Turgenev, Tolstoy, Dostoevsky or Gorky is that of titanic forces pressing on humanity. Witnessing the grossly adverse social and political conditions of their country, Russian writers never seemed to have ceased in their endeavours to reappraise the moral fabric of the society in which they lived. They attempted to ensure an equal and humane treatment for all humanity, and to inspire all men with the spirit of reconciliation. The Russian novel, especially, voices a plea for understanding the abnormal, the underprivileged, the superfluous, and the misunderstood. For such are Onegin, Oblomov, Rudin, Bazarov, Raskolnikov, Nekhlyudov, and in a different manner, Artyzbashev's Sanin. "People are not good or bad," wrote Mirsky about the Russian hero, "they are only more or less unhappy and deserving of sympathy."[21] This belief in the inherent worth of human beings, this sympathy for the downtrodden, this sense of justice and a burning desire to reform society endow Russian literature with a uniquely wide-ranging appeal. In his *Tolstoy and the Novel*, John Bayley made the following profound observation about this aspect of Russian literature: "In the most depressing situation the Russians did not lose their vitality and explosive force of utterance; they have a kind of weird high spirits in the midst of tyranny and gloom, and Pushkin gives us the reason. Russia was not born for this destiny: Poland was. Mickiewicz is a poet of real gloom, as full of backward sorrows as an Irish bard: but for a Russian gloom is a challenge and a stimulant. We can detect this effervescence, this curious discrepancy between the chill of the words and the ardent vivacity of the tone, in Pushkin's statement at the end of the prologue to *The Bronze Horseman*—Pechalen budet moi rasskaz—'mine will be a sad tale'. We detect it in the last sentence of one of Gogol's stories—'it is gloomy in this world, gentlemen'—and in the opening words of Dostoevsky's hero from the underground—'Ja chelovek bolnoi, ja zloi chelovek'—'I am a sick man, a spiteful man'."[22] It was the spirit of challenge and resistance in Russian literature, the moral vigour, the vision of man's relation with society, the various and tenable solutions to the human problem, and the immediacy

[21] Mirsky, *A History of Russian Literature*, p. 170.
[22] Bayley, *Tolstoy and the Novel*, p. 19.

of the experience of the writers that lay behind its immense impact on the Chinese writers.

In a preface to Shen Ying's translation of Turgenev's *On the Eve* (1921), Geng Jizhi started off with a treatise on literature in general, before proceeding to set out his reasons for introducing Russian literature. According to Geng, literature should depict society and life as it is. In so doing, it reveals the ideals of the writer, so that society and life can be improved, and a new life and society formed as a result. This is to him the true value of literature. It is for this quality that Geng thinks that Russian literature should be most valued. The works of Turgenev, Tolstoy, Dostoevsky, Gorky and Andreyev are the most deserving of the label "life literature". He singled out Turgenev's works for praise in particular, for the author's "artistic delineation of the various trends of thought of his time, and of the direction which life takes".[23]

Geng's ideas were far from being singular. Many May Fourth writers believed that the same historical development that set Russia apart from Western Europe was at work in China in the spheres of politics, society and the economy. Their eagerness to find parallels and their transcultural approach to literature and art formed a basis for their sense of having a common cause with Russian literature. Qu Qiubai emphasized that the same turmoil then confronting the Chinese was familiar to the Russians; it was natural that the deep concern and intense sympathy towards the unfortunate and poor permeating Russian literature should be a model for Chinese writers.[24] Shen Yanbing held that the aesthetic quality of the Russian people resides in their ability to bear hardship and stand up against evil forces. Their compassion and spirit of universalism created a literature which echoed around the world. It was this spirit of humanitarianism in literature that he wished Chinese writers would emulate.[25] This view was shared by another noted critic of

[23] Preface to *Qianye*, p. 3.
[24] Qu Qiubai drove home this point in his essay "Lun Puxijin de *Bianerjin xiaoshuo ji*", *QQWJ*, Vol. 2, pp. 541–543; in his "*Eluosi mingjia duanpian xiaoshuo ji xu*", he stressed that "in order to transform society, we are compelled to create a new literature . . . the materials we need do not necessarily have to come from Russia, but the situation in Russia is closely akin to that of China, so that we should introduce Russian literature." Ibid., Vol. 2, p. 544.
[25] Lang Sun (Shen Yanbing), "Xinwenxue yanjiuzhe de zeren yu nuli", *XSYB*, 12.2 (1921.2), p. 2.

the time, Xie Liuyi, who held that Russian literature had been "immortalized" because of her writers' humanitarian stand towards oppression, and their shouldering of the responsibility to educate the people and transform society. He encouraged his readers to learn whatever they could from this great literature.[26] After a detailed discussion of the Russian national character, Zhou Zuoren proceeded to say that Russia was poor in the nineteenth century, and a mist of darkness shrouded its literary works. But this adversity had not created a sense of hatred and disillusionment in the minds of the Russians: it only enhanced their love and sympathy for mankind. It was this great literary tradition, which "wiped out the distinction of classes", that Zhou hoped would inspire Chinese writers.[27] To Lu Xun, the humanitarian concern of Russian literature was unique. He wrote in 1932: "Russian literature has been 'for life' since the time of Nicholas II. Whether its theme is to investigate or solve the problems of life; whether it has degenerated into mysticism or decadence, its central thesis is for life."[28]

Clearly, in their conscious effort to build afresh a national literature, the May Fourth writers reacted sympathetically to that in Russian literature which appeared parallel to the Chinese tradition and experience; they welcomed warmly those elements to which Chinese literature had yet to give expression—specifically the spirit of humanitarianism, cosmopolitanism, Utopian revolution, and the realistic portrayal of life. It was this blending of sympathy with qualities the Russians possessed and excitement at what the Chinese writers lacked that partly sparked off the lively response to Russian literature.

III. The Changed Role of the Intelligentsia

The changed relationship between writer and society in May Fourth China led to the Chinese identification with the Russian intelligentsia, and further enhanced Russian influence. As the nineteenth-century

[26] Xie Liuyi, "Eguo zhi minzhong xiaoshuo jia", *XSYB*, 11.8 (1920.8), p. 7.

[27] Zhou Zuoren, "Wenxue shang de Eguo yu Zhongguo," *XQN*, 8.5 (1921.1), p. 5.

[28] Lu Xun, "*Shuqin qianji*", *LXQJ*, Vol. 4, p. 432.

Russian intelligentsia has been the subject of numerous studies,[29] it will suffice to describe it here in very general terms. It was by and large a non-professional and alienated social group, which emerged in the wake of Russia's gradual cultural Westernization in the nineteenth century. Its members were distinguished from the mass of the population by the degree and quality of their education —more Western orientated, often tinged with a French and German positivism. Mirsky considered the Russian intelligentsia to be the educated classes who were intensely and actively interested in political issues and more or less radically inclined.[30] Many shared the romantic conviction that every man had a unique mission to fulfil if only he could know what it was, and tended to view both personal and social obligation as part of a large collective pattern. This created a general enthusiasm for social and metaphysical ideas, perhaps as a kind of ethical substitute for a dying religion.[31] In fact, what characterized the Russian intelligentsia in general was their monistic outlook, which envisaged the total destruction of the social order and a Utopian revolution as the answer to all human difficulties. From this arose the more specific claims that the state was inherently despotic and oppressive, and that the bulk of the suffering peasants were essentially good, and the expectation that a grassroots destruction of the establishment would liberate men from the whole social and cultural order of the past and present. Their altruistic approach in associating social equality and humanity with revolution, subsequently gave grounds for a general commitment to "socialism" in its several forms.

As a social group, the Russian intelligentsia was comprised mainly of non-professionals. Most of them had no fixed occupation and relied mainly on free-lance writing or occasional teaching for a living. As far as their educational background is concerned, writers like

[29] For detailed studies of the Russian intelligentsia in English, see Richard Pipes (ed.), *The Russian Intelligentsia*; Isaiah Berlin, *Russian Thinkers*; and Ronald Hingley, *The Russian Mind*.

[30] Mirsky, as n. 21, pp. 321–322.

[31] This point is succinctly put by Mme Jarintzov, who says that the typical Russian "cannot go on doubting for very long; his inclination is to make a dogma for himself quickly, and to surrender himself to it wholeheartedly and entirely". *The Russians and Their Language*, p. 124. Also see Nicholas Rzhevsky, *Russian Literature and Ideology*, especially "Russian Literary Tradition".

Dostoevsky, Chekhov or Gorky suffered from the inadequacies of
the official system. Even those who attended universities, such as
Turgenev and Tolstoy, derived little from the formal education
offered there. Alienation was thrust upon them by an oppressive
state and by the fact that the masses inhabited a different spiritual
world.[32] As a result of their alienation, many Russian writers aired
their convictions about human nature and society through their
literary efforts. The result was that the history of the Russian
intelligentsia, perhaps even the history of Russian national
consciousness, was first recounted in the pages of the Russian
novel.[33] As Kropotkin wrote in 1907, "the reason why literature
exercises such an influence in Russia is self-evident. There is no open
political life, and with the exception of a few years at the time of
the abolition of serfdom, the Russian people have never been called
upon to take an active part in the framing of their country's
institutions. The consequence has been that the best minds of the
country have chosen the poem, the novel, the satire or literary
criticism as the medium for expressing their aspirations, their
conceptions of natural life, or their ideals. . . ."[34] Indeed, the early
Pushkin, Lermontov, the Decembrist writers and, in particular, the
men of the "remarkable decade" (to borrow the phrase from Pavel
Annenkov, the famous Russsian critic and literary historian), such
as Herzen, Bakunin, Kropotkin and Belinsky are noted for the
intensity of their involvement in contemporary society. Literature
and literary criticism became almost the only available forum for
political discussion, or a kind of "alternative government", which
offered a second voice, if only indirectly, to challenge established
ideas and behaviour.[35] It is no wonder that Russian writers took
their writing so seriously, and also their responsibility to guide their
country out of the national quagmire. Their moral predicament can
best be summed up in the words of Dobroliubov: "We will be asked:

[32] For a discussion of the inner conflicts of the Russian writers as exemplified
by Turgenev, Tolstoy and Chekhov, see Maurice Larkin, *Man and Society in
Nineteenth-century Realism*, Chapters 10, 11 and 15.

[33] Richard Freeborn, *et al.* (eds.), *Russian Literary Attitudes from Pushkin to
Solzhenitsyn*, p. 1.

[34] Kropotkin, *Ideals and Realities in Russian Literature*, p. vi.

[35] The term "alternative government" is taken from Andrews' study of the
relationship between writer and society in Russia, as n. 20.

why will the environment not manifest its influence on others. Why will it act so fatally on talented natures? The answer is simple. These natures, thanks to their aspirations, run ahead further than others, grasp more than they can carry, and thus often encounter obstacles that they have not the strength to oppose."[36]

A similar sense of commitment and alienation is found in many May Fourth intellectuals.[37] Like their Russian counterparts, many were essentially non-professionals, because unlike scholar-officials of the imperial past, they did not seek careers in the bureaucracy. In any case, the abolition of the civil service examination in 1905 meant that the formal path to officialdom through classical studies was denied them. As Liang Qichao pointed out, the change in the civil service examination in 1898 already "left thousands of old *juren* and *xiucai* without a proper avenue to bureaucratic positions".[38] Many resorted to writing or to somewhat unsteady teaching careers to earn a meagre income. This was made easier and more popular with the emergence of Shanghai as a modern city towards the close of the nineteenth century, and the proliferation of newspapers, weeklies and magazines of all kinds. With the drift of "elite" scholars to this urban centre after the 1898 reform and the Boxer Rebellion in 1900, an elite group of journalists was formed. These chose fiction as one of the chief instruments for the promotion of political reform.[39]

This trend continued into the Republic and developed further in the May Fourth movement, making it possible, even fashionable,

---

[36] Dobroliubov, "Gubernskie ocherki M. E. Saltykova-Shchedrina" (The Provincial Sketches of M. E. Saltykov-Shchedrin), *Sobraine sochinenii*, Vol. 2, pp. 126–127.

[37] Benjamin Schwartz's article, "The Intelligentsia in Communist China: A Tentative Comparison" in *The Russian Intelligentsia* gives valuable insights on the resemblances as well as differences between the so-called Russian and Chinese "intelligentsia". I am indebted to this article for some of the ideas in this section.

[38] Liang Qichao, "Xinzheng zhaoshu gongba", in *Wuxu zhengbianji*, Part one, Chapter two, p. 34. For a study of the abolition of the civil service examination in 1905 and the circumstances leading to it, see Wang Dezhao, *Qingdai keju zhidu yanjiu*, pp. 161–249.

[39] A Ying, for example, listed 50 titles of late-Qing literary magazines in his authoritative *Wan Qing wenyi baokan shulüe*. He also estimated that at least one thousand separate pieces of fiction appeared in this period. See his *Wan Qing xiaoshuo shi*, p. 1. See also Link, as n. 13, p. 135.

for young intellectuals without proper professional qualifications to make a living through writing. Because of their educational experience (most were secondary or teacher training school graduates; some were university graduates and some of these went to foreign universities, mostly in Japan), and their ill-defined status as men of letters, many found that they did not belong to any class in society. Lacking a corporate identity, a lot of them tended either to fall back upon themselves, or relate only to people with similar experiences. This explains to a certain extent the mushrooming of small literary sects with tiny memberships in the 1920s and 1930s. Many conceived of themselves as a band of self-conscious protagonists, standing alone in a bleak world, raising the banner for all to see—the banner of reason, science, progress, of liberty and democracy, of compassion and a better life. They were alienated precisely because of their idealism and their non-conformist leanings, often launching attacks against the corrupt and oppressive government, although their voice was often solitary, and their tone weak. Many accepted the romantic doctrine that every man is called to a mission beyond the mere selfish purposes of material existence. Because they were more privileged or more perceptive, they had a direct duty to help their less fortunate or oppressed brothers towards the light. The following testimony of a young writer on how she perceived her relationship with society can be taken in general: "I need a weapon, like a dissecting knife and a microscope, to dissect and to examine clearly our human society. I need this weapon to carve out all my own sufferings, those of our society, particularly the oppressed, as well as to expose the crimes of the oppressors, and to wage war on the lofty and powerful."[40] The weapon which she needed and discovered was literature.

Like this writer, many May Fourth intellectuals considered that this duty was uniquely binding upon them, and that, if they fulfilled it, as history intended them to do, the future of China might yet be as glorious as her immediate past and present had been dark and empty. Though their aspirations, beliefs and knowledge were often regarded with suspicion or indifference by the vast majority, many took upon themselves the task of transforming society. Both Lu Xun

---

[40] Bai Wei, "Wo zoudao wenxue quandele chuzhong", *WYWX*, p. 15.

and Yu Dafu abandoned their medical studies to take up writing, while Guo Moruo never put his medical knowledge to professional use. Instead of taking up his profession as an engineer, Cheng Fangwu followed the dictates of his heart and devoted his energies to literary criticism. And Xu Zhimo abandoned his ambition to be the Hamilton of China and emerged as the most celebrated romantic poet of his day.[41] In fact, so convinced were the May Fourth intellectuals of the power of literature and so absorbed in themselves as the conscience of society that, as Leo Lee pointed out, their uprootedness and sense of alienation were hidden by their "imagined greatness".[42]

Like many of their Russian predecessors, many May Fourth intellectuals gave priority to the idea of utopian destruction. A prime example is Chen Duxiu's iconoclastic "call to youth" in 1915, where he denounced all the "old and rotten elements"—family, traditions, superstitions—as "savage beasts" which had to be completely destroyed.[43] Chen's call excited May Fourth sensibilities to a high degree. Guo Moruo's first major poem, "Phoenix nirvana" (1920), was nothing but a glorification of the beauty of the destructive impulse. The poet embraced the idea that the highest state of things —that of beauty, perfection and truth: nirvana in his terminology —will rise phoenix-like from the ashes of the old. As he wrote in 1918 to fellow student Zhong Baihua: "Now I wish very much to be like a phoenix, collect some sandalwood, and burn away my present carcass amidst the mournful tunes of the elegies, and from the cold and cleansed ashes a new 'self' will be born again."[44] The poem, as well as the anarchistic writings of Bakunin, and Tolstoy's brand of ethical anarchism (of their impact on the Chinese, more will be said later), touched the heart of many young Chinese in the 1920s. At the same time, Russian works with nihilistic overtones,

[41] Xu Zhimo recounted that when his father sent him abroad to study in 1919, his aim was that his son would return and get a position in banking. But Xu's aim then was to enter politics to "become the Hamilton of China"—taking the American politician as his guide. He further stated that "before the age of twenty-four, poetry was no concern of mine, whether classical or modern." See his preface to the third anthology of his poem, *Manghuji. Quanji*, Vol. 2, p. 340.

[42] Lee, *The Romantic Generation*, p. 295.

[43] Chen Duxiu, "Jing gao qingnian", *XQN*, 1.1 (1915.9).

[44] Guo Moruo, *Sanye ji*, p. 11.

such as Andreyev's *To the Stars*, Artzybashev's *Sanin* and "Shevyrev", and Ropshin's *The Pale Horse*, also achieved popular acclaim. Ba Jin's first novel, published in 1927, was appropriately named *Miewang* (Destruction). Fired by "pure" love for the common people, the nihilistic hero was inspired by yet purer hatred for those whom he conceived to be enemies of the common people—including the common people themselves on the many occasions when they failed to behave as hoped or predicted. Thus, out of a great love for mankind of the future is born a great hatred for human beings; thus the passion for creating a heaven on earth becomes a drive towards destruction, and an espousal of the idea of revolution.[45] This tendency to combine irreconcilable opposites, notably those of love and hate, is reminiscent of a prevailingly Russian position, epitomized in the much quoted phrase of Dostoevsky's nihilist theoretician Shigalyov in *The Possessed*: "Proceeding from unlimited freedom, I end with unlimited slavery."

While commenting on the moral sensitivity of the Russian intelligentsia to the cause of the oppressed, Lu Xun dwells on the general predicament of the intellectuals, "who are always agonized, never content with society. What they see is always the defects. They are prepared to make sacrifices for the future, and society is the more animated for their presence. But they themselves—are tormented both in body and soul."[46] These words, echoing those of Dobroliubov quoted above, exemplified the vigorous yet agonized life of none other than Lu Xun himself. This view is in harmony with that held by the blind Russian poet Eroshenko, who had come to China as an exile in the 1910s, and later made an enormous impact on May Fourth intellectuals. In a talk entitled "The mission of the intelligentsia", he praised the ideals and endeavours, as well as the sufferings imposed on the Russian intelligentsia in their search for a rational society for the common people, and called upon the Chinese men of letters to follow their example.[47] In the same way, Ba Jin championed the cause of Belinsky when talking about the task of the intelligentsia in the mid-1930s. His call to Chinese

[45] For a discussion of Ba Jin's nihilistic hero, see Chapter 6.
[46] Lu Xun, *LXQJ*, Vol. 8, p. 190.
[47] Ailuoxianke (Eroshenko), "Zhishi jieji de shiming", *DFZZ*, 19.4 (1922.2), pp. 107–112.

intellectuals to fulfil the mission that history had assigned to them, echoed that of the Russian master to his fellowmen more than half a century before.[48]

Thus, in their groping for an outlet for expression, many Chinese writers followed the example of their Russian predecessors. Many found in the Russian writers a source of inspiration. The Russian intellectuals demonstrated to them the path of commitment and in particular, that the means of arriving at their goal was literature. As Isaiah Berlin points out, the Russian intelligentsia heralded a new kind of social criticism, which "searches in literature neither for ideal 'types' of men or situations (as the earlier German romantics had taught), nor for an ethical instrument for the direct improvement of life; but for the attitude of life of an individual author, of his milieu, or age or class. This attitude then requires to be judged as it would be in the first place for its degree of genuineness, its adequacy to its subject-matter, its depth, its truthfulness, its ultimate motives."[49] Like the Russian writers, May Fourth writers were noted for their intense involvement in society. Indeed, such an involvement seemed to be a part of their powerful selfhood, of the individuality which has to assert itself against the system. So strong was their approximation of art to life that many were accused of confusing the two, thus derogating from the purity of the former. Ba Jin counters this attack with his usual sincerity: "There is no trace of the artist in me, because I cannot see art beyond life. . . . I am only capable of shouting and yelling in the midst of night. . . ."[50] Like Belinsky some sixty years before, they also believed that literature acted as a forum for political discussion when more obvious channels were closed; that literary works served as a challenge to old beliefs and sought new ones, and that objective truth was discoverable in nature, in society, and in the hearts of men.

In his study of Turgenev's acceptance in America, Gettmann made the interesting observation that the fancied likeness between Russia and America perceived by writers and readers alike contributed significantly to Turgenev's fame in that country, and that literature can cross-fertilize and flourish in a foreign culture in fancy as well

[48] Ba Jin, *Diandi*, p. 36.
[49] Berlin, as n. 29, p. 157.
[50] Ba Jin, *"Dianyi ji dai xu"*, in *Ba Jin wenji*, Vol. 7. p. 7.

as in fact.[51] This also holds true for May Fourth China. While, as Benjamin Schwartz points out, the similarity between the nineteenth-century Russian intelligentsia and their May Fourth counterparts lies in their both sharing the values which are "concomitant of the confrontation of a 'traditional society' with the West", there are also significant differences between the two.[52] However, May Fourth writers' "fascination" for Russian literature, and their readiness to see a common cause with their Russian precursors formed a basis for the Russian influence. Moreover, the Chinese propensity for accepting the Russian view of literature and literary criticism in turn enhanced the development of a Chinese fiction which also made human history and destiny its main subject.

[51] R. A. Gettmann, *Turgenev in England and America*, p. 138.
[52] Schwartz, as n. 37, p. 126.

3 The Russian Hero in the May Fourth Context

In his Nobel Lecture, Solzhenitsyn paid great tribute to literature, which, he said, played a pivotal role in transmitting condensed experience from generation to generation: "in this way it becomes the living memory of nations. In this way it keeps warm and preserves within itself its lost history in a way not subject to distortion and falsification. Thus literature, along with language, preserves the national soul."[1] Solzhenitsyn's tone may seem too bold, and his perception of the importance of literature may sound extravagant to readers who are used to the soft, often self-effacing manner of modern novelists. But he is simply reiterating in this electronic age a century-old tradition which was instituted and refined by the great nineteenth-century Russian masters. Literary historians have repeatedly pointed out the primacy of literature for the Russian people, that the great Russian novels have become a national institution, in which writers document the spiritual history of the nation, and the readers are initiated into it. The pages of the great works: *Eugene Onegin, A Hero of Our Time, Oblomov, Rudin, Fathers and Sons, Crime and Punishment, War and Peace*

---

[1] Alekandr Solzhenitsyn, *The Nobel Lecture on Literature*, tr. into English by Thomas P. Whitney, p. 20.

etc. are vibrant with the different literary images which were born of the writers' endeavour to preserve the national soul. In the opinion of Phelps, whose critical work *Essays on Russian Novelists* had widespread influence in May Fourth China, interest in the human soul was so prominent in the Russian novel that everything else took a subordinate place.[2]

Indeed, "character and introspection" has been regarded as a unique feature of this literary genre.[3] In concrete terms, the Russian novelists transposed the thoughts, doubts, conflicts or even failures of their experiences into the hearts and minds of their literary protagonists. The result is a hero-centred novel, though not in the classical or "Carlylean" sense of the word "heroic".[4] Emphasis is on the moral responsibilities of the characters: it is for their moral worth as human beings and more often than not for their inadequacies, that these characters are being observed and judged. Thus a hero who is in some way inadequate as a human being became a well-known type in Russian literature. This gallery of "unheroic-heroes" includes faltering intellectuals like Pushkin's Onegin, Goncharov's Oblomov, Turgenev's Rudin; blundering types like Tolstoy's Pierre and Levin; or Dostoevsky's circumscribed "underground men", not to mention the nihilists in Andreyev's work or the depraved Sanin in Artzybashev's novel of the same name. Tolstoy made the point when he said to Gorky: "Heroes—that's a lie and invention; there are simply people, people, and nothing else."[5] To the Russian writer, the only hero is truth—whether it is bright or gloomy—a view which is still upheld by Solzhenitsyn at the present day. The writer's primary task is thus to explore, clarify and then generalize human experience. This generalized experience is then embodied in the life and ultimate destiny of the literary protagonists. In his perceptive study of the Russian hero and his heritage, Mathewson wrote that nineteenth-century Russian literature was dominated by two types of hero. The first are the

[2] Phelps, *Essays on Russian Novelists*, p. 75. See also n. 17 below.

[3] Mirsky, *A History of Russian Literature*, p. 171.

[4] See Thomas Carlyle's thesis of "the hero as poet" in his *On Heroes, Hero Worship and the Heroic in History*. This work was translated into Chinese by Zeng Xubai in 1932.

[5] Maxim Gorky, *Reminiscences of Tolstoy, Chekhov and Andreev*, p. 79.

men without hope—Pechorin (Lermontov's *A Hero of Our Time*), Stravrogin (Dostoevsky's *The Possessed*), and Prince Andrei (Tolstoy's *War and Peace*). They are successful in their rebellious search for annihilation. The second are the men with hope and good intentions. Such are Turgenev's ego-centred heroes, Rudin, Lavretsky, and Bazarov, who failed, in spite of themselves, to live as they planned to, or to fulfil the apparent promise of their lives.[6] The common link between these two types is their alienation from other human beings and from purposeful activity. Both types, particularly the second, made a strong impact on May Fourth letters. Before delving into the Chinese image of these Russian heroes, it is useful first to look at the make-up of the Chinese intellectual hero and the circumstances leading to his rapidly achieving popularity in the 1920s and 1930s.

The disintegration perceived at the end of the Qing dynasty did in principle prepare the ground for a prefiguring of the hero racked with anxiety. Distressed at the dilapidated state of the country and desirous to be of use, many late Qing intellectuals, convinced of the social use of fiction, poured their feelings and ideals, and to a lesser extent, their inner conflicts, into the hearts and minds of their fictional heroes. The result is the rising popularity of the autobiographical-intellectual hero-type, though some basic differences distinguish them from the modern hero. We can quote two examples. First, Liu E's protagonist Lao Can, who came to maturity in the twilight period of classical Chinese fiction (1904–1908). Noted for his patriotism, intellect and sense of mission, Lao Can is however different from the iconoclastic May Fourth hero in his single-minded purpose, holding to his conviction that a regenerated Confucianism will bring peace and happiness to all, and lead China back to its former glory.[7] The May Fourth intellectual hero is also distinguishable from another late Qing prototype, the "hero of sentiment" characterized by Su Manshu's Saburō in

---

[6] Mathewson, *The Positive Hero in Russian Literature*, p. 15.

[7] Lao Can's enthusiasm in preaching the gospel of benevolence, his colourful adventures redressing the wrongs of the world and his steadfastness and good humour in the face of obstacles make him something of a Chinese "Don Quixote". As such, the essence of his being differs from the modern Chinese "Hamlets".

Duanhong lingyan ji (Lonely Swan).[8] While a sense of frustration, an intensity of emotion and a delicate sentiment pervade both Saburō and the modern hero, the difference between them lies in the former's singleness of purpose, which guides him through the troubled seas of sentiment. Lacking a frame of reference, the modern hero fails precisely because of his intellectual doubts and his complicated mind, which incapacitate him from spontaneously and unconditionally offering himself to love or to any cause at all. Yu Dafu, whose autobiographical hero comes closest to Manshu's in his delicate sentiment, actually criticizes the romantic monk-scholar's hero as being over-sentimental.[9] This remark underlines their difference in outlook as well as their approach to literature.

Taken in general, the May Fourth writer's aim to intellectualize experience and convert thought into living drama is an important trademark of May Fourth fiction. In some of the celebrated literary types is synthesized the fate of many a young intellectual, and the experiences, conflicts and philosophy of the author. Among the more common qualities of this type of hero is his intellectual freshness: his intense craving for knowledge, his passionate resolve to participate in the affairs of the country, a troubled consciousness of the various problems of China, an awareness of his inability to alter the course of events, and a general malaise at his failure to exert his individuality, both in love and in duty. What Qu Qiubai wrote in 1921 has topical relevance for the entire twenties and thirties. He remarked that a lot of pioneering work needed to be done to bring about China's emergence from a "society-less" state. While his romantic temperament urged him to reach out, to rally the multitude to his call, he was hamstrung by the rational dictates of his mind, and fell victim to the contradictions of his inner self.[10] This sense of dilemma and tragedy runs through many writers and their heroes. Hu Feng also wrote to the same effect that his consciousness had been elevated by May Fourth literature, which

[8] For Manshu's hero, characterized by his monastic bent, his nostalgic attachment to his mother, and his triangular relationship with the two women devoted to him, both loyal and self-sacrificing, love and sentiment are his leitmotif, and sadly, the core of his malady. See Leo Lee's discussion of him, *The Romantic Generation*, pp. 58–78.

[9] Yu Dafu, "Zaping Manshu de zuopin", YDWJ, Vol. 5, pp. 258–260.

[10] Qu Qiubai, "Zhongguo de 'duoyude ren'", QQWJ, Vol. 1, pp. 170–171.

awakened in him not only the message of the individuality of human beings, but also the sorrow of the accompanying disillusion. The May Fourth spirit made an "infantile idealist" out of him, not knowing what to choose, what to devote his idealism to.[11] The rapid turn of events in the 1920s—the anger and frustration that followed the May Thirtieth Massacre in 1925, the immense optimism that was generated with the Northern Expedition against the warlords by the Guomindang, and the sense of betrayal and defeat that accompanied the persecution of the radically inclined intellectuals—created in them a frantic state of mind, divided between light and darkness, hope and despair, unable to find their balance. As the *North China Herald* put it succinctly in May 1930: "the sense of hopelessness one feels so commonly among all Chinese today is perhaps the worst feature of all."[12] Lacking a proper political forum, literature seems for many the only alternative means of expression. Many transpose their most naked thoughts into their fiction, and many characters are based on real-life models. Not infrequently, the writer reduces the models to mere masks through which he presents problems which are his, not theirs. It is often difficult to say whose identity (the writer's or his character's) is swallowed up by whom. The writer becomes totally involved in his characters. In the case of many May Fourth writers, their writing is yoked up with their lives, so that they are, like their heroes, totally caught up in the conflicts of love and hate, thought and action, ideal and reality, and reason and emotion.[13] This close correspondence between life and literature, and a strong sense of the walled-in nature of human consciousness is a feature unparalleled in the history of Chinese fiction.

The profound significance of this blurring of the line between the writer and his fiction, and of that between the writer and his reader, is that the best of May Fourth fiction conveys not only the inner life and conflicts of many intellectuals, but also the "feel" of a national literature. Obsessed by suffering, his own and that of those around him and eager for the regeneration of his country, the novelist was anxious to act out his self-appointed task as the

---

[11] Hu Feng, "Lixiang zhuyizhe shidai de huigu", *WYWX*, pp. 260–261.
[12] Quoted from L. E. Eastman, *The Abortive Revolution*, p. 21.
[13] See Ba Jin's preface to his *Dianyi ji*, in *Ba Jin wenji*, Vol. 7, p. 7.

spokesman of his age, depicting his anguish and malaise in his heroes. The common reader, on the other hand, often worshipped the writer or his protagonist as someone championing his cause, possessing the foresight to read his mind, and the heart to feel for the whole of mankind. Like his counterpart in French literature at the time, the May Fourth intellectual played the triple role of "the hero, the victim and the buffoon of a tortured era which has experienced politics as tragedy, freedom as necessity, and where history has assumed the urgent voice of a fatum."[14]

Thus, in their readiness to find common cause with their Russian predecessors, May Fourth intellectuals saw the Russian hero not only as personifying generalized human experience, but also as representing the experience of a people in distress, anxious to find new expression in life amidst great historical changes. To them, the actions and the failure of the Russian hero reflect with great realism the society in which they themselves live, where traditional values are drastically transformed in the wake of modernization and political upheavals. The Russian hero, therefore, impressed them not just as a universal human type, but as having particular meaning for May Fourth China. Ba Jin was not only voicing his own view when he expressed great sympathy and admiration for the Russian hero, whose aspirations, tastes and character were to him similar to those of the Chinese people, though the latter live in a different age and another land.[15] Likewise, Lu Xun was not just relating his own experience when he proclaimed that Russian literature opened to the May Fourth readers the beautiful soul of the oppressed; that Chinese souls were inflamed when they read the Russian writers of the 1840s, and that they suffered with the characters created by the writers of the 1860s.[16] He was, in short, presenting the view and experience of a great many of his contemporaries, who were able to find what they were looking for in the Russian works, whether it was the superfluous hero, the thwarted revolutionary, the underdog character, or the underground man.

The list of "classical" Russian heroes who had "inflamed" the

[14] Victor Brombert, *The Intellectual Hero: Studies in the French Novel, 1889–1955*, p. 19.
[15] Quoted from Monsterleet, *Note sur Pa Chin*, p. 90.
[16] Lu Xun, *LXQJ*, Vol. 4, p. 460.

Chinese mind easily includes Pechorin, Arkaky Arkakievich (Gogol's "Overcoat"), Devushkin, Goldyakin (in Dostoevsky's *Poor Folks* and *The Double* respectively) of the 1840s; Rudin, Lavretsky, Raskolnikov, Oblomov of the 1860s; Tolstoy's Nekhlyudov of the 1880s; and Artzybashev's Sanin, Ropshin's George, Andreyev's thought heroes, and Gorky's characters in the "lower depths" produced around the turn of the century. In short, two images of the Russian hero caught the Chinese imagination: the injured and contrite portrayed mainly in the works of Dostoevsky and Tolstoy; and the superfluous and nihilistic in those of Turgenev, Andreyev, Artzybashev and Ropshin.

I. The Injured and the Contrite

a. Dostoevsky

We recall from the first chapter that the great works of Dostoevsky —notably *The Brothers Karamazov* and *The Idiots*—were not available in Chinese translation until quite late. Thus the "Dostoevskian" impact was limited and came primarily from two sources. First, from the critical studies of Baring, Phelps, Brandes and Kropotkin that May Fourth writers were familiar with;[17] and second, from his earlier works: *Poor Folks* and *The Double* of the 1840s, and *Crime and Punishment* of the 1860s. In general, Kropotkin and his contemporary critics without exception emphasized the image of the "insulted and injured" in Dostoevsky's work. So popular was this term taken from the author's novel of the same title, that its Chinese translation *"bei wurude yu bei sunhaide renwu"* 被侮辱的與被損害的人物 was persistently used by Chinese readers to represent the fate of the "underdogs" in society —down-and-out clerks, shopkeepers, peasants, workers, prostitutes

---

[17] Baring's *An Outline of Russian Literature* and *Landmarks in Russian Literature*, Brandes' *Impressions of Russia*, Kropotkin's *Russian Literature: Ideals and Realities*, and Phelps' *Essays on Russian Novelists* were among the titles listed by Zheng Zhenduo as some of the most important works on Russian literature; *XSYB*, 14.8 (1923.8), pp. 1–12. For the reception by and impact of these critical works on Chinese critics, see McDougall, *The Introduction of Western Literary Theories into Modern China*.

and the like. In a long treatise on Dostoevsky's thought, Shen Yanbing (Mao Dun) stated in the popular *Short Story Monthly* that although Russian writers had invariably shown their sympathy towards the "insulted and injured" characters, none was as deep and broadminded as Dostoevsky. For him, the most striking feature of this author was his love for mankind. He did not teach people what to love, but about love itself, and placed himself on the same level as those with whom he had sympathy.[18] Mao Dun's exaltation of Dostoevsky's insulted characters not only typified the view of many of his contemporaries in the early and mid-1920s, but also served as a guide to young readers interested in Russian literature.

There is one particular episode in Dostoevsky's *The Double* which was quoted over and again by Chinese writers. So great was its impact on Chinese readers that it is worth quoting in full here. This is the section when the protagonist Goldyakin is described as a rag:

> Possibly if someone wanted, if someone, for instance, actually insisted on turning Mr. Goldyakin into a rag, he might have done so, might have done so without opposition or punishment (Mr. Goldyakin was himself conscious of this at times), and he would have been a rag and not Goldyakin—yes, a nasty, filthy rag; but that rag would not have been a simple rag, it would have been a rag possessed of dignity: it would have been a rag possessed of feelings and sentiments, even though dignity was defenceless and feelings could not assert themselves, and lay hidden deep down in the filthy folds of the rag, still the feelings were there. . . .[19]

What struck the Chinese mind was not the filthy, distasteful image of the "rag"; rather this image became a symbol of the readers'

---

[18] Shen Yanbing (pseud. Lang Sun), "Tuosituoyifusiji zai Eguo wenxueshi shang de diwei", *XSYB*, 13.1 (1922.1), p. 21.

[19] *The Double*, tr. by Constance Garnett, p. 210. This passage is either quoted or has its content related in many places. A random check shows that it appeared in Lu Xun's article "*Qiongren* xiaoyin", Mao Dun's "Tuosituoyifusiji de sixiang", Xiao Hang's "Tuosituoyifusiji zhuanlüe", Chang Feng's "Tuosituoyefusiji de *Baichi*", and Wei Congwu's "*Tuosituofusiji quanji* zongxu". Ba Jin actually used *The Rag* as the title for a collection of his short stories—*Mabuji*. The Chinese appreciation of the social content of Dostoevsky's work is understandable. When his works first generated interest in the West at the turn of the century, Dostoevsky was primarily regarded as a social writer, a champion for the injured and insulted. See Helen Muchnic, *Dostoevsky's English Reputation*.

pity and intense sympathy for the outwardly dehumanized and repulsive, but sensitive and morally superior creature. As the Russian critic Solovev pointed out, a deep feeling of social injustice was evoked in Dostoevsky's early works, and "in the existent order of things the [ethically] *best* people are at the same time essentially the *worst* for society, for which reason they are destined to be poor people, insulted and injured".[20] A similar feeling was also evoked in the May Fourth readers. It was precisely these ethically superior people with hearts of gold who were relegated to the lower depths of society that, according to a Chinese critic, "aroused our sympathy, love and pity".[21]

The Chinese "sympathy, love and pity" for the Dostoevskian injured hero induced some to share the author's general "philanthropic" attitude to life, and others to write under the spell of the Russian giant, or both. Suffice it to mention his impact on a few May Fourth leaders. To Lu Xun, Dostoevsky was a "cruel genius", the "grand inquisitor" who pierced through the deep recesses of the human soul.[22] What impressed Lu Xun most was that his hero invariably suffered mental tortures, but was cleansed in the process of being injured, recuperating, and finally being healed. This release of strong emotion enabled such heroes to find new meaning in life. It was because of this kind of faith in the author and his work that Chinese readers welcomed Dostoevsky as a "humanitarian writer", a term which was used with high regard especially in the 1920s. On this understanding, Mao Dun recommended Dostoevsky to the readers of *Short Story Monthly*, convinced that his work could effectively act as a stimulant to the drowsy and complacent Chinese youth. He wrote admiringly that Dostoevsky's heroes or heroines might have been killers, robbers, or prostitutes, but in the end they were all repentant for their sins. "They have led depraved lives, but their souls are never depraved."[23]

This insight brings to the fore another aspect of Dostoevsky's

---

[20] Vladimir Solovev, "In Memory of Dostoevsky", in P. Debreczeny and J. Zeldin (eds.), *Literature and National Identity*, p. 174.

[21] Chang Feng, "Tuosituoyefusiji de *Baichi*", *Wenxue zazhi*, 2.1 (1947.6), p. 204.

[22] "*Qiongren xiaoyin*", *LXQJ*, Vol. 7, pp. 103–104.

[23] Shen Bing (Mao Dun), "Tuosituoyifusiji de sixiang", *XSYB*, 13.1 (1922.1), p. 6.

impact—the image of the contrite soul. This is patently shown in
the admiration shown for and sympathy showered on Raskolnikov,
the central hero of *Crime and Punishment*. It is worthy of note that
the philosophic plane of the novel—Raskolnikov's inner struggle
to be his own master so that everything is in his power—did not
impress the Chinese readers. Nor did the hero, when he committed
murder in the name of power, thinking that he had the right to do
so, make a good impression. It was rather the "punishment" part
of the book, crystallized in the confession of the hero, which held
their imagination. The deed of murder, which Raskolnikov considered as only a transgression of an external and senseless law,
suddenly became for his conscience a sin, a transgression of internal
ethical truth. For his transgression of external law, Raskolnikov
received legal retribution from without in exile and prison camp,
but his internal sin, as Solovev put it, could be "expiated only by
an internal act of renunciation".[24] Some critics have branded the
hero's renunciation as his "final collapse", as "not a conversion
but simply a defeat of the man from the underground".[25] Chinese
readers reacted otherwise. To noted critics like Zhou Zuoren, Hu
Yuzhi or Mao Dun, Raskolnikov's humbling experience, his eventual
discovery of meaning in his love for the prostitute Sonya, was both
instructive and morally uplifting. The final act of the hero, when
he knelt in front of the heroine and exclaimed: "I did not bow down
to you individually but to suffering Humanity in your person"
touched the hearts of the Chinese critics. Overawed by what he
called the "magnanimous spirit" of the hero, Hu Yuzhi considered
that this line represented "the quintessence not only of *Crime and
Punishment*, but also of the whole corpus of Dostoevsky's
work".[26] In the same vein, Zhou Zuoren wrote engagingly that
a love when it filled the soul could turn it from bad to good,
and that this was the key to understanding Dostoevsky's entire
works.[27] Even with the increasing radicalism of the intellectual
climate towards the late 1920s, when some writers brought in the

[24] As n. 20, p. 177.
[25] Marc Slonim, *The Epic of Russian Literature*, p. 286.
[26] Yuzhi, "Tuosituoyifusiji de yisheng", *DFZZ*, 18.23 (1921.12), p. 79.
[27] Zhou Zuoren, afterword to his translation of W. B. Trites' article on
Dostoevsky, included in *Yishu yu shenghuo*, pp. 349–351.

class element in the analysis of Dostoevsky's "oppressed" hero, his humanitarianism continued to command respect from Chinese readers.[28] Jin Yi, for example, wrote a story in 1942 which is strongly reminiscent of *The Insulted and Injured*.[29]

Zhou Zuoren, to return to him, went on to assert in his article that Dostoevsky chronicled in great detail the condition of Raskolnikov in Siberia, an experience which was based on that of the author himself. But Dostoevsky did not dwell on the turn of events seven years later (i.e. when the hero had finished his sentence). This story was taken up by Tolstoy who related it in the life of Nekhlyudov in *Resurrection*. Zhou's assertion, though far from the truth, is interesting nevertheless. By linking the two heroes together, Zhou was, in effect, taking "poetic licence" to single out the only common denominator between these two characters—their love for a heroine of humble origin who urged them to disown their past and confess their former "sins". At the same time, he overlooked the enormous difference between these two distinctly dissimilar types. Zhou's distortion reveals a prevailing May Fourth concern—the preoccupation with the character who confesses, of whom Raskolnikov as well as Nekhlyudov are eminent representatives.

b. Tolstoy

In his study of Tolstoy, Georg Lukács concluded that the Russian master set the task for writers in Western Europe by his clear vision of the truth to be obtained by means of love, a love embracing all mankind.[30] Love for mankind was just as much Tolstoy's message to the May Fourth writers. It is revealing that of Tolstoy's works, the one which drew the greatest response in China in the 1920s and

[28] For example, Lu Xun, while still admiring Dostoevsky's greatness as the grand inquisitor of the human soul, as he did in 1926, was sceptical of the Russian's tolerance, expressed in his essay "Tuosituoyifusiji de shi" written in 1936, *LXQJ*, Vol. 7, pp. 411–413; He Qifang also related his mingled feeling of sorrow and excitement in reading Dostoevsky—the excitement of being tormented and then immediately embraced, and the excitement of one, who, after tormenting others, immediately kneels in front of the one who suffered and cries for forgiveness, *Xinghuo ji*, p. 140.

[29] Jin Yi, "Renmen" in *Jin Yi sanwen xiaoshuo ji*, pp. 424–448.

[30] Georg Lukács, *Studies in European Realism*, p. 259.

1930s was not his *War and Peace*, or his *Anna Karenina*; but his final major "moral tract"—*Resurrection*. While few read *War and Peace*—a complete translation of the work did not appear in China until 1947,[31] and *Anna Karenina* likewise attracted little attention from the reading public, *Resurrection* was a different matter. Not only did it appear in many different translations, but it was hailed by Zheng Zhenduo in his pioneering *Concise History of Russian Literature* as a great artistic achievement. Zheng was deeply moved by the novel's theme of "Nekhlyudov being saved as a result of love, sympathy and contrition".[32] Another critic described the work as "reaching tragic proportions", while he gave but scant attention to *Anna Karenina* and *War and Peace*.[33] The young novelist Xu Jie admitted that he had "learnt the meaning of a contrite soul" through reading the novel.[34] The single most laudatory remark about the work came from Mao Dun. Every single phrase of Tolstoy's later works, he claimed, of which *Resurrection* is a prime representative, was wrung from the deep recesses of a contrite heart. So moving was the work *Resurrection* that he claimed that every human being, be he a prodigal son, a monster killer or habitual thief, could not refrain from weeping upon reading it. Behind the words of mercy and compassion is the spirit of humanitarianism and non-resistance to evil. In his later works is crystallized the soul of Tolstoy, as well as that of Russian literature. Nobody, according to Mao Dun, has reached such heights before in world literature.[35] Once again, the thrust of the argument is on the image of the contrite heart.

In contrast, contemporary Western readers of the novel had mixed reactions. Of these, the most sympathetic came from Kropotkin, who thought *Resurrection* the most international of all Tolstoy's works, because the problems and contradictions the book raised

---

[31] The translators of the work, Guo Moruo and Gao Di wrote in the preface to their translation that the number of Chinese who have read the entire *War and Peace* amounted to very few.

[32] Zheng Zhenduo, *Eguo wenxueshi lüe*, p. 55.

[33] Chen Shuliang, "Tuoersitai dansheng baizhou jinian", *DFZZ*, 25.19 (1928.9), p. 46. The author was also particularly impressed by Tolstoy's other "confessional" works. He considered, for example, *My Confession* as more important than Tolstoy's other works in explicating Tolstoy's outlook on life.

[34] Xu Jie, "Ni bishang nidi yanjing ba!", *WYFX*, 2.3 (1947.5), pp. 281–282.

[35] Shen Yanbing, "Tuoersitai de wenxue", *Gaizao*, 3.4 (1920.12), p. 97.

were not merely of Russian society, but of "Society the civilised world over."[36] Having said this, Kropotkin had to qualify his statement by admitting that the principal character Nekhlyudov is "not sufficiently living". Mirsky was less enthusiastic in his appraisal. He considered this a lesser work than *War and Peace* and *Anna Karenina*. Nekhlyudov's conversion, much appreciated by Chinese readers, appeared to him to be not a revelation of inner light, but a cold decision to adapt to the moral law so as to escape the stings of conscience and acquire inner peace.[37] To Chinese readers, however, it was not *how* Nekhlyudov arrived at his decision which mattered, whether calmly or with emotion; what attracted them was the action itself: that he confessed his past "misdeeds", severed the ties with what his past represented—high society and its shams —and followed Katiusha to Siberia. The repentant nobleman found new life in his love for the downtrodden and unfortunate—this was the appeal and the romanticism of the story, and its moral for the Chinese readers.

The question remains however—why did Chinese writers and readers find the "Russian contrite characters" so appealing? This has to be answered against the background of the general "populist" leanings of the May Fourth leaders. Their brand of populism can be traced back to the late Qing. Yan Fu advocated the Western idea of the inalienable rights of the individual in the preface to his translation of Huxley's *Evolution and Ethics*. He further linked man's happiness with his capacity to do good: while it is good for individuals to strive for their own happiness, greater happiness is to be found, Yan reasoned, when one cares for the happiness of all.[38] Yan's merging of the two attitudes—to benefit the self and the collective—is reminiscent of Bentham's brand of utilitarianism. The enormous influence of Yan on late Qing and May Fourth ideas is a well-known fact. The search for the greatest happiness for the greatest number had already become one of the favourite slogans of May Fourth intellectuals. Leaders of opinion like Chen Duxiu, Cai Yuanpei, Hu Shi, Lu Xun, Zhou Zuoren, Mao Dun and the

[36] Kropotkin, *Ideals and Realities in Russian Literature*, p. 147.
[37] Mirsky, as n. 3, p. 307.
[38] *Tian yan lun:* (i) "Xin fan", p. 25; see also his article "Lun shi bian zhi ji", in *Yan Fu shiwen xuan*, p. 5.

like all held such ideas during one stage or another of their intellectual development. At the core of their belief was the conviction that all human beings shared a common destiny. If an individual was concerned with his own destiny, he should also be concerned with the destiny of all—thus esteem for individual self-respect was aligned with respect for the masses. This brand of populism acquired an enthusiastic following in May Fourth China, even though many of those who promoted it remained idealists at the time, with no specific programmes to implement their populist ideas, or a clear notion of the analysis of society. In the late 1920s and early 1930s, some young intellectuals even went further to propagate, as the Russian populists did some decades before, the idea of "going to the people". It is not surprising that this "populism" later took on a Marxist character.

In the realm of literature, Chen Duxiu proclaimed as early as 1917 that China's new literature should be for the people, realistic and popular. This theme was taken up and further developed by others. Zhou Zuoren, for example, came up with the term "commoner's literature" (*pingmin de wenxue*).[39] In the same vein, the writers congregating around the Association of Literary Studies formally endorsed the view that literature should champion the cause of the underdog, a position shared even by their arch-rival, the Creation Society, and less surprisingly also by the "proletarian" writers of the late 1920s. It is in this context that the contrition of the rich and highborn like Nekhlyudov in *Resurrection* (or Nezhdanov in *Virgin Soil* for that matter)—who in renouncing the world, rose above it and discovered a new beauty in forgiveness and love—appealed to their conscience, or provided them with examples to follow. The redemption of the mighty was actually described by Zhou Zuoren as "pulling themselves out of an inhuman

[39] Zhou Zuoren, "Pingmin de wenxue", in *Yishu yu shenghuo*, pp. 1–10. For Zhou, one particular feature of this literature is that it seeks to document the happiness and despair, success and failure of the common people; rather than those of the heroic, mighty and highborn. This theme is reiterated in his well-known "Rende wenxue" (Human Literature), in which he sought the introduction of more Western literary works to broaden the outlook of Chinese readers, foster in them a "human conduct", and make possible a "human living". Ibid., p. 30. Mao Dun also considered the propagation of a commoner's literature the foremost task of the writer and the critic, *MWZJ*, Vol. 1, p. 5.

existence".[40] Xia Yan, who adapted *Resurrection* for the stage, told in 1943 of how his heart ached every time he read the work. He was indeed speaking his own feeling when he wrote that it must have been a great spiritual burden for Tolstoy, who was of noble birth (Xia Yan was also born of a relatively rich family), to learn to make himself akin to the people.[41] The May Fourth writers' eagerness to make themselves akin to the people was precisely what caused them great anguish and deepened the sense of futility in their works. Their anguish came as a result of their recognition that it was difficult to reach the people, who possessed a spiritual outlook different from theirs. (Recognizing this weakness of the intellectuals, Mao Zedong later tried to shorten the distance between the "city" and the "country" by forcing the intellectuals to reform themselves and take on a mass outlook.) On a more personal level, many May Fourth writers, brought up in the turmoil of the 1911 Revolution and its aftermath, became acutely conscious of the fact that they were confined to this life alone, a life full of hardship and suffering. The political realities of the 1920s hardened and confused further their fragile minds. It was partly because of this "feeling for the tragedy of life"[42] (to quote from Průšek) that May Fourth writers in their inward gaze looked at human misery with disgust and indignation on the one hand, and self-reproach and compassion on the other. The impulse of the Russian repentant characters to embrace the suffering of the world thus caught their imagination. Tian Han, for example, was full of admiration for what he termed the "Tolstoyan contrite personalities". He found their upward struggle to better themselves morally uplifting, and dismissed those content to remain in the bottomless abyss as "evil personalities".[43]

In his perceptive study of Tolstoy's novels, the noted Russian critic Nikolai Strakhov wrote: "Neither traditional villains, nor traditional heroes are seen. The human soul appears in a great variety of types: it appears weak and subject to passion and circumstances, but

[40] Zhou Zuoren, "Rende wenxue", *Yishu yu shenghuo*, p. 17.

[41] Xia Yan, "Wo maole yici daxian—gaibian *Fuhuo* houji", *Xia Yan lun chuangzuo*, p. 56.

[42] Průšek, "Subjectivism and Individualism in Modern Chinese Literature", *AO*, 25.2 (1957), p. 262.

[43] Tian Han, *Sanye ji*, pp. 58–59.

essentially, in the last analysis, it is guided by pure and good aspiration."[44] In broad terms, a good aspiration also directed Dostoevsky's insulted and injured characters. What is more, they are relegated "underground" by their hyper-sensitivity and the consciousness that they are circumscribed by forces beyond the sway of the mortal human soul. It is both these authors' philanthropic sympathy for the suffering and insignificant, and their efforts to ensure humane treatment for all classes and all people which expressly aroused the awareness of the May Fourth intellectuals and stirred their conscience.

II. The Superfluous and Nihilistic

Whereas the impact of Tolstoy and Dostoevsky depends essentially on their moral approach to problems both personal and social, the fame of Turgenev, Andreyev, Artzybashev and Ropshin in China lies in their "realistic" portrayal of the revolutionary currents, and their pinpointing in varying degrees the mood and yearnings of intellectuals in times of challenge, gloom or defeat. It was the historical circumstances in China, particularly in the 1920s, which were responsible for the enormous impact of these authors.

a. Turgenev

Turgenev was one of the most widely read authors in modern China; his popularity came in the 1920s when he had already acquired a world reputation.[45] His appeal came mainly from his vivid depiction of current social issues, and his ability to capture the predicament of the liberal-minded intellectuals in their search for new expression when confronted with a culture as well as a political and social system in decline. All his novels have a topical reference.

---

[44] Nikolai Strakhov wrote three reviews of *Voina i mir* (War and Peace), all published in *Zaria* between 1869 and 1879. The present quotation is from an English translation of the article in *Literature and National Identity*, p. 142.

[45] For example, the English readers were impressed mostly by Turgenev's art, whereas the American readers approached Turgenev's novels not only as repositories of facts pertaining to a hostile nation, but as serious, artistic narratives of life anywhere.

They are works which chronicle the "body and pressure of time", meaning chiefly the evolution of Russian society and the Russian intelligentsia in the several epochs of the 1840s, 1850s and 1870s. The themes of his many novels, for example: the injustice and ineptitude of the system of serfdom, the recognition of the humanity and wisdom of the peasantry, the conflict between fathers and sons, the unhappiness in the homes of the gentry, and above all, the frustrations of the morally sensitive intellectuals, were all familiar topics to Chinese readers in the 1920s.[46] It is no surprise that Turgenev was highly regarded by Chinese writers. One eminent Chinese critic commented in 1923: "The outstanding characteristic of Turgenev's works is that [in them] he could document the changes of his time. His novels cover a range of more than thirty years. During this time, Russian society witnessed changes from old to new, and the intelligentsia underwent drastic changes. Turgenev was able to discern with a philosophic eye, and render with art and much foreboding, the permutations of contemporaneous intellectual society. . . . It is difficult to think of another writer endowed with as distinctive an artistic genius for mirroring the spirit of the time."[47] This is a fine observation. The question asked by many today whether Turgenev had actually given a true picture of Russia is outside the scope of this study.[48] It is beyond doubt that he was regarded in his day as a leader of opinion on social and intellectual problems.

[46] Mao Dun, for example, mentioned in his "Social Background and Creation" that the conflicts in thought between the obstinate father generation and the enterprising son generation in Chinese society is so acute, that there should be works like Turgenev's *Fathers and Sons* to depict it. *MWZJ*, Vol. 1, pp. 48–51.

[47] Yanbing, *et al.*, "Dujieniefu", in *Jindai Eguo wenxuejia lun*, pp. 9–10.

[48] In his *Turgenev's Russia*, a sympathetic study of the author, Victor Ripp argued that the author's fiction should not simply be regarded as a representation of Russian reality. He suggests that his fiction provided contemporaries with the means to shape their political and social views. While this argument is open to discussion, it is obvious that in May Fourth China, Turgenev's novels were read by many young intellectuals as a guidance to matters political, social or literary. For example, the young writer Xiru declared that after reading *Fathers and Sons* several times, the novel opened new vistas for him, of the ominous signs of the collapse of the father generation, and the courage and nihilism of the son generation, *WYWX*, p. 77. The poet Xin Di wrote that he was unable to forget, twenty years after first reading *Fathers and Sons*, the image of the young iconclastic Bazarov, who dared to wage war against authoritarianism, *Yedu ouji*, p. 47.

However, Turgenev's works were not just of contemporary interest. They deal sympathetically with a perennial human problem—the fallibility of mankind. It is precisely Turgenev's portrayal of this human problem, embodied in his unheroic intellectual hero, that fascinated Chinese men of letters and the reading public. His protagonists are representatives of phases successfully traversed by the Russian intellectual: Rudin is the progressive idealist of the 1840s, Bazarov the militant materialist of the 1860s, Nezhdanov the repentant nobleman of the 1870s. Through them, Turgenev created a famous generation of "superfluous men" (after the title of his short novel, "The Diary of a Superfluous Man"), heroes whose intelligence and aspirations could find nothing to work on or through in the objective social world. Here are people of good intentions, intelligent, sensitive, articulate and passionate, imbued with hope and idealism, who want to transform a corrupt society. But in the end they all discover, partly through their own supine, half-hearted and impractical natures, that the world is intolerably apathetic and effete. Revolt is futile and reform out of the question. They finally fall victims to this decaying social order and waste away. Kropotkin was most illuminating in his analysis of Turgenev and his heroes: "He knew that the true curse of the Russian intellectual is the weakness of his will, the insufficient strength of his desires. Perhaps he felt it in himself. . . . This absence of strong desire and weakness of will he continually, over and over again, represented in his heroes. But this predilection was not a mere accident of temperament and character. It was a direct product of the times he lived in."[49]

Many Chinese writers immediately identified themselves with Turgenev's superfluous man. They found that the ideals, aspirations, and even the half-heartedness of Turgenev's protagonists reflected their own. This is why Turgenev's works were honoured with a great number of translations, greeted with tremendous enthusiasm, and served as models for not a few Chinese writers. I shall here quote a few of the many testimonies to show the impact of Turgenev's hero.

In his autobiography, the well-known writer and critic Cao Juren

[49] Phelps, *Essays on Russian Novelists*, p. 77.

labelled himself the Rudin of China, and talked of the immense appeal of the Russian hero: "there was a time when Turgenev's novels were seen as a mirror of the souls of intellectuals of our generation. We frequently considered ourselves to be Rudins."[50] From the fervour with which Turgenev's novels were received and from the way in which writers identified with his heroes, Cao's remark seems hardly exaggerated. Rudin's hero-type and what he represents stirred the enthusiasm of Qu Qiubai. Like the Russian hero before him, Qu also found himself torn between heart and intellect. He felt that he had fallen victim to the conflicts of European and Chinese culture, and that his primitive drive was hampered by an "unhelpful society". Citing Rudin as an example, Qu labelled himself a "superfluous man".[51] According to Liang Yuchun, Turgenev's hero won not only the admiration of the May Fourth readers, but what was more important, their hearts, because he was so similar in type to the May Fourth intellectuals. Liang was enchanted by the respect Turgenev showed his impractical heroes. This, together with his sardonic attitude to the highborn and rich, is for Liang a unique feature of his work, which is much more interesting than those which only depict the weak to enlist one's sympathy.[52] To complement this view, we can add Guo Moruo's frank assertion in a letter to Cheng Fangwu, citing their identification with Nezhdanov, the protagonist of *Virgin Soil:* "We have had a taste for literature, but we treat it lightly; we want to come close to the masses, but we also have a little of the aristocratic spirit: we are lazy, doubting, we lack the courage to put into practice [our convictions]. We are indeed China's 'Hamlets'. This is precisely the reason I love to read *Virgin Soil*."[53] Guo's remark summarizes the attitude of the May Fourth writers. It is true that the character of Turgenev's torn apart intellectual, who often fails because of the objective social environment, but also more often than not out of his own human weakness, can be found in most people in the world. But the magnitude of his impact on the May Fourth intellectuals,

[50] Cao Juren, *Xiaoshuo xinyu,* p. 12

[51] Qu Qiubai, as n. 10.

[52] Liang Yuchun, *Lei yu xiao,* pp. 39–40.

[53] Guo Moruo, "Guhong—zhi Cheng Fangwu de yifengxin", *Moruo wenji,* Vol. 10, p. 297.

who identify without reserve with the hero and his failures, is truly remarkable. His typology is tailor-made for the liberal- and social-minded, but at the same time impractical and half-hearted intellectuals of the 1920s and 1930s.

b. Artzybashev

While Turgenev's works develop the "liberal predicament" of the morally sensitive intellectuals, those by Artzybashev express a different element dormant in their psyche—their yearnings in the wake of suppression and defeat.

Writing in 1925, two years before Artzybashev's death, Mirsky commented that "at present no one regards him as a significant writer but only as a curious and, on the whole, regrettable episode in the history of Russian literature".[54] Other notable literary historians of the time, such as Masaryk and later Marc Slonim, were equally derogatory in their appraisal. They saw his work, notably *Sanin*, as "sensational", as concentrated exclusively "on the portrayal of sex and violence", and as over-indulgent in describing the bestial nature of man. "Regrettable" may be Mirsky's word for Artzybashev's writings, but Chinese readers thought otherwise. Indeed, Artzybashev's fame reached its peak in China at this time, especially after the Northern Expedition of the Guomindang in the late 1920s. His *Sanin* was translated more than once, and in 1934 quickly became one of the most sought after books in the Beijing University Library. Well-known men of letters wrote enthusiastically about his works, and young men considered themselves Chinese Shevyrevs and Sanins. One such example is the young poet Lu Yishi, who is said to have shared the nihilistic temperament of Shevyrev.[55] And Gao Changhong likened Lu Xun's (the translator of "Shevyrev") first meeting with him to that of Shevyrev heckling Aladiev, his meek young neighbour.[56]

Artzybashev's popularity in a foreign country like China in the 1920s is not difficult to understand. His work presents the lives

[54] Mirsky, as n. 3, p. 403.
[55] Hu Lancheng, "Lu Yishi", in Yang Zhihua (ed.), *Wentan shiliao*, pp. 271–275.
[56] Gao Changhong, "Xiegei *Panghuang*", in *Zoudao chubanjie*, p. 34.

and thought of young revolutionaries. Punitive expeditions, mass executions, death-throes and bloodshed fill the pages of his revolutionary tales with gruesome power. Shevyrev, the hero of the work of the same name, was utterly disillusioned and sought to end his life, believing that human society, to the improvement of which he had devoted himself completely, was beyond redemption. Lu Xun was particularly moved by the hero's compassion. His view of this work influenced that of many of his followers and readers. He saw Shevyrev as torn apart by love and hate: a hate that originated in his broadminded love of mankind, and culmimated in his final act of revenge on society. However, he disapproved of Shevyrev's way of taking revenge: by firing at the masses whom he considered at least as culpable as the oppressive government. In Lu Xun's own words, he was "horrified" by this act of violence.[57]

The Chinese intellectuals gave a similarly qualified reception to *Sanin*. Different, if not less nihilistic, was the manner in which Sanin, the protagonist of the novel, expressed his emptiness and despair after an abortive attempt to topple the oppressive government. His is a manifestation of the mentality of bourgeois youth who sought to forget the unpleasant experience of the stillborn revolution, emancipated themselves from human conventions and beliefs, and became intoxicated in sensuous pursuits.[58] While Sanin's "emancipation" won him popularity in Russia, particularly after the abortive 1905 Revolution, Chinese readers, though fascinated by his typology, adapted this work to their own tastes. It is noteworthy that apart from a few exceptions (Mao Dun's *Zhuiqiu* [Pursuit] is one of them), Chinese writers did not seize upon the theme of sadness and despair in Artzybashev's work, nor did they stress the bloodshed, sexual licence and sense of the insanity of

[57] Lu Xun, *LXQJ*, Vol. 3, p. 357.

[58] *Sanin* is Artzybashev's most important novel. Though written before 1905, it only appeared in the immediate aftermath of the abortive 1905 Revolution (in 1907) when a wave of disillusionment with public ideals swept the intelligentsia. Personal enjoyment and freedom from morality became the order of the day. Sanin's philosophy is simple: "I do what I want to do and can do"; "man should be as free as a bird". It became a sensation of the time and acquired immediate popularity, though conservative critics condemned its immorality and modernists pointed out its lack of literary merit.

human life that dominated it. Instead they found in his work a new type of hero in the protagonist Sanin. Sanin certainly does not possess the traditional heroic qualities; but his forthright courage enables him to defy all human conventions, and stand firm against opposition. He is thus a source of strength, and appeared to them as an image of the totally emancipated man. In 1929, a young writer profusely admitted her indebtedness to the author; she wrote, "he is the centre of my adoration, because he makes me open my eyes, and plunge into the current of the times with courage. Owing everything to him, I am no longer stifled by so-called morality and faith."[59] Sanin's hero-type was especially appealing when at the time the Chinese themselves were trying hard to assert their own individuality and do away with all sorts of corrupt and outmoded conventions. Perhaps Zheng Zhenduo's remark about Sanin, that he "embodies something that lies latent in all human beings", that he is "representative of the spirit of the new, strong, and brave"[60] sums up the attitudes of the Chinese writers.

On a more general level, this concern for the fate of the revolutionaries reflected some of the burning problems of the time. The 1920s were a period of unrest and turbulence. Many intellectuals who were reaching out for a more humane society were persecuted first by the warlords and then by the Guomindang. In the wake of suppression and defeat, a sense of disillusionment enveloped the intellectuals. Artzybashev's works, concentrating on the afflictions of revolutionaries before, during and after their defeat, therefore, had a strong attraction for the conscience-ridden Chinese intellectuals. Commenting in 1927 on Artzybashev's story "Morning Shadow", the well-known critic Qian Xingcun (A Ying) explained the relevance of his work to Chinese readers:

> Artzybashev's description is a realistic reflection, a reflection of the literary trend that prevailed after the October Revolution. Sadness and despair reigned; this is also a truthful reflection. A sense of despair and sadness also pervades the young Chinese following recent revolutionary events. It will ultimately be reflected in our own creative writings. For

[59] He Shaoxian (pseud. Shaoxian), "Xifeng chuilai de hua", *YS*, 5.27 (1929.9), p. 51.

[60] Xiti (Zheng Zhenduo), "Azhibasuifu yu *Shaning—Shaning* de yiben xu", *XSYB*, 15.5 (1924.5), p. 5.

the time being, there is no need for such creations, for Artzybashev has already placed them before our eyes.[61]

Not only had Chinese readers taken Artzybashev's work to heart, but, they also did not have to wait long before novels with an "Artzybashevan" flavour began to take shape in their native land, notably in Ba Jin's *Destruction* (1928), and Mao Dun's trilogy on the intellectuals, *Eclipse* (1928).

c. Ropshin

Chinese intellectuals who read Ropshin's *The Pale House* also found in it a revolutionary sentiment, the hero of the novel was not a revolutionary, but a cold-blooded terrorist. Unlike Artzybashev's Shevyrev, who was hamstrung by the uncommunicative masses, Ropshin's George was concerned only to carry out the orders of his superiors. Also, unlike revolutionary heroes of the previous decades (for example, those in Stepniak's works)[62] who were totally devoted to the organization and to the cause of the people, and ready to sacrifice themselves at any time for their faith, Ropshin's George was an egoist as well as a sceptic. For him, life had no meaning, and he had no higher motive for killing than the question: "Why shouldn't one kill? And why is murder justified in one case and not in another?"[63] He argued that he could not understand why to kill in the name of this or that is considered right, while to kill in the name of something else is wrong. At the end George found that suicide was desirable in itself—as a means to escape from this stale variety show which was life—and he shot himself.

[61] Qian Xingcun on Artzybashev's "Morning Shadow" in "Eluosi wenxue manping", *XSYB*, 19.1 (1928.1), p. 194. Presumably by October Revolution, Qian actually meant the 1905 Revolution. Artzybashev wrote that the feeling of defeat of his protagonist Sanin came not as a result of the 1905 Revolution, as it was commonly thought, because his work was completed before the Revolution. See the preface to the English translation of the work.

[62] For example, Stepniak (pseud. of Sergei Kravchinskii, 1851–1895) describes the life of the nihilist terrorists in his novel *The Career of a Nihilist* and his pamphlet *A Life for a Life*, in which he also gives concise expression to the ethical theory of the terrorist revolution. For a brief description of Stepniak's views, see Masaryk, *The Spirit of Russia*, Vol. 2, pp. 193–205. Ba Jin translated sections of Stepniak's *Underground Russia* into Chinese, included in his *Menkan*.

[63] *The Pale Horse*, English translation, p. 5.

Contemporary reaction to this controversial hero-type was decidedly mixed. Masaryk, who reflected one school of thought, was disturbed to see the emergence of a new type of terrorist who was riven by mental as well as moral chaos;[64] while Vengerova, the English translator of the novel, thought differently. Despite the pessimistic tone of the work, said the translator, there was a "suggestion of hopefulness in the struggle for the establishment of idealistic values, in the attempt to make the will conform to the standards of enlightened thought".[65] Chinese sentiments frankly sided with the latter. They also viewed the work hopefully, finding two aspects of the work particularly potent. First, it met their criterion of "realism"—in that it movingly documented the spirit and thought of the time; and second, it delineated with insight the development and transformation of a revolutionary soul.

In an article entitled *"The Pale Horse* and the Russian Social Movement", Qu Qiubai examined the work from the point of view of the environment that bred it. He regarded it as encapsulating Russian social thought in the decade between the 1905 and the October Revolution. Russian terrorism, he reasoned, was the result of the vile social environment, and the "Georgian-type" of young man was but its natural offspring. They were representatives of the rebellious young who were utterly opposed to the dark and indulgent life. Underneath the cold surface of these assassins, Qu claimed, were the most sincere, honest and ardent of hearts which pined for love and social justice.[66]

This point of view was shared by other fervent advocates of the work. In his preface to the translation of the novel, Zheng Zhenduo wrote that Russian society was thirsting for change at this juncture, and Ropshin's *The Pale Horse* describes a section of Russian national life better than any other book of its kind. It laid bare the psychological transformation of some terrorists, and, therefore, constituted "a must for those who are intent on reading about and investigating the Russian revolutionary movement".[67] Such was

[64] Masaryk, as n. 62, pp. 444–456.
[65] Vengerova, *The Pale Horse*, Introducton, p. vii.
[66] Qu Qiubai, *"Huisema yu Eguo shehui yundong"*, XSYB, 14.11 (1923.11), pp. 1–10.
[67] Zheng Zhenduo, *"Huisema yizhe yinyan"*, XSYB, 13.7 (1922.7), pp. 1–2.

essentially the view of Shen Yanbing, who also dwelt on the reflective aspect of the work in great detail.[68]

Appreciative as they were of the "social realism" of the novel, Zheng and others would not have been so united in their compliments had it not been for the interpretation of the type of the hero George. Shen Yanbing made this point clear at the beginning of his article: one might indeed hate or love, admire or pity this ringleader of the terrorist group, but one could not remain indifferent. Shen's reaction to "the metamorphosis of this soul in a particular environment" was one of sympathy and understanding. George's action in killing, Shen argued, was his only way of keeping himself alive when others were chasing him as a cat chases a mouse. His indifference was the paradoxical outcome of an acute sensitivity: if there could be no pure love in life, there could be no fear of death either, hence his final abhorrence of life. A confirmed evolutionist at this time, Shen related the behaviour and thinking of the hero to his social environment, and extolled the author's "greatness" in describing the hero's metamorphosis with great delicacy.[69] Moving a step further, Zheng Zhenduo and Yu Pingbo regarded the hero's sentiment as typifying the tiredness of and the scepticism about life of at least some modern men. Zheng related George's coldness and egoism to the phenomenon of the modern age.[70] (Zheng's concept of "modern" was that of catching up with the times, which in May Fourth China was considered not only desirable, but essential.) More philosophical by nature, Yu Pingbo viewed the hero's life and thought as representing "a tremendous tragedy in the struggle for life."[71] The hero saw everything as futile, be it the revolutionary fervour of a terrorist, or the drowsy numbness of love. At the end, the only reality for him was, "my revolver is with me"—suicide. The solution to the problem of life lay not in living, but in not living. In the seemingly contradictory action of the hero— an egotist ending his own life in suicide—Yu saw epitomized the sorrow of modern man: the never-ending conflict between love and

[68] Shen Yanbing, "*Huisema xu*", *Huisema*, pp. 1–8.
[69] Ibid.
[70] Zheng Zhenduo, as n. 67.
[71] Yu Pingbo, "Ba *Huisema* yiben", *XSYB*, 14.10 (1923.10), p. 1.

hate, passion and intellect. George was to Yu a conflict incarnate, but an admirable one, nevertheless: "I can say with certainty that his hate is but a transformation of his love. He said that he dies out of hatred for society, but underneath he gives up his life for love of this world."[72] George's death was but an appropriate end to the greatest problem of all, that is, the problem of life and its fulfilment.

It is interesting to observe the Chinese critics' reaction to the controversial George. By fixing him solidly in his environment, and explaining away his egoism, they were able to find meaning in his endeavours. George's blood-letting terrorism and his nihilistic ending of his own life were accepted by Chinese readers with a tolerant smile. For them, his intelligence and conscientiousness compensated for his apparent lack of heroism and charm, although he was not lacking in will-power. Indeed, Shen Yanbing considered that George's strength of purpose might provide an example and a stimulus to the apathetic youth of China who were a major cause of concern to the May Fourth leaders.[73]

d. Andreyev

Andreyev's reputation in China was due to the fact that, like Ropshin, he succeeded in capturing the mood of the Russian youth at the turn of the century, particularly after Russia's defeat by the Japanese in 1904, and the failure of the Revolution in 1905. His appeal was, however, more wide-ranging and multi-faceted. Defeat is, no doubt, the dominant theme of Andreyev, and it seems that he had some mental quirk which forced him to dwell on the abnormal and diseased. The outcome is that his work is not only decadent, but decidedly pathological. "He has deepened the universal gloom of Russian fiction", noted one critic, "not by descending into the slums with Gorky, but by depicting life as seen through the strange light of a decaying mind."[74] Mirsky thought Andreyev's message for the Russians was a "thorough nihilism and

[72] Ibid., p. 3.
[73] Shen Yanbing, as n. 68, p. 8. Lu Xun also expressed his concern in many of the essays written at this time. See especially his collections of essays *Refeng* and *Fen*.
[74] Phelps, as n. 49, p. 269.

negation";[75] human life, society, morals, culture are all lies, death and annihilation is the only reality, and "madness and horror" (the opening words of his work *Red Laugh*) are the only feelings that express human understanding of the truth. This view is shared by many other Russian critics.

May Fourth writers, however, responded in a different manner. Andreyev was one of the most avidly read writers in the 1920s, and his works were amongst the first to appear in Chinese—Lu Xun translated "The Lie" and "Silence" in 1908. There is also a deep humanitarian spirit in Andreyev's work, and it was to this that the Chinese writers responded, as well as to the vividness with which Andreyev depicted Russian reality. May Fourth leaders like Lu Xun, Mao Dun, Zhou Zuoren, Zheng Zhenduo and Geng Jizhi, who were awakened themselves to see the life endured by the suffering masses, were specially captivated by Andreyev's compassionate spirit towards the weak and the suffering, exemplified by his *Red Laugh* and *The Seven Who Were Hanged*. Apart from arousing their conscience, these works also achieved the effect of wiping away the boundaries and distances between people.[76] On this understanding, Mao Dun rated him a first class writer.

However, Andreyev was too complicated a writer to be taken just as humanitarian. This the May Fourth writers knew. They were well aware of his dual attitude to life—his heart which was determined to live life, and reason that abnegated it.[77] Andreyev's negative aspect of life—the gloom and pessimism which enveloped his works—posed a challenge to the Chinese writers. They were unwilling to accept his despair. Mao Dun's reaction can be said to represent one school of thought. A determinist at this time, Mao

[75] Mirsky, as n. 3, p. 398.

[76] Zhou Zuoren made this point in his note to the translation of Andreyev's "Ben Tobit" (Chitong), *XQN*, 7.1 (1919.12), pp. 69–70. Andreyev actually mentioned this as an important aim of his *The Seven Who Were Hanged*. See his letter to the American edition of the work, 1909, p. 11.

[77] Wei Suyuan mentioned in his "Xu *Wang xing zhong*" that Andreyev's works can be epitomized in the author's dual attitude to life: between belief and scepticism, desperation and revolution, *MY*, 1.10 (1926), p. 408. Mei Chuan, the translator of *Red Laugh*, also said to the same effect that Andreyev's theme is above all "a fervent endeavour to dissolve the incongruity between a curse on the reason for life and praise of the passion for it". "*Hongdexiao* yinyan", *YS*, 5.15 (1929.6), pp. 64–65.

Dun argued that the defeatist tone in Andreyev's works was the natural flavour of literature after great changes and calamities.[78] Andreyev was, moreover, for him, the spokesman of his age, when the boredom, disappointment and despondency of young people in Russia reached its peak, especially after their defeat in the Russo-Japanese War in 1904.[79] It was thus Andreyev's "realism" which appealed to Mao Dun, Zheng Zhenduo and the like. Lu Xun was also appreciative of Andreyev's ability to depict the gloom of Russian life. The writer's ability to dissolve the difference between the inner world and its outward manifestations was to Lu Xun realism of a higher order which he called symbolic realism.[80] By this, Lu Xun apparently meant the author's blurring devices which obscured surface differences and left his world ambiguous.

This is the limit to which Chinese writers went in accepting Andreyev's gloom. They hardly shared his belief in the insanity of humanity. For many May Fourth intellectuals, brought up in Kropotkin's notion of "anarchism", human misery is due to the working of an oppressive order, and with its eventual destruction light will shine through again. Thus, attracted as Mao Dun was by Andreyev's abstract conception of the "iron round of destiny", he later embodied his rejection of it in his determination to take the brave Scandinavian goddess of destiny as his spiritual guide.[81] Li Jiye, who translated The Black Masks in 1926, hoped to abandon the play one day with the same fervour as he received it.[82] Li Dichen also read To the Stars with cautious optimism. He admitted that the Chinese intellectuals, like Andreyev, might also be plagued by the contradictory forces of the will to live and its abnegation, and he hoped that "the damnable abnegation will not appear in the masses if they have hope for the future".[83]

All in all, inspired as the Chinese men of the 1920s were by Andreyev's depiction of the conflicts between intellect and feeling, passion and reason, they responded to his attitude to life according

---

[78] "Andeliefu sihao", XSYB, 11.1 (1920.1), p. 4.
[79] "Andeliefu", DFZZ, 17.10 (1920.5), p. 67.
[80] LXQJ, Vol. 10, p. 185.
[81] Mao Dun, "Cong Guling dao Dongjing", XSYB, 19.10 (1928.10), p. 1146.
[82] "Xu Hei jiamianren", MY, 2.1 (1926), p. 42.
[83] "Du Wang xing zhong", MY, 1.11 (1926), p. 520.

to their perception of what constituted human misery. What they were looking for was personal solutions. Because they were oppressed by the gloom and boredom of Chinese life, they drew close to Andreyev's works, which some twenty years before painted with vividness and force a no less oppressive Russia. But for them, unlike their Russian counterparts, Andreyev's message of "horror and madness" had little meaning. In 1930, Qian Qingcun published his full length study of the Russian writer, in which, as might be expected, he was critical of Andreyev's "decadent" tendencies. Despite his many criticisms, he acknowledged the Russian as "a genius who prefigured the style of urban impressionism".[84] Yet Qian's study, detailed as it is, did not shed much new light on the writer. What it did show, rather, was the leftist leanings of writers like himself—they now broke their restraint and denounced the other aspect of Andreyev's work—its morbidity. The influence of this "pathological genius" was beginning to pass its peak.

III. Conclusion

Thus, we see in this first phase of Russo-Chinese literary contact that there was a conscious effort by Chinese men of letters to propagate those elements in Russian literature which they thought were most suited to the cultural, social and political climate of their native soil. They tried to borrow from Russian literature in order to enrich their national life. In the process of borrowing, they rejected those elements they found were either unsuitable or undesirable. This emphasis on the content of Russian literary works resulted in the rise to popularity of some fine writers, as well as some mediocre ones. The fame of secondary writers like Artzybashev and Ropshin rose to such heights in the 1920s that it almost equalled that of Tolstoy and Turgenev.

More specifically, the image of Tolstoy and Dostoevsky in May Fourth China was represented chiefly by their contrite or insulted

---

[84] Qian Xingcun, *Anteliefu pingzhuan*, pp. 135–136. Qian's study, totalling some 140 pages which appeared in 1931, is to date the only full length study of Andreyev in Chinese. Qian indeed had much to say for the author's modernist technique, and his reflecting the life of the urban intelligentsia.

characters. The novels in which these characters appear—*Resurrection, Poor Folks, The Double* are some of the most "reflective" of their works—were more socially and ideologically inclined and as such, more translatable. At the same time Dostoevsky's more beguiling and complex characters like Ivan and Dimitri Karamazov —with their inner lust and irrationality, and their vision of a spiritual life that begins in alienation from routine morality—were hardly grasped by the Chinese readers. Likewise, prophetic as Tolstoy was, the unique and grand attraction of his writing (John Bayley calls it nicely: "the morning freshness of a morning already irrevocably in the past")[85]—his insulating himself to look back into the heart of the Russia of old, from which he derived his principle of non-resistance—was beyond the reach of May Fourth writers. Thus, Tolstoy's celebrated character-types—Anna, Prince Andrei or Pierre —hardly attracted any attention in China, while Nekhlyudov, a much lesser artistic type, became a model for emulation. The importance of both Tolstoyan and Dostoevskian characters therefore lay in their moral vigour, and their ability to heighten the moral sensitivity of Chinese writers and readers. Chinese writers might use the symbol of the "rag" or the image of the contrite soul in their fictional works, holding them up as a mirror for their moral inadequacies, but the actual "typological" influence of these heroes on their Chinese counterparts was not as marked as the more "socially and ideologically" inclined heroes of Turgenev, Artzybashev or Andreyev.

The superfluous, nihilistic or egoistic heroes in the "reflective" works of Turgenev, Artzybashev, Ropshin or Andreyev, who either provided the relevant social message or reflected a similar revolutionary situation to that of their Chinese readers, stirred them to the depths. These heroes, as one writer observed, might not be the most lovable; they were nevertheless the most admirable.[86] Indeed, one of the most fruitful products of this process of cross-fertilization was the emergence of the "unheroic-hero" in Chinese fiction, one with an unmistakable Russian flavour, be he "Turgenevan", "Andreyevan", "Artzybashevan" or "Ropshinian". Like

[85] John Bayley, *Tolstoy and the Novel*, p. 34.
[86] Kai Ming, "Tuoersitai de shiqing", *YS*, 14 (1925.2), pp. 1–2.

Pushkin's Onegin, the Chinese heroes have an abundance of *amour propre*, a dryness of soul, a strong tendency to dream, and an embittered mind seething with futile activity. As a rule, they fail in their battle against life, fall back defeated, and poison themselves. Like many a Russian tormented type, they are profoundly unhappy, because they see farther than their fellows. They are indeed "heroes of their time" (to borrow a phrase from Lermontov)—inseparable from the moment in which they live, expressing the spirit of a particular decade, and sometimes almost a particular year. In their fate can be read the history of their own age, as it was seen by their creators, who saw themselves as the spokesmen of a people in chaos. In the following section, I shall delineate the typology of the intellectual hero of Lu Xun, Yu Dafu, Mao Dun and Ba Jin, for they are representative of the intellectual types of the fiction of the period, and of the different aspects of Russian influence.

Part II: The Hero of His Time

4 Yu Dafu's Superfluous Hero

I. Autobiography and Fiction

The saying that "all literary work is nothing but the author's autobiography", I feel is absolutely true! Objective attitude. Objective description. No matter how objective you are, if and when a pure objective attitude, a pure objective description is possible, then there will be no use for the talent and soul of an artist; and the reason for the existence of the artist will disappear.[1]

There is a sense in which to pay tribute to Yu Dafu is to resist the biographical spell, to withstand the temptation to react to his work as one might react—in simultaneous identification and repulsion—to his character. Yet the spell is irresistible. The reminder of the gap between the life and work of a writer seems irrelevant, not because the two are naturally irreconcilable, but because Yu Dafu is an autobiographical writer who makes himself the protagonist in his fiction, and, as Leo Lee remarked, attempts to

[1] Yu Dafu, "Wuliu nian lai chuangzao shenghuo de huigu" (1927), *YDWJ*, Vol. 7, p. 180. Page numbers of Yu's creative works from *YDWJ* will appear in brackets after the citation.

go beyond himself to create visions of himself through his writings.[2]

As a person, Yu is one of the most pathetic of all modern Chinese writers. His life (1896–1945) is a story of unchecked passion in all its transformations—its obsessions, its morbidities, its guilts, its remorses; interspersed with moments of illumination.[3] He was the youngest child of a strong-willed and down-trodden mother, who had to shoulder the burden of raising the family after the premature death of her husband. Yu's feeling of closeness and indebtedness to his mother was to become one of the main motives of his writings. In his student days in Hangzhou and Jiaxing, he spent his time in voracious reading,[4] and surrendered to introspection, fantasy and romantic dreams of grandeur. He would roam along the quiet paths and hill tracks of Hangzhou composing poems. He grew up in a place rich in history and romance, and this place held a life-long fascination for him.

These dreams and fantasies soon gave way to the realization of the dark realities of the time. China at the turn of the century was the "sick man of Asia", an ailing monarchy encumbered with a

[2] In his study of Yu Dafu, Leo Lee employed the Eriksonian scheme to analyze the author's confusion of identity and psychological problems. See *The Romantic Generation*, pp. 81–123. Lee's study remains to date one of the most illuminating. Though my intepetation of Yu's hero-type differs in some ways from his, I am indebted to him for the many ideas in his essay.

[3] For a detailed biography of Yu Dafu, see Itō Toramaru *et al.* (ed.), *Iku Tatsufu shiryō*; Anna Doleželová, *Yu Ta-fu: Specific Traits of His Literary Creation.* Yu's own autobiography up to his sojourn in Japan, "Yu Dafu zizhuan" (1–7) published periodically in *Renjianshi* (1934.11–1935.4) and "Xue ye" in *Yuzhou feng* (1936.2), and his diaries of episodes of his life from 1927–1935 are valuable sources for understanding his life and thought. Included also in *YDWJ*, Vol. 3.

[4] According to his autobiography, Yu had already become something of a bibliophile and a good poet (in classical style) in his student days. Three works influenced him greatly at the time: an anthology of poems of Wu Meicun; a book describing the origins and impact of the Boxers by an anonymous writer; and a collection of essays, poetry and memorials written during the Sino-Japanese War in 1894, entitled *Putian zhongfen ji.* He was also well grounded in Chinese classics, especially literature. He mentioned reading the voluminous *Zizhi tongjian, Tang Song shiwen chun, Baixiang cipu,* and *Xihu jiahua*—every tale of which he read more than twice. See his autobiography 5 and 6 in *Renjianshi*, 23, pp. 33–36; 26, pp. 25–28. He was also fond of *Hongloumeng, Xixiang ji, Hua yue hen,* and particularly *Taohua shan* and *Yenzi jian, YDWJ*, Vol. 7, p. 177.

corrupt administration and outmoded conventions. The young Yu Dafu abhorred the wretched condition the country was in, especially the hard lot of the destitute and ignorant peasants, but felt unable to do anything to help alleviate their deprivations. He was fond of reading books dedicated to a righteous cause, and felt the urge to join the struggle for a just and more accommodating China. But during the revolutionary struggle to overthrow the Manchus in 1911, he found himself "standing outside the revolutionary whirlwind, doing nothing beyond clenching tight his empty fists, and shedding a few idle tears of an observer".[5]

The feeling of being an onlooker, a morally conscious intellectual unable to find his path of commitment, oppressed the mind of the precocious seventeen-year old, and continued to do so throughout his entire life. Amidst this inner restlessness and confusion came his years of study in Japan (1913-1921). His experience in these eight years left an indelible mark on his mind. Reminiscing over this period in 1931, he wrote: "I had witnessed the gradual decline of my motherland. I had experienced the humiliating insult of coming from a foreign country. My feelings, thoughts, and experiences were steeped in sorrow and despair. Like a young widow newly deprived of her husband, I lacked strength and courage. I conveyed my pity and sorrow in my story 'Chenlun' (Sinking), which in those days caused an uproar."[6] Estranged from his native country, and failing to find proper outlets to relieve his intense feeling, he turned to sombre and sado-masochistic relationships with women. Public houses and brothels became his favourite haunts.

His last year's sojourn in Japan coincided with his first literary success. The next few years (1922-1927) were the most turbulent in his life, as he wandered listlessly between the north and south of China. These were also the most productive in terms of literary output. (It is mainly on the short stories written in this period that I centre my study.) He founded the Chuangzao she (Creation Society) with Guo Moruo, Cheng Fangwu, Zhang Ziping and Zheng Boqi, advocating a form of romanticism in literature. He wrote prolifically, and moved from one job to another, unable to settle

---

[5] "Zizhuan, 7", *YDWJ*, Vol. 3, p. 439.
[6] "Chanyu dubai", *YDWJ*, Vol. 7, p. 250.

down in the country from which he had been disassociated for so many years. The difficulties that he encountered with the Creation Society, with his career, with the corrupt government, and above all with his family during these years—he was married to a woman he did not love—increased his restlessness and unhappiness. Entangled in social, psychological and moral dilemmas that he could not escape, he gave in to the compounded pressures, and saw himself as a "superfluous man". Writing with bitterness in 1927, he concluded:

> Seeing the opportunists run rampant at a time when the entire country is in a state of frenzy, while we the conscience-ridden can neither do nor say anything, but must just sit down and wait for death. . . . This is our true sorrow, our real dilemma.[7]

His misery grew into a state of almost tragi-comic indifference, into a dream-like alienation. It was only relieved by his love affair and subsequent marriage to Wang Yingxia in June 1927. There followed a few calmer years under the protective shadow of his beautiful, shrewd and sociable wife. He seemed for a while to settle down, first in the bustle of Shanghai, then in the tranquility of Hangzhou. He did a lot of leisure travelling during this period, and produced a good many travel notes which are reminiscent of the travel essays of classical literature—being relaxed in mood and formal in style. Most of the short stories written at this time (and there are not many of them) were engagingly set in the "hills and lakes" of idyllic Hangzhou and Fuyang, his native village. This peace of mind, however, came to an abrupt end with the breakdown of his marriage in 1938. His self-imposed exile in Nanyang (Malaysia and Indonesia today) ended, after some years of unsettled life, when he was executed by the Japanese in 1945.

There is a kind of hideous rhythm in the pattern of life of Yu Dafu, if anything so disrupted can be termed a rhythm at all. Like the "superfluous man" in his creation, his life is riven with all kinds of contradictions which act and interact upon each other. He was sensitive yet ineffective, by turns confiding and mistrustful, cowardly and assertive, conceited and diffident, innocent and perverse, restless and slothful, filial and ungrateful. His inner life is made up of a

---

[7] "Riji wenxue", *YDWJ*, Vol. 5, p. 263.

strange combination of intellectual insight, unbounded imagination, heightened consciousness, high vulnerability, and an unremitting sense of shame and remorse. The irony of it all is that he understands only too well that he is circumscribed by these conflicts, and in his morbid delight, he seems to be exciting himself with his own torment.

All these conflicts are amply reflected and represented in Yu's own fiction. In fact, taken as a whole, his fictional works represent an enlarged view of his personal life, and his ideals about the nature of human destiny in a particular social milieu. The specific traits of Yu's literary creation, and the relation between his life and works can be, and have been, fruitfully dwelt upon.[8] My concern here is specifically with the typology of Yu's hero, the superfluous man, and the relation with his Russian precursors. We must also consider his relationship with the Chinese heritage and the Japanese *watakushi-shōsetsu* (!-novel). As most of his autobiographical short stories were written in the 1920s, I will concentrate on his short stories of this period. Discounting the autobiographical element, it is my contention that Yu Dafu's hero owes most to the influence of nineteenth-century Russian literature. Before looking into this relationship, it is important first to discuss his relationship with Western European literature, especially with the romantic hero.

II. The Romantic Hero?

Much has been said about the Western European literary influence on Yu Dafu's fiction. C. T. Hsia says that Yu's first volume of short stories, "while obviously showing the strong influence of Western romanticism . . . [influences] are also traceable to the Chinese literary tradition".[9] J. Průšek observes that the life and works of Yu Dafu recall "figures in European romanticism of the beginning of the late nineteenth century—a Byron, or a Czech Mancha,

---

[8] See Doležalová, as n. 3; and Lee, as n. 2.

[9] C. T. Hsia (ed.), *Twentieth-Century Chinese Stories*, p. 1. He also mentions in *A History of Modern Chinese Fiction* that "a Wertherian self-pity exaggerates alike the hero's love for nature and the ache in his heart", p. 104.

including their tragic end".[10] Leo Lee likens Yu's hero to the "Wertherian type".[11] The critics' opinions of Yu's hero-type are indeed diverse. Whether he is "Wertherian" or "Byronic", or something else, is worth further investigation.

It can be asserted with confidence that Yu's relationship with Western romanticism is easily discernible. As we have already seen, he was a founder member of the Creation Society, which strongly advocated Western romanticism (or its offshoots). The leaders of the society emphasized the individualist approach to creation, and believed (as far as one can tell) in the beauty and perfection of literature. Goethe, Heine, Shelley, Byron, Whitman, Spinoza, Nietzsche were at one time or another among their favourite writers.[12]

While the young "Creationists" rallied under the banner of "Western romanticism", it must be pointed out that the society was loosely organized, and their understanding of the concept and the movement was essentially emotional and divided. This can be seen from the constant quarrels and abrupt changes or modifications of literary viewpoint among the founders in the few short years of the Society's history.[13] What bound them together in the first place were their general romantic attitudes towards life and literature. Zheng Boqi, one of its founders, made this point clear. He said that most members had had the experience of living in a foreign country for a long time, and had become extremely nostalgic. The pressures they had undergone while abroad, and their disgust with the conditions at home, aroused in them a spirit of rebellion. Their mingled feelings of nostalgia, humiliation and disillusionment filled them with "gloom and anger" upon returning. At the same time, their rejection of rationalism in philosophy and naturalism in literature left them with a hankering for an anti-rationalist literature.[14] This comment provides the background for understanding the romantic tendencies of many "Creationists", and above all, the hero-type of Yu Dafu's fiction.

[10] J. Průšek, *Three Sketches of Chinese Literature*, p. 79.

[11] Lee, as n. 2, pp. 280–281.

[12] Zheng Boqi, "Introduction", ZXD, Vol. 5, pp. 11–12.

[13] See Li Helin, *Jin ershinian Zhongguo wenyi shichao lun*, pp. 95–114, 143–167. See also the relevant chapters in Marián Gálik's *The Genesis of Modern Chinese Criticism*.

[14] Zheng Boqi, as n. 12, p. 12.

As Yu Dafu is a person of undisguised romantic temperament, who talks of the superiority of the artist, of beauty being the core of art, of delivering oneself from "Weltschmerz" in literature, and who claims that some of his short stories may have been unconsciously influenced by the German "Ich-erzählungen" form of literature,[15] one would expect his hero-type have some affinity with the Western romantic hero. Let us start by examining the typology of the hero in "Sinking" for this purpose, as he is supposed to have a close association with Western romanticism, and the German romantic hero in particular.

"Sinking" (1921) has little plot or characterization, something that is typical of all of Yu Dafu's short stories. Everything in the story is seen from the viewpoint of the single central character, who can be closely identified with the author himself. The story is about the spiritual malady of the protagonist when in Japan as a student. Without friends, at odds with his family, and distressed by the state of affairs in his own country, the hero falls into some form of "megalomania" and "hypochondria", to use his own words. In his unbearable moments of psychological distress, he longs for the body and love of a woman, but is oppressed by his sense of inferiority at being a "Shinajin" (Chinaman). He releases his sexual impulse through masturbation and various sexual deviations. One day, afraid that his act of spying on the daughter of his landlord taking a bath may have been discovered, he flees the house. Later, in an intoxicated mood, he courts a waitress in a brothel. The next day, having left the brothel full of remorse and confused as to his own identity, he contemplates suicide.

At the root of the hero's "hypochondria" are the dissonances and inner conflicts of his mind. We can detect that beneath his timid and pallid looks is a character who greatly prizes his individuality. He has tried to reach out of his tiny cocoon, but the hypocrisy and shallowness of his colleagues repel him and he retreats further into himself, wrapping himself up in all sorts of idle dreams. He escapes from people, and tries to soothe his "Weltschmerz" through the romantic grandeur of nature. He becomes the "child of nature", and in his frequent "idyllic wanderings", he finds comfort in the works

[15] *"Dafu zixuanji xu"*, YDWJ, Vol. 7, p. 255.

of Heine, Wordsworth and Gissing. In one of those rare and fleeting
moments when he feels himself liberated from ennui he says:
"forgive, forgive! I have forgiven ye all who have wronged me.
Come ye all and make peace with me!"[16] But more often than not,
after these fleeting moments comes even greater distress. And he
resorts to self-abuse—masturbation and masochism.

From the above, we can see the characteristics of the "unre-
deemed Weltschmerz" in Yu's hero—the introspection, the isolation
and quest for solitude, the unbounded craving of the soul as well
as the perpetual dissatisfaction, the ennui and the resultant melancholy, the disgust with life and the attempted flight for relief
to nature or even to suicide.[17] This "Weltschmerz", one notices,
has been anticipated in Rousseau's *Rêverie d'un Promeneur Solitaire*
as well as in Goethe's *The Sufferings of Young Werther*, both works
familiar to the author of "Sinking".

Can we take it that Yu's hero is a "Werther" or "Byron" in the
Chinese context, as critics have claimed? While it is undeniably true,
as Průšek puts it, that in "Sinking" Yu "returns to the description
of the aberrant mental states of a young man and also the tragic
conclusion of 'Drowning' (Sinking), motivated only by emotional
disturbance and gloomy moods, recalls the suicide of young
Werther",[18] we can go beyond these general traits and discern
certain fundamental differences that distinguish Yu's hero from his
European counterparts.

It is common knowledge that the European romantics laid
particular emphasis on their right to an inner life. To them, the
impetus towards action comes entirely from the individual. Inward
activity is given priority over all external standards, all practices
and moral achievements. As Werther says: "We very often find
that we get farther with our tacking and tardiness than others with
their sailing and rowing."[19] Hand in hand with this subjectivist

---

[16] "Chenlun", English translation under the title "Sinking" in *Twentieth-Century Chinese Stories*, as n. 9, p. 25.

[17] For a discussion of romanticism in general, see H. G. Schenk, *The Mind of the European Romantics: An Essay in Cultural History*. I am indebted to the author for some of the ideas in this section.

[18] As n. 10, p. 87.

[19] Goethe, *The Sufferings of Young Werther*, tr. by B. Q. Morgan, p. 81.

outlook goes the belief that the ability to comprehend nature and the world, the passion for true love, is confined to an élite whose superiority lies in the fact that it is endowed with perception, and capable of experiencing the emotion of love in a deeper and more intense manner than other beings. "I am quite aware that we are not equal and cannot be equal,"[20] says Werther. This marked élitist notion is characteristic of the European romantics—in Rousseau, Goethe, Byron, Coleridge, Friedrich Schlegel, and the later George Sand and Victor Hugo. As a critic remarked recently: the romantic hero does in some ways still fulfil the traditional heroic role. His attractive appearance often makes him a sort of *homme fatal*. He is almost invariably a gentleman, a member of the leisured class at ease financially. Both his good looks and his freedom from mundane concerns raise him to the level of an idealized, glamorous figure sharply distinguished from the characteristic modern anti-hero with his petty subsistence-level anxieties, his frequent physical imperfections, his embroilment in the grotesque messiness of daily living. Such problems are alien to the Romantic hero who exists, as in Caspar David Friedrich's painting, *Mountaineer in a Misty Landscape*, on a lofty mountain-top high above everyday reality.[21] The existence of such an "aristocratic" and anti-egalitarian leitmotif has induced some scholars to interpret the romantic movement as "the swan song of the European nobility".[22]

In their literary works, a conflict between inner values and outer forms—the State, society, the professions, religion and morality—is presented in which the hero tragically asserts his subjective values rather than renounce them and submit to standards which are meaningless for him. He affirms the inward energy he feels, in its richness and its torment, despite the catastrophe it brings. Goethe's Werther is a good example. When Werther's ardent love is denied fulfilment because the conventions forbid it, there is a catastrophic explosion. To destroy freedom thus is too much. He chooses death, asserts his right to commit suicide and defends it. He is full of confidence and tranquility, one can almost say a sense of joy when

---

[20] Ibid.

[21] Lilian Furst, *The Contours of European Romanticism*, p. 42.

[22] Schenk, as n. 17, p. 13.

he commits suicide: "All is still about me, and my soul so calm. I thank you, God, for granting me in these last moments this warmth, this strength."[23] As Lionel Trilling points out, Werther is "in all things the sincere man; even in his disintegration he struggles to be true to the self he must still believe is his own".[24] Irony— the capacity to scorn oneself, and central to the modern intellectual hero—is totally beyond his comprehension. The Faust myth—the myth of the modern Prometheus—who is a characteristic product of the Renaissance, symbolizes, in Goethe's hands, the theme of human struggle against the barriers imposed by authority and custom. Goethe's heroes have been described as rebels who opt against "practical occupations, social conventions, religious sanctions, against the state, the study, the family; this rebellion is their glory, though it is often impure and unclear, a composite of good and bad, egoism and selflessness".[25] Much more can be said of the rebelliousness of the Byronic hero, a familiar theme that hardly needs elaboration here.

Moreover, this subjectivist outlook of the romantics directs their attention to their own selves, rather than to other people and how they live, or to the prevalent social evils. Even in the case of the relatively few romantics, such as Blake, Wordsworth and Byron, who are aware of and appalled by the evils of modern industrial society, their moral significance lies not in the attack on particular social evils, but in the depiction of the dissonance of man in modern society, of the metaphysical contradiction between inner values and social forms. The heroes in their works are caught in a web from which there is no escape. We admire and love them, yet they must perish, through no fault of their own. Such is the fate of Goethe's Werther, Chateaubriand's René, and Jean Seneaucour's Oberman.

A close examination of Yu Dafu's hero, however, shows that he belongs to a different category. Instead of a confident hero asserting his ego with a seriousness verging on pomposity, we have a weak and vacillating hero bitterly torn apart by his conflicts. At the core of his malaise and self-pity is a deep inferiority complex. For

---

[23] As n. 19, p. 157.
[24] Lionel Trilling, *Sincerity and Authenticity*, p. 52.
[25] Roy Pascal, *The German Sturm and Drang*, p. 310.

instance, his consciousness of being a "Shinajin" oppresses him with a sense not only of racial but even of sexual inferiority. This atrophying sense of uncertainty and inferiority is an essential factor in bringing about his isolation and alienation. Whenever his Japanese classmates laugh and joke in his presence, his face will redden because he thinks they are laughing and joking at his expense. When he lacks the courage to accost the Japanese girls, as his classmates have done, he turns upon himself:

> You coward, you are too cowardly. If you are so shy, what's there for you to regret? If you now regret your cowardice, why didn't you summon up enough courage to talk to the girls? Oh, coward, coward! (p. 24)

This image of an over-sensitive, morbid, humiliated and submissive youth runs through the pages of "Sinking". Even when he is drunk, he fails to shake off his inferiority complex and assert himself in his moment of intoxication. When the waitress asks where he comes from, "his pallid face reddened again; he stammered and stammered but could not give a forthright answer. He was once again standing on the guillotine. For the Japanese look down upon the Chinese just as we look down upon pigs and dogs. They call us Shinajin, 'Chinaman', a term more derogatory than 'knave' in Chinese. And now he had to confess before this pretty young girl that he was a Shinajin." (p. 29)

This underdog mentality of the hero is most patently manifested in the final scene, when he contemplates suicide. He is beset by feelings of shame and remorse, of being deserted, "insulted and injured" (p. 33)[26] and unable to free himself from oppression. Though both Werther and Yu's hero seek death, their feelings upon giving themselves over to it are as different as can be:

> How could I have gone to such a place? I really have become a most degraded person. But it's too late to regret, too late to regret. I may as well end my life here, since I'll probably never get the kind of love I want. And what would life be without love: Isn't it as dead as ashes? Ah, this dreary life, how dull and dry! Everyone in this world hates

---

[26]Yu has here used the term immortalized by Dostoevsky's novel of the same title.

me, maltreats me—even my own brother is trying to push me off the edge of the world. How can I make a living? And why should I stay on in this world of suffering? (p. 32)

Thus, we have in Yu's hero a man who fails to live up to the challenge of his time, who is driven to the edge of the cliff not only by objectionable social pressures but also by his own wavering character and shortcomings. He is remarkably different from the Western romantic hero. While he submits to fate with remorse and regret, the romantic hero meets death with defiance and gallantry. Failure is to the latter more noble than success, and herein lies his heroism.

In a word, Yu's hero shows the general traits of the romantic hero—the contradictoriness, dissonance and inner conflicts, the romantic wanderlust and intoxication with nature. But the core of his sorrow, his outlook on life, and his attitude to love and death, show some fundamental differences.

In addition, this feeling of the "insulted and injured" also governs Yu Dafu's understanding of the European romantic and decadent writers, such as Rousseau, Max Stirner, Theodor Storm, George Gissing and Ernest Dowson. From his opinions of these writers, one gets the impression that he identifies more with the writers than with their works, with the exception of Goethe's Werther, whose confidence and courage his own hero regrets that he lacks.[27]

Of these men of letters, Rousseau appeals to Yu as a social misfit, a wanderer, at times persecuted and at others believing himself a spiritual exile. He shares with Rousseau a sense of solace in nature, a feeling that he can be in intimate communion with it.[28] As to Stirner, his ability to endure life despite a broken family, and an unrequited love affair, fill Yu's mind, "a hundred years later, ten thousand miles away, a good-for-nothing superfluous man . . . with both immense grief and admiration".[29] His fellow-countryman Theodor Storm's nostalgia for his country and his solitary life is very much shared by Yu, who at the time of writing his

---

[27] "Fengling", *Guoqu ji*, p. 53, 1922.7.
[28] See his "Lusao zhuan", *YDWJ*, Vol. 6, pp. 1–18; "Lusao de sixiang yu tade chuangzuo", *YWDJ*, Vol. 6, pp. 19–35.
[29] "Ziwokuang zhe Xudeerne", *YDWJ*, Vol. 5, pp. 141–148.

essay on him, was in "spiritual exile" in Japan.[30]

This identification with an author's despair, disillusionment and loneliness also explains, to a certain extent, Yu's liking for the English decadents: Ernest Dowson, George Gissing and the "Yellow Book" writers.[31] He saw both Dowson and Gissing as sensitive and poverty-stricken intellectuals. Their writings are a reaction to their sense of being swallowed up in the faceless masses of the commercial and industrial metropolis; they reflect the modern pressures of society on individuals, and herald the "twilight of decadence" of contemporary society.[32]

The fact that Yu Dafu sees most of the romantic writers whom he loves and admires as victims of a vile social environment, just like his fictional heroes, leads one to think that his outlook on life and literature presupposes a stand quite different from that of the European romantics. This is clearly brought out by the author's perception of romanticism. In line with Chinese tradition, Yu put strong emphasis on the social responsibility of the writer—a point which is at variance with the European romantics. He distinguished between romanticism and what he called "sentimentalism" (*xunqing zhuyi*). Both "isms" are related, he wrote, in that they have human feeling as their core. But the romantic writer is governed by idealism, pinning his hopes on the future. He is moreover "impulsive, illusory, quixotic and destructive. . . . Reason and thought become in him the total captive of feeling." Works of sentimentalism, on the other hand, are the offspring of someone whose prime is over, whose life is consumed. With the little strength which still remains, he is only capable of sighing for the bygone days which are no more. This unremitting sense of nostalgia "is but a testimony to his present lack of strength and steadfastness, and a camouflage for his present bitter loneliness". Himself lacking in valour and pertinacity, Yu judged that the tone of these works is necessarily melancholic and resentful, nostalgic and fatalistic. It is when a country faces rapid disintegration or is on the verge of collapse that these works are most popular.[33]

---

[30] "Shidumu", *YDWJ*, Vol. 5, pp. 107–116.

[31] "Jizhong yu *Huangmianzhi* de renwu", *YDWJ*, Vol. 5, pp. 169–188.

[32] Yu Dafu has written extensively on this topic in his article "Shenmo jiao shijimo wenxuesichao", *YDWJ*, Vol. 6, pp. 287–289.

[33] "Wenxue gaishuo", *YDWJ*, Vol. 5, pp. 79–83.

These words are autobiographical. A close examination shows that Yu's melancholic and humiliated hero reveals strong traits of "sentimentalism" as he defines it, and at the same time betrays a marked resemblance to the celebrated insulted and superfluous heroes of nineteenth-century Russan literature, especially in the works of Turgenev and Dostoevsky.

III. The Superfluous Man

Before focussing our attention on the typology of Yu Dafu's superfluous man, it is worthwhile looking into his contact with Russian literature, and literature in general. He writes that when he was an eighteen-year-old, he was admitted to the matriculation class of Tokyo First High School. In spite of the heavy work load, he managed to read in his spare time the English translations of Turgenev's novelettes "First Love" and "Spring Tide". His contact with Western literature, once established, continued like a hurricane, and he swept on from Turgenev's works to Tolstoy's, and from Tolstoy's to those of Dostoevsky, Gorky and Chekhov. This obsession with Russian novels, Yu stressed, "may have induced in him a pathological morbid state of mind in those years."[34]

Indeed, Yu's voracious reading of Russian literature has left an indelible mark on his own writings. He has extensively referred to and commented on Russian literature in his works and diaries. Among the Russian writers that he mentioned are Pushkin, Lermontov, Gogol, Herzen, Goncharov, Turgenev, Tolstoy, Dostoevsky, Artzybashev, Bunin, Blok and Ehrenburg. He translated Turgenev's celebrated article "Hamlet and Don Quixote" into Chinese and called it the "best piece of literary criticism".[35] His plans to translate into Chinese Turgenev's *Rudin, Smoke,* and "Spring Tide", and Lermontov's *A Hero of Our Time* were un-

[34] As n. 1, p. 178.
[35] Preface to his translation of Turgenev's "Hamlet and Don Quixote", *YDWJ*, Vol. 7, p. 247.

fortunately never carried out.[36] His fascination with Russian literature made a deep impact on his works—an aspect by and large ignored by current scholarship on Yu Dafu.

In an essay on the nature and function of literature published in 1923, Yu stressed the point that:

> Art should aim at an unstinting naturalness, for peace among nations, for righteousness, intoxication with beauty, a burning sense of sympathy, and a selfless love.... Art is the sympathizer with the downtrodden, and the defender of love. In her realm the differences between countries and races disappears.[37]

While stressing the importance of beauty and naturalness, Yu's humanitarian and cosmopolitan views on literature clearly echo the characteristic concern of nineteenth-century Russian literature and literary criticism.[38] Specifically, he has immense sympathy for the sufferings of Dostoevsky's Raskolnikov, whom he called a "baleful soul", a victim of autocratic bourgeois society.[39] He considers the impotence of Goncharov's Oblomov and the coldness of Artzybashev's Sanin, both notably "unheroic heroes", as protests by their authors against the lethargic, oppressive and inhumane society of their times.[40] Moreover, he is full of admiration for the Russian emigré writer Herzen, and feels deeply for his plight as one misunderstood and rendered rootless by his native Russia. While praising the Russian writer for his integrity, he urges Chinese youth to learn from his courage and moral vigour, and be prepared to die for their country.[41] It is clear from the above studies that Yu shares the Russian idea that literature is a representation, albeit

---

[36] See his diary of 1927.1.10 in *YDWJ*, Vol. 9, p. 44.

[37] "Yishu yu guojia", *YDWJ*, Vol. 5, pp. 149–154.

[38] See n. 41 below.

[39] "Weibing", *YDWJ*, Vol. 1, p. 110.

[40] "Wenxue shang de jiejidouzheng", *YDWJ*, Vol. 5, p. 139.

[41] "He Ercang", *YDWJ*, Vol. 5, pp. 164–168. The bulk of the material in the essay was taken from Kropotkin's *Ideals and Realities in Russian Literature*, pp. 271–275. Kropotkin's humanitarian approach to anarchism and to literature made a great impact in China in the 1920s. Famous men of letters such as Zheng Zhenduo, Hu Yuzhi and Ba Jin have long been known as advocates of his ideas. It does seem that Yu Dafu was one of their company.

subjective, of the moral fabric of society, and can be a means by which to campaign for the insulted and injured.[42] This understanding of his literary view is essential for a thorough appreciation of the typology of his hero.

The I-hero

> Living in this world, one has to do something. But for a superfluous man like myself, castrated by higher education, what is there I can do? (YDWJ, 7:155)

In calling himself a "superfluous man", as he does so many times in his writings, even entitling one of his stories "The Superfluous Man" (Lingyuzhe), Yu Dafu is repeating a term first used by Turgenev in Russian literature.[43] Knowing Yu's indebtedness to Turgenev as a writer, it is not in the least surprising to see him using the same appellation for himself and his hero. As Yu himself confesses: "Amongst the many foreign writers, great and mediocre, I feel most attracted and closest to Turgenev. I have the longest connection with his works, and will never get tired of them. When I first started to read fiction, and applied my pen to write some myself, I was totally spellbound by this tender looking, sad-eyed and long-bearded Northern Giant."[44] Yu's profuse acknowledgement to Turgenev is hardly exaggerated. His morally sensitive, intelligent, pathological and pessimistic intellectual hero has much in common with the Turgenevan superfluous man, notably Rudin and Chulkaturin in "The Diary of a Superfluous Man". Moreover, the particular dream-like state of alienation, coupled with a bitter, penetrating and obsessive talent for introspection, brings his hero close to the

---

[42] In the preface of the first issue of *Chuangzao yuekan*, Yu Dafu reiterates this theme, and claims that they themselves are underdogs, and would like to use the magazine to campaign for the cause of the insulted and injured, *YDWJ*, Vol. 7, pp. 290–291.

[43] Apart from his short story "Lingyuzhe", Yu Dafu calls himself and his hero by the name of "the superfluous man" in several places: in his short story "Niaoluoxing", in "Huanxiang ji", in his essay "Stirner", as n. 29. There are many other instances where he used similar terms with the same effect, e.g. "most listless and useless" in *"Zai hanfeng li danxingben xu"*, *YDWJ*, Vol. 7, p. 230, and "the alienated dreamer" in "Fengling", as n. 27.

[44] "Tugeniefu de *Luoting* wenshi yiqian", *YDWJ*, Vol. 6, p. 176.

"underground man" of Dostoevsky, another Russian writer Yu esteems.

Before delineating Yu's intellectual hero, one point needs to be made clear. As the bulk of his short stories are autobiographical in nature, it is essential to take the stories which dwell on the same theme as a whole, and see them as extended portraits of the life and activities of one single protagonist. Taken separately, the portrait is limited to a particular occasion or episode in the hero's life, and presents a scattered and dissected image of a hero who is in fact the same person disguised under various names. Moreover, since the main concern of the author is to show his own dilemmas through his short stories, his meaning can best be grasped when we consider these stories, written in the 1920s, to be in the nature of a chronicle. As the viewpoint of the stories is largely restricted to a single perspective, it is difficult for the reader, as for the hero, to assess the realities of the situation with any kind of objectivity. The fruitful approach is for the reader to yield, along with the protagonist, to the enveloping mood, and see how in these works the author tried to create visions of himself through this hero.

Yu's hero, then, is a man in his late twenties, and he reaches his early thirties in the later stories. (Most of the stories I am discussing were written between 1921-1927.) His lean and pale-looking face, with its sad eyes deeply sunk behind the protruding cheek bones, conveys the image of a much battered, sickly and melancholic young man. He returns after eight years in Japan to the strange milieu of Shanghai. Feeling unsatisfied and unfulfilled, he shifts from one job to another, and moves up and down the country. He takes up writing and translating, as many of the men of letters of his time do, but often gets the cold shoulder from his editors. His family life is unhappy. Having dutifully married a woman he does not love, and feeling too ashamed to go home to his mother as a social misfit, he shuns home whenever possible.

Homeless and friendless and without a fixed job or any prospect of getting one, our hero is confined to a solitary existence. He becomes a listless, wandering soul, and haunts the city of Shanghai day and night. As the hero in "Chunfeng chenzui de wanshang" (Intoxicating Spring Nights) describes it, "on such aimless, spring-intoxicated nights, I would wander purposelessly about not returning until almost daybreak".[45] In "Huaixiang bingzhe" (Homesick) we are told that "when dusk and nightfall meet, in the boundless countryside, his (the hero's) head facing the vast and misty canopy of heaven, he staggers on slowly, not knowing who he is, nor what he ought to do, where he is heading. He trudges along whichever way his feet lead him. . . . To employ the expression now current, his present state of mind is like the numbness of Oblomov." (1:147-148)

Why is the hero haunted by this "Oblomovian numbness"? Why is he overshadowed with this dream-like state of alienation? Why does he call himself a "pitiable character in a tragicomedy"? We need to go into the social, psychological, and above all, moral dilemmas he is thrust into in order to answer these questions.

In "The Superfluous Man", the protagonist cries in despair: "I am a superfluous man and nothing more. I am entirely useless to mankind and society. A superfluous man! A useless man! Superfluous! Superfluous. . . ." (3:88)[46] This feeling of futility appears again in "Qing yan" (Bluish Smoke):

> Time flies by, but my career, my position, and my future . . . oh, oh, I have endured endless hardships. Thinking that I had some things firmly in my grasp, but when I unclench my fist, all I can see is a wisp of bluish smoke drifting away in the air. (1:229)

What is revealed here is the self-reproach and self-pity of a man whose desire to be of use to mankind and society is unfulfilled, who tries in vain to commit himself to something or somebody. Herein lies his superfluousness.

First, in terms of social relationships. After eight years of modern education in Japan, our hero comes home, aspiring to the ideals of liberalism and democracy, believing that many social problems of the day can be solved through intellectual means. Literature, with its titanic influence, which can infuse into the mind of the authorities what is just and beautiful, and awaken the people from their lethargy, is to him an effective means by which to bring about a

---

[45] "Chunfeng chenzui de wanshang", tr. by George A. Kennedy as "Intoxicating Spring Nights" in Issacs (ed.), *Straw Sandals* (hereafter Issacs), p. 76.

[46] *YDWJ*, Vol. 3, p. 88. It should be noted that the words "a superfluous man, useless man" are in English in the original, showing that they are obviously borrowed.

more accommodating China. With friends who "love and share the same ideas in literature", they have taken it as their task "to devote all their efforts to scourge the evils of the time, and to save society from decadence". But alas, their "all our struggles cannot withstand one single blow from the wealthy and powerful" (1:274–275).[47]

This concern that "the corrupt run rampant, the evil ride roughshod", and despair at the hopelessness of the situation remain the constant theme of Yu's fiction, and the main obsession of his hero. Along with his gradual loss of confidence in himself goes his loss of faith in his country. China used to be for him both his root and his pride. He deems it his responsibility to restore her people to their former dignity. But his ideals are gradually eroded by the harsh realities. A close friend tries to solve his problem. "What a pity", he says, "that you were born in this time. When China is being torn apart . . . Your sorrow is inevitable. If you had been born ten years earlier or later . . ." To this our hero replies: "Even if a country has to experience immense sufferings, even to the extent of being devoured, there are still people like Sienkiewicz who will persist with their heroic struggle. In China, Lu You's famous lines 'When the conquering armies Northward go. At the familial altar do not fail to tell thy sire' were composed when sighing for his lost country." He thinks that the cause of his sufferings lies not in the turbulent time, but in that "a person like myself whose passion is withered . . . is no longer a chauvinist" (1:231). (The word "chauvinist" is in English in the original. He presumably used it to mean a patriot.)

His predicament is further complicated by his relationship with his family. In "Niaoluo xing" (Wistaria and Dodder), a short story written in letter form to his wife, the hero quotes the following stanza from A. E. Housman's "Shropshire lad":

> Come you home a hero
> Or come not home at all
> The lads you leave will mind you
> Till Ludlow Tower shall fall.[48]

---

[47] For a personal revelation, see Yu's essay "Beiguo de weiyin", *YDWJ*, Vol. 3, pp. 91–95.

[48] "Niaoluo xing", tr. by Edgar Snow as "Wisteria and Dodder" in idem (ed.), *Living China: Modern Chinese Short Stories* (hereafter Snow), p. 252.

These lines epitomize the moral dilemma of the hero vis-à-vis his family. We are given insights into the inner life of the hero. Upon his return from Japan, he wanders around Shanghai instead of going home immediately, even for a brief visit. This reluctance to go home, to go back to Fuyang, his native town that he has often longed for, reveals a confused situation. First of all, being a graduate of a foreign university, he is expected to come home with distinction—wealth, power, and position, so that he can bring glory to his family and ancestors. Because of our hero's reluctance to compromise, and his lack of steadfastness, he has no success with his career, and lives in abject poverty. Though nearing thirty, he is still accepting aid from his mother: "Oh! I have studied so long, and when will I be able to carve out a career for myself? Even these few dollars . . . are from my mother. What use am I at all to my mother, to my family?" (3:89) He is therefore unable to face the prospect of returning home. When at last his return home becomes imminent, he makes a heartfelt prayer: "Heavenly Father! Just let it be that none of my acquaintances shall see me disembark. I couldn't stand it having them see me return in disgrace." (Snow, p. 255)

His relationship with his estranged wife further exacerbates the situation. Submissive to parental authority and totally against his own conscience he has entered into an "unwanted union" with his wife, which brings unhappiness to both sides. Imprisoned in this impossible position, he vents his frustration by bullying his wife:

> Why don't you die? . . . "Why not? It is only when you are dead that it becomes possible for me to live! What are you, actually? Why should I labour like an enslaved animal for you? Oh, for a little freedom— freedom from this endless drudgery, freedom to live! . . ." (Snow, p. 258)

Not that his wife deserves this harsh treatment; on the contrary, her unstinting loyalty, tenderness and moral humility act as a constant challenge to his moral faculties, and further sharpen his dilemma. Entrenched in such intricate social, psychological and moral dilemmas, Yu's hero becomes, in his own words, "a solitary trespasser on his way to exile". All he can do is to put up an impotent protest: "And now it isn't we who are responsible for the tragedy of today, but our parents, not us, but China!" (Snow, p. 249) No wonder when the factory girl in "Intoxicating Spring Nights" asks our hero the simple and straightforward questions: "Where is your home? Why don't you go home?", he is rendered speechless:

> Her question awakened me suddenly to a realization of my predicament. Since the previous year I had been growing more lifeless day by day until I had almost completely lost track of such thoughts as "Who am I?" "What are my present circumstances?" "Do I feel happiness or sorrow?" Her question brought vividly to mind the various stages in my half year of misery and left me staring stupidly at her without a word to offer. (Issacs, p. 74)

The irony of it all is that he is drawn into this faceless existence precisely because he values his individuality and his ideals.

This said, it is important also to observe that the hero's humiliated dignity, and in particular, his morbid delight in humiliation, is not only due to the conflict of an individual with his stagnant environment. It is, in essence, due to the conflict within the individual himself, and the meaninglessness of his existence.

It can be said that the greatest failure of our hero as a person is his inability to translate his desires into action, and his lack of will-power to dedicate himself to something or some person completely. The half-heartedness makes him a divided person, which in turn generates a morbid sense of self-pity and self-denigration: "My past life is nothing but a sequence of failures. . . . Now I am even deprived of that feeling of 'sweet bitterness'. Even the last weapon of the fool—'to dream with wide open eyes'—is snatched from me by fate."[49] What we have here is a person driven to his wits' end, a self-tormentor who derives some strange delight from his torments. He is well aware of his weakness, nor has he any doubts about his intelligence and education. As he says: "As far as intelligence and education go, I am not amongst the lowest category of the two hundred million people in China. Why am I in such a wretched situation?" (3:26) He vacillates between self-humiliation and self-assertion. He thinks that if he is driven to the path of suicide, he will get drunk, and "end up by killing one or two people . . . if it happened to be a rich man I killed so much

---

[49] "Fengling", in *Guoqu ji*, p. 58

the better for society, but if poor and miserable then I would be doing him a service by ending his vegetable career" (Snow, p. 253). He is thus suffering from the contradiction between the world perceived by his internal sensitivity to humanity's coarseness and an awareness of longing for something better. He wants to be his own master, but his own hypersensitivity enables him to understand his own limitations and the difficulties facing him too well. He falls before jumping the first hurdle, and is never able to get up again. This shame at capitulating turns into bitterness against himself, and he defines himself once and for all: a superfluous man useless to mankind, to society, and to his family.

He envies ordinary, simple people. For instance, the simple country folk who are firmly rooted in their land and soil, who build up a healthy and congenial family relationship are for him the happiest people in the world. He is but a "rootless wanderer", a "foreigner to his own native soil" (3:29–34) compared to them. Underneath this envy is his presupposition that true human relationships can only be achieved through simple and unsophisticated companionship. He cherishes his understanding and friendship with the good-natured and kind-hearted rickshaw driver. When the latter is forced to commit suicide, our hero is filled with real anger—one of the rare occasions that he is really angry—and curses the well-to-do passers by: "Pigs, beasts, what are you staring at? My friend, this poor rickshaw driver has been hounded to death by you. What more do you want to see?" (1:299)

This attitude towards simple and compassionate people is further emphasised in the hero's relationship with the factory girl, Ermei. Even in her darkest moments, Ermei still shows great sympathy for the suffering of others, and the hero says:

> Her delightful simplicity suddenly aroused in me a curious emotion. I wanted to put my arms out and take her to me, but my reason told me, "Don't make a slip again. Don't you realize the position you are in? Are you set on poisoning this innocent young virgin? Beast! You have no right to love anyone now." (Issacs, p. 82)

This realization of what is genuinely superior shows up his own unworthiness in greater relief.

As his degradation progresses, he comes to the realization that he is a clown, whose mode of existence is defined by his ugliness.[50] This process reaches its climax when he understands that intelligence and intellect are worthless. He is but a muddled and graceless creature: "Oh, oh, you two-legged creature, you vain-gloriously consider yourself a being supreme among all creation. Your feelings and thoughts are at best a collection of contradictions. Dare you talk of reason, of philosophy?" (3:26) Upon realizing his own unworthiness and debilitating self-consciousness, Yu Dafu's superfluous man has become something of a Dostoevskian "underground man".

IV. Relationship with Russian Literature

It is not difficult then to see the affinity of Yu Dafu's superfluous hero to the Russian heroes, notably Turgenev's Chulkaturin and Rudin,[51] and to a lesser extent, the "underground man" of Dostoevsky. As we will recall, Yu acknowledges his indebtedness to Turgenev for his own writings, and he is fascinated by the "baleful soul" of the "mad and crazy" Dostoevskian hero in the wet snow. We can trace the relationship between Yu's superfluous hero and his Russian precursors through their social relationships and psychological malaise.

Relationship with Rudin

Let me start with the social dilemma facing the superfluous man. As Richard Freeborn points out in his study of *Rudin*, "The superfluity of the 'superfluous man' is to be interpreted chiefly in social terms, as of someone, a man of often real talent, who can find no place for himself in the society of his time."[52] We see here

---

[50] See his "Shiyiyue chusan", *YDWJ*, Vol. 1, p. 344. This idea is again reiterated in his diary of 1926.12.7. He composed a poem on his thirtieth birthday and called himself a clown. See *YDWJ*, Vol. 9, pp. 29–30.

[51] It should be pointed out that Turgenev frequently made use of such devices in composing short stories as told by an narrator who gathered with friends for an evening, extracts from diaries, exchange of letters. Many of his stories are first person narrations. "The Diary of a Superfluous Man" is one such example.

[52] Richard Freeborn (tr.), *Rudin*, p. 9.

the similarity between Yu's hero and Rudin. Though the two differ enormously in appearance and temperament, they share the distinctive frailty in character which is instrumental in bringing about their downfall. Rudin is tall, personable, plausible, eloquent and inspiring. As Lezhnev, his old schoolmate says of him, "he has enthusiasm, and that, believe me, for I speak as a phlegmatic man—is a most precious quality of our time."[53] Yu's hero, on the other hand, is pallid, sickly, taciturn and diffident. Despite these differences, both Rudin and Yu's hero are idealists arguing that intellectuals should devote themselves to the service of the country to bring about a more just and humane society. Rudin relies on his eloquence and oratory to propagate his ideas, as in the spellbinding addresses he makes in Darya Lasunsky's house. Yu's hero has tried to realize his ideals through the media—newspapers and magazines. Their aspirations, however, are doomed to be stifled, because the intolerably hostile, indifferent and effete society they try to transform works against them. They become, so to say, divided characters. As Richard Freeborn says, in the superfluous man "the head and the heart are mutually antagonistic; he betrays signs of disillusionment and emotional indifference, a mind that prides itself on cynicism and a precocity that cloaks itself in haughtiness."[54] Such symptoms are shared by both Rudin and Yu's superfluous hero, despite their differences in appearance and temperament.

The make-up of these "divided characters", however, is not only due to hostile social forces from outside. Their own weakness of character is also an important factor. Both Rudin and Yu's hero are lazy and weak. They lack consistency and endurance. Their wishful thinking often leads them to take their dreams for accomplishments. It is true that both have a strong moral thrust, but they cling to the notion of duty in vain, since they lack the capacity to dedicate themselves to someone or something completely. Rudin's farewell to Lezhnev summarizes his own failings: "And yet was I really fit for nothing, was there really nothing on this earth I could do? . . . I've hardly succeeded in reaching a definite position or stopping at a known point of view when fate drags me down from it . . . I've begun to be frightened of it

[53] Ibid., p. 157.
[54] Freeborn, *Turgenev, The Novelist's Novelist*, p. 20.

—my fate, that is . . . I'm tired now . . . I've had enough."[55] The same fate befalls Yu's hero. He says in despair: "Let me say it once and for all. I am now a lonely, solitary wanderer, . . . without tears, without pity, without a career, without friends . . . without anything. I have nothing . . . nothing, nothing . . . All I have is an empty heart, a heart like dead ashes." (1:339) Thus, what binds Rudin and Yu's hero together is their failure as people, apart from both being half-hearted intellectuals caught up in a hostile environment. They are made of paper. When faced with a genuine crisis that calls for courage and resolution, both crumble and collapse. However, similar though the roots of their superfluousness may be, one basic difference distinguishes them from each other. Rudin is an "external" character. He is to be understood through his speeches, his actions and his relation to other people. Yu's hero is an introvert. It is his inner state of mind—his self-analysis, self-reproach, and self-pity—that determines his existence. In point of fact, it is Turgenev's first superfluous hero—Chulkaturin in "The Diary of a Superfluous Man"—that we find sharing the morbid existence of Yu's hero.

Relationship with "The Diary of a Superfluous Man"

"The Diary of a Superfluous Man" is one of Yu Dafu's favourite works, if not the favourite. He writes in his diary of October 14, 1932: ". . . this is the third time I have read Turgenev's 'The Diary of a Superfluous Man'. The experience of reading the work of a great writer is like that of chewing an olive. The harder you chew it, the more tasty it becomes." In the entry for the following day, he writes:

> The few lines of poetry sung by the German teacher in "The Diary of a Superfluous Man", which reveal the intense pining for his far-off fatherland, are full of meaning
> "Herz, mein Herz, warum so traurig
> Was bekummert dich so sehr?
> 'Sist ja schon im fremden Lande—
> Herz, mein Herz—was willst du mehr?"

---

[55] As n. 52, pp. 175–178.

Furthermore, the last poem cited in the story,
   "And about the grove
   May youthful life rejoice
   And nature healed
   Glow with eternal beauty"
is also very meaningful. Unfortunately, I am unable to translate it into
Chinese. (9:193–194)

Yu's fascination with "The Diary" merits a detailed comparison
between his superfluous hero and Turgenev's Chulkaturin. He, in
fact, has compared a character of his, who is lost in despair and
in unrequited love, to the Russian hero (2:374).

The reason for Yu Dafu's fondness for Turgenev's story can easily
be understood. We have here the vivid confession of a hero in
despair. Like Yu's hero, Chulkaturin is a pallid, sickly looking man.
He is stripped of his pride in his thwarted love for Liza, and is held
in contempt by the prince, whom he challenges to a duel out of
jealousy. He overhears himself being openly insulted by the woman
he loves passionately: "She went on quickly, 'if you knew how I
loathe that T . . . (Chulkaturin, sic.),' I always fancy I see on that
man's hands . . . his blood."[56] What breaks his heart most and
drives him to suicide is the fact that while denouncing him, Liza
wishes her seducer, the prince, who has since left her, happiness
with a wife.

"The Diary" is the hero's narrated monologue before his death.
What distinguishes the story is not its plot, but the vivid description
of the psychological trauma and spiritual malaise of the protagonist.
As Chulkaturin confesses, he is "apprehensive, reserved, and
irritable, like all sickly people" (ibid., p. 16). He admits the folly
of his own self-consciousness: "I analysed myself to the last thread,
compared myself with others, recalled the slightest glances, smiles,
words of the people to whom I had tried to open myself out, put
the worst construction on everything, laughed vindictively at my
own pretensions to 'be like everyone else'—and suddenly in the midst
of my laughter, collapsed utterly into gloom, sank into absurd
dejection and then began again as before—went round and round,

[56]Turgenev, "The Diary of a Superfluous Man", tr. by Constance Garnett, in
The Novels of Ivan Turgenev, Vol. 13, p. 89.

in fact, like a squirrel on the wheel, whose days were spent in harassing, fruitless exercise."(Ibid.) We can see that from this constant process of self-examination he derives a certain masochistic pleasure.

This excessive self-consciousness and the constant doubts concerning his own worth prevent him from acting. As he himself says: "The misfortune of solitary and timid people—who are timid from self-consciousness—is just that, though they have eyes and indeed open them wide, they see nothing, or see everything in a false light." (p. 36) These few lines underline the paradox of the superfluous hero. His sensitivity and excessive self-consciousness enable him to analyze himself and society as such, but this self-consciousness also separates him from the rest of society. He is conscious of the hypocrisy and self-deception of those who believe themselves to be better. The irony rests in the fact that while he is unsure of himself, he feels his superiority at the same time by virtue of his self-knowledge and sensitivity. As he says, he is not devoid of "penetration and the faculty of observation", and can come up with ideas that are "not absolutely commonplace" (p. 18). But his trouble is that he has neither the will nor the strength to see his ideas through; and when he acts, he is overwhelmed by his hypersensitivity, and very often makes a fool of himself, as is exemplified in his unrequited love for Liza.

Were Chulkaturin less conscious of himself, his thwarted love might only cause him some momentary suffering and unhappiness, and he would start afresh without undue difficulty. But his self-consciousness works upon him, and it readily takes the form of self-degradation and self-humiliation. Feeling himself battered about, and aware of the meaninglessness of his existence, he arrives at the following conclusion:

> Superfluous, superfluous . . . that's a capital word I have hit on . . . Superfluous—that's just it. To other people that term is not applicable . . . People are bad, or good, clever, stupid, pleasant, and disagreeable; but superfluous . . . no. Understand me, though: the universe could get on without those people too . . . no doubt; but uselessness is not their prime characteristic . . . But I . . . there's nothing else one can say about me, I'm superfluous and nothing more. A supernumerary and that's all. (p. 15)

The term "superfluous man" may indeed be "not applicable to other people", as Chulkaturin admits, but it is nonetheless the very essence of Yu Dafu's hero, and a term he employs consistently to describe himself and his fictional hero. The mental state and psychological dilemma of his hero echo those of Chulkaturin, and so does his relationship with other people.

Like Chulkaturin, Yu's superfluous man is a timid and insulted character. His hypersensitivity also induces him to "dream with wide opened eyes", and often makes a fool of him. He, too, will analyze himself to the last thread at the slightest provocation by other people. For instance, the surprised stare of a girl whose luggage he offers to carry is enough to reduce him to a state of frenzy and despair. He dismisses himself: "Oh, I am wrong. I am out of my mind. My little sister, please do not be mad with me. I am not a rascal, nor a pickpocket either. Please forgive me. I am so sorry, I deserve your reproachful looks." (3:26) Likewise, when he was still in Japan, a glance at the beautiful girls in the street would remind him of his own inferiority: "Coward, coward."

Both heroes suffer torments from the insults of their supposed lovers. Just as Chulkaturin is openly insulted by Liza, Yu's super-fluous hero in "Yinhuise de si" (Silvergrey Death) experiences the same kind of public insult from Jinger. While he is having a quiet drink in Jinger's place, "suddenly a man in his thirties comes in. Upon seeing him, Jinger leaves to talk to him immediately, and he is left to engage in idle chit-chat with her mother. After more than half an hour Jinger is still laughing and chuckling with the man. He leaves the house in impatience, like a beaten animal." (1:8-9) Filled with jealousy and hurt pride, both heroes revert to a form of masochistic revenge. They purposely expose themselves to ridicule and humiliation, and consequently to suffering, in which they take a sardonic and masochistic pleasure. Upon seeing Liza dancing with the prince, Chulkaturin "happily felt full of wrath" and invited an ugly young lady to dance with him, thinking this would affront them. Yu's hero resorts to getting drunk in front of Jinger, believing that thus he will assert himself and get his revenge.[57]

[57] The masochistic choice of an ugly woman has parallels in Yu Dafu's works also. In "Mangmangye", *YDWJ*, Vol. 1, pp. 116–146, instead of choosing a beautiful courtesan, the hero has his eyes on the ugly Haitang, whom he describes as having "monkeyish looks, a pair of dull eyes, and a long face".

Above all, Yu's hero in "The Superfluous Man" is more or less in agreement with Chulkaturin when he defines the core of his existence. The words of both, the tone of their utterances, and the disjointed way they express them are strikingly similar:

> I am a superfluous man and nothing more. This is the crux of the whole issue. All other thoughts are but secondary . . . I am a superfluous man and nothing more. I am utterly useless to mankind and society. A superfluous man! a useless man! superfluous! superfluous! (3:88)[58]

Apart from the similarities in mentality, the atmosphere in which the two heroes arrive at their conclusion, and their intense feeling of loss are also alike. Both Turgenev and Yu Dafu are careful to build up the sombre atmosphere by setting their stories in dismal weather. Yu's hero in "The Superfluous Man" is actually likened to a solitary wanderer in the vastness of the cold, wintry Russian countryside. (It is quite conceivable that Yu Dafu may actually have Chulkaturin in mind here.) The atmosphere of dislocation is given due emphasis in the last lines of Chulkaturin's diary. What he sees in these final moments are fleeting objects—spots on the walls, the old yellow face of his nurse, the hissing samovar, his own pen and hand. All these things come revolving round him. Yu's hero also experiences similar fleeting visions towards the end of the story. He has lost completely his sense of purpose and direction. As the rickshaw driver pulls him along, he feels emptiness and numbness. All he sees are "a lot of lights and passers-by, and many fleeting objects that I can neither specify nor describe. They keep revolving round me on every side." (3:90)

From the above similarities, one can summarize the character of Yu's superfluous hero in the words of a critic's comment on Turgenev's Chulkaturin and Hamlet:[59]

> Hamlet and Chulkaturin are as much dreamers and idealists as Rudin, but in them Turgenev analyzes the condition of a disillusioned spirit which has withdrawn into itself and cut off from the world. In their bitter solitude, Hamlet and Chulkaturin are consumed by their egos and both turn to masochism. Turgenev emphasizes their humiliating

---

[58] As n. 46.

[59] "Hamlet" here refers to the superfluous hero Hamlet in Turgenev's "Hamlet of the Shchigrovsky District" in his *Sketches from a Hunter's Album*.

self-pity and their emotional weakness: at the same time, these portraits
are marked by profound psychological insight into the complexities of
their spiritual dilemma.[60]

So pertinent is this description that it can be applied to Yu's hero
without altering one single word. What we can add though, is that
Yu Dafu succeeds in telescoping Rudin's liberal predicament and
Chulkaturin's morbid self-pity into one and makes it part and parcel
of his own version of the superfluous hero. Indeed, the complexities
and subtleties of Yu's superfluous hero remind us of Dostoevsky's
"underground man", Dostoevsky's hypersensitive and bookish
protagonist, who sees through the follies of society, who is aware
of the futility of trying to break out of the confines of the "stone
walls", and who proclaims that men with heightened consciousness
like himself are but scoundrels, and that the "best definition of man
is—a creature who walks on two legs, and is ungrateful". In the
same vein, Yu's hero also comes to the realization that he is
circumscribed by his own consciousness, that he is "born for a time
of rebellion", and treads a path that is "full of thorns", and that
he is but a worthless "two-legged animal". Just as the man from
the underground is humiliated by the genuine superiority of Liza,
the prostitute, Yu's hero admits he is a beast before the innocence
and simplicity of the factory girl Ermei. Patent as these similarities
are, one should be careful to point out that Yu's hero lacks the
characteristic spitefulness and morbid sense of superiority that
distinguish Dostoevsky's underground man.

Relationship between the Hero and the Heroine

A further area of similarity between Yu's fiction and that of the
Russian writers is in the relationship between the hero and the
heroine. Russian fiction in general, and that of Turgenev in particular, depicts a situation wherein the heroines are either strong, and
pure, or passionate, as opposed to the hero who is weak and ineffective. It is very often the case that the strong-willed and
determined heroine acts as a challenge to the weak and wandering

---

[60]Eva Kagan-Kans, *Hamlet and Don Quixote: Turgenev's Ambivalent Vision*,
p. 34.

hero. In his failure to live up to the challenge is revealed the hero's unworthiness, shame and superfluousness.

Critics have unanimously categorized Turgenev's heroines into two types. While determination, pride and strength of will are qualities common to both, the first type is pure, innocent, courageous, and truthful to her feelings, and her outer calmness conceals an ardent heart. Natalya in *Rudin* and Liza in *Home of the Gentry* are notable examples. The second type is usually a more mature woman, governed by an unflagging will and passion, and a yearning for absolute possession. They are sometimes called "predatory women", because of their cruelty. To this category belong Madame Odintsov in *Fathers and Sons*, Madame Polozov in "Spring Tide", and Clara Militch in the novel of the same title. Interestingly enough, Yu Dafu's heroines fall neatly into these two categories, though there are relatively few of them in his fiction. And they all serve to underline the superfluousness of the hero.

The hero's wife Quanjun, the factory girl Ermei, and Lian, the sister of his friend, fall into the first category of heroines. All can be labelled "insulted and injured" women. Quanjun is married without her consent into the Yu family. She has to bear with her irresponsible and ill-tempered husband, a demanding mother-in-law, and the burden of running a household reduced in fortune. She bears all this with great humility, perseverance and understanding. Her equanimity and purity of mind in accepting her fate without grumbling, and her dutiful love towards the hero provoke his moral scruples, and force him into a kind of identity crisis. Does he love her? Is he a burden to her, or vice versa? He can find no way out of the maze, and is tragically plagued by his half-heartedness—having "a wife that he does not love but cannot help not loving". Before her moral humility and single-mindedness, the hero is stripped of his pride and moral worth, and is clearly shown to be a "superfluous man" who is worthless in this world, one without whom the world will lose absolutely nothing (1:216).[61]

Ermei and Lian also display similar traits of courage and humility.

---

[61] "Niaoluo xing", *YDWJ*, Vol. 1, p. 216. See n. 48. I have departed from Snow's translation here. Snow aims at a more free rendering of the story, as he pointed out in his Introduction.

After the death of her father, Ermei is all alone in the world, without friends and relatives. She can only survive at subsistence level, and under the constant threat of being seduced by her foreman. Lian is maltreated by her mother-in-law. She is forced to go home to live with her mother after her husband's death, which she is accused of having hastened through her evil influence. (2:323–324) This is certainly one of the most severe forms of punishment and disgrace that can be imposed on a daughter-in-law. Both women endure their sufferings with great tenacity and resignation. The hostile environment can do nothing to dampen the naturalness and emotional spontaneity that are innate in them. Knowing hardship only helps to augment their interest in the fate and well-being of others. As in the case of Natalya, Lian's innocence and seriousness of purpose highlight the central paradox of the sophisticated and unfulfilled hero—his admiration for emotional spontaneity of the heart, which contrasts strongly, he believes, with his own heightened consciousness.

The second sister in "Guoqu" (The Past) belongs to the second category—the "predatory woman". She is charming, vivacious, and has a capacity for cruelty. Most of the young men in the neighbourhood cannot resist "falling into her love net", being constantly "hustled and teased" by her. The protagonist Li Baishi also attends to her needs, no matter how demanding, does what she pleases, and bears her insults. As he confesses: "Curiously enough, though she teased me and belittled me like this, I hadn't the slightest sense of resentment towards her. I even considered being tormented as my constant glory, my source of happiness." (1:376) This irrational quality of love is linked to the masochistic enjoyment of the pain it causes: "Any time I disobeyed her orders, she would raise her plump hand and slap my face without hesitation. As for me, I felt an inexpressible sense of satisfaction after being vilified by her. Sometimes because I wanted this 'favour' of hers, I would deliberately disobey her orders, and invite her to beat me, or to kick me in the midriff with her pointed shoes. If I felt she hadn't kicked or beaten me enough, I would taunt her: 'I do not feel the pain, that's not enough, keep on kicking me, keep on beating me.'" (1:377)

The peculiar relationship between Yu's hero and heroine in "Guoqu" is reminiscent of that which exists between the young I-figure and Zinaida in "First Love" by Turgenev. The images of a weak and submissive hero and a strong and experienced heroine are strikingly similar. Yu's second sister shares Zinaida's physical attraction and possessive character. Both are charming and combine the outward traits of an innocent maiden with a yearning for absolute possession. Zinaida's feline beauty—she has huge grey eyes, and golden hair, and is "tall, tender, in her movements so imperious, so caressing, so mocking and sweet"—subjugates all the men who approach her: "It amused her to arouse their hopes and then their pains, to turn them round her finger, (She used to call it knocking their heads together), while they never dreamed of offering resistance and eagerly submitted to her."[62] Arrogance, cruelty, and tenderness alternate in her behaviour from movement to movement. The young hero is her total captive: "She amused herself with my passion, made a fool of me, petted and tormented me. There is a sweetness in being the sole source, the autocratic and irresponsible cause of the greatest joy and profoundest pain to another, and I was like wax in Zinaida's hands." (p. 283) He describes his submission in a humiliating comparison with a beetle tied by its leg, turning around and around a post, and even more cruelly, compares Zinaida in this relationship with a cat playing with a mouse. The pain, however is not limited to the emotional plane. The physical pain he suffers after the jump from the high wall in response to Zinaida's challenge is transformed into a highly pleasurable, and masochistic experience:

> But the feeling of rapture I experienced then has never come a second time in my life. It turned to a sweet ache in all my limbs and found expression at last in ecstatic hops and skips and shouts. (p. 284)

The many similarities between "First Love" and "The Past"; the masochistic relationship between the hero and the heroine; the centre of action taking place in the heroine's house, a lot of it around the card table; the heroine's luxurious life being supported by an older person and the release of her sensual passion with the inexperienced hero—lead us to think that certain episodes of "The Past" have been inspired by Turgenev's first short story, one well loved by Yu Dafu.

It is clear in Yu's treatment of the relationship between his hero

[62] Turgenev, "First Love", as n. 56, Vol. 11, p. 283.

and heroine, that he constantly exposes his hero as a failure, as an underdog in relation to the genuinely superior, or the wilfully possessive woman.[63] The hero is either unable to withstand the challenge posed to him, or submits with a morbid delight. He willingly concedes his own cowardice and inferiority. Such an inferiority complex on the part of the hero is seldom found in Chinese literature.

From what has been said above, we can safely talk of a Russian, especially a "Turgenevan" influence on Yu Dafu's work. We have seen that Yu's hero is different in substantial ways from the confident and assertive European romantic hero, but shares a marked similarity with the Russian superfluous man. His failure in character, the liberal predicament tormenting him, his morbid delight in humiliation, and his submissiveness in relation to the heroine are akin to his Russian precursors, notably Chulkaturin and Rudin. In a discussion of the contrasting issues in Russian fiction—the opposition of imitative and indigenous, of town and country, of new and old, Richard Freeborn points out that such relationships "establish a formula" in Russian fiction:

> The relationship only begins when the hero finds himself in the milieu that is unfamiliar to him, either through long dissociation or simply because he has had no previous knowledge of it, and the result is that the hero appears in the milieu as a relative stranger, whose very strangeness and newness are a source of fascination to the heroine. The contrast afforded by the presence of the hero in the strange milieu is at once both social and psychological. His social affinities contrast with the social characteristics of the strange milieu in which he finds himself. When the heroine falls in love with him, as is usually the case, the love is represented as a challenge to his character, which he can either accept or fail to live up to, and the extent to which he suceeds or fails reveals the extent of his moral worth.[64]

---

[63] A word can be said of Yu Dafu's unfinished story "Renyao", *YDWJ*, Vol. 1, pp. 281–287. Yu wrote in his diary of 1926.11.8 (*YDWJ*, Vol. 9, p. 11) that he had read Turgenev's "Clara Militch" but did not think it very good. He said that his unfinished story "Renyao", when finished, might be better. There are certain parallels between the two stories. Both heroes are meek and innocent, both fall in love with an actress who has an inexplicable charm. Both stories are shrouded in mystery. As Yu's story is unfinished, it would be futile, however, to push the comparison further.

[64] As n. 54.

Such a "formula of relationship" is also traceable in Yu Dafu's short stories. We see that Yu's hero also returns as a relative stranger to a milieu from which he has long been dissociated. His liberal and cosmopolitan ideals, which he cannot shed, act on him and constitute his "strangeness" and "newness". In this social context the extent of his moral worth is revealed through his failures. Nor is his tragedy an isolated one. It reflects the severe constraints and conflicting demands society imposed on intellectuals in the May Fourth era. On the one hand, these people denounced union without love, marriage without consent, and autocratic authority. On the other, their liberal education demanded that they be rational and responsible, both towards their family and towards their country. On such conflicts of love and hate, home and exile, freedom and authority, and on their interaction, the social, psychological, and above all, the moral dilemmas of Yu's intellectual hero are founded and they illustrate the predicament of the Chinese intellectual in general. In the final analysis, it was the objective environment of China in the 1920s that occasioned the "Russian-flavoured" short stories of Yu Dafu.

V. Chinese Heritage and Japanese Influence

While we have seen the affinities of Yu Dafu's hero with the Russian superfluous man, our study will be severely limited unless we examine his relationship with the Chinese heritage, since Yu is demonstrably one of the few modern writers who is well grounded in classics, a good poet in the classical style, and a copious reader of classical Chinese literature. As Průšek has dealt perceptively with some of the general aspects of his writing in relation to traditional Chinese literature,[65] I will only concern myself with the depiction of the hero in his short stories.

[65] Průšek, as n. 10, pp. 90–98. Examples of the affinity of Yu's works with the Chinese heritage are not difficult to trace, especially in his travel notes written in the 1930s. The short story "Shisanye", *YDWJ*, Vol. 2, pp. 155–169, where the *caizi* hero roams along the hills and lakes of Hangzhou in pursuit of his lover, echoes some of the romantic tales in *Xihu jiahua*, a work that fascinated Yu Dafu (see n. 4).

A Modern Caizi and Mingshi

Critics have talked of Yu Dafu as a modern *caizi* (profligate litterateur). In a recent study of the author, Lee Ou-fan defines a *caizi* as a scholar with a "talent" for literature, and more important, a knack for love. He makes a distinction between the modern and traditional *caizi*. For him, the former was "modernized" with foreign fads and new-style thinking, whereas the old-style *caizi* might still "weep over Black Jade's poetic burial of the withered flowers in the *Dream of the Red Chamber*, or find his passion inflamed by the furtive rendezvous between the two lovers in the *Dream of the West Chamber* (*Xixiang ji*). The new style *wenren* preferred to invoke the love-affairs of Byron, the sad ending of Keats or Shelley, or even the daring amours of George Sand."[66] Lee considers Yu a modern *caizi*, the writer's admiration for the literary talent of the late Qing *caizi* poet Huang Zhongze, and his identification with the latter's moral principles cause Lee to see them both as solitary and talented men of letters suffering from "the humiliation inflicted upon them by a philistine society which could never appreciate true genius".[67]

In his predisposition towards wine and women, and his literary talent, Yu's hero is, no doubt, a *caizi* at heart. However, it is important also to distinguish between two archetypes in the *caizi* tradition: Zhang Sheng in *Dream of the West Chamber* and Hou Fangyu in *Taohua shan* (Plum Blossom Fan), a play that Yu Dafu loved above all others.[68] Zheng's wit, dalliance, and light-hearted follies together with his exhibitionist approach to literature make him a classic case, and Hou, while no less lacking in charm, is known for his moral sensitivity. He opposes corrupt officials selling out to the Manchu conquerors, and refuses to compromise with the callousness and obsequiousness of his time. In his seriousness of purpose, he is only treading in the footsteps of the enlightened, righteous and loyal scholar-officials of old, such as Qu Yuan, Du Fu, Lu You, Fang Zhongyan, Wen Tianxiang and many others

[66] Lee, as n. 2, pp. 38–39. For the sake of consistency, I have taken the liberty to change the original romanization in the quotation into *pinyin*.
[67] Ibid., p. 118.
[68] As n. 4.

throughout the ages. Yu's hero unmistakably belongs to this second type, though lacking the eloquence and charm of young master Hou. We have a display of literary talent à la Hou when the hero of "Sinking", in an intoxicated mood, starts composing a *lüshi* (regulated verse poem in heptasyllabics) in a brothel:

> Drunk, I tap the railing and feel the chillier because of the wine;
> Rivers and lakes again turn bleak in the dead of winter.
> The mad poet with his profound pity for the parrot
> Was spared through death—his bones buried in the Central Province—
> The further ignominy of another talented youth
> Exiled to Chang'an with the title of grand tutor.
> It's not too hard to try to repay a life-saving meal
> With a thousand pieces of gold,
> But how many could pass through the capital
> Without heaving five long sighs?
> Looking homeward across the misted sea,
> I, too, weep for my beloved country. (p. 30)

The theme of worry for the country, of exile from the "Central Province", the intense sorrow, and the sombre tone remind us of many of the poems of the Tang poet Du Fu, in particular his *Qiuxing* (Autumn Meditation) poems.[69] In fact Yu's hero identifies with the misfortune of the great poet. He laments that his "thinness" is not a result of illness, over-drinking or intense melancholy. It is "the thinness of Du Fu, the affliction of wearing an academic cap".[70] Here, Yu's hero is referring to the famous semi-autobiographical poem of that poet, whose intellectual predicament he in some ways shares. Du Fu's poem is worth quoting at length:

> Those who wear silk underwear never starve, An academic cap is apt to ruin a life. If my venerable elder will quietly listen, I shall humbly offer my dissertation.
>
> When I was still in my youth, I was a candidate for the Imperial examination. With thousands of volumes worn by reading. Whenever I took a pen, my thoughts were inspired. My prose was thought to rival

---

[69] For a discussion of Du Fu's life and thoughts in English, see William Hung, *Tu Fu, China's Greatest Poet*; for the "Qiuxing" poems, see pp. 227–235. A translation of "Qiuxing" by A. C. Graham is included in *Anthology of Chinese Literature*, pp. 252–255

[70] "Haishang tongxin", *YDWJ*, Vol. 3, p. 76.

Yang Xiong's. My poetry was regarded as approaching that of Cao Xie. Even the great Li Yong wanted to be my acquaintance. And the brilliant Wang Han wished to lodge near me. I thought, of course, I was extraordinary, and would immediately climb to an important position, To help my soverign to succeed better than even the best, And to restore the purity of culture and civilization. But all these hopes were sadly shattered, I gleaned to live in an unwilling hermitage. Now for more than three years on a donkey's back, I have been foe on the spring air of the flowery capital. Mornings, I knock on the doors of rich youth, Evenings, I follow in the dust of the fast horses. Left-over wine and roast that is cold I swill together with my pride and my tears.[71]

These afflictions, the daunting poverty and frustrated ambition, the sentiment that "Literature seldom leads to a life of worldly success; Demons are usually pleased to meet their victims",[72] are only too familiar to Yu's hero. In one of his nostalgic moments, Yu Dafu hankers for the Jin dynasty (265–419), when he could have listened to the wailing of Ruan Ji, and seen Tao Qian begging for food; or in the late Ming, when his agony would have been relieved by seeing the gallant and romantic events of the Donglin group of *caizi* (of whom Hou Fangyu mentioned above was a representative) and their relations with the beautiful and righteous courtesans in Qinhuai River (in the Southern capital, Nanjing).[73] Such are the archetypes of Chinese literati that Yu admires. Like Ruan Ji before him, who was "unable to make the great leap of the spirit that might have satisfied at least the part of his complicated mind that yearned for the freedom of the soul", and whose tears were "the only release left to him to resolve the irresolvable contradiction that finds such passionate expression in his poetry",[74] Yu Dafu and his hero often find momentary relief in tears. And wearied of the battles of life that he cannot stand up to, he sometimes contemplates retreating

[71] Du Fu, "Feng zeng Wei Zuocheng zhang ershier yun", English translation by Hung, as n. 69, p. 52.

[72] Du Fu, "Yi Li Bai", ibid., p. 149. Yu Dafu quoted these two lines of Du Fu as a preface to his short story "Cai shi ji", on the Qing *caizi* Huang Zhongze, whom Yu admired. *YDWJ*, Vol. 1, p. 194.

[73] "Haigu miluanshe de duyu", *YDWJ*, Vol. 3, p. 122.

[74] Donald Holzman, *Poetry and Politics: The Life and Works of Juan Chi, A.D. 210–263*, pp. 223–224.

to the mountains and lakes of a far-off land to allow his tormented soul to recuperate, a course often adopted by the *mingshi* (honourable non-serving scholars), for example, among whom Tao Qian is one of the most famous and admired.

Thus, in Yu's hero are mingled elements of what might be termed the "profligate litterateur" *caizi*, and the high-mindedness and frustrations characteristic of the morally sensitive *mingshi* literati— Tao Qian, Ruan Ji and Du Fu. One basic factor, though, distinguishes his hero from his Chinese precursors. While these high-minded writers felt the pressures of frustration and humiliation, they nevertheless countered them with consistent pride and dignity. Underlying Ruan Ji's weeping, Tao Qian's seclusion, Du Fu's sorrow or Huang Zhongze's bitterness is their righteous anger. In Tao Qian's famous utterance: "How can I bend my back for five pecks of rice and earnestly pay court to such a yokel" is the sense of superiority common to them, by virtue of their intellect, scholarship, talents, sensibility and moral uprightness. They seldom believe that their misfortunes and agony may be due to their own foibles or weaknesses. They are therefore different from Yu's hero, who is diffident and recoils into himself, blaming himself for his failures. As we have seen, this "underdog mentality" is by and large responsible for his boundless self-pity and ultimate superfluity. As I said earlier, this concept of the hero as the "underdog", as the "insulted and injured", seldom figures in Chinese literary tradition. It seems therefore that here Yu Dafu is mainly inspired by Russian literature, which has immortalized the down-trodden and superfluous heroes— Gogol's Akaky Akakievich, Goncharov's Oblomov, Turgenev's Rudin and Dostoevsky's Raskolnikov.

Influence of the Watakushi-shōsetsu

Some consideration needs to be given to another oriental factor, the general impact of Japanese literature on Yu Dafu's works. Cheng Ching-mao maintains that Yu's insistence that "all literature is autobiographical" reflects the general defence made by Japanese *watakushi-shōsetsu* (I-novel) writers against the critics who accused them of being too subjective, too personal, and too indifferent to the outside world, and the point that is "most revealing is Yu Dafu's use of the term *zixuzhuan* (*jijoden* in Japanese, a term preferred by Japanese naturalist writers to *watakushi-shōsetsu* when referring to the very private autobiographical nature of their creative works)".[75] Quite conceivably, from the etymological point of view, the affinities between the terms *zixuzhuan* (autobiography) and *jijoden* may very well imply, as Cheng points out, a Chinese borrowing of a term originally Japanese. We may, however, be overstating the case if we conclude from this that Yu's autobiographical works are derived from the Japanese.[76] We must also take into account the fact that Yu Dafu's favourite works— Rousseau's *Rêverie d'un Promeneur Solitaire*, Goethe's *The Sufferings of Young Werther*, and Turgenev's "The Diary of a Superfluous Man"—were all partly autobiographical and confessional in nature. Thus, the *zixuzhuan*, though having Japanese overtones, need not be limited to the Japanese variety of a genre not originally Japanese. Moreover, many of the writings of the old Chinese literati that Yu admires are of the most intimate nature—notes written down for personal communications, diaries, letters and so on.

On the other hand, we will be equally off the mark if we ignore the impact of the *watakushi-shōsetsu* on Yu Dafu. After all, the well-known "I-novel" writer Satō Haruo was a personal friend of Yu, who in 1923 expressed his admiration for Satō's "Rural Melancholy", "Fingerprints", "Li Po" and "Pruned Flowers".[77] He was also impressed by another important "I-novel" writer of short stories, Kasai Zenzō, as he states in his diary.[78] Certain general similarities can be discerned in the works of Satō and Yu. Apart from the autobiographical strain common to both, there is an attempt to depict the sensory view of nature, and the magic of the vague, limitless, unspeakable world of melancholy invented by modern sensitivity. More specifically, as the noted Japanese expert

[75] Cheng Ching-mao, "The Impact of Japanese Literary Trends on Modern Chinese Writers", in *MCL*, pp. 81–82.

[76] Yu Dafu was not the only writer in the 1920s to use "zixuzhuan" instead of "zizhuan" or "zixu" for autobiography. In fact, it was a common practice for writers to use this term thus. Zhou Zuoren used it many times, for example, in *Yutian de shu*, p. 124; and so did Mao Dun in his work *Zhuiqiu*, Zhang Yiping in his autobiographical essay, "Wode zixuzhuan lüe".

[77] "Haishang tongxin", as n. 70, p. 73.

[78] Diary of 1927.1.6, in *YDWJ*, Vol. 9, p. 40.

on Yu Dafu, Itō Toramaru, observes in his article on "Sinking", the "hypochondria" and sexual frustrations in the young protagonist echo the main concerns of the Japanese "I-novel", and those of the writings of Satō Haruo.[79]

What strikes me as most "Japanese" in Yu's writings is his obsession with the sexual impulses of the protagonist. As Sokichi Tsuda points out in his detailed study of sexual love in Japanese literature, the explicit representation of sexual delight in love, of carnal passion, has been a tradition in Japanese since the *Tale of Genji* and *Tale of Ise*.[80] With the advent of naturalism in modern Japanese literature at the turn of the century, "straightforward description" (*rokotsu no byosha*) became the byword of the day, and added fuel to the burning fire of a detailed and pathological description of sexual love and sensuous impulses. The well-known novelist of the time, Tanizaki Jun'ichirō, for instance, writes without the least reservation about such sexual abnormalities as masochism and fetishism. His detailed description of the young man in *Akuma* licking the soiled handkerchief of his sweetheart became well known as "the epitome of aestheticism of the time".[81] Such sexual abnormalities are also given equally explicit treatment in Yu Dafu's fiction. To quote but a few examples: feeling sexually frustrated, the hero in "Mangmangye" (Deep Night) goes out to acquire a handkerchief and some old needles that have been used by a young woman. Upon returning home, he keeps smelling the "fragrance" of the handkerchief, and cannot resist piercing his cheek with the needle until he bleeds and he is swept by "a sense of joy" (1:133). In another instance, the hero in "Huanxiang Ji" (Reminiscences on Returning Home) imagines that he breaks into someone's house, and taking hold of a pair of woman's laced shoes, he indulges in toying with them and smelling them, and finally takes them away with him (3:41–42). Such a fetishistic and morbid delight in the peculiarities of sexual love is seldom displayed so prominently in Chinese and Western European literature, or in Russian lit-

---

[79] Itō Toramaru, "'Chinron' ron", *Chūgoku bungaku kenkyū*, No. 1.

[80] Tsuda Sōkichi, *An Inquiry into the Japanese Mind as Mirrored in Literature—The Flowering Period of Common People Literature*, tr. by Fukamatsu Matsuda, pp. 202–225.

[81] Nakamura Mitsuo, *Modern Japanese Fiction, 1868–1926*, p. 13.

erature.[82] It is no wonder that Yu's short story "Sinking" came as a great shock to the Chinese reading public of his time, and he was immediately denounced by many, including some liberal intellectuals, as an "erotic" and "decadent" writer. This repugnance is still felt by some today. Yu Dafu countered that "those who have never lived in Japan will never quite understand the true value of his work; those who have no sincere feeling for literature or art have no right to criticise this work".[83] The precise meaning of this statement is not very clear. But it can safely be deduced without distortion that the so-called "decadent" description are sincere reflections of his thoughts and feelings, and their portrayal is closely related to his eight years' sojourn in Japan. To hazard a guess, this "close relation" may be elaborated to mean the influence of the Japanese attitude to sex, and/or the depiction of sex prevalent in Japanese literature of the time, and his own sexual frustrations.

VI. Strangeness and Familiarity: A Central Paradox

Yu Dafu's hero seems then to be a mixture of everything. He betrays streaks of Wertherian sorrow, the literary talent of the old style *caizi* and *mingshi*, the heightened consciousness of the Dostoevskian underground man, and above all, the superfluousness of the Turgenevan hero. From the Chinese literary point of view, we have in front of us a "strange" hero—strange in that he calls himself a Chulkaturin when disappointed in love, strange in that in his solitariness he imagines himself wandering in the vastness of the Russian countryside, strange in that he calls his numbness an "Oblomovian numbness", strange in that he invokes the Mona Lisa as an example of paramount beauty. Yet he is at the same time so familiar—his ideals, his sufferings, his intellectual predicament, and his "thinness" (which he calls "the thinness of Du Fu") have

---

[82] While it is true that some Chinese fictional heroes may feel a fetishistic delight, for example, in the tiny feet of women, as in the opening chapter of *Jin Ping Mei*, where the author describes "the silken hose, the tiny feet", they seldom do so as explicity as is done in Japanese literature.

[83] Quoted from Zhou Zuoren, "'Chenlun'", appeared in the literary criticism page, *Chen Bao fujuan*, 1922.3.16.

frequently been the lot of Chinese men of letters, old and young, past and present. In his "strangeness" and "familiarity" lies the paradox of the typology of Yu Dafu's superfluous man, an instance of the rather "peculiar" effect of literary influence.

As we have seen from the situational and specific parallels, and from the direct borrowings, there is a demonstrable Turgenevan influence on Yu's fictional works. The very concept of the "super-fluous man", so central to Yu's autobiographical short stories, is a direct borrowing from this 'Northern Giant'. Interestingly enough, it is precisely the "strangeness" of the Turgenevan superfluous hero that gave him a greater hold over Yu's contemporaries.

In the circumscribed Turgenevan hero, Yu has found a prototype who is full of goodwill and high moral sensibility, but because of his weakness of character, his intelligence and aspirations can find nothing to work on or through in the objective social world confronting him. He vacillates between self-assertion and self-denigration, between self-appreciation and self-pity, blending together what Turgenev calls the "Hamlet and Don Quixote" qualities.[84] He is a stranger to Chinese literature. Seldom has there been a Chinese fictional hero who is as oppressed by his frustrations, and yet so conscious of his physical and moral failure. Inspired by the Turgenevan model, Yu Dafu is able to give ample expression to the "divided character" that rapidly emerged in the May Fourth period, of which he is a cardinal example. That his hero-type is so little Wertherian (even less Byronic), in spite of the fact that Yu was arguably equally well exposed to Western romantic litera-ture, is itself revealing. The meaning that these romantic heroes and writers hold for him lies in their intense sorrow, their *Weltschmerz*—a feeling much shared by Yu himself. He is less impressed by the way they face up to their impending fate, overwhelmed (as he is) by the Turgenevan solution. For Yu's hero, his failure is a source of shame and remorse; there is nothing honourable about failure, as there is for so many romantics. He feels that man's predicament can only render him superfluous, and his outlook on life is essentially pessimistic, even though he aspires

---

[84] It should be remembered that Yu Dafu rendered this article into Chinese in 1928.

to a more free, egalitarian and compassionate society. He also lacks the characteristic pride of the Chinese *mingshi* scholars. He may share their discontent and final gesture of escape, but setting up as a recluse in a far-off land is to him an admission of failure— failure to face up to life and reality.

Thus, Yu's hero may appear at first glance to be a mixture of everything. But this is not simply a "hotch-potch". There is a conscious effort by the author to unify these elements, however "strange" and disparate, into an organic whole. What we have is a new unity that gives meaning and richness to the portrayal.

At the same time, a double bond of "familiarity" is central to this influence. As I have said in the second chapter, the readiness of the Chinese men of letters to find a common cause in nineteenth-century Russian political, social and intellectual history, and to see parallels with the Chinese environment in the May Fourth period is basic to their receptiveness to the Russian literary influence. We see that the conflicts suffered by Yu's hero—the conflicts between old and new, love and authority, honour and ignominy, freedom and responsibility—are common conflicts plaguing many May Fourth intellectuals. They are also familiar conflicts oppressing Turgenev's superfluous man, though the extent and slant may be different. Just as Yu's hero is rendered rootless and homeless by his failure to come to grips with the conflicts confounding him, the tragedy of Turgenev's hero has been described as "the tragedy of a politics of homelessness and homesickness".[85] Just as Turgenev's hero is to be understood through his conflicts, so is Yu Dafu's. His hero quarrels and argues with himself, and the division within himself gives a somewhat Dostoevskian tinge to his motivation. The result is that the hero, in terms of his contradictions and impulses, appears more lifelike, more "realistic" than the conventional depictions. There is a tendency in Yu Dafu to destroy the notion of character altogether. His hero can be seen as a "problem in-carnate"—the solving of his problems knows no end, and there seems no conclusion to his conflicts. He is circumscribed. He is super-fluous. In his superfluity is seen a new meaning and a universal

[85] Irving Howe, "Turgenev: The Politics of Hesitation", in *Politics and the Novel*, p. 128.

dimension—something hitherto lying dormant in the Chinese literary tradition. The new unity is the result of the paradoxical blending of the qualities of "strangeness"—Russian influences—and "familiarity"—indigenous literary tradition and social environment.

In the final analysis, it is in this new unity that the real strength of Yu's hero and his writings reside. Russian literary influence is to be interpreted as a "living model" that has left an indelible mark on Yu's attitude to life, that has, as he says, induced in him a "pathologically morbid state of mind". This explains why, of all the Russian writers, he particularly likes Turgenev, Dostoevsky and Lermontov, and of the fictional heroes favours Rudin, Chulkaturin, Raskolnikov and Oblomov. This distinctively "Russian attitude"—cosmopolitanism, sympathy for the down-trodden, numbness and lethargy, and the underdog mentality—has become inseparable from his own attitude to life, and in turn becomes equally inseparable from his autobiographical short stories. Not infrequently, an otherwise "Russian" phenomenon becomes, through Yu's own making—by combining it organically with the indigenous forces—his own vision or an enlarged vision of himself and of life in general, so that an attempt at a structural analysis of his works becomes quite often superfluous, in the ordinary sense of the word. In trying to be himself, the superfluous man in his short stories becomes both an independent and representative figure. In his superfluousness is revealed the moral fabric of his time, as well as the social, psychological and moral dilemmas facing the conscientious intellectual in an age of turbulence and transition.

5 Mao Dun's Defeated Hero

I. The Literary Circle in the 1920s

...up to the eve of the May Thirtieth Incident (1925), the entire
wentan (literary circle) was shrouded in despair and uncertainty. Despite
the apparent differences between [the realists' ability for] stark observation and bleak smiles, and [the sensualists'] urge for sensual pursuits
and intoxication, inside they share the same ennui and uncertainty. The
literary world then, which had been heading towards the crossroads,
could only linger irresolutely there.[1]

Mao Dun, 1936.

Such was the situation of the literary circle in the mid-1920s.
Many men of letters were indeed at the crossroads. Faced with
corruption and malpractices from above, and encroachments
from abroad (the May Thirtieth Massacre), the optimism that
blossomed with the Literary Revolution gradually wilted away.
The initial success of the Northern Expedition in 1927, which first
caused great rejoicing among the liberal and social-minded intellectuals, was immediately offset by the brutal repression that
followed. Tens of thousands of radical intellectuals were tortured,

---

[1]Mao Dun, "Preface to *Daxi*", ZXD, Vol. 2, p. 12.

jailed, or executed. Although scattered revolts and demonstrations continued to flare up, the revolutionary movement in the big cities was losing momentum. Pessimism and despair swept over many city-dwelling intellectuals.[2]

In the years of moral disintegration and defeat, the most cherished ideals and illusions of the conscience-ridden intellectuals were crushed to pieces. Some writers offered an escape into sensualism and decadence, while others simply mirrored their own gloom and disillusionment in their fiction.[3] Never quite before in Chinese history had the literary scene been so thickly veiled by such clouds of pessimism, nihilism and moral lassitude. Many compared this period with the "age of decadence" in Russian literary history, when, in the wake of the defeat by the Japanese in 1904, and the failure of the Revolution in 1905, Russian nihilism reached its peak. The intellectual heroes of Mao Dun (1896–1981)[4] in his early works (1927–1931), reveal traits remarkably similar to those of the nihilistic heroes of Andreyev and Artzybashev. In his search for a way to mould his defeated hero types, Mao Dun is both consciously and sub-consciously under the spell of his Russian precursors. But first we must examine his initial attitude to literature.

II. Initial Attitude to Literature

Any discussion of Mao Dun's outlook on literature, especially during the 1920s when he was less orthodox in thought, will draw our attention to the pseudonym "Maodun" (inconsistency/conflict)

[2] See Eastman, *The Abortive Revolution: China under Nationalist Rule, 1927–1937.*

[3] A good example of these two attitudes would be the decadent works of Zhang Ziping, and the realistic ones of Ye Shaojun, notably *Ni Huanzhi* which Mao Dun commented on at length.

[4] Mao Dun's autobiography *Wo zhouguode daolu* offers new information about his life and activities during the May Fourth period. By relating his many behind-the-scenes activities, the author tries to show with eagerness his closeness to the Party during these years. While the author attempts to be consistent in his autobiography, he left untold his many inconsistencies in this period, as his testimonies made at the time show. Marián Gálik also drew out Mao Dun's contradictions in his study *Mao Dun and Modern Chinese Literary Criticism.*

which the author chose for himself.[5] Mao Dun's evolution in these initial years of writing makes an interesting study, as Gálik's account clearly demonstrates,[6] though his approach to literature remained essentially unchanged. As a leading May Fourth intellectual, Mao Dun embraced the patriotic yet cosmopolitan spirit prevalent at the time. Literature was for him the artistic expression of an all-embracing outlook, an ethical view of history and of man's place in the cosmos. The constant tendency of Western literary history, he reasoned, was nothing less than "to make literature more re-presentative of the life of all mankind of its time, to express more adequately man's emotional life, with all its sufferings and yearnings, and to represent him in his struggle against and entreaties to unfathomable destiny."[7] Only the works which could represent the feeling of the common man, provide an aesthetic education, help towards building a rational moral society, and wipe away human barriers were to him real literature.[8] He was in this initial period less concerned with whether works were realistic, symbolic or mystical in nature.[9] This promethean and utilitarian way of thinking affected his approach to literature, and gave rise to many of his conflicts in this period.

While Mao Dun tirelessly campaigned for promethean ideals in literature, there was another side to him which was just as pervasive. He was at heart an evolutionist, and also a determinist and a realist. His literary viewpoint in the 1920s was often characterized by these two forces in him—promethean and determinist—which often

[5]Mao Dun mentioned that he had actually chosen "maodun" (矛盾) as his pseudonym for *Disillusion*, to reflect the many contradictions in himself. Ye Shengtao however changed " 矛 " to " 茅 " (also *mao*), which sounds more like a proper surname. See his *Autobiography*, Vol. 2, pp. 5–6.

[6]As n. 4. Gálik's study remains to date the most meticulous on Mao Dun's views on literature. I am indebted to him for some of my interpretations in this section.

[7]"Xinwenxue yanjiuzhe de zeren yu nuli", *XSYB*, 12.2 (1921.2), p. 2 (pseud. Lang Sun). Also *MWZJ*, Vol. 1, pp. 27–28. For a checklist of Mao Dun's names and pseudonyms, see Gálik, "The Names and Pseudonyms Used by Mao Tun", *AO*, 31 (1963), pp. 80–108.

[8]"Chuangzuo de qiantu", *MWZJ*, Vol. 1, p. 55.

[9]"Wenxue he ren de guanxi ji Zhongguo gulai duiyu wenxuezhe shenfen de wuren", ibid., p. 25; also "Yinianlai de ganxiang yu mingnian de jihua", ibid., pp. 67–68.

acted on or against each other. As a confirmed evolutionist, he was convinced of the evolutionary stages which literary history passes through—from classicism to romanticism, then to realism/naturalism, and finally to the neo-romanticism of the modern age.[10] Neo-romantic literature was to him ideal for China, as it not only represented the spirit of modern man, but can also "show mankind the right way."[11] However, he was also impelled by his determinist instincts to believe that May Fourth literature must, like its counterpart in Europe, first experience the wave of realism/naturalism before it can proceed on to neo-romanticism.[12] His view on literature in the early 1920s was thus, as Gálik puts it, "characterized by a historical look at reality and determined by the principle of social and psychological determinism."[13] While he formally endorsed realism in Chinese literature, he nevertheless had doubts about what he considered its deficiencies. Here we see the promethean and determinist forces in him striking a discordant note.

It is true that at this time Mao Dun shared Taine's view of literature, that being shaped by its socio-political environment it must necessarily reflect its epoch.[14] He was nevertheless uneasy about the effect of realistic literature on the reader; it was prone to show the dark side of humanity and society, and was often pessimistic. Because of his promethean ideal he wanted literature "to take up the enormous task of awakening the masses and filling them with strength."[15] The answer he found to his inner conflict, between a determination to see things as they really are and the desire to have them better, was that of an uneasy compromise. A

[10] See his "Wenxue shangde gudian zhuyi, langman zhuyi he xieshi zhuyi", XSYB, 11.9 (1920.9), pp. 1–19; see also "Xiaoshuo xinchaolan xuanyan", MWZJ, Vol. 1, pp. 6–11.

[11] See Gálik, "Mao Tun's Struggle for a Realistic and Marxist Theory of Literature", in The Genesis of Modern Chinese Literary Criticism, p. 196.

[12] As n. 10.

[13] As n. 4, p. 82.

[14] See especially his article "Wenxue yu rensheng", MWZJ, Vol. 1, pp. 110–114. Mao Dun adopted Taine's theory that factors of race, milieu and epoch govern a piece of work, and added a fourth, the personality of the writer. In invoking the last factor, one sees that Mao Dun was less deterministic than his French predecessor. See also "Shehui beijing yu chuangzuo", ibid., pp. 48–51; "Wenxue yu zhengzhi shehui", ibid., pp. 115–117.

[15] "Da zhuanbian shiqi he shi laine?", ibid., p. 160.

classic example is his reaction to Max Nordau's *Degeneration*. Nordau held that contemporary works of naturalism and decadence showed symptoms of regression and neurosis. Mao Dun argued to the contrary. These symptoms, he explained, merely manifested man's disagreement with humdrum living and his cries of resistance. They signalled man's true awakening.[16] His purpose is therefore to promote a literature which is realistic yet not lacking optimism. This is what he argued for in his important article "Naturalism and Modern Chinese Fiction" (1922).[17] In it, he gave his unqualified support to the technique of the Western naturalist school. Such a technique, he argued, is even observed by neo-romantic writers like Maeterlinck. While he disapproved of the sadness and fatalism of naturalism, he defended it by relating it to the social reality of the time which the writers but faithfully reflected. This is why he favoured works of symbolism, which to him not only reflect, but can also harmonize conflicting human feelings, reduce the gloom of realism, and act as a fruitful transition to neo-romanticism.[18] Such an understanding also accounts largely for his high regard for the works of Andreyev, a point I will amplify later.

By the same token, he advocates neo-romantic works because besides wiping away the exaggerated criticism and despair of realism, they lead the reader to the correct *Weltanschauung* and the spirit of self-consciousness. Romain Rolland's *Jean Christophe* was for him until the mid-1920s the ideal neo-romantic work.[19] Profuse also was his praise for *Clerambault*, which shows not only Rolland's ideal of an absolute free will, but also exposes the hypocrisy of the intelligentsia in their attempt during the World War to deceive the soldiers on the battlefield.[20] He was also attracted by the spirit of optimism and the symbolic technique of Rolland's play *Liluli*.[21] However, Mao Dun soon took back a lot of the praise he had

---

[16]"Qingnian de pijuan", *XSYB*, 13.8 (1922.8), pp. 1–2.

[17]"Ziranzhuyi yu Zhongguo xiandai xiaoshuo", *MWZJ*, Vol. 1, pp. 83–99.

[18]As Gálik points out in his study, Mao Dun did not distinguish clearly between symbolic and neo-romantic works. An example is his analysis of G. Hauptmann's *Die Versunkene Glocke* (The Sunken Bell), which was considered as symbolic in one place, and neo-romantic in another. As n. 4, pp. 74–75.

[19]Ibid., pp. 40–41.

[20]"Ouzhou dazhan yu wenxue", *XSYB*, 15.8 (1924.8), pp. 34–38.

[21]"Leguan de wenxue", *MWZJ*, Vol. 1, p. 135.

lavished on Rolland, and with it his approval of Western avant-garde literature. In his long treatise *On Proletarian Art (Lun wuchan jieji yishu)*, written at the time of the May Thirtieth Massacre and its immediate aftermath, the instincts of Mao Dun the promethean were deeply stirred. In this article, he criticized avant-garde writers for their subjective approach, which deformed objective reality, and rendered their works incomprehensible. To him, avant-garde literature betrayed "abnormal pathological symptoms". By comparison, proletarian literature, which showed the healthy spirit of the common people, the proletariat, was healthy. It was in this connection that he took issue with the so-called "people's art" advocated by Romain Rolland, which seemed now simply to reflect the utopian ideals of the capitalist intelligentsia. The spirit of the proletarians was best captured by Gorky, whose work, Mao Dun reasoned, vividly depicted the suffering spirit and the enormous mission of this class.

Attracted as Mao Dun was by proletarian literature at this time, it is however significant that he did not idealize it. Instead, he allowed a discussion of its possible pitfalls to occupy the bulk of the article. In short, he feared that this infant art might become too polemical in nature, that its subject matter might be too restricted (partly as a result of the narrow scope of its writers, a point which he later expounded in detail), and that its artistic form might take time to develop, due to the "organic evolutionary" principles of literature.[22] Here, we see clearly the promethean and determinist forces in Mao Dun working on and checking each other. This balancing act is even more clearly marked in "The New Mission of the Writer", another article written at the same time. He saw that literature should guide its readers to a bright and better future, but writers should at the same time not shy away from real life, even while they concentrated on depicting and eulogizing the future ideal world. They should first and foremost care for the suffering and the needy of the present generation, and champion them. Lacking such sentiments, Mao Dun postulated, they certainly could not show the correct path which is the future.[23] While Mao Dun adopted a class interpretation of literature, which differed from the

[22] "Lun wuchan jieji yishu", ibid., pp. 182–199.
[23] "Wenxuezhe de xinshiming", ibid., pp. 217–219.

national and universal standpoint he had hitherto stood for, it is important to point out that his approach had not changed. The writer may indeed have "a new mission", but he still held that literature is indisputably the truthful reflection of reality.[24]

It was in this frame of mind that he wrote in the late 1920s that "social organizations change more violently from day to day. The so-called good and fine human society lies in the distant future. Hence, analytical and critical realism has a long, long way to go to reach this remote future."[25] Interestingly, he even came to the defence of naturalism, saying that although it was not a healthy literary current the new anti-naturalist-isms also have their pathological symptoms.[26] It is true, as Gálik points out, that in 1929, after Mao Dun's own bitter experience, shattered illusions and defeats, he began "to look upon literary problems from the aspect of a far more objective historicism. Literature proved to be more complex than his reflections had been. Consequently Mao Dun went back to his positions of 1924, particularly to that period when he wrote about the war literature".[27] This was the period when Mao Dun was full of praise for Andreyev. It is therefore not surprising that when he made his debut as a novelist in 1927–1928, it was his determinist instincts which got the upper hand, and the works of Andreyev and Artzybashev which made their presence felt. Thus a brief discussion of his attitude towards Russian literature will be of value.

Mao Dun's enthusiasm for Russian literature, especially in the early 1920s, has been dwelt upon in the previous chapters. His preference for Russian literature sprang mainly from a belief that it possessed the essential qualities of great literature—universality, humanitarian appeal, and a deep concern for the common people. As he saw it, Russian writers were preoccupied with social revolution and the betterment of the life of all. The Russian "cause" im-

---

[24] Ibid., p. 217.

[25] *Xiyang wenxue tonglun*, p. 21.

[26] Ibid., p. 283. As we know, Mao Dun was at this time critical of the so-called "proletariat" art of young writers like Jiang Guangci, which is formalistic, empty and lacks real feeling. See his "Huanying *Taiyang*", *MWZJ*, Vol. 1, pp. 261–264.

[27] As n. 11, p. 211.

mortalized in their literary writings was a "reflection of the national
spirit of Russia, which literary writings of no other country can
measure up to".[28] Tolstoy and Dostoevsky, as we have seen, represented in his mind the acme of Russian humanitarianism.[29]
Although his infatuation with these two authors cooled off with
his advocacy of proletarian literature in the 1930s, his admiration
did not.

What is more complicated, and correspondingly more interesting,
is his response to the writers of the "silver age" of Russian literature:
Andreyev, Artzybashev and Ropshin. It is in Mao Dun's reaction
to them that his promethean and determinist instincts are thrown
into sharp contrast. On the one hand, he approved, and even
admired these writers for their "realistic" depiction of life in Russia
in the first years of this century, when, he reasoned, Russia was
strikingly similar to China in the 1920s; on the other, he had second
thoughts about the unheroic types in their works, people who are
either nihilists, egoists or sensualists. He felt obliged to make a stand,
as he did in the beginning of his article about the controversial
George of Ropshin's *The Pale Horse*. Rather than take issue with
George's nihilistic egoism, he extolled the author's "greatness" in
describing delicately "the metamorphosis of this soul in a particular
environment". He defended George's action against the society in
which he lived, and even showed admiration for his individual
strength.[30] About Andreyev's works, he agreed that some of these
tend to be nihilistic and decadent, but he still considered him a first
class writer with a profound humanitarian appeal and a deep concern

[28] "Eguo jindai wenxue zatan, xia", *XSYB*, 11.2 (1920.2), p. 1. Mao Dun's
strong orientation towards Russian literature contrasts with his attitude towards
other "realistic" literature. Dickens, he argues, also depicts the life of the poor,
but he lacks sincerity, and his works betray signs of "the upper class writing for
the lower class". Maupassant's delineation of the dark side of society is realistic,
even naturalistic, but he lacks compassion. Whereas Russian writers can reduce
people to "tears and contrition", Maupassant can only arouse their anger and
bitterness. "Eguo jindai wenxue zatan, shang", *XSYB*, 11.1, (1920.1), p. 2. He was
also sceptical of Zola's materialistic mechanical determinism. See "Ziranzhuyi",
as n. 17.
[29] See nn. 10 and 26 in Chapter Three.
[30] See nn. 56 and 61 in Chapter Three.

for the common people. He took considerable pains to explain that Andreyev "lived in the revolutionary era of 1905. Witnessing numerous losses and sufferings, killings and bloodshed, he concluded that human destiny is all misery. A defeatist tone resounds in his works. This is the natural flavour [of literature] after great changes and calamities."[31] In "World War and Literature", a major article written in 1924, Mao Dun, while taking note of the pessimism in Andreyev, praised the author's anti-war sentiments, and his championing the cause of the little man. He mentioned especially the author's *The Confession of a Little Man during Great Days* and *The Sorrow of Belgium*. Twice in the article he hailed Andreyev as a great writer.[32]

Mao Dun's attitude revealed the potentially conflicting forces in him. From the determinist point of view, it is only natural, if not inevitable, for Andreyev to write about defeat and disillusion; but on the other hand, Mao Dun's belief in the inspirational power of literature urges him to seek for works that depict man's ability to rise above his environment. This attitude also governed his appraisal of Artzybashev's works. He found the Russian writer's decadence difficult to accept at first, but soon came to admit that this is the result of an emerging trend in Russia around the turn of the century, and Artzybashev could not have written otherwise. He further reasoned that such works emerged as a result of the sociopolitical environment of the writer. Despite his disappointment the writer strove to live and to act; such obstinacy made him an easy target for sensualism or egoism.[33] By adopting such an attitude, Mao

---

[31] "Andeliefu sihao", *XSYB*, 11.1 (1920.1), p. 4. Mao Dun's conflicting views on Andreyev's works are further revealed in that while on the one hand quoting Seltzer's remark that "Andreyev arose, with his mysteriousness and decadence, depicted the new hopes and new strivings" in the second part of "Eguo jindai wenxue zatan", he told readers on the other hand (in "Tongxin—fanyi wenxueshu de taolun", *XSYB*, 12.2 [1921.2], p. 2) that he would be reluctant to translate Andreyev's *Savva, The Black Masks, The Wall, The Governor* and *Satan's Diary* into Chinese because of their nihilistic content, though he considered those good works of literature.

[32] As n. 20, pp. 15, 31.

[33] Mao Dun advocated the translation of Artzybashev's revolutionary tales such as "Shevyrev" and "The Millionaire", but was doubtful about *Sanin* for its sensualism, though he thought highly of the work. As n. 31, "Tongxin".

Dun was in actuality anticipating something that he was to argue in his own defence, after the publication of his first trilogy *Eclipse* in 1928, when the work attracted exceptionally hostile harangues from the ultra-leftists.[34] This is how he described his pessimism in 1928 in the wake of defeat: "Having truthfully lived and experienced the most complicated chapter of life in China, I have become steeped in disillusion and in life's contradiction. Despondent and in solitude, I am nevertheless still governed by the will to live. I try to use the cold ashes of my life to transmit a ray of light amidst this confusion and gloom. This is how I came to write [my first novel]."[35]

This gloom and despair, coupled with his witnessing the trend towards nihilism and decadence sweeping over the intellectuals of the time, gave his realist and determinist instincts the ascendency over his promethean vision. He wrote in his preface to *Ye qiangwei* (Wild Rose) of the "dull and oppressive reality": "life is truly like a wild rose and to assert that it has no thorns is a deep self-deception, while to hate it because of them, leads to nothing".[36] When he came to depict the moral disintegration of the intellectuals after the Northern Expedition, of the "thorns" that pricked his defeated heroes, it was Andreyev and Artzybashev, who wrote in and about a similar situation in Russia some twenty years before, who provided a live model for Mao Dun.

In the following pages, I will study Mao Dun's defeated hero types in the light of Russian influence. I will address myself to these questions: What sort of Russian flavour do we find in his early intellectual types? To what extent are his heroes drawn from life and to what extent are they contrived? How does this influence shed light on Mao Dun's art in his early endeavours as a novelist and his claim to be a chronicler of Chinese society? I will begin by

[34] Mao Dun wrote considerably less between 1925–1927, the years immediately preceding his first creative effort. A crucial factor was his active participation in the Northern Expedition, which brought him to Canton and Wuhan. His determinist views on literature were strengthened upon witnessing the "great changes and calamities" of the late 1920s, as his critical and creative writings of that period show.

[35] "Cong Guling dao Dongjing", *XSYB*, 19.10 (1928.10), p. 1138.

[36] "Xiezai *Yeqiangwei* de qianmien", *Mao Dun lun chuangzuo*, pp. 51–52.

briefly looking into the three types of intellectuals in these works: the pessimists, the decadents and the rationalists.

III. The Defeated Hero

Qu Qiubai wrote in a comment on Mao Dun's *Three Friends* (*Sanrenxing*, 1931) that "there is no 'ideal' hero in his works, there are rather prototypes of the ideal 'unheroic-hero'".[37] This remark can be extended to describe Mao Dun's other early works—*Eclipse* (1927–1928), *Rainbow* (*Hong*, 1929) and *Road* (*Lu*, 1931).[38] In each of these the hero disintegrates before our eyes, either degenerating into self-pity and disillusion, taking refuge in sensualism, or remaining locked up in his intellect, unable to act. As Wang Zhongzhao, who also plays the role of observer and commentator in Mao Dun's early works,[39] remarked: "All of them (the intellectuals) are busily searching for something. All have their own visions of life, but they are all disillusioned. Despite their differences in disposition and mentality, they are rent with the same disillusionment. The authority of fate—is this the authority of fate? The sorrow of our modern age—is this inescapable?" (p. 174)[40] Mao Dun provided the answer himself. He had one of his characters, Manqing, describe this as "the sorrow of the fin-de-siècle . . . which consists of the sorrow of disillusion, the anxiety to do good, and

[37] Qu Qiubai, "Tantan *Sanrenxing*", *QQWJ*, Vol. 2, p. 340.

[38] It should be pointed out that the ten volume *Mao Dun wenji* published in Beijing between 1958–1961 contained considerable revisions by the author. Many of the more pessimistic passages of his early works were struck out. I have here adhered to his early editions: *Disillusion, Vacillation, Pursuit*, and *Rainbow* published in 1930; *Three Friends* in 1931; *Road*, a 1935 reprint of the original 1931 edition; and *Twilight*, 1933.

[39] Susan W. Chen points out the many similarities between Mao Dun and his character Zhongzhao, and holds that the author injects his own experiences and moods into the character, as well as using him as a mouthpiece of his own views. "The Personal Element in Mao Dun's Early Fiction", *HJAS*, 43 (1983). I go further to argue that he is about the only living character in Mao Dun's early works, partly because of this "live" model.

[40] Průšek wrote that in this work Mao Dun sees around him "nothing but dissolution and death. There can be no more convincing document of the feeling for the tragedy of life with which youth of that time was filled." "Subjectivism and Individualism in Modern Chinese Literature", *AO*, 25.2 (1957), p. 265.

the impulse towards decadence . . ." (ibid., p. 5).[41] In these works
Fate is depicted as all-encompassing, unfathomable and destructive.
His heroes have either become totally submissive to her will (like
Shi Xun in *Pursuit* and Wei Yu in *Rainbow*), are playthings in
her hands (like Jing in *Disillusion* and Zhongzhao in *Pursuit*), or
have adopted the role of her willing accomplices (like Dinghui in
Disillusion and Qiuliu in *Pursuit*). So ubiquitous and irresistible is
her dark hand that "The Symphony of Fate" would make an ideal
title for all these works taken together.

This sorrow of the fin-de-siècle and the author's preoccupation
with it are what distinguish and unite Mao Dun's heroes in his
"Symphony of Fate". They are notable for their inner life—the
problems that characterise the life of the soul, with its premonitions,
its yearnings, searchings and failings. Political and social events serve
mainly to bring into focus the author's preoccupation with the
abstract concept of the "iron round of destiny". Indeed, Mao Dun's
obsessions, coupled with the abstract and schematic depiction of
the characters, marks the difference between Mao Dun's early works
and those immediately following—works like *Twilight (Ziye*, 1932)
and *Village Trilogy (Spring Silkworm, Autumn Harvest* and *Bleak
Winter*, 1932–1934) justify Mao Dun's reputation as the chronicler
of Chinese society in the 1930s. One of the most salient differences
lies in the character of his heroes. True, many of his heroes in this
second phase are also injured and crushed, but their "failure" is

[41] This speech is interesting in several ways. First, it reflects Mao Dun's own
pessimism about the situation of the time. Mao Dun claims (in "Tongxin—
ziranzhuyi de lun zhan", *XSYB*, 13.5 [1922.5], pp. 1–3) that in this era of the
"fin-de-siècle" the enlightened youth are capable of penetrating vile reality with
their own eyes. The most agonizing sorrow is not so much the horridness of ugliness
as the crippling of ideals, and the really brave man is he who is not despondent
and disappointed, he who keeps on striving upon seeing ugliness. This constitutes
for him the reason for advocating naturalistic literature. We see clearly here Mao
Dun's determinist outlook. Second, the wording and tone of this speech echo
Andreyev's in *The Life of Man* (which Mao Dun referred to in his note in
"Andeliefu", see n. 50 below) which begins: "I have traversed many towns and
lands, and nowhere have I seen a free man. . . ." Manqing's speech also contains:
". . . I traversed many towns and lands, . . . and everywhere I have witnessed
such sickness. We, . . . the wandering youth, also have our sorrow. . . ." Third,
it is interesting to see him using the European term "fin-de-siècle" to define the
malaise.

no longer caused by the inescapable authority of Fate. Mao Dun emphatically points out that the underlying cause of their suppression is the macro-economic and market forces prevailing at the time. They are unfortunately caught up in a web of conflicts when they attempt actively to resist the established order, and become the unwilling victims of evil capitalism. Such is the tragedy that befalls Wu Sunfu, Mr Lin and Lao Tongbao. Moreover, Mao Dun has replaced his early schematic, nihilistic or submissive intellectual types with real, stubborn and courageous people, who are true embodiments of their indigenous environment.

So plain are the differences between the works of his first and second phase (though the interval between them was only a few months) that one wonders whether these works did in fact originate from the same hand. Several factors are pertinent. The most obvious is Mao Dun's pessimism in the wake of defeat in 1928. It is beyond doubt that Mao Dun's own demoralization, and his witnessing the disintegration of those around him account by and large for the prevailing pessimistic and sentimental nature of the earlier works. It is also clear that he allowed his own tormented feeling to invade these works. While this "subjective" approach differs from the objectivity and control which characterize the works from 1932 on, works written at a time when Mao Dun was less disturbed, it offers no explanation for the abstractness of his types. On the other hand, the marked affinities between some of these defeated heroes and those of his Russian precursors—Andreyev's resigned heroes, Artzybashev's sensualists and Ropshin's egoists—give grounds for the belief that Mao Dun the apprentice novelist drew examples from his Russian predecessors. One can go a step further and argue that the difference between his early and later works is accentuated by his borrowing Russian conventions which he shook off later, a point I will develop in the course of this chapter.

The Pessimists

Scepticism, disillusionment and submission (in that order) are the catchwords for Mao Dun's pessimistic early heroes. In the wake of defeat, a sense of numbness and negation overshadows them. Some, like Jing, Shi Xun, and Wei Yu have become reconciled to the power of fate. Others degenerate from scepticism into nihilism, which is the path of Hui in *Three Friends.*

Jing (in *Disillusion*) is Mao Dun's first intellectual type, and in portraying her Mao Dun has produced a prototype for all of his early heroes. As a character, she lacks life. Her actions are motivated by a conflict of ideas, rather than one of personality. Historical and personal events serve as rather crude devices to bring to the fore her internal conflicts. Since taking part in the demonstrations at her Provincial Girls' School the previous year (the story is set in Shanghai in the late spring of 1926), and upon seeing many of her classmates abandoning the true objectives of the movement, Jing has become "shattered and disappointed with everything". Mao Dun takes pains to depict her inexperience and innocence. For instance, she is horrified that her very experienced friend Dinghui has chosen revenge on Man as her aim in life: "She could never imagine that underneath this loving face was hidden such hatefulness and ugliness" (p. 6). Finding the ugliness in life unbearable, Jing prefers to destroy the world and to end her own life (p. 32).

On the other hand, her altruistic instincts make her want to believe that compassion is the highest of all sentiments. She pities Dinghui, whom she regards as "a victim of fate". Her vulnerable character is grasped by Baosu, who poses as an unrequited lover, and succeeds in seducing her. The irony is that not only is Baosu a "woman killer", he is also a shameless imposter and agent of the corrupt government. The realization of this provokes the most intense emotional upheaval in Jing. As the narrator comments: "She does not want to think of the past, and dares not think of the future. Human beings are but the playthings of destiny. Who can escape the taunts of destiny? Who can say that his plans for today will not be swiftly smashed to pieces by the malicious hand of destiny? The blows of her past experiences are severe. Jing dares not have confidence any more, dares not have hope. She decides thereupon to live mechanically, and . . . will comply with the dictates of destiny in the future." (pp. 45–46)

However, "two opposing forces", as the narrator has it, emerge, which symbolize Jing's inner conflicts. They are personified as "The New Ideal" and "Past Experiences", and they wage a battle in her mind:

Past Experiences: "All hopes will result in despair, all beautiful visions are themselves ugly. Poor thing . . . the more you struggle, the higher is your record of suffering and defeat."

New Ideal: "Is life worth living without hope? The difference between mankind and animals lies in the former's ability to hope. Hope will necessarily bring disillusion, but disillusion is not suffering. The real suffering is a life without hope or purpose."

Past Experiences: "The intangible net of destiny overshadows you on all sides. All struggles are futile."

New Ideal: "Destiny is the meaningless self-pity of the defeated, the way the cowardly explain away jeers. Man's future can only be determined by his own will-power and effort." (pp. 52–53)

As the battle goes on, Jing is temporarily won over by the guidance of the "New Ideal", and she emerges from her lethargy. As the narrator observes wryly: "the next day she went on board the *Changjiang* with Miss Zhao, intent on seeking her new life according to the dictates of destiny, though at the moment there was no trace of the word 'destiny' in the mind of Miss Jing" (p. 53). She goes to work for the new revolutionary government established in Wuhan after the first successes of the Northern Expedition, only to be disillusioned once more. She detests the pseudo-progressiveness and hypocrisy that hide behind the mask of many so-called revolutionaries, who "are madly looking for sensual pursuits, new and strange sexual stimuli . . ." (p. 63). She retreats again, and meets the wounded soldier, Lieutenant Qiang, in her capacity as a nursing assistant. They fall in love. Just as Jing is strong enough to gather up her altruistic instincts again to try to soften the "futuristic"[42] or war-loving stance of Qiang, he is summoned once more and chooses to answer the call. Jing is again frustrated by fate:

The worsening of her situation has aroused Jing's scepticism about all things. Are nice words, highstrung phrases, or things that appear good reliable? Jing has experienced all these, and is overcome by disillusion. . . . (p. 86)

---

[42] Mao Dun has borrowed the concept "futurism" current in European literature around the time of the First World War to depict the enthusiasm for war in the "weilai zhuyizhe" (futurist) Qiang Weili, a name that signifies the adoration of strength and power. As the chief writer on Western literature in the *Short Story Monthly*, Mao Dun was well informed of current literary trends. He published in October 1922 an article entitled "Weilaipai wenxue zhi xianshi", *XSYB*, 13.10.

The deterioration of her situation and the continual mishaps she has experienced remind us of Jing's own reasoning in distress—"who can say that his plans for today will not be swiftly smashed to pieces by the malicious hand of destiny?"

Even more sketchy and schematic than Jing is Shi Xun in *Pursuit*. He totally lacks personality, and merely exists to illustrate the powerful sway of the "iron round of destiny". Even his name, which means "the round of history", is symbolic. He himself reminds us of this role by repeatedly saying that "history goes in circles" (p. 57); "all that I see are circles. Human nature also has its circle, one static, and one in motion" (p. 21). For him, life is but a bunch of contradictions—between reason and emotion, truth and deception; only suicide can tip the balance.

Like Shi Xun, the purpose of Wei Yu's existence in *Rainbow* is further to illustrate the powerful sway of Fate. He is a total weakling, who feels all the time that "the fist of Fate has clenched on him tightly" (p. 32). His lover Mei, desperate when her father tries to force her to marry someone she detests, takes the initiative and arranges a meeting with Wei Yu to discuss plans for escape. To her surprise and disappointment, he opts for submission: "I am not worthy of your love . . . I'm not worthy of enjoying human happiness. I should not cast over your future bliss my own dark shadow. . . ." (p. 20) This "submission" scene closely echoes Turgenev's *Rudin* where Rudin is totally unmanned before the spontaneity of Natalya. However, Wei Yu is an infinitely more unheroic figure than Rudin. Though the Russian superfluous hero is made of paper, he at least has high passions and loftly ideals. Wei Yu has none of these compensating qualities. He sees his action as embodying the Tolstoyan principle of non-resistance to evil, a term that he (mistakenly) equates with resignation.

Thus, what draws Jing and Wei Yu together is the fact that they are both playthings in the hands of Fate, though the latter's co-operativeness makes him unheroic. Indeed, such is also the fate of Xu the sceptic who becomes a futile "Chinese Don Quixote", and Hui the nihilist who ends up in madness in Mao Dun's *The Three Friends*.[43]

[43] Qu Qiubai sighed that there is no *way* in "the way of the *Three Friends*" (a literal translation of the title *Sanrenxing*), as n. 37. Ye Ziming thought that this

A student caught up in the conflict of love and his career, Xu faces the immediate prospect of unemployment, and feels himself unworthy of the girl whom he admires. He decides to withdraw from the struggle, and philosophizes to her: "... there is no other way. I've decided to love you only in my heart and to adore you— Fate—this mischievous fate." (p. 9) He sees everything as in a state of uncertainty, and "feels that an invisible force dominates everything, and that any effort to resist would be futile" (p. 22).

His mother's untimely illness, which causes him to abandon his examination—thus putting his future career at risk—and go home immediately, further increases his sorrow. In a moment of intense spiritual malaise, Xu senses that he is not able to establish a direct bond between his personal existence and the laws of nature: "the past and the present, the realm of imagination and reality are all muddled up", and "everything is predestined, all ill omens are predestined. There is no escape, there is no way out—no way out!" (p. 31) In total frustration, he casually looks up at the sky and remembers Andreyev's play *To the Stars*, where the hero Ternovsky proposes that the immortality of the soul is infinitely more important than human passion. At this juncture, Xu's thoughts take a new turn. He cannot agree with Ternovsky's contempt for social life, nor with his cosmic view of the world. For him, to die unfulfilled is tragic. Therefore he summons up enough courage to try to break out of the four walls where he is trapped. He becomes, as the author puts it, a Chinese Don Quixote. But his efforts to alleviate the sufferings of Qiuju, the maid, only hasten her death, and his attempt to murder the monstrous landlord who tries to coerce one of his students into marrying him brings about his own demise.

If Xu's conflict of ideas reminds us of Andreyev's pessimistic heroes, Hui's character type resembles that of the Russian nihilists, whose existence is governed by the overrriding instinct to destroy. The earth, he holds, must be purged with fire, and the old world obliterated. Human convention, art and science, all things good or bad, need to be swept away to prepare the way for something new.

-----

work represents only the author's pattern of thought. It is not realistic. The character depictions are a failure, and even Yun, the "positive" hero in the work, lacks life, *Lun Mao Dun sishinian de wenxue daolu*, p. 84.

He burns with frenzy: "... one day this volcano in the earth will explode and burn many poisonous insects and monstrous animals to death. With them will also vanish many innocent and pitiable objects...." (p. 95)

Obsessed with his melodramatic dream that one day a miracle will come where evil will be purified to make way for the heavenly Kingdom, Hui believes nobody on earth can do anything. He treats everything with a cold contempt. His friend Yun is outraged by his "assumed superiority": "Hui, ... I hate your indifference, your 'superman-like' manner of smiling. You appear to be perfect, a superior being in front of those pitiable beings. You induce them to forget that they are lying in the dirt, and you yourself are in the same position. You rely on your smile to spread your virus of intoxication." (p. 100)

For such a fanatical nihilist, who thinks that morality is only rationalization, and a new type of superman is needed to live beyond the stultifying categories of good and evil, human communication is an impossibility. As he laments repeatedly: "Men can never understand each other."[44] The only reality for this avenger lies in an unknown world, in madness.

Hui's type is fascinating despite the simplified and abstract depiction. His instinct for utopian destruction reminds us of many a Russian nihilist. As a matter of fact, his type shows striking similarities to Andreyev's Savva.

We should also notice Xin in *Road*, who reminds us of Mao Dun's comments on Dostoevsky when he reasons: "It is better to enter prison than to be at school. It may actually be better to be a real sinner than a mental sinner. In this vile society of ours, sinners are good people and prison is a school for youngsters." (p. 131) When he realizes that man should fight for his future, and that sacrifice is nothing, a new road opens ahead of him, though he does not know where it leads. Thus, Xin serves as a transitional figure in Mao Dun's development from the first to the second phase of his

---

[44] Hui utters this on three occasions: first, after he receives Yun's letter chiding him for his nihilism (p. 98); second, after he has read Ke's diary of a revolutionary (p. 102); third, in disagreement with the students' call to petition the Nanjing Government (p. 116).

fictional writing, where scepticism, disillusion and submission are no longer hallmarks.

Certain broad themes emerge. All Mao Dun's early heroes are haunted by the traumatic experience of their past, and seeing their future in complete disarray, they recoil from the torpid reality of their surroundings. They endure an estranged and isolated existence, and become resigned to the idea that man is limited to his individual consciousness, that man thinks he is embracing the universe while he is only a slave to the laws of thought and existence that were not created by him and which he is not at liberty to alter. Mao Dun's delineation of the inner life of his intellectual heroes, concerned with their intellect rather than their personality, their psychological malaise rather than concrete action, accounts largely for the simplified and schematic pattern of their presentation—a presentation that is reminiscent of Andreyev's.

The Decadents

> I detest Shanghai, detest the foreigners, detest the silver-tongued shopkeepers in the big department stores, detest the conductors in the trams, detest my landlord, detest the vagabonds who eye girls on the street . . . It is true, though I don't know why, that the whole of Shanghai has become my enemy. . . .
>
> Zhou Dinghui in *Disillusion* (p. 1)

Dinghui's feeling of revulsion is the culmination of her disillusionment in trying to find the meaning of life in the bloody struggles of China in the late 1920s. Dinghui is a returned student frustrated in her endeavours to secure a job, and utterly disgusted with the bestial nature of man: in Dinghui's own words: "ever since the first time she was cheated by a man, she has toyed with the idea of revenge on men", and is always seeking ways to taunt them (p. 25). Her life becomes one of total aimlessness. She drifts from one place to another, enduring a decadent existence, seeking only her revenge. Compared to the shadowy figure of Dinghui, Zhang Qiuliu in *Pursuit* is a more actual and sentient creation. One is forced, perhaps paradoxically, to sympathize with her conflicts, rationalizations, and even her decadence. She remains today one of Mao Dun's most passionately depicted heroines.

From the very beginning, our attention is arrested by the eloquent and passionate voice of Qiuliu:

> Yes, we want to form a club. We are a group of people who adore action
> in preference to a quiet life. But in this time of turbulence, we are
> rendered entirely superfluous. Not that we are unable to find jobs—if
> we forget our dignity, we can undoubtedly muddle through. We have
> thought of concentrating on our studies, but we are no supermen. We
> have passions. We cannot concentrate on our studies in this age of fire
> and blood, at a time when demons run rampant. We see everywhere
> around us shameless and despicable people. We hear of many events
> that will reduce us to sorrow and tears. Though our blood is boiling
> inside us, we can find nothing to do. We are not worthy to be officials
> or landlords, nor are we able to become robbers or bandits. In such
> a turbulent time, our existence is almost wholly negative. We don't even
> know whether we still survive. We remain listless and despondent all
> day. We spend half a day here in the student association, we kill off
> an afternoon over there in a dance hall. In utter despair, we laugh,
> we yell, we cuddle, we kiss. We contain our tears, we seek sensual
> pleasures, and we become decadent. But are we content to squander
> our lives like this? We still want to go forward. This is what's behind
> our intention to form a club. (pp. 9–11)

In Qiuliu's speech are reflected the major political and moral
issues confronting the sensitive intellectuals of the time. As a weary
student in Shanghai, disillusioned at the outcome of the Northern
Expedition, Qiuliu is torn apart by a desire for excitement and a
fear of mediocrity in her search for the meaning of life. She
recognizes two paths open before her: "one will lead you to
brightness, but there will be much suffering, and many thorny
pitfalls; another will lead you to decadence, there you will find
comforts, satisfaction for your sensual passions, and the exaltation
of the flesh." (p. 61)

She wavers between the two poles, which the narrator describes
as the "angels" and "devils" in her. Has she "the courage to do good,
or the guts to become decadent?" (p. 62) she asks. Her impulsive
and sensual desires encourage her to choose the latter. As she reveals
to Manqing: "I am searching for violent sensual pleasures. I want
to go to dance halls, cinemas, hotels, restaurants. I even want to
go to Hell, to see blood. Only in so doing will I find meaning in
life." (p. 69) And she becomes once and for all, as Mao Dun puts
it, "a sensual egoist" (p. 71).

After this, the mental activities of Qiuliu the egoist are interesting to observe. As Mao Dun points out, she has found new bearings in her thoughts. She reasons: "I am my own arbiter. I should have complete freedom to treat my body in whatever way I like." (p. 77) No law, morality or convention can bind her. To her, love has no spiritual or moral value, "there is no such thing as love, there is only momentary joy" (p. 92).

However, underneath her individualistic appearance and passionate outcry lurks a lonely self. Decadence is but a momentary escape. In her calmer and more frightening moments of coldness and indifference, a desperate voice cries out from her innermost self: "Zhang Qiuliu, you are a lone wolf . . . You don't believe in love, country or society. You're always self-confident, you're never sorry for your past. Why should you weep? You should laugh frantically. You should be angry—take revenge, destroy. You should not take revenge on any single person, but on everybody. Throw away your dancing fan, take up your revolver." (p. 122)

Thus, Qiuliu's life alternates between her destructive despair and frantic passion. Despite her daring and vehemence, her fate seems, as her friend Zhongzhao observes after she has contracted V. D., "to be all shadowed in darkness" (p. 171). Her individualist egoism cannot, after all, protect her from the "iron round of destiny".

In the character of Zhang Qiuliu, Mao Dun has created a heroine who is capable of passion, who is open and unafraid. She stands for the warm, the impulsive, and as such is the obvious vehicle for passion. In her battle between decadence and altruism, individuality and mediocrity, feeling and intellect, her vision is dominated by irrationality. Qiuliu is indeed a "strange and romantic" person, as Zhongzhao comments. Never before has there been a Chinese heroine who is so passionately decadent, yet so sure of her actions, even her failures. Her sweeping rationalizations and moral anarchism are closely akin to those of Artzybashev's Sanin and Ropshin's George.

The Rationalists

Unlike his resigned pessimists and wilful decadents, some characters in Mao Dun's early novels seek a rational way of life. They are rationalists in the sense that they see ways in which man can achieve goodness and happiness amidst the chaos of the world. To them, harmony with mankind and a purpose in life are more important than lofty ideals and high-flown words. Their tragedy invariably lies in the fact that they are all crushed by the grindstones of destiny. The three rationalists in Mao Dun's early works are Wang Zhongzhao and Zhang Manqing in *Pursuit*, and Mei in *Rainbow*.

Self-sufficiency is the key to Zhongzhao's character. He knows what he is seeking and sets his priorities right. He aims, first and foremost, to be a "healthy man both spiritually and physically". What worries him in this time of turbulence are not the burning political and economic issues of the day, but "saving oneself from distress and uncertainty, from empty words and frivolity" (p. 22). As a journalist, he would like to see the pages that he edits become "the pulse of the city", to serve the function of diagnosing the state of health of society.

The core of his existence is his self-contentedness—his "half-pace" philosophy (*banbu zhuyi*). Given that the present restrictions do not "permit us to walk forward step by step", he argues, "we may as well walk half a pace. It is better to do so than not to walk at all." (p. 33) His reaction to the curtailment by the editor-in-chief of his plans to reform the social news page is one of "tolerance" and "patience". When even his "half-pace" philosophy encounters difficulties, embodied in the editor's obstruction of any reform, his feeling of self-sufficiency is once more activated. The narrator observes: "He was not as sensitive to the blow as the first time . . . He holds the belief that, having struggled against crippling defeats inch by inch, he will eventually see the day of his total success. . . ." (p. 39) The guiding light in his darker moments is the image of his beloved Miss Lu. She is the source of his happiness, the wellspring of his courage and the embodiment to him of the Scandinavian goddess—"the courageous Verdandi" (p. 168). No wonder that it is a tragic blow to him when she is fatally injured. With her loss he also loses the source of his strength, his self-sufficiency. A sharp and shrill voice sounds in his ear: "This is the last and final blow. You may succeed in capturing your illusion, but the moment you grasp it, it utterly changes its appearance in your very hands." (p. 175)

As for Wang the self-sufficient rationalist, who "only searches for something that appears to be beautiful to our rational faculties" (p. 135), his failure can only be accounted for by the forces of the chaotic world that lie beyond his comprehension. His self-sufficiency—his rationalizations, spirit of compromise and calculated optimism lead him nowhere. In a world governed by mysterious and irrational forces, his striving for order and harmony is doomed. Wang's confident remarks come as a powerful dramatic irony: "Now is the time when man's intelligence overcomes fate, overcomes nature. The successful man has his unwavering reasons, the defeated his irretrievable shortcomings. The disappointed man has too many illusions, and holds his head too high, so that he can only see the rainbow in the sky, but ignores the pitfalls at his feet." (p. 174)

The same fate befalls Zhang Manqing of the same work. He first emerges in the novel as a tired revolutionary, when his "experience of last year drives home to him the message that society is corrupt and politics is chaotic", a stark contrast to his former idealism. A rationalist, he pins his hope on education and at the same time yearns for the repose of a happy family. Things seem to be working his way at first. As his teaching career seems to be making a little headway, he marries a fellow teacher Miss Zhu, who he believes possesses the qualities of an ideal wife—"a tender, taciturn person who does not indulge in high-flown words, who does not despise modest things" (pp. 20–21). But he soon discovers that Miss Zhu is petty, possessive, and materialistic, and looks upon education as a way to officialdom. He also comes to realize that the educational system is controlled by a weak and sycophantic set of people, who are antagonistic to any change. With both ideals in complete disarray, he queries, in the true spirit of a rationalist, whether it is due to his own inability, or whether his ideals are defective in themselves. His only conclusion is that human life is just "a bunch of contradictions and inconsistencies" (p. 167). He airs his views to Zhongzhao: "Now that my last hope is vanquished. . . . The more I think, the more sceptical, and the more decadent I become." (ibid.) And we hear no more of him.

Thus, Manqing's search for a rational way of life—a life founded on the child's freedom of the spirit, on simplicity and moral humility is inevitably frustrated. His friend Zhongzhao's doubts on the day of their marriage: "will not an accident also happen to them? Mutable Destiny is watching from all sides. Can you definitely exclude it?" not only sounded but *were* ominous. One is prompted to ask at this juncture: how should one go about searching for a rational way of life? what is the moral worth of one's struggles? If numbness and negation is not Mao Dun's answer at this time, he offers no clues as to what the alternative might be.

Like Zhongzhao and Manqing, Miss Mei in *Rainbow*, Mao Dun's second novel, also searches untiringly for a rational way of life. She struggles and manages to fly out of the "bamboo cage" of her life with her husband. After regaining her freedom, she endures for a while a "chaotic life". Her experience as a school teacher and as tutor to the warlord of her province discloses to her a vivid picture of the pettiness and corruption in education as well as government circles. She resumes her flight, and finally leaves her native province Sichuan, for Shanghai. Her feelings upon leaving this "prosperous state" are beautifully captured:

> ...the wonderful scenery of the Gorge of the Witch (Wuxia) had moved her profoundly. Reminiscing over her past, was it not full of changes and hidden corners? Had she not overcome the difficulties every time? She had now courageously reeled in half of the thread of life, interwoven with brightness and darkness; what would her future be? She saw it as a maze. She had no illusions, nor was she pessimistic. She only waited silently, like an experienced boxer on his mark, waiting for the moment to avenge himself on his opponent. These vissicitudes of life had left a deep imprint on her youthful years. (p. 3)

While in Shanghai, Mei is awakened by the massive student movements. Just as she is about to participate in them, the novel ends abruptly.

It is unfortunate that Mao Dun was unable to finish the novel and thus fulfil his aim, as he said in the afterword to *Rainbow*, of "depicting the grand epic of the events of the past ten years in China" (p. 273). Judging from the pessimism that shrouds his previous work *Eclipse*, and the ones immediately following, *Three Friends* and *Road*, works that actually take up from where *Rainbow* leaves off, I find it is difficult to agree with some Mao Dun scholars, who, basing themselves on the rather sketchy last chapters about Mei's arrival in Shanghai, argue that Mei has thus emerged as a heroic figure.[45] Had Mao Dun finished writing this "intended epic" of his, I venture to suggest, Mei's reaction to the abortive Revolution of 1927 would have been much like those of the pessimists or decadents before or after her. Mao Dun's own words are the best testimony. In the postscript of the May issue (1929) of the *Short Story Monthly*, the editor writes:

> As to Mao Dun's novel *Rainbow*, the novelist has written in a letter to us: "*rainbow* (hong) is a bridge. It is over this bridge that Proserpine (the Goddess of Spring) returns to this world from the underworld. The 'rainbow' which often appears at dusk is the illusory beauty before darkness. It is transient. It has an inexplicable charm but itself is an illusory mirage. This is the theme of *Rainbow*, a symbolic title. Following from this, you may also think that no matter whether in subject matter or in thought content, it is a work that marks the transition to a new direction after the *trilogy* (i.e. *Eclipse*). As to that new direction, it is the theme of another novel *Xia* (Dawn) which I have given much thought to but dare not write in haste."[46]

The stress that Mao Dun places on the illusory nature of the "rainbow" drives home the point that when darkness overshadows the sky, the illusory beauty that has adorned the evening will soon

---

[45] For example, Ye Ziming thinks that "the author has depicted a character who is as bright as the rainbow. She symbolizes brightness and reflects the fact that the author is again full of confidence for future revolutions" (p. 78); Fan Jun thinks that "in the May Thirtieth Demonstrations, Mei has emerged as a brave warrior" ("Mao Dun de *Shi* he *Hong*", *Wenxue yanjiu jikan*, Vol. 4, p. 249); Liu Shousong is more circumspect. Taking note that the later chapters of the work are too contrived, he asks his readers to think that were Mei to "experience the 1927 Revolution, would she continue to struggle forward along the revolutionary path, and thoroughly reform herself in the process, or would she take another path?" ("Lun Mao Dun de *Shi* yu *Hong*", *WXPL*, 2 [1963], p. 39).

[46] "Zuihou yiye", *XSYB*, 20.5 (1929.5), p. 901. This theme is also put forward in his prose "Hong", where he concludes that "hope which is like a rainbow is disheartening"; and in another essay entitled "Wu" (1928), he curses the "thick fog which has devoured everything, which has enshrouded the entire earth". "Wu" (Thick Fog) can only "reduce you to sorrow and despondency, so that you are like a man sinking in the marshes, all struggles are futile." Mao Dun tries to give an explanation to this passage in his *Autobiography* (Vol. 2, pp. 32–33). He did admit that given the situation of the time, Mei's hope and forward movement is but a vanity.

be swallowed up. On the other hand, one should admit the "beauty" of this "rainbow", however transient. Compared to Mao Dun's other heroes or heroines of this period, Mei is less sketchy, and has more personality and feeling. In fact, it is her stubborn insistence on attaining a rational way of life that keeps her walking on the treadmill of life. The author encapsulates Mei's own thought of herself and her past as follows:

> As she is by nature active, forward looking and restless, the aspects of the May Fourth spirit that most affect her are individualism, individual rights and freedom of development. Of all these only the philosophy of Tolstoy that she came across first has left in her a vision of a rational way of life, a desire for a harmonious relationship with mankind, and it is this inner strength that prompts her to summon up enough courage to leave Chengdu, and commands her to stride forward in a combative spirit. . . . (p. 209)

What separates Mei from Manqing and Zhongzhao, fellow rationalists, is that while the latter two search for a rational way of life through their own self-sufficiency, Mei's strivings are governed by discontent, rejection, and above all passion. This makes her a more personable and attractive character.

The "Symphony of Fate" indeed makes an appropriate title for these works taken as a whole. In them life strides along, hard and idealistic at first; later some softer and more conciliatory ideas attempt to make their mark, but without success. Fate proceeds ruthlessly along her chosen path. The tempo is set by the mood, movements and interaction of the three types of thematic heroes. The low moaning of the pessimists, the sombre sighs of the rationalists, and the penetrating cries of the decadents form a strangely delicate and vibrant cadence, and imbue the "Symphony" with a heavy and uncanny rhythm. A harmony is reached, albeit an unsatisfactory and disturbing one, through Mao Dun's emphasis on the common feeling of approaching catastrophe, through the pervading chill of alienation, and through the abstractions of the typology. It is a harmony which echoes the concerns and the artistic treatment of such Russian writers as Tolstoy, Andreyev and Artzybashev.

IV. Relationship with Russian Literature

Writing about the characteristics of Russian literature in "the silver age", Marc Slonim remarks that in the wake of the defeat in 1905 and its aftermath, individualism and healthy nationalism turned into an egotistical gratification of the appetites, or bombastic chauvinism. The reaction against the ascetic morality of the revolutionary easily degenerated into debauchery or outright hedonism. Sexual pleasure and aesthetic enjoyment were proclaimed far superior to the antiquated ideas of public service or political activity. It was "typical of Russian intellectuals that they were not satisfied with merely gratifying their desires. They sought to prove that in doing so they were asserting their moral superiority and were accomplishing an act of liberation."[47]

Similar traits of defeatism also mark the early intellectual heroes of Mao Dun. Commenting on the weariness of many young people in the early 1920s, Mao Dun had actually compared them to the Russian intellectuals at the turn of the century, whom he believed to be equally wearied. "Their coldness", Mao Dun claimed, "is their reaction in anger and bitterness to a hostile reality, and they choose to ignore the burning issues of the day."[48] According to him, this mood is best reflected in the pessimistic heroes of Andreyev and the decadent heroes of Artzybashev, both novelties in the Chinese literary tradition.[49] It is therefore intriguing to find many similarities between his own fictional heroes in this early period and those of precisely these Russian writers. As I see it, there are broadly three main sources of Russian "influences" that one can speak of, namely, Andreyev, Artzybashev and Tolstoy.

The Influence of Andreyev

It is difficult to assess Andreyev's influence on Mao Dun's pessimistic heroes. One cannot detect many similarities in the outward traits (except in the case of Andreyev's Savva and Mao Dun's Hui), and

---

[47] Marc Slonim, *From Chekhov to the Revolution: Russian Literature 1900–1917*, pp. 164–165.
[48] As n. 16, p. 1.
[49] "Tongxin", as n. 31.

the affinities can all too easily be summarily dismissed as mere parallel developments. Where there is, however, an important similarity is in the abstract pattern of the characters. Andreyev's characters follow a simplified abstract pattern, with few onward actions. This is where his influence on Mao Dun is outwardly felt. In general, one can compare the intellectual heroes of the two writers in two areas: the writers' philosophic conception of reality and their abstract conception of character.

M. J. Olgin's essay on Andreyev provides us with a starting point. In 1920, Mao Dun translated Olgin's essay into Chinese.[50] His intense interest in Andreyev's works and in Olgin's interpretation of the author is manifested in the meticulous and illuminating annotated commentary attached to his translation. One paragraph in particular Mao Dun considered exceptionally enlightening. I will quote this in full here, as it provides some valuable insights not only into Mao Dun's attitude to Andreyev, but also into his own fictional works:

> Andreyev is the spokesman of the Russian intellectual who was awakened by modern progress from the sluggishness of a patriarchal system to the realization of the complexity of life. The Russian intellectual was suddenly put before enormous problems. The alternative of either heroic sacrifice for a common cause or cowardly abstinence from life's constructive work loomed up before every self-conscious individual. Life itself was undergoing catastrophic changes. Everything was shaking, yielding, giving way to new forms. It looked as if a powerful hand had tossed all structures asunder, revealing the very foundations. Russian intellect was feverishly scrutinizing life, revaluing the most harrowing problems. It was in the nature of Russian surroundings to tinge all these gropings with the dark colors of sadness, loneliness, pessimism. Andreyev was the writer destined to embody this spirit of intellectual unrest in striking artistic pictures.[51]

Some twenty years later, when life in China was undergoing catastrophic changes, when attempts at constitutional reforms had failed, when encroachments from abroad were increasing, when after the Northern Expedition the repressive measures of the Guomindang

---

[50] This essay, which is a chapter of M. J. Olgin's *A Guide to Russian Literature*, pp. 230–239, was rendered into Chinese by Mao Dun under the title "Andeliefu", published in *DFZZ*, 17.10 (1920.5), pp. 60–68.

[51] I quote here from Olgin's original, p. 232.

against intellectuals had aggravated, it also seemed to many intellectuals that a powerful hand had burst everything asunder. Like Andreyev before him, Mao Dun was also "the writer destined to embody this spirit of intellectual unrest in striking artistic pictures". His comment on Andreyev has a direct bearing on his own works. Taking into account the fact that modern literature is in the main influenced by philosophy, he writes that Andreyev lived in an epoch where man is "not only sceptical of the might of science, but also of man's resistance to nature. Because of Russia's recent external defeat, and internal autocratic rule, the boredom, disappointment and despondency of young people reached its peak. Everybody adopts a pessimistic attitude towards human destiny. Andreyev is the person who shouts at the top of his voice."[52] No wonder then that Mao Dun is able to see a lot of affinities between the "fate" of many Chinese young people and that of their Russian precursors.

a. The general philosophic plane

In his detailed study of Andreyev, James Woodward perceives that "almost from the beginning his (Andreyev's) works show a dualistic conception of reality, a polarization of metaphysical unity and harmony and phenomenal diversity and discord". According to Woodward, the term "first reality" is employed by Andreyev to denote the ephemeral, the world of man's empirical existence, a world dominated by the principle which Schopenhauer termed the *principium individuationis*. On this plane man is a prisoner within the walls of his individuality, and his intellect is the instrument by means of which he endeavours to pierce them. But its struggles are eternally frustrated, its powers do not extend beyond the "first reality". The whole impetus of Andreyev's thoughts is towards "the establishment of contact with the 'other plane', the transcendence of the empirical ego".[53] Andreyev's preoccupation with this distinction between two realities, two levels of life, is amply displayed in his plays—*To the Stars, The Life of Man, Anathema* and *Savva*—plays much to Mao Dun's liking.

[52]"Andeliefu", as n. 50, p. 67.
[53]J. B. Woodward, *Leonid Andreyev: A Study*, p. 29.

In *To the Stars* (1906), the astronomer Ternovsky poses persistently the question of the immortality of man. He argues that man is so insignificant compared to events in the universe that one cannot be concerned about the fate of individuals. He criticizes people who think only about their own life and death and consequently live in a state of fear. If only one can hear the "voice of the stars", he suggests, one will become the "son of eternity". In the end, when Ternovsky's daughter-in-law Marusya brings the news that her husband, who was arrested in a futile revolutionary attempt, has gone mad in prison, Ternovsky still maintains that "there is no death for man, there is no death for the son of eternity",[54] Marusya, however, cannot accept his indifference to life on earth, and suggests that his ideas are lacking in essential humanity.

While in *To the Stars* Andreyev confirms his concern to establish a contact with the "other plane", the contradiction between his ideas is clearly shown in *The Life of Man*—where he emphasizes man's helplessness to change his predetermined path. The play is allegorical and the characters are generations of types, called simply Man, Man's wife, or Someone in Grey, supported by groups of people like a chorus, such as "old woman" or "friends of man". Man, the protagonist, goes through five stages of life—the pain of birth, youth, the prime of life (represented by a ball he gives), old age and finally death—in all of which he is accompanied by the sinister symbolic figure, Someone in Grey. The latter announces in the Prologue Man's inevitable destiny: "Limited in vision, he will see the step to which his unsure foot is already raising him. Limited in knowledge, he will never know what the coming day or hour or moment is bringing him. And in his blind ignorance, worn by apprehension, harassed by hopes and fears, he will complete submissively the iron round of destiny."[55] From poverty and sorrow Man rises to wealth and happiness and becomes an artistic and socially indispensable architect. It would appear that with such powerful spiritual weapons as the intellect and the soul he may easily

---

[54] *To the Stars*, tr. into English by Maurice Magnus, p. 83.
[55] *The Life of Man*, in *Plays by Leonid Andreyeff*, tr. into English by Clarence Meader and F. N. Scott, p. 68.

fortify his position. But wealth and power are the beginning of an end to his life. He does display some defiance of fate—he curses it when his son dies: "Hereby I curse thee, and all that thou hast given me! I curse the day whereon I was born, and the day whereon I shall die! I curse my whole life, its joys and its sorrows! I curse myself,my ears, my eyes, my heart, my tongue, my head! All those things which thou hast given me I fling back in thy face, thou Fate, thou Demon! Cursed be thou—aye cursed for ever!"[56] But his rebellion is vocal only. In reality, he has no alternative but to proceed in his fated circle, as predicted by Someone in Grey in the prologue.

The "iron round of destiny" is the tragedy of Man, as it is of *Anathema* in his play of the same name (1909). Anathema, "someone accursed", dashes himself in vain against the "tightly closed" iron gates that open the way to the "supreme wisdom of the universe". Aware of the contrast between his own view of the world and the "essential harmony", which he suspects exists but to which he, like the vast majority of men, is blind, he makes it his purpose to reveal to the world that life is fundamentally unjust. But like Andreyev's other heroes, he remains the prisoner of his own logic and intellect, and the way remains barred.

These plays of Andreyev, as Woodward points out, reflect "the perpetual conflict between Andreyev the man and Andreyev the philosopher, of the failure of the man ever to measure up to his abstract ideal or to find the peace of mind which, he believed, that ideal afforded".[57] Andreyev presents a unique spectacle of duality—a duality or contradiction between ideas which renders his philosophy unintelligible. While his body proceeds obediently, like that of Man, to describe the "iron round of destiny", his mind returns again and again to preach the virtue of self-transcendence.

From Mao Dun's detailed commentary on Olgin's essay, it is clear that he is impressed not only by the philosophic content of Andreyev's plays, but also by the contradictions inherent in his ideals. In fact, Mao Dun goes as far as to rehearse Andreyev's debate on the "two realities" in his early works. I would like to begin this

[56] Ibid., p. 127.
[57] As n. 53, p. 160.

discussion by quoting his reaction to *To the Stars*, a play referred to many times in his writings:

> ... *To the Stars* ... asks stoically for the meaning of life, but the whole play is steeped in pessimism, offering no solution. Look at the astronomer in the play. He detests the life of the common people, he says that they are like wax men, lifeless and soulless. He researches in astronomy, and feels the world beyond this world is full of wonderment, and that affairs in this world cannot be compared to it. He says: "In our world someone dies every second, and in the universe probably a world is destroyed every second. How can I cry and fall into despair on account of the death of one man?" So he is practically unmoved by the death of his own son. But he is unable to alleviate his wife's sorrow for her son, or his daughter-in-law's sorrow for her husband. Andreyev announces through this play the conflicts between emotion [worldly] and ideals [other-worldly] in life. The astronomer's solution is beyond normal thinking. What he seeks is an abstract world, one that not everybody can understand.[58]

Nor is the attempt of Savva, the protagonist in his play of the same title, to seek a way out in anarchism of any avail. According to Mao Dun, "the outcome is that he (Savva) is being utilized by the bad people. Not only that, he also encourages the ignorant masses into further believing the bad people."[59] Neither is Andreyev able to arrive at any satisfactory answer to the problem of life in *The Life of Man*. The sense of futility in the play is for Mao Dun even greater than in *To the Stars*, and "the shouts of the meaninglessness of life are intense". What underlies Andreyev's sense of frustration and pessimism, Mao Dun stresses, is not death. He writes about Andreyev's play *Lazarus* that the "horridness of death is not in the cessation of life, but rather in the inexplicable, quizzical grey mist, and the impenetrable darkness that lurks behind 'death'".[60] Only

---

[58] "Andeliefu", pp. 63–64. Mao Dun again singled out this episode in his essay "Shenme shi wenxue", *MWZJ*, Vol. 1, pp. 151–152. Though disagreeing with Ternovsky's stand, he nevertheless sees this "optimistic feeling is ingrained in the pessimism of Russian nihilism". He wrote to the same effect in his *Autobiography* that the work of Andreyev is powerful, though frightening. Vol. 2, p. 41.

[59] "Andeliefu", p. 64.

[60] "Lanshalesi", *DFZZ*, 17.10 (1920.5), p. 111. Pseud. Mingxin; note by Yanbing.

in *Anathema*, Mao Dun thinks, does Andreyev seem to have come up with a temporary answer, when the protagonist only asks for immortality, not empirical existence.

From Mao Dun's interpretation of Andreyev's plays, one sees that while no less preoccupied with the idea of man in the hands of fate (as one may recall, he considers that one of the functions of literature is to represent man struggling with unfathomable destiny), he has reservations about Andreyev's "other-worldly" ideas. Especially in his earliest works, Mao Dun's protagonists, like Andreyev's dramatic heroes, come up against the wall of fate which determines the lot of man with implacable cruelty. Like Andreyev before him (especially in his story "Wall"), Mao Dun also employs the same image to underline the fact that his heroes are trapped within four walls—the walls of their own intellect and ideals, and of social contradictions. In *Pursuit*, we see the characters depicted as "one chasing another, and knocking at the light-yellow walls one after another" (p. 3). In *Disillusion*, the hero, riven with conflicts, is like "a fly knocking blindly at the window" (p. 32). Xu in *Three Friends* recognizes that he is "trapped between the two thick walls of social contradiction" (p. 30). Just as Man curses in the wake of his defeat, so does Dinghui in *Disillusion*. In both cases, cursing is all they are capable of. The tone and rhythm of Dinghui's curses echo Andreyev's hero:

> She tries hard to capture the happy moments of the past. But when she thinks of her happiness, sorrowful and dark images are immediately conjured up. She madly bites her own lips. She curses her whole life, curses all her past experiences, she curses herself. . . . (p. 24)

If the fate of Mao Dun's characters in *Disillusion* and *Pursuit* reminds us of Andreyev's Man, Anathema, or Lorenzo in *The Black Masks*, the restaging of Andreyev's debate on immortality and revolution by Xu and his girl friend Qing in *Three Friends* represents Mao Dun's rejection of Ternovsky's argument in *To the Stars*.[61]

Both Qing and Xu begin life in *Three Friends* as the "Andreyev"

[61]Whereas Andreyev attempts to find a way out on the metaphysical plane, by "other-worldly" means, as Mao Dun calls it, Mao Dun's solution is confined to the "worldly". This remains an acute difference between his "thought" hero and those of Andreyev.

type of pessimist, believing everything is predestined and that man's strivings towards harmony and order are doomed to be frustrated. However, as their inner conflict heightens, things take a new turn. This is how the author describes Qing's feeling upon breaking off with Xu:

> Gradually she became so tired, with the tiredness that followed emotional excitement. She raised her head, and stared aimlessly at the sky outside the window. The dark canopy of the sky, which appeared to be very low, glittered with numerous stars. All of them seemed to be full of life. A slightly reddish ray of light suddenly cut across the sky, and fell towards the southwest. "A falling star", she thought mechanically. Her thought was captured by the mysteriousness and vastness of the universe. Reality seemed to have receded on all sides. Her virgin heart was again filled with liveliness and joyousness. (p. 10)

One does not need much guesswork to discern that Qing's reaction to the falling star, her awe at the mysteriousness of the universe, and her ease of mind hark back to Ternovsky. However, it is in Xu's arguments and actions that we see most explicitly Mao Dun's position. Xu's reasoning is a concrete extension of Mao Dun's comment on *To the Stars* that we saw earlier. In his despair, Xu is at first attracted by Ternovsky's reasoning that "the misery in this world is nothing, every second a planet is destroyed in the universe" (p. 33). Then his reasoning takes a new turn. He cannot accept Ternovsky's so-called generosity, he reasons to himself thus:

> True that every single second a planet is destroyed in the universe, but this planet has endured for thousands of years, and its destruction is the inevitable course of nature. Destruction is the ultimate end of everything—being and non-being. There is nothing to feel sorry about. But the destruction of a young budding shoot is pitiable. And he, Xu, is a budding shoot that has already encountered freezing snow. All his ways are blocked. The ray of hope has become dimmer, and is becoming even fainter. (ibid.)

Xu's understanding of an untimely destruction has dragged him from the metaphysical back to the social plane, and, as we have seen, acts as an impetus to his subsequent quixotic actions.

On the other hand, in the character of Hui in *Three Friends*, Mao Dun comes close to suggesting, as Andreyev has done in *Savva*, that anarchism is not only no panacea for the sickly symptoms of society, but is indeed a "virus of intoxication". Mao Dun writes that Savva's preaching of the "gospel" of anarchism can only "encourage the ignorant masses into further believing the bad people". He puts in the mouth of Yun, the only "positive" hero in *Three Friends*, the comment that Hui the "Chinese style nihilist" is also trying, by his propagation of nihilism, to invite the ignorant masses "to forget that they are lying in the dirt", and believe in his "virus of intoxication".

Many similarities exist between the typology of Savva and Hui. In fact, Hui is the only character in Mao Dun in whom one finds specific similarities with an Andreyevan hero. Both are disgusted with civilization and human conventions. Both believe that destruction is the sole weapon for bringing about a new world. Savva says: "We have got to destroy everything, the old houses, the Universities, science, the old literature, the old art! . . . What I wish is to free the earth, to free Thought . . . To break the prison in which ideas are hidden away, to give them wings, to open a great new, unknown world. In fire and thunder, I wish to overstep the boundary of the universe."[62] Hui, as we have seen already, believes that everything should be destroyed, and only a miracle can right all wrongs. He also believes in fire and thunder. As he proclaims to Qing: "A hurricane is coming. The volcano is about to erupt. All dirt, all misfortunes, all grievances will be destroyed by the lava ejected by the volcano. All chains and manacles will be broken. . . ." (p. 120) Both find communication with others impossible. Savva's new gospel of a new life encounters a wall of incomprehension. Almost every tirade of his concludes with the question "Do you understand?"—but no one does, and this silent response is clearly intended to denote life's rejection of the reformer. The same walls of incomprehension surround Hui. Nobody, he reasons, understands his plans for the salvation of this world. He repeats again and again in frustration: "men are unable to understand each other." Their extremes lead both Savva and Hui to defeat. Savva is murdered by the people he wants to save, and Hui is driven to madness upon seeing the failure of his "grand designs".

[62] As n. 51.

The marked similarities between Andreyev's Savva and Mao Dun's Hui suggest that Mao Dun may actually have had the image of the Russian hero before him when he came to create his own. Like Andreyev's Savva, the pitiful and tragic end of Mao Dun's hero expresses the destructiveness of anarchism.

It is clear that Mao Dun sets out to address the problems of his age, and uppermost among them the problem of individual isolation; he was drawn to the pessimistic ideas of Andreyev, who had "magnified to grandiose proportions all the features of his contemporaries, and combined them all in himself".[63] Like Andreyev before him, Mao Dun also synthesized the dark realities of his era "under a very powerful magnifying glass". However, what makes Mao Dun's pessimistic hero more "Andreyevan" is the abstract conception of character, his following the "Andreyevan" device, in the words of Olgin, of "substitut(ing) abstraction for living human beings, (of) transfer(ring) the place of his tragedies into imaginary realms".[64]

b. The abstract conception of character

To begin with, I will quote Olgin again for two reasons: his lucidity of argument, and more important, his possible influence on Mao Dun:

> Andreyev is never content to write a story for the story's sake. Every story or play of his represents a problem. The scheme is somewhat like this: Granted a man is put in certain conditions and made to suffer certain experiences, what would be the spiritual or moral effect? The surroundings and conditions thus become of subordinate importance; the centre of gravity is put into the spiritual or moral reaction ... Andreyev is one of the first to introduce *schematization* into Russian literature.[65]

External environment merely works as a "backdrop" in Andreyev's plays. Once it has made its impact, it becomes non-essential, a set

---

[63] K. Chukovsky, *Ot Chehova do nashikh dney, Literaturnye portrety, Kharakteristiki*, 1908, p. 238. Quoted from Woodward, as n. 53, p. 60.
[64] As n. 50, p. 233.
[65] Ibid.

of merely unavoidable details. It is the effect it exerts on the heroes that is the centre of concern. It is not hunger, ambition, or even love—the passion of the traditional hero—but thought in its sufferings, joys, and struggles that becomes the true hero in these plays. As Kaun points out in his study of Andreyev, the "favourite situation" in his works is that of thought struggling with darkness, striving for understanding, and dutifully breaking down under the inexorable force of the inexplicable.[66] In depicting the "thought" of his heroes Andreyev resorts to his schematization. In short, all his characters lack any concrete, external life. They are defined by their static qualities, by the conflicts they symbolize. The essence of the protagonist is a step by step movement towards his doom. Such is essentially the typology of Man, Lorenzo and Anathema. Furthermore, the conflicts of the protagonist, the evil forces enshrouding him are enlarged to the extent of being personified. Each of these forces is assigned a definite "role", mainly to show the pitfalls, sufferings or struggles of the protagonist, as Someone in Grey, Friends, Enemies of Man in *The Life of Man*, The Thing in *The Black Masks*, or Guardian in *Anathema*. The forward movement of the protagonist is often brought about by the recurrent advances of these "personified" forces. All these elements combine to create the impression of "abstractness" and "schematization" in Andreyev's plays.

We see to a lesser extent a similar schematization also pervading Mao Dun's works. As we have said earlier, Mao Dun's early fiction is centred around a particular problem: the spiritual reactions of his heroes in the wake of defeat in the late 1920s. Political and social events serve mainly to define the situation that his heroes are thrust into. His characters are also schematic.[67] We are not told of their appearance, interests or characteristics. They have little external action, little development. Mao Dun emphasizes, and amplifies their psychological malaise and their failings to such an extent that they are exposed to us in their step by step movement,

---

[66] A. Kaun, *Leonid Andreyev: A Critical Study*, p. 217.

[67] This schematic device is clearly seen also in his short stories of this period, such as "Shi yu sanwen", "Chuangzao" and "Semang". The device is reminiscent of what Olgin says of Andreyev's stories and plays. See n. 50 above.

escorted by remorseless fate—a device which is reminiscent of Andreyev. We see that most "schematic" of Mao Dun's characters, like many of the Andreyevan heroes, only exist for an abstract notion—Shi Xun for "the circle of human nature", Dinghui for her railing against man, and Wei Yu for his non-resistance. Something which makes Mao Dun's more complicated characters even more "Andreyevan" is the technique of personifying "inner forces". Thus, when Jing in *Disillusion* suffers the severest inner conflict, Mao Dun adopts an essentially schematic device to depict it—he personifies her unhappy past in "Past Experiences", and her guardian spirit in "New Ideal". Their arguments about the purpose of life, the moral worth of one's strivings, and the destiny of the individual, echo not a few of the arguments of Someone in Grey in *The Life of Man*, and the Guardian in *Anathema*.[68] This device of personifying the hero's inner conflicts is used again in the depiction of Zhang Qiuliu in *Pursuit*. When confronted with a critical choice, the "good angel" shows the way to brightness and hope, while "the devil" encourages her along the path of decay and degeneration. This portrayal of the "conflict between good and evil in the human heart", Mao Dun pointed out once and again half a century later (in his *Autobiography*), is an important thematic device in Russian literature.[69]

To sum up, the typology of Mao Dun's pessimistic heroes betrays signs of the "Andreyevan" influence. Taken as a whole, their passive acceptance of fate, their strivings with the intellect, their schematic existence, and their abstract thoughts and notions, are reminiscent of the Andreyevan hero, though in specific cases, for instance, in Xu's rejection of Ternovsky's outlook on life, Mao Dun breaks with Andreyev's thought. The influence of Andreyev is quite understandable. In the postscript to his study, Woodward sums up succinctly Andreyev's art and his age: "The isolation and rootlessness of the intellectual in contemporary Russian society, the intrinsic perils of a predominantly rationalistic culture, the inevitable bankruptcy of an assertive individualistic philosophy of life, the

---

[68] It is interesting to note that Mao Dun used exactly the same term "New Ideal" to describe the Guardian in Anathema. See "Andeliefu".

[69] See his *Autobiography*, Vol. 1, p. 290, Vol. 2, p. 21.

irreconcilability of abstract ideals and mundane reality, the relation of man to his neighbour and to the universe as a whole— these are the problems to which his thoughts were constantly directed, problems which had inspired some of the best known works of nineteenth-century Russian literature, but which from the turn of the century to 1917 acquired an unparalleled ascendency in Russian intellectual life."[70] Such are also the problems to which Mao Dun's thoughts are constantly directed. It is therefore no surprise that he sees in Andreyev's heroes a model for the many conflicts of his own fictional heroes, and that he himself is influenced by the "great Russian", as he calls him, in both outlook on life and artistic presentation.

The Influence of Ropshin and Artzybashev

Unlike the influence of Andreyev, which is somewhat difficult to grasp, that of Artzybashev and Ropshin is fairly straightforward. Their influences are mainly centred on the typology of Zhang Qiuliu, the most egotistical and sensual heroine, if not the first, in modern Chinese fiction. Were Qiuliu a Russian heroine, she would undoubtedly be labelled by Russian literary critics as a disciple of Artzybashev's Sanin.

It is interesting to observe that when Qiuliu's friend Long Fei makes advances to her, and reminds her that love is holy, Qiuliu chides him saying: "Go and seek holiness yourself. Don't you dare to bind me with these words. For me, there is no such thing as love, there is only momentary joy." Then, "disregarding him, Miss Zhang walked slowly towards the desk, sat down, and started reading *The Pale Horse* translated by Zheng Zhenduo" (p. 42).[71]

---

[70] As n. 53, p. 278.

[71] Mao Dun wrote a preface to Zheng Zhenduo's translation of *The Pale Horse* (pp. 1–8). He is conscious that the novel may eventually do harm, and he warns his readers against its individual anarchism. Despite this, he recommends the novel for two reasons. First, the author truthfully depicts the social and political reality of his time; second, the splendid portrayal of the hero George, whose thought, words and deeds are motivated by reality. He knows no difference between love and hatred, good and evil, joy and sorrow, life and death; he is a man deeply steeped in loneliness. Such "nihilism" is also reflected in the typology of Zhang Qiuliu.

The link with Ropshin's *The Pale Horse* sheds light on the unbridled egoism of Qiuliu. As we have already seen, Ropshin's George is an extreme egoist. His defiance of everything results in a belief in nothing but himself: "What God could I pray to not to abandon me? To whom could I appeal for help and protection? I am alone. But since there is no one to protect me, I must protect myself. Since I have no God, I shall be my own God."[72] His reasoning is also echoed in Qiuliu. In her despair and loneliness, she reasons that "I should be my own arbiter. I should have complete freedom to treat my body in whatever way I like." (p. 77) Like her predecessor George, she denies that she has any higher motive, and denies the relevance of love, country and society as such. Like George before her, she also thinks of death and revenge: ". . . destroy and take revenge. You should not take revenge on any single person, but on everybody." (p. 122) However, unlike the cold-blooded George, Qiuliu is described as a "sensual egoist". Her unquenchable thirst for sensual pursuits is in many ways a copy of Artzybashev's Sanin.

In the characters of Sanin and Qiuliu, both Artzybashev and Mao Dun have depicted a class of people who experienced the mental and spiritual strain of the revolution and who have consequently become wearied and numbed. From the fictional point of view, both are schematic, spending long hours philosophizing over the moral worth of their actions. It is their particular style of thought— their moral anarchism in life, that binds them together. Mao Dun explains the decadence of Artzybashev's Sanin thus: "When man's disappointment has reached its peak, he will easily become pessimistic and despondent. When the despondency and passion reach their climax, and at the same time his will to live is stronger than ever, he will easily degenerate into egoism."[73] Such is also the root of Qiuliu's torments, as we have seen from her passionate outburst at the beginning of *Pursuit*. In fact, Mao Dun used the same term, "sensual egoists"[74] to describe both characters.

For Sanin, "man is vile by nature", and this world is full of miseries

[72] Ropshin, *The Pale Horse*, tr. by Z. Vengerova, p. 41. For a more detailed description of the typology of George, see Chapter Six.

[73] "Wei xinwenxue yanjiuzhe jin yijie", *Jiefang yu gaizao*, 3.1 (1920.9), p. 99.

[74] He called Artzybashev's literature a "total egotistical literature", ibid.

and sufferings that man cannot overcome. He believes the task of changing the world "lies outside the pale of our existence . . . Our role is a passive, an auxiliary one." (p. 98) Each improvement in this world "has always been achieved by bloodshed, anarchy and revolt . . ." (p. 184). He thus comes to the conclusion that the aim of life is to enjoy it to the full: ". . . enjoyment is the aim of human life", he says to Sarudine, "paradise is the synonym for absolute enjoyment, and we all of us, more or less, dream of an earthly paradise" (p. 34). To gratify man's natural desires, Sanin argues that man should be as free as a bird, give himself unhesitatingly to every attainable pleasure, and do what he wants to do or can do. He has the right to enjoy love-making without fear and without scruple. Chastity, which to him is an attempt to suppress one's natural desires, is "all humbug" (p. 247). Only those who find joy in living should live. For him, whatever lies beyond or behind his sensations is purely hypothetical; "life is only worth living for today" (p. 202).

It is interesting to find an almost identical attitude to life in Mao Dun's Qiuliu. We see that like Sanin, she is also weary of the revolutionary age, though neither author has revealed the past history of his hero to us. Seeing the miseries in life but lacking the courage to tread the thorny path, Qiuliu has come to terms with the "devil" and reasons that enjoyment is the only reality. She refuses to be hamstrung by morality, conventions or laws. "Everything that brings enjoyment is moral" (p. 139), she anounces. And she counters such arguments as human decency in the same way as Sanin does, with a cold contempt, believing it to be human deception in disguise. Just as Sanin retorts to his friend Youri's preaching of the principle of non-resistance, Qiuliu dismisses her friend Shitao's tolerance of life, and her worries about the future. She says, "I never think of the future. I only exist for the present. I never hesitate. Whatever I want to do now, I will do it in an instant." (p. 11) This belief that life is only worth living for today is also shared, as we have seen, by Sanin. For such a "sensual egoist", life has no meaning while culture and convention are merely a blind for one's instincts. This outright sensualism and egoism make her typology akin to those of Sanin and George, and represent a new departure in the Chinese literary tradition.

The "Influence" of Tolstoy

Unlike the case of Andreyev and Artzybashev, the typological "influence" of Tolstoy on Mao Dun is of a more general kind. One does not find "counterparts" of the Tolstoyan hero in Mao Dun's works. What Tolstoy contributes most to Mao Dun's heroes is his philosophy of life, and the self-sufficiency of his fictional characters.

As we have seen earlier, Mao Dun was deeply impressed by Tolstoy's humanitarianism, though he rejected the Russian writer's extreme views quite early on.[75] By 1927–1928, his enthusiasm for Tolstoy's works waned, though he still admired him as a great writer.[76] He writes in his celebrated essay "Cong Guling dao Dongjing" (From Guling to Tokyo):

> Zola's attitude to life can at least be described as "cold observation", and is contrary to Tolstoy's passion for life . . . I like Zola, and I like Tolstoy too . . . However, when I come to write my novels, I am closer to Tolstoy. Of course I am not so fanatical as to compare myself to Tolstoy, and my life and thought do not resemble this great Russian writer much . . .[77]

It is true that by 1928, Mao Dun's thought did not much resemble Tolstoy's, though it is still possible to discern traits of "Tolstoyanism" in him. One should distinguish between two levels. While advocating compassion and sincerity, sympathy towards the downtrodden, and a rational way of life, Mao Dun rejected Tolstoy's principle of non-resistance. This is manifested in his depiction of Wei Yu and Mei in *Rainbow*. Wei Yu, who embraced Tolstoy's principle of non-resistance, is held in contempt by Mei, who complains that this belief of his is only "an 'anaesthesia' for the self-gratification of the cowardly" (p. 41), and his character utterly lacks any compensating quality that can arouse sympathy from the

---

[75] For example, he wrote in "Da zhuanbian", as n. 15, that he disapproved of Tolstoy's advocacy of an extreme form of "art for life".

[76] By the late 1920s, Tolstoy's popularity in China had receded. Even Ba Jin, one of the most fervent advocates of Tolstoy, has created in Juexin (in *Jia*) a pitiable character who espouses Tolstoy's principle of non-resistance, see Chapter Six.

[77] As n. 35, pp. 341–342. Mao Dun was essentially interested in Zola's objective method of creation, not his materialistic mechanical determinism, as he pointed out in his article on "Naturalism", see n. 17.

readers. He is depicted by Mao Dun not only as an unheroic, but as a negative character.

It should be stressed that Mao Dun's ideas on Tolstoy's principle are superficial and distorted. He is led into taking non-resistance at its nominal value, as nothing more than mere submission. For Tolstoy, his non-resistance is a programme of Christian anarchism. Believing that God is all-benevolent, that men have a right to be free and also equal, that coercion is evil, and that all these are eternal truths, Tolstoy strives to discover and expound them, and awaken the spontaneous interest, the imagination, love, curiosity of children or simple folk and above all to liberate their "natural", moral or emotional and intellectual forces; this would achieve harmony within men and between them. For him, as Isaiah Berlin points out, "there exists a sure path to complete harmony in which everything fits and is at peace; with the corollary that knowledge of man's nature gained from observation or introspection or moral intuition, or from the study of the lives and writings of the best and wisest of men of all ages, can show us this path."[78] For Tolstoy, man's task is to develop along these lines, and not seek to alter himself, or force himself into a mould. Herein lies the core of his principle of non-resistance. It is therefore a programme of action, or in the words of Berlin, "a declaration of war against the tyranny of states, societies, churches, against brutality, injustice, stupidity, hypocrisy, weakness, above all against vanity and moral blindness".[79] Clearly the meek and timid Wei Yu could hardly be called an adherent of Tolstoy's principle. One is inclined to think that the opposite is true.

In fact, it is Mei's striving for a rational way of life, encouraged by the idea that she should develop her natural qualities, and that human beings have a right to be free and equal, which is Tolstoyan. She herself admits her indebtedness to Tolstoy. Of all the current philosophic thinking prevalent in the May Fourth era, she confesses that "only the philosophy of Tolstoy that she came across had left in her a vision of a rational way of life, a desire for a harmonious relationship with mankind, and it is this inner strength that prompts

[78] Isaiah Berlin, "Tolstoy and Enlightenment", in *Russian Thinkers*, p. 254.
[79] Ibid.

her to summon up enough courage to leave Chengdu, and commands her to stride forward in a combative spirit." (p. 209) Though she chides Wei Yu for his principle of non-resistance (which she equates with submission), ironically, her ideals in life are more akin to the Tolstoyan principle than those of her one-time lover, who first introduced her to the Russian writer.

From the fictional point of view, what I find most "Tolstoyan" is Mao Dun's depiction of his rationalists, especially Wang Zhongzhao. In a discussion of the characteristic Tolstoyan hero, John Bayley makes the observation that "when crisis or alienation comes to one of Tolstoy's characters it comes from outside, like a thief reconnoitring and breaking into an orderly house ... In terms of the construction of the novel, the dramatic principle of the *nadryv* is replaced in Tolstoy by the static principle of *samodovolnost*—self-sufficiency, or self-esteem. When that is gone, the Tolstoyan character is lost indeed."[80] Viewed in this light, the typology of Wang Zhongzhao in *Pursuit* can be said to be sufficiently "Tolstoyan". Self-sufficiency and self-esteem are the essence of his existence. Fundamental to his concept of life is that enduring human wish to make sense, to create harmony, to see life as simple and clear, and to absorb it entirely into his consciousness. (To this goal Manqing's behaviour is also directed, though as a type he is less clearly defined.) As we remember, he claims confidently that he is "not an ambitious man who longs for the idealistic world of supreme beauty and truth", he only "searches for something that appears to be beautiful to our rational faculties".[81] Unlike other characters, all of Zhongzhao's troubles come from the outside, and he tries to solve his problems through outward means. His "half-pace" principle betokens his outlook. This principle is governed by his self-sufficiency—his confidence, self-esteem. Moreover, he is incapable of passion. The woman whom he proclaims to love represents to him merely the embodiment of the human pattern of goodness, rationality, dignity, and simplicity. He remains an intellectual rationalist to the end, like many of Tolstoy's characters. In a sense, one is tempted to think that of all of Mao Dun's early

[80] John Bayley, *Tolstoy and the Novel*, p. 43.
[81] *Zhuiqiu*, p. 135.

intellectual heroes, Zhongzhao is closest to a *real* character, in that he is unable to understand or believe what is going to happen to him, whereas others readily kowtow to the "iron round of destiny" even before their eventual defeat. Zhongzhao believes that he alone holds the key to life's mysteries. (In this he is carrying out his other function, as the commentator in the work.) However, Mao Dun's questioning of the "principle of half-pace" is clearly seen in that, instead of giving Zhongzhao a happy ending, which he could easily have done (as Tolstoy gives to Pierre in *War and Peace*), he has made him undergo the loss of his ideals, his confidence, and above all, his self-sufficiency.

Whether Mao Dun aimed to create a "Tolstoyan" character is not clear. Judging from his fondness for Tolstoy, it is quite conceivable that this may have been his intention. Be that as it may, Wang Zhongzhao's consistency with the self-sufficient Tolstoyan character is worthy of our attention.

Apart from the typological parallels, one may also discern certain general Tolstoyan "influences" in Mao Dun's works. Mao Dun may have had Tolstoy's *War and Peace* in mind when he attempted to make *Twilight* a true replica of Chinese society in the 1930s, making it a multiform work concerned with multifarious themes. The same influence may be present in his efforts to identify the major characters by details about appearance and gesture, inviting the reader's instant recognition. More specifically, the opening chapters of *Twilight*, in which the various major characters are brought together and introduced, and the antagonisms are revealed through the funeral of the father of the protagonist Wu Sunfu, are reminiscent of the opening chapters of *War and Peace*, where the Christmas party scene serves a similar function.

Discussing Russian modernism (1893-1917), E. Lampert refers to "a polarity between a bewildering and chaotic outer world and the inner private one that failed to connect".[82] Such was essentially the phenomenon that Mao Dun responded to in the late 1920s. Steeped in pessimism, overwhelmed with the abstract notion of the incoherence of the cosmic bond between man and the nature of the

---

[82] E. Lampert, "Modernism in Russia, 1893-1917", in M. Bradbury and J. McFarlane (eds.), *Modernism, 1890-1930*, p. 147.

world, Mao Dun in his "Symphony of Fate" has marshalled his heroes to be taunted, toyed with, and finally annihilated. It is now time to ask ourselves several questions. In what ways has the "Russian influence" affected Mao Dun's works? To what extent are his heroes drawn from life? And above all, given Mao Dun's abstract heroes and schematic depictions, how should one interpret the claim of Mao Dun to be a "realistic" writer in this early period?

V. Fiction and Reality

The main differences between Mao Dun's works up to the end of 1931 and those that followed have already been discussed. In his second phase, Mao Dun is no longer obsessed with intellectual phenomena. City life, country life, the state of the economy, the political climate—all these are intricately interwoven in works such as *Twilight* and *Village Trilogy*. More markedly still, the heroes in these works, for example, Lao Tongbao in "Chuncan" (Spring Silkworm), are concrete, rounded, and endowed with personality. No longer is "fate" inexplicable, no longer is there the abstraction that permeates his earlier works. In a word, these works are infinitely more "realistic", and the author's depiction is far more "objective".

One is obviously tempted to ask the reason for these conspicuous changes. Critics hold the view that Mao Dun has in his second phase "shaken off his pessimism of the revolutionary era"[83] of the late 1920s. Some go further and point out that Mao Dun has come to see social and political developments in Marxist terms. These are plausible and valid reasons, but lie beyond the scope of this study. The central question, namely, why Mao Dun's earlier pessimism led him to produce certain characters with strong Russian overtones, is, however, left largely unanswered.

It is not easy to find an answer to this question, and for two reasons. First, Mao Dun was depicting a certain type of person prevalent at that time. As he says in "From Guling to Tokyo": "The only thing I was concerned about was not allowing my individual subjectivity to sneak in, and moreover, to make the characters in

[83] Ye Ziming, as n. 43, p. 82.

Disillusion and *Dongyao* (Vacillation) respond to the revolution in a manner consistent with the objective situation of the times."[84] There is no dispute as to Mao Dun's intention in these early works to depict the "objective reality" of the late 1920s and early 1930s, a phrase he used himself so often that it has become a catchword. In fact, critics have consistently referred to Mao Dun's skill in depicting social reality. Průšek thinks that "Mao Dun's endeavour to seize and communicate reality is characterized by his pre-occupation with topical reality . . .".[85] This is a fair comment. In Mao Dun's own words, his *Eclipse* springs from his decision to portray the three different periods endured by modern youth in the tidal wave of revolution: (1) the exuberance on the eve of revolution and the disillusionment when coming face to face with it; (2) the vacillation during the intensification of the revolutionary struggle; (3) after the disillusionment and vacillation, the unwillingness to accept loneliness and the desire still to undertake a final search.[86] His ability to draw from the demoralized intellectual types of the late 1920s models for his defeated heroes is manifested in the immediate success of these works among the young intellectuals of the day. Many of his contemporaries saw the image of themselves in Mao Dun's heroes. One critic was filled with gratitude upon reading *Disillusion*, for "it created in me an indescribable and complicated feeling, . . . he has forcefully expressed in great detail what I had wanted to express all through, and uttered for me the words that I had wanted to say but could not . . .".[87] Another critic recounted that *Eclipse* had made him "feel unconsciously that a certain force was commanding my eyes to carry on line by line. I felt that I seemed to have experienced some of the episodes described [in the novel], and at least should know a few of them [the characters]."[88]

While Mao Dun's skill at depicting the so-called "objective reality" is beyond doubt, when one gets down to the *typology* of his defeated

[84] As n. 35, p. 1139.

[85] J. Průšek, *Three Sketches of Chinese Literature*, p. 10.

[86] As n. 35. p. 1139.

[87] Zhang Mianyue, "*Huanmie* de shidai miaoxie", in Fu Zhiying (ed.), *Mao Dun pingzhuan*, pp. 69–70.

[88] Xin Yi, "*Zhuiqiu* zhong de Zhang Qiuliu", ibid., pp. 85–86.

heroes, the above explanations provide no more than the source of, the background to, or the central contradictions in their personalities.[89] One is still left largely blank as to *why* these defeated heroes take on such an "abstract" and "schematic" form, and whence comes the equally abstract notion of the "iron round of destiny". This leads to the second reason. Mao Dun provided the clue himself by pointing out that the tone of *Pursuit* is "utterly pessimistic . . . I admit that this stark pessimism is my own, though the discontent, despondency and the eagerness for an outlet is an objective reality."[90] This remark can safely be taken to describe his early works as a whole. In other words, his defeated heroes are overshadowed by his *own* pessimism. They are circumscribed by his *own* philosophy. It is, I think, this very pessimism that resulted in Mao Dun's susceptibility to the "Andreyevan" and "Artzybashevan" influence, when he sees a common cause underlying the state of Russia at the turn of the century and the state of the China of his time, in his own words, "a defeatist tone is the natural flavour of literature after great changes and calamities". The "Russian influence" is made all the more likely by Mao Dun's already strongly Russia orientated literary outlook, with his special admiration for such writers as Tolstoy, Andreyev and Artzybashev, and his predilection for depicting the "thought" of his characters. The typology of his early defeated hero is thus a combination of the indigenous elements—the nihilistic and defeatist outlook on life of many Chinese intellectuals, together with the author's own natural pessimism and the borrowings from the Russian forerunners who were depicting a parallel situation some twenty or more years before. It is such a combination that makes Mao Dun's hero at the same time a familiar figure, and yet equally a stranger to the Chinese literary tradition.

Given this Russian influence, the question to ask is: how has it affected Mao Dun's works? I would venture to suggest that from

---

[89] As a recent study points puts, two main themes—the theme of politics, recent history, and revolution intertwined with while simultaneously pulling against personal liberation, psychological alienation, and the individual's search for self-fulfilment—provide a central contradiction in Mao Dun's early works. John Berninghausen, "The Central Contradiction in Mao Dun's Earliest Fiction", in Merle Goldman (ed.), *MCL*, p. 257.

[90] As n. 35, p. 1140.

the fictional point of view, such an influence is essentially a deleterious one. It is strange and indeed disturbing to see him produce these abstract and schematic characters. As the most fervent and articulate advocate of realism in modern Chinese literature, Mao Dun has always been preoccupied in his critical writings with "concrete" character portrayals. One would at least expect the character type of Lao Tongbao to be his ideal "realistic" hero. As recently as 1925, two years before he wrote his first novel, Mao Dun warned in his excellent essay "Renwu de yanjiu" (On Character Depiction) against "type" characters, who are portrayed solely by means of traits characteristic of their background, class, profession, or position, with the result that they are not a harmonious grouping of the general and the individual. He considers such "type" characters a failure, and recommends that the "non-typical", the individualized character should be created.[91]

When we examine Mao Dun's own early fictional heroes, we see that he has slipped precisely into the pitfall he warned his readers against—though the "type" is an intellectual one. One important reason for this "slip", I think, is due to the Russian influence, and above all, the "Andreyevan" influence. Again, Mao Dun's remarks made in 1925 provide an appropriate guide to his work a few years later. He says in his "On Character Depiction" that one main reason why "typical characters" emerge is because "a certain type of fictional hero has been in vogue on the literary scene. Being influenced, certain writers start to imitate . . . If a writer falls in with already established types, the outcome of his creation of character can only be typical. The suggestive power of these established types is immensely powerful. Not only have others been overshadowed by them without realizing it, but frequently the authors who created these character types themselves also unconsciously took these archetypal characters as their blueprint. Consequently, they become a prototype for their own characters."[92] This is a penetrating look into the psyche of the writer. It is also self revealing. When Mao Dun started to write his novels in 1927, he was spellbound by the

[91] "Renwu de yanjiu", *XSYB*, 16.3 (1925.3), p. 8. For a study of Mao Dun's views on the questions of creation and literary technique, see Gálik, as n. 4, pp. 126–138.

[92] "Renwu de yanjiu", pp. 8–9.

already popular pessimistic hero-types of Andreyev, the Sanin-like characters of Artzybashev, the George-like characters of Ropshin, and he admits his "closeness to Tolstoy". The process that he described above took place in his own case. This is how his "type" characters came about.

To go a step further, Andreyev was the first (as Olgin remarked), to introduce "schematization" into Russian literature, and he was noted for his abstract heroes. Many of these are in fact dramatic heroes. Possibly the visual effect of the stage helps to offset a lot of the so-called "schematic" defects, if they can be considered defects at all. We have seen that it is precisely these dramatic heroes—Ternovsky, Man, Anathema and Savva, that impressed Mao Dun most, and he has to a certain extent borrowed some of the "dramatic techniques" of Andreyev for his own fictional writings, for example, the device of transferring the place of his tragedies onto a plane of discourse rather than action, the personification of inner forces, the stage by stage movement towards a predetermined end. Many of these "schematic" devices, however, appear to be unsuitable for the "fictional" mode, which requires more complicated situations, more interactions and development of characters and events, more concrete descriptions, and fewer abrupt and dramatic changes. He amplifies the inner conflicts of his "thought" heroes without at the same time bringing in adequate supporting actions and events. For instance, Xu's changes in *Three Friends* are sudden and dramatic, and so are those of Jing in *Disillusion* and Qiuliu in *Pursuit*. On the other hand, Shi Xun, Wei Yu, or Hui only exist to illustrate the mercilessness of fate. (Only Zhongzhao, the least "Andreyevan" character of all, comes to life.) Such typological abstractions actually induce one to think of many of Mao Dun's early heroes as "symbolic"—as the titles of most of the novels suggest.[93] Consequently, when one talks of the early Mao Dun as a "realist", one should distinguish between two levels. Mao Dun is "realistic" in depicting historical trends, in capturing the mood of the intellectuals of his time, but on the "fictional" level, his abstract and schematic typologies can hardly be called "realistic". His early works lack the

---

[93] As we may remember, Mao Dun himself reminds us that the title of *Rainbow* is symbolic. He also dwelt at length on the symbolic nature of his early works in his *Autobiography*, Vol. 2, pp. 6–38.

concrete and detailed description, the detached observation that is a prerequisite for all realistic writings. Indeed, one does not need to go far to look for an ideal "realistic" hero—his own Lao Tongbao created in 1932 is a cardinal example.

All in all, Mao Dun's earliest works are unsatisfactory and chaotic in many ways. The shortcomings in style and technique—all betray the hand of an apprentice novelist in his first literary efforts. Even more disturbing, however, is the way the expectations and aspirations of his characters are disappointed and undermined less by their own shortcomings or force of circumstances than by the author's own assumption of human fallibility and his obsession with the hostility of fate. Mao Dun the pessimist has yet to be liberated by Mao Dun the Prometheus. The formerly contradictory forces of idealism and realism will be unified in the typology of Duo-duotou in *Village Trilogy*, his first positive hero.

6 Ba Jin's Estranged Hero

I. Introduction

It is noteworthy that on Ba Jin's recent visit to France, his first since he left it in 1928, the then 75-year-old author made a special trip to the burial ground of Herzen in Nice, to pay tribute to the great Russian romantic exile who died in France more than a century before, and who has commanded his deep respect since youth.[1] In fact, Ba Jin has it as one of his major undertakings to translate into Chinese Herzen's *My Past and Thoughts* in the remaining years of his life—the first volume was already published in 1979. In the postscript to his translation, Ba Jin wrote movingly of Herzen's influence on him: "*My Past and Thoughts* can be said to be my

[1] Alexander Herzen (1812–1870), famous Russian thinker and publicist. Having left Russia in 1847, Herzen spent the rest of his life in Western Europe, though his words resounded over Russia, and his influence was overwhelming. His reputation can best be summed up in Isaiah Berlin's remark: "Herzen's ideas have long since entered into the general texture of Russian political thought—liberals, radicals, populists and anarchists, socialists and communists, have all claimed him as an ancestor." Introduction to *My Past and Thoughts*, Vol. 1, p. xxxv. Other than *My Past*, Herzen's major works include *From the Other Shore* and *The Russian People and Socialism*. For Ba Jin's reminiscence of Herzen, see *Random Thoughts*, Chapter 16.

teacher. I first read it on February 5, 1928, when I bought a copy of Mrs. Constance Garnett's translation of the work. Then I had not yet finished writing my first novel *Destruction*. Though my experience was simple, a glowing fire burnt in my heart. I wanted to pour out my feelings, speak my love and hate, and use my pen to convert into words and paragraphs my 'blood and tears'. Later on, in my several attempts to translate sections of *My Past and Thoughts* I had the express wish to learn from the author how to turn feeling into words. Now that I am doing a complete translation of *My Past and Thoughts*, I cannot say that I no longer have such a motive. I will learn [from the author] to the last breath of my life."[2] After all these years of hardship and enforced inactivity,[3] it is interesting to see that, now aged four score and more, Ba Jin's admiration and enthusiasm for Russian literature has hardly declined (he finished re-translating Turgenev's *Virgin Soil* in 1974).[4] He is still bearing the torch for a culture which has inspired many Chinese to pursue the ideal of cosmopolitanism and the way of revolution. In this chapter, I intend to examine Ba Jin's indebtedness to Russian

[2] *Wangshi yu suixiang*, pp. 395–396. Herzen's memoirs *Byloye i dumy* was first published in the original Russian in five volumes by Slovo, Berlin, 1921; and it was from this edition that Constance Garnett made her translation, *My Past and Thoughts*, first published in London between 1924–1927. Ba Jin acknowledged that his translation is largely based on the Garnett translation, while making references to Vol. 8 of *The Complete Works of Herzen*, published by Moscow in 1965. Postscript to *Wangshi*, p. 397.

[3] See his essays about his experiences during the Cultural Revolution in *Random Thoughts*. See also "Lianyu zhong de shenghuo" by Wang Xiyan which appeared in the book of the same title.

[4] *Virgin Soil* was translated into Chinese by Ba Jin in 1944 under the title *Chunü di*, published in the *Wenhua shenghuo congshu* of which Ba Jin was the chief editor. Ba Jin mentioned in the preface that his translation was based on Constance Garnett's and R. G. Townshend's translations published in 1906 and 1922 respectively, and that he had not the Russian original to refer to. This has been the general pattern of Ba Jin's translation of Russian works. He normally bases his translation on a standard English version, if one is available, while consulting the Russian original at the same time. A case in point would be his recent re-translation of *Virgin Soil*, and also his translation of Herzen's *My Past*. This is presumably because he reads English better than Russian. However, Ba Jin has also directly translated from the Russian original, e.g. Turgenev's prose-poem "The Threshold" in the work of the same title, see n. 19. Sometimes he consults various translations of a Russian work before he makes his own, as in his translation of Kropotkin's *Ethics: Origin and Development*, see n. 10.

writings. As the Russian presence is most keenly felt in his early fictional works, I will confine my study to these first years of his literary output, when he was, among other things, consciously learning from the Russian masters.

II. Response to European Writings

a. Romain Rolland and Zola

In a letter to Fr. Monsterleet in 1948, Ba Jin told of his development as a writer. According to him, Chinese classical novels never had a profound impact on his writings. He liked Dickens and some Western novels (which he did not specify), but he read these for pleasure. In contrast, Russian novels had meaning for him: he began reading Russian novels when he was eighteen, and "liked them tremendously, because the conditions of life in Russia closely resembled those of the Chinese people of that period. The characters, the aspirations and tastes of the Russians were somewhat similar to ours." Among the French novelists, Hugo, Romain Rolland and Zola were his favourites. Also, the writings of the anarchists Emma Goldman and Alexander Berkman, and the memoirs of some revolutionaries, "left a deep imprint" on him.[5]

From Ba Jin's own account, we can therefore identify three main sources of foreign impact on his writings: French novels, Russian novels, and the works of some revolutionaries—most of them Russian anarchists. I will try to assess the importance of these

[5] Ming Xingli (Jean Monsterleet), *Ba Jin de shenghuo he zhuzuo*, pp. 50–53. In an interview with a French journalist in Paris in May 1979, Ba Jin said that his early works were influenced by Turgenev and Tolstoy. As to French writers, he pointed out that he was familiar with the works of Zola, Maupassant, Hugo and Rousseau, though he did not use the word "influence" or "impact". He further mentioned that his agonized or courageous heroines owe much to, first, the heroines in the great classical Chinese novels, and second, to the revolutionary maidens in Russian novels. *Le Monde*, May 18, 1979. However, since most of Ba Jin's early heroines are outgoing and revolutionary by nature, and have little in common with the heroines in classical Chinese novels, his earlier remark to Fr. Monsterleet that Chinese classical novels had little impact on his early writings seems to be more convincing. For a recent study of Ba Jin's life and works, see Olga Lang, *Pa Chin and His Writings*.

influences on Ba Jin's works, with special reference to his estranged
heroes.

First, the French writers. Ba Jin spent some twenty-two months
in France as a young man (1927–1928), and was well exposed to
French writings. It is possible to see connections in some of his early
works. The sadness and sorrow of Jean Christophe in Romain
Rolland's novel over his failure to see his universalist ideals through,
and his frustrations as a result of his enforced exile from his native
Rhineland were shared by Ba Jin and his romantic heroes. Ba Jin
began reading Rolland's novel in France, at a time when he was,
albeit temporarily, in spiritual exile from his motherland. The
affinities between Christophe and Ba Jin's intellectual heroes,
however, rest mainly on the level of an idealistic youth seeking the
meaning of life. Whereas Christophe grows in artistic and moral
stature as he acquires experience, and becomes almost a symbol
of the genius who wins through to joy by suffering, Ba Jin's early
heroes almost all either die frustrated, or attain "fulfilment" through
destruction. A more explicit source of influence are the works of
Zola. Ba Jin's early novel *Mengya* (Germination), a deliberate
attempt to reflect the life of Chinese coal-miners, bears certain
thematic resemblances to Zola's *Germinal*—though lacking the
experimental objectivity and physiological determinism that
distinguish his French counterpart.[6] Taken as a whole, especially
in typological terms, the French influence is not as pronounced as
the Russian. The "conditions of life" in France in no way "closely
resembled those of the Chinese people". This is actually the view
of Juehui in *Jia* (Family), who can be said to speak for the author himself. Finding the "cannibalistic" Confucian conventions
unbearable, he bursts out: "'Why is there so much misery in the
world?' At this moment, he remembers what his French teacher had
said the other day: 'In France, youngsters of your age don't know
the meaning of tragedy.' But he is a youth of China, and already
tragedy is weighing him down."[7] Ba Jin explicitly draws our
attention to this fact. Repudiating the contention that his heroes
have antecedents in French novels, he wrote in 1935 that Flaubert,

[6] For a more detailed discussion of French literary influence on Ba Jin, see Lang,
Pa Chin and His Writings, pp. 245–254.
[7] *Jia*, p. 362; English translation, *Family*, p. 244.

Zola and George Sand would have been incapable of creating his heroes, since they lived in an entirely alien world.[8] Moreover, well versed as Ba Jin is in the French language, he has not published any translation of French literary writings. Significantly, his first novel *Destruction*, one of the most "Russian-flavoured" of his works, was written during his sojourn in France.

If the number of translations can be taken as an indication of the translator's affection for the works he translated, then Ba Jin's sympathy unmistakably lies with nineteenth-century Russian literary and revolutionary writings. Russian writings made up the bulk of his translations.[9] A first glance shows that he translated into Chinese works by Pushkin, Garshin, Turgenev, Stepniak, Gorky, Aleksey Tolstoy and Yaroshenko, and writings of Herzen, Kropotkin, Vera Figner, Alexander Berkman and Emma Goldman. The Polish playwright Leopald Kampf's work *On the Eve*, which describes the life and death of Russian nihilists, can also be put into the category of "Russian" translation. The writers featured most prominently in his translations are Kropotkin and Turgenev. Ba Jin rendered most of Kropotkin's works into Chinese singlehanded, and the translations of Turgenev's works include the novels *Fathers and Sons*, *Virgin Soil*, and a good number of short stories and prose poems. Ba Jin's relationship with the Russian writers, notably Kropotkin, Turgenev, Tolstoy, Artzybashev and Ropshin, deserves to be treated in some detail.

b. Kropotkin and the Russian revolutionaries

Ba Jin came across Kropotkin's celebrated essay "An Appeal to the Young" when he was fifteen. His reactions upon reading it are worth quoting in full:

> ...I got hold of a pamphlet. This was an abridged version of Kropotkin's "An Appeal to the Young". I hadn't imagined that such a work ever existed. In it was all that I wanted to say but was incapable of clearly expressing. The arguments were so lucid, reasonable and

---

[8] Ba Jin, "*Aiqing de sanbuqu* zuozhe de zibai", in *BJZJ*, p. 313.
[9] For a comprehensive list of Ba Jin's translations, see Lang, as n. 5, pp. 351–353.

convincing! The provocative tone burnt to ashes the heart of a fifteen
year old. I put the pamphlet beside my bed and read it every night.
My tears dropped on the pages until my eyes failed me and I began
to laugh. . . . From that time on I understood the meaning of justice.
This understanding enabled me to reconcile the feelings of love and
hatred.[10]

It is easy to understand Kropotkin's impact on Ba Jin. His ideas
on social revolution, on the destruction of the unjust world of
inequality and baneful government, and the vision of a new, peaceful
and fraternal world arising from the ashes of the old, had special
relevance to the Chinese situation in the 1920s. "An Appeal to the
Young" which dwells on the necessity of a revolutionary whirlwind
to sweep away all that is rotten, is one of his most eloquent and
provocative essays. To the teenager Ba Jin, who was brought up
in a secluded environment of love and protection, who had just
learned about the cruelties of society, and seen through the injustices
disguised under the cloak of love,[11] the works of Kropotkin were
a bombshell. He tried to put these generous, humanitarian and
regenerating ideas into practice, and to bring to mankind a spirit
of devotion, self-denial and heroism. With friends he formed a
society, and considered himself an anarchist.[12]

Indeed the writings of Kropotkin were to remain a source of
inspiration and comfort to Ba Jin throughout his early period,

---

[10] Ba Jin, "Wode younian" in *Duanjian*, pp. 7–8. Peter A. Kropotkin
(1841–1921), Russian revolutionary and geographer, the foremost leader and
theorist of the anarchist movement. He shunned material success for the life of
a revolutionist, and did more than any other figure to further the libertarian
cause in Europe and around the world. His major works include *Memoirs of a
Revolutionist* (1899), *Conquest of Bread* (1892), *Mutual Aid* (1902), and *Ethics:
Origin and Development* (1924). "An Appeal to the Young", one of the best known
and most influential of Kropotkin's pamphlets, was first published in *Le Révolté*
in 1880. It was translated into English and published by Modern Press in London
in 1885. Li Shizeng translated this pamphlet into Chinese while studying in Paris,
and it was first published by the anarchist Shijie she in Paris before the 1911
Revolution in China, and a later reprint appeared in *Min Sheng*, Canton, after
1913. See Lang, as n. 5, p. 293. Ba Jin did a re-translation of this pamphlet, most
likely from French and English versions, which was later included in *Yige
fankangzhe de hua*, a translation of Kropotkin's *Speeches of a Rebel* by edited
and translated Bi Xiushao.

[11] See *Ba Jin zizhuan*, especially Chapters 1 and 2.

[12] See *Yige fankangzhe de hua*, p. 11.

especially in times of distress. As he wrote in the preface to the translation of Kropotkin's *Ethics: Origin and Development*: "At the time when the revolution was crushed in Russia, Kropotkin frantically wrote his *Ethics*, and I was moved by the same spirit when at the time of the great massacre of Chinese people I put all my strength into the translation of this book."[13] So deep was his respect for Kropotkin that he urged his brother to learn from the Russian's noble character and shining example. If he could act according to Kropotkin's principle of love and sympathy, wrote Ba Jin, then there would not be a moment in life that he would feel the pangs of conscience, nor would he do anything unfaithful to himself or to others.[14]

Enthusiastic as Ba Jin was for Kropotkin's writing at this time, one sees in his early works that his heroes did not conform to the latter's idea of revolution by natural evolution, nor to his belief in man's natural leaning towards social responsibility, the basic tenet of his notion of mutual aid. Instead of the self-centred individual, who sought changes through cataclysmic transformation, Ba Jin's depiction is closer to Bakunin's style of anarchism, and akin to the belief held by many Russian revolutionaries, whose writings Ba Jin greeted with high acclaim.

Ba Jin first encountered the stories of Russian revolutionaries in Leopald Kampf's play *On the Eve*, which centres on the right to kill to achieve a new society. Its impact on Ba Jin was astounding:

> It is probably ten years ago that a fifteen year old youth was reading this little book. At that time he had just embraced the ideal of loving mankind and loving the world; he had the childish illusion that a new society in which everybody shares happiness would rise with tomorrow's sun and that all evils would instantly vanish. Reading the little book in this frame of mind, he was indescribably stirred. That

---

[13] Translated by Lang in *Pa Chin and His Writings*, p. 125. *Ethics* was translated from Russian into English by Louis S. Friedland and Joseph R. Piroshinikoff, and published in New York in 1924. Ba Jin wrote in the preface to his translation of Volume 2 of *Ethics* (*Rensheng zhexue: qi qiyuan ji qi fazhan*) that while working on this volume, he consulted English, French, Japanese, Spanish, German and Esperanto translations of the book. Ba Jin most probably based his translation on the English translation. See Lang, p. 137.

[14] Ba Jin, "*Wode zizhuan* yiben xu", in *Sheng zhi chanhui*, p. 137.

book opened for him a new vista and let him see the great tragedy of a generation of youth in another country striving for the liberty and happiness of the people. In that book the fifteen year old formed for the first time the hero of his dreams, found moreover his life's career. He introduced that book to his friends as a precious jewel. They even copied it down word by word, and because it was a play, they played it on stage several times. This child was myself, and that book was the Chinese translation of *On the Eve*.[15]

What touched Ba Jin most were the conflicts betwen life and death, duty and love, reason and passion among the protagonists. As he commented, the play not only faithfully described the "moeurs" of the Russian nihilists, it also dealt with their conflicts in depth. The same sort of conflicts, as we will see, haunted Ba Jin's own intellectual heroes later.

In the same vein, the stories and memoirs of many Russian revolutionaries also filled Ba Jin with enthusiasm. As he wrote to Fr. Monsterleet: "I love to read books that others do not read, ...books written in the very blood of living people."[16] The memoirs of Herzen, Kropotkin and Emma Goldman;[17] the stories of the Russian terrorists Vera Figner and Sophia Perovskaya moved him to the verge of tears.[18] He recalled how his heart was filled with joy and fervour when he first read Turgenev's prose poem "The

---

[15] Ba Jin, "*Qianye* yiben xu", p. 126, English translation (with minor adaptations) from C. T. Hsia, *A History of Modern Chinese Fiction, 1917–1957*, pp. 240–241. This play by Leopold Kampf (1881–?), written in German under the title *Am Vorabend*, was first performed in New York in 1907, and in the Théâtre des Arts in Paris in December 1907 for several months, with tremendous success. An English translation under the title *On the Eve* was published in New York in 1907. Ba Jin wrote in 1936 that this play "has had a tremendous impact in China, it won the heart of a generation of Chinese youth", *Menkan*, p. 108. *On the Eve* was re-enacted in Ba Jin's *Chun*, Part II, Chapters 1, 4 and 5. The example of Anna, Kampf's heroine, helped Gao Shuying to make up her mind to leave the despotic family. See also Chapter One, n. 1.

[16] *Ba Jin de shenghuo he zhuzuo*, p. 55.

[17] Herzen's *My Past and Thoughts*, Kropotkin's *Memoirs of a Revolutionist*, and Goldman's *Living My Life*, 2 vols.

[18] Both Vera Figner (1852–1949) and Sophia Perovskaya (1853–1881) were members of the executive committee of the Narodnaia volia (People's Will Party). The latter was arrested and executed shortly after the attempted assassination of Alexander II in 1881, the former was arrested in 1883 and spent twenty years in solitary confinement. Also see Chapter 1.

Threshold",[19] which is an apotheosis of Sophia Perovskaya. The example of these women revolutionaries was conducive to the creation of his beautiful and steely heroines—who are such a contrast to the meek and wavering heroes. For example, Hui the heroine of *Lei* (Thunder) looks to Emma Goldman for spiritual encouragement; Lina in *Hai di meng* (Dream of the Sea) gallantly bears her sufferings thinking of those endured by Sophia Perovskaya. Li Peizhu in *Dian* (Lightning), the most beautiful of Ba Jin's early creations and his favourite heroine (in the author's own words), finds her revolutionary vocation upon reading the memoir of Vera Figner. As Ba Jin wrote of Li Peizhu: "this Vera-like heroine is entirely my own creation. I have not modelled her on anybody, but the memoirs of the women revolutionaries in various countries that I have read have imparted valuable insights to me."[20]

That the actions of these Russian revolutionaries succeeded in evoking Ba Jin's deep sympathy is understandable. The testimony of a Russian revolutionary in court provides us with the reason: "It is not necessary to have been a tiger from the first and by nature in order to display tigerish qualities. Social conditions exist by which lambs are converted into tigers."[21] In the first decades of this century, many Chinese youths also turned into tigers; their incentive for revolutionary action was the offspring of a mingled love for humanity and justice and loathing for the vile social environment. Many of the more committed and courageous became true revolutionaries, but there were also a good number of half-hearted intellectuals, whose frustrated ideals and eroded enthusiasm resulted in divided personalities. It was these maimed or would-be tigers who became the central concern of Ba Jin's early novels.

c. Turgenev, Artzybashev and Ropshin

If the Russian revolutionaries appealed to Ba Jin as people with quixotic qualities, the heroes in the novels of Turgenev, Artzybashev

---

[19] In his postscript to the translation of *The Threshold* (*Menkan*) Ba Jin stressed that the moving story and realistic portrayals alone are sufficient reasons for these works to last.

[20] Ba Jin, "*Aiqing de sanbuqu* zongxu", in *BJZJ*, p. 299. Ba Jin admitted his indebtedness to the Russian heroines for his own creations. See *Ba Jin de shenghuo*, as n. 5.

[21] Quoted from Masaryk, *The Spirit of Russia*, Vol. 2, p. 112.

and Ropshin revealed to him the psychological malaise suffered by many Russian intellectuals—their fantasies and illusions, cynicisms and despairs, which more often than not led them to destruction. The intellectual heroes of Ba Jin's novels, who represent a unique fusion of inner sincerity and ideological contradictions, of mixed fact, fantasy, prophecy and despair, have much in common with their Russian counterparts. Their "unheroism" makes them more akin to the Russian fictional heroes than to the Russian terrorists in real life.[22]

In his *Yi* (Recollections), Ba Jin mentioned that he preferred Tolstoy, Dostoevsky and Artzybashev to Shakespeare, Dante and Goethe, because the Russian writers have a more admirable attitude to life.[23] Suffice it to say here that Dostoevsky's impact on Ba Jin results mainly from a general plea on behalf of the plight of the insulted and injured,[24] whereas Tolstoy's is mainly from the moral authority of his person, his force as an advocate of personal and social regeneration, and his concept of art as a vehicle for moral rearmament. His principle of non-resistance to evil, however, was not particular esteemed by the Chinese writer. An example of this attitude is shown in Ba Jin's reaction to *The Power of Darkness*. Admitting that it may not be Tolstoy's intention in the play to resist evil, Ba Jin insists nevertheless that the play "kindles the flame of righteousness in the hearts of the readers", and arouses them "to struggle against the present social order, and to uproot the power of darkness".[25] A further case in point is the much battered character Gao Juexin in *Family* who is the embodiment of Tolstoy's doctrine of non-resistance to evil. He is closely portrayed as a

[22] Lang holds that the spirit and content of Ba Jin's novels and short stories owed more to his reading of the historical accounts of the Russian populist movement than the Russian novels, as n. 5, p. 237. I do not share her view, as this study of Ba Jin's heroes will show.

[23] Ba Jin, *Yi*, pp. 172–173. Though Ba Jin did not specify what exactly this attitude is, one can safely deduce that it is the sympathy towards the injured and insulted that distinguished nineteenth-century Russian writings.

[24] Ba Jin only quoted Dostoevsky once, as Lang points out. Nevertheless, he named a collection of his short stories *Mabuji* (The Rag). He compared the filthy rag to the insulted and injured, who, in their wretched state, still transmit rays of light that brighten his very heart—see his preface to the collection. Also see Chapter 3 for a discussion of Dostoevsky's injured hero.

[25] Ba Jin, "Heian shili de kaocha", pp. 84–85.

character to be pitied, rather than someone to emulate.[26]

The works of Turgenev, Artzybashev and Ropshin in particular, had quite a profound influence on Ba Jin's novels, especially his early works. In his *"Gongnü Ma Dalan* yiben xu" (Preface to the Translation of *Les Mauvais Bergers*), Ba Jin singled out Artzybashev and Ropshin:

> Of the recent Chinese translations of Western literary works, there are only three for which I have a deep feeling. The first is "Shevyrev" by Artzybashev; the second is *The Pale Horse* by Ropshin, and the third is this work. The first two are Russian works of fiction, and are significantly different from this one. Lu Xun thinks "Shevyrev" is a story about "anger and righteous indignation". As to *The Pale Horse*, the hero George is an extremist who denies everything. He does not even believe in revolution, despite being a member of a terrorist group.[27]

Ba Jin knew Artzybashev's works well;[28] his presence can readily be detected in some of his early writings. His young intellectual hero Chen Zhen (in *Fog*), for example, is addressed by friends as Pasha Afanasiev (Artzybashev's hero in *Morning Shadow*). Chen's diligence, his shining example to his colleagues and his untimely death, leaving an unaccomplished task behind, are reminiscent of Pasha. Feng Wenshu the heroine in Volume III

[26] Ba Jin depicts Juexin as an admirer of Liu Bannung's "philosophy of compliant bows" and Tolstoy's "principle of non-resistance", Chapter 6. They are a solace to him, permitting him to believe in the new theories of the May Fourth Movement while still conforming to the old feudal concepts. He is undoubtedly the most pathetic of Ba Jin's early characters. As the eldest son of the big patriachal family, the best he can do is to make himself "befuddled". Accused of being a weakling, he can only counter with resignation: "certainly you've triumphed . . . you resist everything, you have contempt for everything, and you've won. But your victory has deepened my defeat. They heap upon me all their resentment against you. . . . I kept my bitterness inside me. No one knew. It's all very well for you to talk about resistance, struggle. But who can I say those fine-sounding words to?" *Family*, pp. 300–301.

[27] As n. 13, pp. 119–120. *Gongnü Ma Dalan* is the Chinese title of Octave Mireau's play *Les Mauvais Bergers*, translated by Yue Ying and published in 1928. I had previously been unable to identify the original work. Ba Jin kindly told me the title after reading my article "Ba Jin and Russian Literature".

[28] C. T. Hsia holds that there are three translations of *Sanin* and Ba Jin translated one of them, *A History*, p. 584, n. 12. Olga Lang, however, has not included *Sanin* in the list of works translated by the author. I have not come across any mention of Ba Jin having translated *Sanin* into Chinese, other than Hsia's.

of *Huo* (Fire) uses Sanin's individualistic and anarchistic arguments against Christianity with the Christian Tian Huishi. Certain episodes in Ba Jin's fiction also have parallels in Artzybashev's works. A case of direct borrowing would be the climactic scene in *Lightning*, where the secret police break in to search for the revolutionary Min, but kill his friend Fang instead, and the subsequent crowd scene where Min overhears the onlookers denouncing the dead man; is almost identical to the incident in "Shevyrev", where Shevyrev's friend Aladiev is killed in mistake for him, and Shevyrev hears the crowd accusing the revolutionary who had laid down his life for them.[29] The device of Artzybashev in using dreams to reveal the protagonist's past sorrows and inner conflicts which impel him to action is echoed in many of Ba Jin's novels and stories.[30] But it was Artzybashev's "Shevyrev" which exerted the most influence on his writing. He recalled recently that during the time of writing *Destruction*, he often recited a sentence from Lu Xun's translation of the work, that people "are awakened in spirit to see their putrid corpses". He had the heart to do something before it was too late. His first novel *Destruction* was written in such a frame of mind. It is no wonder that Du Daxin, the central figure of the work, bears the strongest resemblance to Artzybashev's Shevyrev.[31]

As for Ropshin, we have seen the immediate recognition of his *The Pale Horse* when it appeared in Chinese in 1922. As a hero type, George is undoubtedly different from the traditional terrorists, such as Stepniak's heroes,[32] in that he is both a philosopher and a practical terrorist. As the historian Masaryk observed: "As I read [*The Pale Horse*], I feel that I am making the acquaintance of a new type of terrorist, and of a real terrorist, not an imaginary one."[33]

[29] "Shevyrev", translated into English by Percy Pinkerton, in *Tales of the Revolution*, pp. 87–90.

[30] For example, in *Miewang*, *Si qu de taiyang* and *Xinsheng*, and many of his short stories. I will go into more detail about this in my discussion of *Miewang*. Chinese classical novelists did employ the technique of dreams too, but quite unlike the way that both Ba Jin and Artzybashev used it.

[31] *Chuangzuo huiyilu*, p. 82.

[32] Ba Jin translated three chapters of Stepniak's *Russian under the Tsars* in *Menkan* (pp. 75–106), based on the English original. See also Chapter 3, n. 50.

[33] Masaryk, Vol. 2, p. 445. It should be pointed out that Zheng Zhenduo freely made use of the materials from Masaryk's study of *The Pale Horse* in his preface to the Chinese translation.

It is therefore interesting, not to say intriguing, to see that Li Leng, the protagonist of Ba Jin's third novel *Xinsheng* (New Life) displays ample affinities with George. In fact, as we shall see, so patent is the similarity between the characters at one point that one can talk of a direct borrowing by Ba Jin.

Discussing his indebtedness to Turgenev's writings, Ba Jin said that "when I learned to write short stories, Turgenev was my first teacher. . . . Some of my early stories about people relating their own experience were most probably inspired by him."[34] He pointed out that his story "First Love" was partially modelled on Turgenev's story of the same title.[35] And the prose poem "The Threshold" of the Russian master moved him to tears, as we have seen. He expanded this poem into a short story, and gave it the same title. Quoting the poem towards the end of the story, the "girl on the threshold" portends to the I-hero the coming of a bright future.[36] At the same time, Turgenev's poem "The Russian Language" was his "anchor and only source of support" when he was in temporary exile in Japan in 1935. It kindled his spirit for the mother country. So touching was the poem to him that he was constantly reciting it to himself when he was writing *Fire* in 1938.[37]

Much more can be said of Turgenev's influence.[38] Leaving aside the Turgenevan superfluous hero, a subject I will go into later, his presence is most felt in *The Dream of the Sea*, a story about Lina, a girl of aristocratic blood. Disgusted with the sycophants and dandies around her, she finds new life in the lowly-born Yang—a young revolutionary fighting for the freedom of his motherland. She marries him and accompanies him in his revolutionary struggles. He is fatally wounded, and charges her to throw his dead body into the sea—the sea of freedom for his country. After many dangers and difficulties, she fulfils Yang's last wish, and becomes a committed revolutionary herself. It is obvious that *The Dream of the Sea* and *On the Eve* share the same theme: the fight for the independence

[34] Ba Jin, "Guanyu wode duanpianxiaoshuo", *Ba Jin wenji*, Vol. 7, pp. 472–473.

[35] Ibid., p. 474.

[36] "Zai menkan shang", included in *Jiangjun*, pp. 120–147.

[37] As n. 31, pp. 56, 70.

[38] Lang, *Pa Chin*, pp. 234–236.

of the hero's mother country. There is also a similar story-line. Both works depict the conversion of the heroine of high society into a revolutionary by the hero of humble birth—the struggles against foreign aggression—the untimely death of the hero—and the heroine fulfilling the wish of the hero by carrying the corpse a long way and throwing it into the sea. Lina and Yang can without equivocation be regarded as the Chinese equivalents of Yelena and Insarov in Turgenev's novel. (Even the names show similarities: Lina and Yelena, Yang and Insarov—the first syllable of *Insarov* would be *Yang* in Chinese.) Ba Jin has made use of Turgenev's story to depict a similar Chinese situation: in the wake of the Japanese invasion from 1931 onwards (*The Dream of the Sea* was written in 1932), many patriotic Chinese youths did in fact join the forces fighting the Japanese.

On the Eve is also read with great enthusiasm by the Gao brothers in *Jia*, Ba Jin's most famous and popular novel written in 1931. The romantic outbursts of the dilettante sculptor Shubin in *On the Eve*: "We're young, we're not monsters, not fools: we'll conquer happiness for ourselves" are quoted many times by Gao Juehui, the youngest brother and the most powerful figure of the novel. Juehui's eager espousal of the egoistic cause of Shubin, who when pressed by his friend Bresyenev to say whether there are higher values than happiness for oneself, frowns and replies: "That's all right for the Germans: but I want love for myself: I want to be number one"[39] —instead of being inspired by the selflessness of the protagonist Insarov—offers fresh insights into his primarily individualistic character. He holds the individualistic view that the world is a tragic place: "People lived only to destroy themselves, or to destroy others. Destruction was inevitable, no matter how he struggled" (*Family*, pp. 301–302). He is determined that "no matter what happens, I must go my own road, even if it means trampling over their dead bodies" (ibid.)—meaning those who stood in his way.

To put the Russian influence into perspective, we must now consider the extent to which his estranged intellectual heroes—the central concern of his early works—live in the shadow of their Russian counterparts, and in what way they are Ba Jin's own

[39] Turgenev, *On the Eve*, pp. 29–30.

creation. By putting the Russian influence into perspective, we will be able to understand more acutely the typology of these heroes.

III. The Estranged Hero

> "Let's go. Follow me. Between Hamlet and Don Quixote you must choose one. You should be a Don Quixote", he said. Thereupon he grabbed my shoulders and dashed for the door.[40]
>
> Ba Jin, "Chunyü" (Spring Rain), 1934.

"Spring Rain" ends with the wavering young man turning over a new leaf, and finding himself a committed, happy person. By alluding to the celebrated article "Hamlet and Don Quixote" by Turgenev,[41] Ba Jin revealed his resolve to create Don Quixote-type characters, whose freedom from reflection and questioning would make them efficient, and whose dedication to noble causes would prompt them to action. Up to this time most of Ba Jin's heroes had been wandering and brooding intellectuals, heroes with Russian overtones. These Hamlet-like heroes are of particular interest.

a. Destruction *and "Shevyrev"*

Ba Jin began writing his first novel *Destruction* between 1927–1928, when he was in spiritual exile in France. As the title suggests, the novel is about the disillusionment, struggle, and the ultimate destruction of the protagonist Du Daxin, a student turned revolutionary. Du's personal tragedy—his mother has died sighing for love; the cousin that he loves, submissive to parental authority, marries somebody else she has never met before, and then becomes an unhappy widow—breaks his "big heart" (*daxin* in Chinese). Not only this, all around him he encounters unhappiness and oppression. As he recalls, during the time of famine the rich people hoarded up food and sold it at high prices, and the poor were compelled to eat grass, maggots, and even one another. Is there

---

[40] "Chunyu" in *Chenmo ji*, p. 168. It should be noted that in his 14-volume *Collected Works* published in the 1950s, Ba Jin has expurgated from the original versions some of the more nihilistic or pessimistic passages.

[41] This article was translated by Yu Dafu into Chinese in 1928. See Chapter Four, p. 96.

any such thing as justice and love in this world? he apostrophizes.

The common people's indifference, and their hostility towards the revolutionaries further exacerbate his growing disgust for human society. As he observes after the accident where a poor man is run over by a rich man's car, and the rich man orders his chauffeur to drive on, throwing down a few dollars for the poor man's body to be carried away: "everything is quiet and calm . . . Judging from the yellow faces of the owners and shopkeepers behind the shop-windows, one cannot imagine that any blood-letting incident ever happens in their lives, nor can one guess that a car knocks over and kills somebody, a boy is beaten black and blue for shop-lifting and dragged to the police station, that fighting breaks out incessantly, that warlords oppress the people. No one can believe that hooligans and bandits run rampant, that the army ride rough-shod over the people, that revolutionaries are being massacred like dogs and pigs" (Shanghai, 1939, pp. 51–52). In disgust, he quotes Garshin in his diary: "Wolf does not eat wolf; but human beings devour each other with pleasure" (p. 128). His anger is transformed into hatred of the oppressors—the rich and unfeeling masses alike. With hate comes his determination to take revenge—to avenge the people being eaten, to avenge the workers suffocating under "the red smoke coming out of the chimney". The lines of the Russian populist Ryleev: "Those who first rise against oppression must meet with destruction. I know this, but my fate is already sealed" (p. 80), fire him with a demoniacal satisfaction. Hate, he reasons, can vanish only with destruction, and only then is love possible. Under the spell of redemption through hate, he rejects the love of Li Jingshu despite his own love for her.

His afflictions reach their climax with the execution of his comrade Zhang Weiqun. In front of him is the much tortured body, close to death, of the once lovely young idealist. The crowd clamour around as if coming to a play. Out of boredom they jeer at the clumsiness of the hatchetman. They condemn the revolutionaries who have laid down their lives for them (pp. 175–187).[42] Du's fire

---

[42] This scene recalls that of Lu Xun in "A Q zhengzhuan" especially about the superstition and ignorance of the masses. The cynicism displayed is also reminiscent of Lu Xun. Ba Jin admitted that he was "enlightened" by Lu Xun's *Nahan*, *Panghuang* and the short stories that he translated, as n. 34, p. 166. Traces of the

of revenge reaches its height upon hearing these remarks. As he trudges home, he finally realizes that this city has no resting place for him, "not only this city, but indeed the entire world. He is the most solitary soul. His thoughts, his hopes and sufferings are totally incommunicable to others. Not only are the people around totally unrelated to him, they are his enemies" (p. 189). In utter despair, he tries to carry out his plan to assassinate the governor-general. The latter is only slightly hurt, and Du commits suicide on the spot.

The publication of *Destruction* immediately aroused a heated discussion on the typology of Du Daxin. The figure of someone who seeks and ends in destruction, who gets his inspiration from Ryleev and Garshin was indeed a novelty in Chinese literature. Critics branded him "an anarchist", "an individual nihilist", and "a personification of Kropotkin's anarchism, Tolstoy's humanitarianism, and Artzybashev's nihilism".[43] Diverse though their views were, they acknowledged that Du Daxin is a new kind of hero.

Let us first look at the possible influence of Kropotkin and Tolstoy. Although Kropotkin urges people to revolt against the corrupt old social order, his concept of revolution rests on the natural evolution of a free society, a concrete process in which revolutionaries must be aware of the consequence of their actions. From this he derived his concept of mutual aid, which has little in common with Du Daxin's belief in an apocalyptic form of destruction. As to Tolstoy, pulsating through his writings is his belief in the innate goodness of man, especially in the simplicity and singlemindedness of the people, and in the attainment of happiness through tolerance and spiritual regeneration, as the character of Platon in *War and Peace* and Nikita in *Master and Man* exemplify (and as is apparent in his parables). Life for Tolstoy, in the words of a critic, "was an aspect of vitality, of being fully committed to existence—*Zhizn*, life with a capital L".[44] Du Daxin on the other hand, finds the common people repulsive. His active

---

influence of Lu Xun's translation of "Shevyrev" on *Miewang* are not difficult to find. Ba Jin used almost the same words as Lu Xun's version in the climactic scene when the hero comes to realize that he is tormented both by the oppressors and unsympathetic masses.

[43] Ba Jin, "*Miewang* zuozhe de zibai", pp. 5–6.

[44] John Bayley, *Tolstoy and the Novel*, p. 54.

strivings for the destruction of human society by violence come as an antithesis to Tolstoy's non-resistance to evil.

This being so, what sort of hero is Du Daxin? Ba Jin throws light on his own creation: "a person who hates mankind, who hates himself, can only end up in killing or being killed, or by committing suicide. There is no other way but death . . . I abhor his destruction through violence, but I am unable to prevent it, and I can only weep over his death."[45] Hate, revenge and destruction crowned the existence of Du, and we find the same sentiments permeating Artzybashev's Shevyrev.

☐ *The prototype in Artzybashev's Shevyrev*

The similarities between "Shevyrev" and *Destruction* are striking. Both stories revolve round the theme of love and hate, revenge and destruction. Shevyrev is a university student turned terrorist. He narrowly escapes arrest in an abortive revolutionary attempt, but his beloved wife and his comrades are all executed. All alone, hunted by the police, and aware of his imminent arrest, he poses as a worker, awaiting his moment of revenge. The agonizing thought that the indifferent masses oppress him as much as his pursuers further excites his anger. In utter despair, he takes revenge—by firing at the policemen and the crowd alike.

It is obvious that there are similar story-lines in "Shevyrev" and *Destruction*, and both writers dwell on a similar theme. The similarities between the two are in fact too many to relate in full detail here. I will only concern myself with the typology of the intellectual hero. The similarity between the two appears right from the very first scene. The cold penetrating looks of both heroes, laden with sorrow, haunt those they meet. The "grey metallic eyes" of Shevyrev induce Aladiev to think in his first encounter that "this Shevyrev would never under any circumstances prove false either to himself or to the certain something hidden within his soul" (p. 14). Likewise, Du's looks, his "lean face, protuberant nose and gleaming eyes" pierce the heart of Li Leng upon their first meeting. To him, "words cannot describe the tormented appearance of this man" (p. 3). Their personal tragedy—the execution of Shevyrev's

[45] As n. 43, pp. 7–8.

wife, the death in unfulfilment of Du's mother, and the "living death" of his beloved cousin—is closely linked with the oppressive established order enveloping them. Both abandon their former belief that love will redeem the world, and turn to a hatred for humanity. Admitting that he "hates mankind", Shevyrev reacts with contempt and cynicism to Aladiev's idea of love, self-sacrifice and compassion. Were these attainable, and "really instinctive to us", Shevyrev argues, "those who are well-fed could never bear to see others starve and die; there would be no masters and no servants . . ." (p. 20). In the same vein, Du rejects Li Leng's concept of universal love: ". . . this so-called love, peace or natural beauty are monopolized by the very few like you. At least for me, or for the one who was knocked over and killed by the car, or for the many who have been frozen or have starved to death, these things are non-existent. That's why I want to curse life" (pp. 63–64). In consequence, both see it as their task to bring justice to mankind through the apocalyptic redemption of society. Shevyrev declares his reign over the world: "I am the lord of thy life . . . I shall bring to justice all of you who for so long have crushed the life out of us, who have robbed us of sunshine and beauty and love, who have condemned us to a joyless life of eternal slavery . . ." (pp. 43–44). Du deems it his responsibility to "avenge his comrades", vowing that "all those who have built their happiness on others' sufferings must meet with destruction" (pp. 189–190).

In both characters, their abomination of the masses is the catalyst of their decision to take revenge. The recognition that their all-out efforts to bring justice to this world are futile brings to the fore their instinct to destroy. Moreover, the death of their friends precipitates their final act of revenge. The death of Aladiev, Shevyrev's only "friend", in defiance of the police not only crystallizes his hatred, but also drives home to him his solitariness: "in this frightful life-and-death struggle all those whom he had met were his enemies. Not one had attempted to hide him, or to detain his pursuers, or even to make way for him" (p. 100). Feeling that "what was going on had nothing whatever to do with his own tremendous misery, it is as if his woes did not exist" (p. 106), he finally fires straight at the mass of unconscious spectators. With a cold-blooded, brutal joy, Shevyrev feels that he has "avenged the insults, the sufferings, and the ruined lives of which he knew so much" (p. 108)—his wife, his comrades, and the forerunners of reform.

The circumstances leading to the death of Du also strike a parallel. Witnessing the death of his comrade Zhang Weijun, Du is also tormented by the thought that he is the loneliest being in the world. Like Shevyrev, he too thinks that the people around are his enemies: "Not only are the people around totally unrelated to him, they are his enemies" (p. 189). As in Shevyrev's case, reckoning that "all these people need to be destroyed before him" because of their intransigence, antagonism and support of the oppressors, Du finds his mission in "avenging and dying for the numerous oppressed and suffering"[46] (p. 230)—his mother, his cousin, and his fellow revolutionaries.

One hardly need elaborate on the pronounced typological affinities between the two heroes, in their acts, their conception of the world and of life at large, their emotional life and human relationships, their ultimate fate and the circumstances leading to it. Both stories revolve round the mental state of the one single protagonist, and as such follow a similar pattern of development. Moreover, both works use dreams as a thematic device: Shevyrev's dream about his victimized wife inflames him with hate and remorse, and his dream about the desperate ironmonger challenges him to take revenge. Du's dream about his cousin reminds him of his deep sorrows, and his dream about Zhang Weiqun's widow impels him to take immediate action. In both cases, the hero's final attempt is abortive.

One can safely talk then of Artzybashev's Shevyrev as a prototype of Ba Jin's Du Daxin, even if Du lacks the cynicism towards human life of Shevyrev, who takes the position that everything in life is nothing but lies. Du, on the other hand, is obsessed with the central problem of whether to love or not to love (he is drained of his love towards Li Jingshu by his concern for duty), destroy or not destroy. His conflicts here remind us of those between love and responsibility in Leopald Kampf's *On the Eve*. In his reasoning and inner contradictions, Du epitomizes the intellectual predicament of his age, but he is unusual in being a "Hamlet" who opts for the extreme.

[46] See n. 42 on Ba Jin's borrowing.

On a more personal level, the dilemma of Du Daxin was an extension of that of Ba Jin. He writes of his spiritual malady at the time of writing *Destruction*:

> I am searching for a bright future, for human love, for my ideal hero. But now my love has been betrayed, my ideals vanquished. Only darkness and solitariness remains. Accustomed to being insulted by others, and having witnessed too many human tragedies, I have had enough of all this, though it cannot ruin my heart. . . .[47]

This flicker of life was to lead him to write *Xinsheng* (New Life), a continuation of *Destruction*.[48]

b. New Life *and* The Pale Horse

New Life (1931) is the diary of Li Leng, who embodies the spirit of universal love in *Destruction*. Laid low by the horrifying death of Du Daxin, he has lost his hope for human society. The diary is about his dejection, despair and his road to ultimate spiritual salvation.

To Li Leng, human society, the habitat of the selfish, ignorant and repellent, is now meaningless and chaotic, and beyond redemption. He goes a step further than the nihilistic Du Daxin, envisaging destruction as the ultimate end, and faces human society with a contemptuous indifference: "No one can say that I have never lived, and no one can deny my right to live. I live for myself, other people have nothing to do with me, nor I with them" (p. 9). For him, "I" with a bold capital is the be all and end all of things. The world will cease to exist with his destruction.

He is akin to Dostoevsky's underground man when he says: "I feel everything is strange to me . . . I am traversing alone the desert of the human heart" (p. 24). He says he is not the madman

---

[47] Ba Jin, "Wode xin", pp. 3–4.

[48] Ba Jin wrote that he blamed the Chinese people for their ignorance in the first twenty-two chapters of *Destruction*, but since they are not devoid of hope, and "to be fair to the Chinese masses, I left a ray of hope in Chapter 22, saying that their victory comes four years later. I have also laid the foundation of my trilogy: *New Life* and *Liming* (Dawn). *New Life* is the diary of Li Leng, *Dawn* is the history of Li Jingshu." As n. 43, pp. 8–9. Ba Jin, however, has never come round to writing *Dawn*.

in Zarathustra's mouth, but one can hardly deny traces of the madman in his egoistic approach to life, especially in his concept of the man-god. He goes to the extreme when he extends Feuerbach's idea of "man is to man the summit of all existence", to "I am to myself the summit of all existence" (p. 19).

Ironically, however, he is but another extreme form of "Hamlet". The conflicts between reason and emotion, love and hate never for one moment quit his mind. In spite of his bold declarations, he has deep affection for his sister Jingshu and her friend Wenzhu. His admiration for his friend Mingdong, who writes with the aim of transforming society, further confirms the fact that his negation is half-hearted. The most acute irony of all is that he vehemently abjures love, but becomes precisely the captive of a love that finally transforms him. It is love for Jingshu and Wenshu, and anger at the way foreigners ride roughshod on Chinese soil, and the way his brothers and sisters are abused by them, that finally turn him into a man of action.

He is imprisoned for being a revolutionary. While waiting for his execution, inner tranquillity and peace have taken the place of contemptuous indifference in his heart:

> My heart is tranquil. I am not excited, nor have I any fears. I have come to the border of life and death with calmness of heart. I have no pity, no remorse. I am not grieved, and I have no tears. I will walk this last step with valour. I am no longer on the road of destruction. (p. 237)

Death comes as a glory to him; he goes to his execution willingly and speaks of wearing a crown of thorns (pp. 225, 235, 237).

Li Leng is a new type. Never has there been a Chinese fictional hero who embraces egoism to such a degree—"I am to myself the summit of all existence." A comparison with Ropshin's *The Pale Horse* will shed some light on this aspect of Li Leng's character.

□ *The prototype in Ropshin's George*

The Pale Horse was one of Ba Jin's favourite novels. A careful comparison shows not only that the two works have similar traits, but also that Ba Jin deliberately uses *New Life* as an antithesis to *The Pale Horse,* as the titles of the two works suggest.

There are many similarities between Ropshin's George and Ba Jin's Li Leng in the early stages of the two novels. Both are disillusioned revolutionaries who find no purpose in life. Li Leng chides his sister and friends for believing in love and compassion, and George admits that he is unlikely to believe in Christ, in socialism, or in anything at all. Both are lone wolves governed by their selfish desires, who have nothing in common with the people around them:

> George—
> I rise. The people are bustling in the square under my window like black ants, each intent on his personal cares, on petty everyday interests. I despise them. (p. 105)
> Li Leng—
> I hate to go out. I detest those despicable, sly faces that fill the streets. Men are like pigs who only crave for food: they eat blindly, eat all day long, eat to pass the time. (p. 37)

Finding the world around them repulsive, both retreat into themselves and view human life with complete cynicism. Both become extreme rationalists, believing that their law is the law. At this juncture, their concerns and reasoning are almost identical. George is overcome by severe egoism: "What God could I pray to not to abandon me? To whom could I appeal for help and protection? I am alone. But since there is no other one to protect me, I must protect myself. Since I have no God, I shall be my own God!" (p. 41) His words immediately remind us of Li Leng's: "I am to myself the summit of existence."

George thus accepts Nietzsche's superman; and he is in line with Dostoevsky's "underground man" in that he sees everything with rancour. His entire reasoning recalls Feuerbach's "Homo homini deus". As a terrorist what worries George at the early stage of the novel is not destruction. He is concerned with the problem of the right to life and death. Why should he kill Governor X or Y? He questions, and knows no answer. Later, he conceives a personal hatred for the Governor. Overpowered by jealousy and vengeance, he sets out to assassinate him. He also challenges and kills his friend

Elena's husband because he cannot endure not having the exclusive possession of his wife. We are thus given insights into his moral chaos as the story develops. Killing or destruction is not governed by a higher motive, but by a desire to satisfy his ego. In the end it becomes perfectly clear to George that he cares nothing either for any individual or for the world at large: "I am on the border of life and death, words about sin mean nothing to me. I may say about myself: 'I looked up and saw the pale horse and the rider whose name is Death.' Whenever that horse stamps its feet there the grass withers; and where the grass withers there is no life and consequently no law; for Death recognises no law." (p. 70) To this utterly cynical person, life is but a dull puppet show. Destruction becomes desirable in itself. One autumn day, he says his last word: "My revolver is with me" (p. 180) and kills himself.

George's development is therefore a downhill movement—from a will to live to utter despair and desolation, from cold reasoning to moral chaos. He finally dies a desperate egoist. By contrast, Li Leng's path is an upward struggle. All is vanity and a lie to him in the early chapters of the novel. He toys with the idea of ultimate destruction. In invoking "I" as the centre of existence, underscoring his contempt for human society, the early Li Leng is more or less in the same position as George finds himself in towards the end of The Pale Horse. Both have reached "the border of life and death", a phrase which both novelists employ. After this, George continues downhill to destruction, while Li Leng is redeemed through love. Both meet death at the end of the novel, and refer to it in the same words, as the "crown of thorns". But for George, it is only a crown of death; for Li Leng, it is a crown of glory. Though both greet death voluntarily and with calmness, George's attitude remains one of cold indifference and emptiness, the consequence of hopelessness. The calmness of Li Leng, on the other hand, is an expression of love and magnanimity, knowing that his life is at one with many other lives striving for the well-being of the human race.

As the two novels develop, New Life unmistakably becomes the antithesis to The Pale Horse. The postscript that Ba Jin gives to his novel is a direct challenge to Ropshin's motto at the beginning of his work. Both are quotations from the Bible:

Ba Jin's Postscript:

"A kernel of wheat falls to the ground and dies, it remains only a single seed. But if it dies, it provides many seeds." —*John* XII 24 (p. 239)

Ropshin's Mottos:

". . . and behold the pale horse; and his name that sat on him was Death." —*Revelation* VI 8

"But he that hateth his brother is in darkness, and walketh in darkness, and knoweth not whither he goeth, because darkness hath blinded his eyes." —*I John* II 11 (p. 1)

In using the diary form to describe the tormented path of his revolutionary hero, and in dressing him in a cloak of extreme egoism, Ba Jin is undisguisedly influenced by Ropshin's *The Pale Horse*, which, among other things, is also a story in diary form. However, *New Life* is not a Chinese version of *The Pale Horse*. It is meticulously constructed, as we have seen, as an antithesis to Ropshin's novel. Why take such pains? The answer lies in Ba Jin's effort to paint a full picture, in his own view, of how the "George-type" of hero should and would develop in the Chinese context. This type of young man had already taken flesh in China in the 1920s. As Ba Jin wrote in the preface to his second novel, *The Dead Sun* (*Siqu de taiyang*, 1930): "I am depicting the activities of a petty bourgeois intellectual during the Incident (May Thirtieth Incident, 1925). The novel delineates his blind actions, disillusionment, and his final awareness. Should the reader find my hero somewhat naïve and ridiculous, then I invite him to have second thoughts, since most petty bourgeois intellectuals are like that." Ba Jin wants to depict in *The Dead Sun*, and in fact in all his novels of this period, the life of intellectuals in a time of turbulence and transition; they are necessarily unbalanced, unsettled, more often given to reflecting upon their doubts and conflicts than to facing their problems with the decisive and undivided will they need for their purpose. They are tragic in the absolute sincerity of their divided minds. When he set out to depict these intellectuals, it was almost inevitable that he would touch upon the traits of character of the "George-type", since *The Pale Horse* was one of his favourite novels. But Ba Jin's divergences from *The Pale Horse* are at least as telling as his borrowings. In Li Leng's transformation we see the hopeful prophecy of a new life—the vision of a new and regenerated China rising above the sad tale of shattered lives and cruel destinies.

c. The Trilogy of Love *and* Rudin

If the protagonists of *Destruction* and *New Life* are essentially revolutionary "Hamlets" troubled by their abstract vision of life, those of *The Trilogy of Love*—*Wu* (Fog, 1931), *Yu* (Rain, 1932) and *Dian* (Lightning, 1932)—are people more concerned with existence, both their own and other people's. In Ba Jin's own words: "the *Trilogy* is about characters, not love. . . . Turgenev is said to have used the love theme to blind the eyes of the Russian censors, and his six novels are still somewhat erroneously considered love novels. I may have been influenced by him, I may have been influenced by others. I observe my characters, and depict them through love."[49] Indeed, the presence of Turgenev is keenly felt in the first two parts of the *Trilogy*. Ba Jin's morally sensitive but wavering intellectual types have strong antecedents in the celebrated "Turgenevan" superfluous man, in particular Rudin. This can be seen particularly in two of them—Zhou Rushui and Wu Renmin, each dominant in separate parts of the *Trilogy*.

☐ *Zhou Rushui, Rudin and Lavretsky*

In *Fog*, the first part of the *Trilogy*, the capriciousness and failure of the protagonist, Zhou Rushui, are delineated. After seven years' studies in Japan, leading a cosmopolitan life, Zhou comes home to China with the dream of "returning to the countryside". He believes that therein lies the future of the country: "every enlightened person should leave the city, to work in the country—to run farms, schools, cooperatives, and all other kinds of public and productive organizations. They should teach and help the peasants" (p. 39). In the idyllic tranquillity of the seaside resort he is drawn into a romance with Zhang Ruolan—the sensitive, poetic and intelligent heroine, who combines a disarming candour with strong personality. All would be ideal were it not for Zhou's hesitations.

It is revealed that Zhou is already married with a son. More than

[49] As n. 8, p. 316. Ba Jin also drew attention to the fact that many of the characters in the novel have real-life models, many from no other than his own friends. As n. 20, pp. 266–273.

ten years before, he was given a wife under parental authority. Later, imbued with the May Fourth spirit, he managed to persuade his father to allow him to enter university, and then to study in Japan. The love affair with Ruolan revives in Zhou the sad memory of his unhappy marriage. Should he abandon his wife at home, a woman he has never loved, and who is now a burden to him? This would sever his ties with his family. Can he bear to be called an unfilial son? And endure the curse of society? Love or duty—that is the question. His father's plea for his immediate return to take up a position in the government further complicates the matter. This would mean an end to his ideal of "returning to the countryside".

Ruolan learns of Zhou's dilemma, and decides to resolve the deadlock. She invites Zhou to a meeting in the shrubbery near their guest house. Described as having the courage of the "Slavonic women", she reveals her love and offers her hand: "I can give up everything for you, I hope you will be a useful man" (p. 94). To her bitter disappointment, Zhou recoils from her proposal: "I am not worthy. I am a coward . . . I regret having met you. You and I are not destined to live together. I hope you will forget me later. Our union is entirely impossible. I must go home. There's where my duty lies" (pp. 96–97). But where is home? He learns later that his wife died two years earlier. Ironically his father urges him to marry somebody he loves.

On a personal level, the failure of Zhou Rushui is unmistakably due to his inability to dedicate himself to someone or something completely. We learn that he joined some socialist societies, but never participated in their activities; he translates, but is never able to finish the work. He talks of his principle of returning to the countryside, but draws back before realization is even in prospect. In his half-heartedness, Zhou discovers himself to be a superfluous character, in the manner of Turgenev's Rudin.

The affinities of both characters lie as much in their general sense of unfulfilment as in their relationship with the heroine. Just as Rudin feels his superfluousness: "at thirty-five, still to be trying to set about doing something" (Penguin Classics, p. 144), Zhou also reflects as he approaches his thirties: "I don't want to enter the civil service; to return to the countryside, this is quite improbable if I go home; I have nothing to do . . ." (p. 46). Their greatest revelation of their weakness however, is in the test of love. The heroines in both cases, Natalya and Ruolan, are pure and fresh, possessing emotional spontaneity. Both courageously take the initiative and offer their love, but bitterly discover the pusillanimity of the hero. When meeting for the first time, in the sombre environment of the Avdyukhin pond, Natalya expects Rudin to act, and break away from the possessive spell of her mother Darya Lasunsky. Rudin's reply is worth quoting in full:

> Submit to fate ... There's nothing else for it. I know only too well how bitter, how difficult, how unendurable it can be. But judge for yourself, Natalya Alexeyevna, I'm a poor man ... true, I could work; but even if I were rich, would you be in a condition to endure the violent rupture with your family and your mother's anger? ... No, Natalya Alexeyevna, it's not to be contemplated. Evidently you and I are not destined to live together and the happiness of which I dreamed is not for me! (p. 127)

Here, we see Rudin totally "unmanned", submitting to his own weakness of will, to the family and social forces at work. He is stripped of his former grandeur and finally leaves "with a sense of shame". Ba Jin clearly has this episode in mind when he depicts his own climactic scene in *Fog*. Ruolan's freshness, her invitation to the hero, her willingness to sacrifice everything she possesses, are all reminiscent of Natalya. (Ruolan, as we remember, is described as having the courage of "Slavonic women".) Zhou's answers: "I am a coward", and "we are not destined to live together" echo those of Rudin. The failure of both is a failure of character. Lacking the courage to commit themselves, both seek refuge in a notional "duty" rather than in action.

In general terms, Zhou's tragedy is also akin to that of Lavretsky in Turgenev's *Home of the Gentry*—the Russian intellectual comes home, trying to break away from the West that has become contaminated and turning to the traditional purity of Russia; and he is doomed to be frustrated. His cosmopolitan experience, which he cannot undo, makes him unfit for the task of reaching the heart of Russia. As Irving Howe puts it, the tragedy of *Home of the Gentry* is "the tragedy of a politics of homelessness and homesickness".[50]

---

[50] Howe, *Politics and the Novel*, p. 128.

The same can be said of Zhou Rushui's tragedy. He is tired of cosmopolitan living in Japan, and returns home with a dream of tilling the land.[51] But what is home for him? It is a home characterized by autocratic authority, outmoded convention, widespread corruption, a home that holds intellectualism in contempt, and regards education as only a means to officialdom. Zhou's yearning for free love and the development of individuality, the result of his foreign education, makes him unfitted for this environment, which demands conformity and submission. On the other hand, when he makes contact with the outside world, symbolized in his love affair with Ruolan, he is also doomed to be frustrated.

□ *Wu Renmin and Rudin*

Like Zhou Rushui, Wu Renmin in *Rain* is also oppressed by the sense of frustration and loneliness engendered by the intolerably humdrum and enervating society around him. Contrary to the diffidence and passivity of the "bucolic" Zhou however, Wu is impulsive, and governed by passionate emotions. But common to both is their sense of loneliness and desolation. Ba Jin describes Wu thus:

> Wu Renmin in *Fog* is buried in his personal sadness. I use the word sadness because his afflictions are slow, fractional, and personal. Before the shock he experiences [the death of his sweetheart, his wife and his best friend], Wu's commonplace existence seldom arouses our interest. Death carries off his wife, and with that his love. . . . Thereupon his passion accumulates, and he loses his sense of balance. Friends cannot understand him, and he lacks a strong faith as his guide. . . . He gropes,

---

[51] In the early 1920s in China, the Japanese utopian social movement, the *atarashiki mura* (new village), based on the philosophy of mutual assistance and humanitarianism espoused by Kropotkin, Tolstoy and certain idealistic socialists, caught the fancy of some intellectuals, amongst them Cai Yuanpei, Chen Duxiu, and the Zhou brothers. During a trip to Japan in 1919, Zhou Zuoren visited New Village. So impressed was he by the Japanese experiment that upon returning he wrote several articles propagating the movement. Most notable among these is "Xincun de jingshen", in *XQN*, 7.2 (1920.2). For the historical existence of this village/rural community movement in China, see Chow Tse-ts'ung, *The May Fourth Movement*, p. 425, nn. 54, 55.

but ends up in a cul-de-sac. He desires action and warmth, but is only steeped in loneliness, tormented by the idea of death. And loneliness is something more awful than death. Loneliness cannot drain away his passion, it only adds fuel to the fire. His passion grows, and becomes a volcano. When this volcano erupts, Wu will meet with total destruction.[52]

Wu opts to evade his mental torments through company. With a discerning eye and an articulate tongue, he is able to compel others to admit their weaknesses. Eloquent and convincing though he is, what does he stand for? The answer is necessarily vague. As a man of ideas, he tries to demonstrate the importance of believing in ideas. Commitment and dedication are words which flow expressively out of his mouth. He soliloquizes on the importance of a meaningful life, on laying down his life for the ideal: "My melancholy and impetuousness may estrange me from some comrades; but in them a new life is fermenting. . . . My old habits may be difficult to shake off, and I am not sure whether I will attain a new life, but I will do my utmost to struggle for one. If ever I fail, I am prepared to meet complete destruction . . ." (p. 132). This raises the whole question of the Chinese intellectuals' duty to devote themselves to the future welfare of their country, a task that demands the subordination of the ego to some higher cause. Wu Renmin is able to proclaim with force in the early part of the novel: "Suffering is our strength, suffering is our pride" (p. 164). But the moment of truth comes when he descends from this pedestal, and retreats into a self that he understands all too well. His weakness as a person is unveiled. We are given insights into his inconsistencies. He easily gives way to his passions. For example, he may have been attacking scathingly the evil of prostitution; but in his utter loneliness, he feels the urge to go out and "chase after the wild chickens" (prostitutes). From this point on, we witness the downward slide of Wu, his "loud-mouthedness", and his growing apathy. He "falls into the love-net" of Hong Zhijun, and reneges little by little on the values he had passionately championed earlier. Injustice, China's destiny and a new life, bother him no more. Wine, roses and women swiftly take

[52] As n. 8, pp. 314–315. Wu Renmin appears as a supporting character in *Fog* and goes on to become the protagonist of *Rain*.

the place of suffering as his strength and pride. In short, he becomes a selfish person, and he loses his former eloquence. His unheroism reaches its climax when he asks Fang to lend him some money for his honeymoon. Fang is a fellow comrade who he knows administers a sum set aside to finance revolutionary causes.

In Wu Renmin's gradual downfall is epitomized the plight of many an unfulfilled hero. Like Rudin, the Russian hero whom he positively identifies with, Wu remains until he sinks into ignominy, a man of ideas and no action. While agreeing with friends who compare his impracticality and "loud-mouthedness" to Nekrasov's Sasha, the Russian superfluous hero who argues and boasts much, but achieves little, Wu sees himself as closer to Rudin:

> ...Yes, I am always lonely. I am impetuous and passionate. I boast a lot and accomplish little. I am like Rudin...Yes, I feel like Rudin. I can never compromise and understand people. I try in vain to befriend everybody, hoping that they will understand me. Oh! how I'd like to smash this world to pieces with my fist. (pp. 156–157)

In another instance, he sighs in melancholy:

> Yes, I am all alone, a wandering man. Some friends call me Rudin. I am like him, drifting from one place to another with my good intentions, derided and misunderstood. (pp. 196–197)

In his proud abrasive manner, his moral sensitivity, his vulnerability, and above all, his eloquence and enthusiasm, Wu is unmistakably Rudin in a Chinese context. The final vindication of Rudin by his life-long friend Lezhnev: "He has enthusiasm; and that, believe me—for I speak as a phlegmatic man—is a most precious quality in our time. We have all become intolerably rational, indifferent and effete; we have gone to sleep, we have grown old, and we should be grateful to anyone who rouses us and warms us, if only for a moment" (p. 157) can also be applied to Wu Renmin, who speaks with religious fervour of man's service to humanity, to his own country, or to the liberation of his people, and whose words enter into the moral consciousness of his contemporaries. But unlike Rudin, who dies an unfulfilled superfluous man, we see that towards the end of *Rain*, Ba Jin has prepared the way for his protagonist to depart from his unheroism: "Wu Renmin stands on the verge of destruction. By simply raising his foot, he will fall into the bottomless abyss. Fortunately faith comes to his rescue. When his tears are dried up, he will become a new man."[53] He in fact becomes a dedicated revolutionary in *Lightning*, the third part of the *Trilogy*.

Together Zhou Rushui and Wu Renmin combine to make a perfect Chinese version of Rudin. Zhou, while lacking Rudin's silver tongue and enthusiasm, shares his central paradox—his dedication to principles and causes, but failure to commit himself to one thing or one person. Like Rudin he is totally unmanned by the natural spontaneity of the heroine. In turn, Wu Renmin's belief in ideas, coupled with his characteristic inconsistencies, not to mention his personal identification with Rudin, all remind us of the Russian hero. These typological affinities reveal Ba Jin's conscious borrowing and adaptation of the celebrated Russian archetype in depicting a parallel phenomenon in China, though the specific sorrows of his heroes and their way of dealing with their problems remain Chinese.

Marking the above parallels, it is pertinent to point out that just as Rudin is an arch-example of the Russian "liberal predicament" (in the words of Isaiah Berlin), Ba Jin's superfluous heroes likewise symbolize the tragedy of Chinese liberalism in general. Take the case of Zhou Rushui. Born twenty years earlier, he would have been a filial son, obediently married and dutifully bringing up his family. Had he gone abroad, he would most probably have come home to be an enlightened "parent official" (Chinese conception of a district magistrate), the pride and delight of his parents. But having imbibed the May Fourth spirit, along with a Western-oriented liberal education, and a striving for moral good, he is not prepared to serve the corrupt government, which in any case has no place for him. He is dislocated in place and time. His liberal ideals have to succumb to the call of duty, to the authority of Confucianism—filial piety and family solidarity. The crux of the whole issue—marriage without love—is the supreme emblem of Confucian authority, under which numerous love aspirations are denied, numerous ideals stifled. In trying to depict the conflicts of the May Fourth intellectuals: between intellect and feeling, action and hesitation, ideal and reality, Ba Jin finds concrete examples in the celebrated Russian superfluous hero

[53] Ibid., p. 315.

who belongs to that foreign tradition which now set the tone for the lives of Chinese intellectuals.

In short, the first fictional heroes of Ba Jin carry strong Russian overtones. Du Daxin's affinity to Shevyrev, Li Leng's sharing of George's extreme egoism, and Zhou Rushui's and Wu Renmin's superfluous existence—not to mention his Vera Figner-like revolutionary maidens—highlight Ba Jin's indebtedness to Russian literature in the early stages of his development as a novelist. The Russian "influence" either takes the form of a direct imitation, such as the modelling of Du Daxin on Shevyrev, or a variation of a Russian archetype, as in the case of Li Leng, or the simple identification with a Russian hero-type, which accounts for the influence of the Turgenevan superfluous man. The end result is that his early heroes are like Chinese intellectuals in Russian cloaks, though their overall accent is Chinese. Since the heart of these early works, as Ba Jin mentioned time and again, lies in characterization, it is pertinent for us to ask the following questions: Why did Ba Jin the "idealist" portray these estranged and unheroic types? And why did his heroes put on this Russian cloak when the world of high fashion was in Paris, London or New York? To attempt an answer, one needs to delve into the intellectual predicament of the time.

IV. The Intellectual Predicament

It is clear from the Chinese response to Russian literature that, for the 1920s intellectuals, the Russian hero held up a mirror to themselves. They showed the same blend of softness and slackness, with an infinite capacity for taking pains; and the same inspired energy in the face of seemingly insuperable obstacles. They saw in the Russian hero the paradox of the passive resister—who, though utterly defeated, persists in resisting in his own personal or small way, if only in the mind. Just as in Russia, the "superfluous man" and "revolutionary Hamlets" also became one of the "cursed questions" of many Chinese intellectuals. Many positively identified with a Russian hero, as with somebody actually drawn from life, somebody who epitomized their own sorrows and failings. The revealing remarks of the writer and journalist Cao Juren underlined the common feeling of many Chinese men of letters:

> There was a time when I considered myself a Rudin. I remembered the
> letter Rudin sent to Natalya upon leaving her: "It is my strange, almost
> comic fate that I am ready to surrender myself completely, greedily,
> utterly—and yet I can't. I will end up sacrificing myself for some
> nonsense in which I don't even believe." What a pity! Upon reflection,
> I am like that too.[54]

Nor was Cao's identification with the Russian hero an isolated
phenomenon. Guo Moruo likened himself to Nezhdanov, Turgenev's famous superfluous hero in *Virgin Soil*,[55] Gao Changhong
to Aladiev, Shevyrev's counterpart in Artzybashev's story.[56]
In the view of Zheng Zhenduo and Shen Yanbing, the "George-
type" of intellectual became prominent in China of the 1920s.

It is the situation of the 1920s in particular that gave rise to the
Chinese Rudins, Shevyrevs and Georges. To many a romantic
idealist, the May Fourth Movement heralded the advent of a new
era, in which all that was rotten would be swept away by the
whirlwind of anti-feudalism and anti-imperialism. However, the
rapid turn of events in the 1920s—the anger and frustration that
followed the May Thirtieth Massacre in 1925, the immense optimism
that was generated with the Northern Expedition in 1927, and the
sense of defeat that accompanied the persecution of radicals after
the expedition—created in many intellectuals a frantic state of mind,
and left them swaying between light and darkness, hope and despair,
unable to find their balance. Lu Xun's laconic remark in 1931 on
the Chinese men of letters, stripped of its sardonic overtones, reveals
succinctly their ingrained dilemma:

> Quick to kindle, quick to calm down, and even quick to grow decadent,
> men of letters can always find reasons and precedents from the classics
> to justify their shifts of allegiance. For instance, if they need help they
> quote Kropotkin's doctrine of mutual aid, while when they want to
> fight they use Darwin's theory of the survival of the fittest . . .[57]

---

[54] Cao Juren, *Wo yu wode shijie*, p. 320.
[55] Guo Moruo (pseud. Guo Dingtang), "*Xinshidai* xu", *Xinshidai*, p. 3.
[56] Gao Changhong, "Xiegei *Panghuang*", in *Zoudao chubanjie*, p. 34.
[57] Lu Xun, "Shanghai wenyi zhi yipie", English translation from *Selected Works
of Lu Xun* (hereafter *SW*), Vol. 3, p. 134.

Underneath their shifts of allegiance (disregarding the opportunists) was their failure to commit themselves to one doctrine or one thing, a failure engendered by their self-critical and complex minds. As one commentator wrote in 1935, the sufferings of many "petit bourgeois" intellectuals in the May Fourth period were indeed intense, but "lacking a firm commitment to revolt, and not resigned to fall behind, their attitude towards the stark reality could only be one of discontent. They were consciously vacillating, wandering and hesitating. In literature, they were only capable of depicting life that is tragic, society which is stolid, and of channelling their disgust towards the degrading social environment. This venting of grievances was the offspring of a humanitarian attitude towards life."[58] For many morally conscious intellectuals, literature seemed their only outlet. Many transposed their most naked thoughts and experiences into their literary works. Like their Russian precursors, they also saw themselves as the conscience of their age, and literature as a kind of moral and social criticism. The superfluous hero who featured in classical Russian literature thus provided them with a live model. Rudin's ineffectuality presented to them the quintessence of the conflict of the morally sensitive but physically weak in their groping for a way to commit themselves in a time of conflict and vicissitude. Shevyrev's aspirations and sufferings, his conflicts between love and hate, commitment and revenge were shared by many Chinese writers. So were the psychological malaise and the will to act of Ropshin's George (though without his revenge on society at large), as exemplified by Ba Jin's Du Daxin and Li Leng. It was against this background that Ba Jin the novelist made his literary debut in 1928.

As a child of the May Fourth Movement (when the Literary Revolution swept over Beijing and Shanghai in 1917, Ba Jin was still a thirteen year old in Chengdu), Ba Jin was understandably obsessed by the "cursed" Russian hero-types. In the conflicts of the frustrated Russian hero, he saw focussed his own problems. He wrote frankly of his own writings: "My writing synchronized with the path of my life. I am always honest with myself and with others, and this honesty landed me in conflicts, conflicts that I cannot shake

[58] Wang Fengyuan, *Zhongguo xinwenxue yundong shuping*. Quoted from Li Helin, *Jin ershinian Zhongguo wenyi shichao lun*, pp. 78–79.

off. I am totally caught up in the web of these conflicts of love and hate, thought and action, reason and emotion, ideal and reality, which overshadowed my life and works."[59] When he tried to translate these conflicts into literary writings, a generation of estranged heroes ensued. Du Daxin's belief in redemption through destruction, Li Leng's dangling between egoism and altruism, Zhou Rushui and Wu Renmin's superfluous existence, despite their Russian overtones, crystallize Ba Jin's own inner conflicts. Their undisguised typological affinities to the Russian hero spring, in simple literary terms, from Ba Jin's conscious borrowings from the available Russian sources that inspired him as an apprentice novelist. (When Ba Jin became a writer of greater stature as he matured, the Russian influence noticeably diminished though it never completely vanished.) In a broader perspective, Ba Jin may in actuality be drawing his characters from real life, given the prevalence of Chinese Rudins, Shevyrevs and Georges at the time. This is supported by Ba Jin's own statement that his characters, especially those in the *Trilogy*, are mainly modelled on his friends, and that he moulded them according to their reactions to given situations. His "Russian-flavoured" heroes, therefore, represent the culmination of his own spiritual conflicts, his orientation towards Russian literature, coupled with his depiction of the prevailingly "Russian" intellectual types of the 1920s. In these passionately depicted heroes of his, fiction and life are yoked together. (As he himself said: ". . . in my works are mingled my blood and tears. This is no lie. There is no trace of the artist in me, because I cannot see art beyond life."[60]) Their estrangement poignantly reveals not only the author's bitterness towards the established order, but above all, his frustration upon seeing youth wasting away, love thwarted, ideals denied and life wasted. All this signifies to him, on a deeper level, the common conflicts of all men. On the other hand, his beautiful and steely heroines' natural spontaneity, purity of motive and selfless dedication instil life into the otherwise rather hopeless situations of his early novels. Nevertheless, their role is largely subsidiary,

[59] Ba Jin, *"Dianyi ji daixu"*, in *Ba Jin wenji*, Vol. 7, p. 7.
[60] Ibid.

functioning as symbols of his own ideal yearning. Their typology, drawn in the main from Ba Jin's reading of the memoirs of women revolutionaries in other countries, especially those in Russia, further heightens the tragic effect of his works. The estranged intellectual heroes—embodiments of the frustrated "men of the 1920s"—are seen as even more unheroic by contrast.

In his illuminating paper on Turgenev, Isaiah Berlin wrote that "the dilemma of morally sensitive, honest, and intellectually responsible men at times of acute polarization of opinion has since his time, grown acute and world wide".[61] The Chinese situation in the 1920s supports his observation. The May Fourth Movement had awakened these young intellectuals, and planted in them the seed of the liberation of the individual, the equality of men and women, the right to a rational way of living, and the vision of a new and strong China rising from the ashes of her shattered past. Attaining their adulthood in the mid-1920s, many were first pulled into the orbit of the May Thirtieth Massacre, which to them bared the fangs of imperialism and revealed the dangers courted by all reformers. Then came the atrocities of the Nationalists after the Northern Expedition. The "sorrow of disillusion" became a real experience for many. So did it, too, for Ba Jin and his heroes. However, entwined in this hostile environment, Ba Jin was not destitute of hope. He met this environment with obstinacy, as Turgenev did half a century before, envisaging that the current of life would go on in this "turbulent stream":

> The life current moves on all the time, without a moment's rest, because it is unstoppable. Nothing can check it. Along its course, it shoots forth a variety of sprays, which contain a variety of elements such as love, hate, joy and pain. All these congregate into the main stream of the life current, moving on with a tremendous force that can wipe out mountains, heading towards a definite sea or ocean. What this sea is, and how long it would take for the life current to reach it, are questions to which nobody has a definite answer.[62]

---

[61] Berlin, *Fathers and Children*, the Romanes Lecture (Oxford, 1971). Included in *Russian Thinkers*, p. 303.
[62] Ba Jin, *Family*, pp. 1–2.

The life current moves on, but nobody knows when it will end up in its definite sea—in these prophetic words Ba Jin sums up his own predicament, the intellectual predicament of his time and the time to come with sharpness of vision, poetry, and no small degree of truth.

7 Lu Xun's Awakened Hero

I. The Lonely Reformer

> When I was young I, too, had many dreams. Most of them I later forgot, but I see nothing in this to regret. For although recalling the past may bring happiness at times it cannot but bring loneliness, and what is the point of clinging in spirit to lonely bygone days? However, my trouble is that I cannot forget completely, and these stories stem from those things which I have been unable to forget.[1]
>
> Preface to *Nahan* (Outcry), 1922

In order to attain a better understanding of Lu Xun's fictional works,[2] it is worthwhile delving into the inner world of his early life, and trying to detect how past events helped to shape his stories.[3] The importance of this intimate, poetic and often

[1] *LXQJ*, Vol. 1, p. 415. English translation in *SW*, Vol. 1, p. 33. Citations of Lu Xun's works in English, unless otherwise specified, are from *SW*. *Outcry* is a more appropriate translation for *Nahan* than *Call to Arms*.

[2] A considerable number of works on Lu Xun's fiction have been published in Chinese in the last few years. Not many of these are, however, very instructive. Hanan's article, "The Technique of Lu Hsun's Fiction", which appeared in *HJAS* in 1974, remains one of the most reliable.

[3] Zhou Xiashou's (pseud. of Zhou Zuoren) *Lu Xun xiaoshuo li de renwu* sheds much light on this aspect of Lu Xun's art. See also Leo Ou-fan Lee's psychohistorical study of Lu Xun's early life, "Genesis of a Writer: Notes on Lu Xun's Educational Experience, 1881–1909", in Merle Goldman (ed.), *MCL*.

melancholic returning to the past in the stories lies not so much in his regret and nostalgia, as in this rediscovery of the microcosm of Chinese society familiar to him, where he could exercise his acumen "not only in analysing other people, but more ruthlessly analysing my own self to the last fibre all the time".[4]

As a writer of fiction, Lu Xun's output is relatively small—twenty-five short stories in all; yet his popularity and influence have remained unsurpassed to this day. His first collection *Outcry* (1918–1922), and his second, *Wandering* (1924–1925) were written during one of the loneliest and darkest periods of his life. Reminiscing in 1932 about the period leading up to the Literary Revolution in 1917, he said: "I had seen the 1911 Revolution, the second revolution, Yuan Shikai's assumption of the imperial title, and Zhang Xun's restoration of the monarchy, and all this had made me rather cynical. I gave up hope and lost heart completely."[5] Neither the political autocracy, the economic bankruptcy, nor even the "cannibalistic morality and tradition" of Chinese society oppressed him as much as the plight of the frustrated reformer. He expressed this succinctly in the preface to *Outcry:* "If a man's proposals met with approval, that should encourage him to advance; if they met with opposition, that should make him fight back; but the real tragedy was for him to lift up his voice among the living and meet with no response, neither approval nor opposition, just as if he were stranded helpless in a boundless desert completely at a loss. That was when I became conscious of loneliness."[6]

The poignancy of his desolation was even more accentuated at the time he wrote *Wandering.* Having witnessed the dispersal of his fellow reformers who had clustered around the magazine *New Youth*, Lu Xun recounted the loss of his former "fellow feeling" which urged him to issue a call "to encourage those fighters who

---

[4]"Xie zai *Fen* de houmian", *LXQJ*, Vol. 1, p. 284. Průšek attaches much importance to the predominantly reminiscent and lyrical character of Lu Xun's short stories, referring to this tendency in his short stories as "the penetration of the epic by the lyric and the breaking up of the traditional epic forms". See his article, "Lu Hsun's 'Huai Chiu', a Precursor of Modern Chinese Literature", *HJAS*, 24 (1969), p. 174.

[5]*SW*, Vol. 3, p. 200.

[6]*SW*, Vol. 1, p. 36.

are galloping on in loneliness, so that they do not lose heart".[7] China, he observed in 1922, had "no flowers, no poetry, no light, no warmth, no interests, not even any curiosity".[8] Tormented by this gnawing loneliness and lethargy, Lu Xun in his stories depicted with unmitigated sadness the fate befalling so many solitary reformers—an intellectually honest and morally sensitive hero, groping for a brighter future, was caught in the web of a hostile environment, purged of his ideals, and finally made to compromise his principles. Between this awakened intellectual of Lu Xun, and his counterparts in the Russian short stories that Lu Xun translated into Chinese there are some striking similiarities.

In his investigation of Lu Xun's literary relationship, mainly with the works of Russian writers, Patrick Hanan demonstrates that in choosing an artistic tradition with which to work, Lu Xun was drawn "primarily to Gogol, Sienkiewicz and Sōseki, with their range of ironic techniques, and only secondarily to Andreyev and literary modernism".[9] Hanan argues convincingly that Lu Xun's experimentation with the ironic mode represents something quite original, and the study of literary relations provides little more than a starting point for studying the technique of his fiction. It is indeed a delicate task to study foreign influences on Lu Xun, especially when the author himself stated that as his skill matured, he gradually "escaped from the influence of foreign writers in his later stories".[10] The emphasis of the present undertaking is to see how the typology of Lu Xun's solitary hero, a major preoccupation of his "intellectual" stories, was inspired by, or adapted from certain images or conventions which are embedded in Russian literature, and to study what shape literary transformations take in a writer of Lu Xun's stature.

I will begin with an examination of Lu Xun's literary attitude in

---

[7] Ibid., p. 38. In 1932, Lu Xun recounts his desolation in this period: "Later the *New Youth* group broke up. Some of its members rose to high positions, some went into retirement, some moved forward. And I, after seeing this transformation of my comrades of the united front, was left with the label 'author' and went on pacing up and down in the desert." *SW*, Vol. 3, p. 201.

[8] *LXQJ*, Vol. 1, p. 382.

[9] As n. 2, p. 75.

[10] *LXQJ*, Vol. 6, p. 239.

the *Outcry* and *Wandering* period, in relation to his response to Russian literature.

II. Response to Russian Literature

> Lu Xun's closeness to us lies in his personal characteristics as a humanitarian writer. It is fair to say that humanitarianism in nineteenth century Russian literature originated from "The Overcoat" by Gogol, a short story depicting the Russian "little man." The distinctive quality of Lu Xun's humanitarianism is exemplified in his "The True Story of A Q", a story depicting the Chinese "little man"; Lu Xun's closeness to us Russian readers is further evidenced in that, like our classical writers, he is a critical realist, that is to say, one who exposes and scourges old social conventions and the forces that oppress people and curtail the individuality of the "little man."[11]
>
>   Fadeyev, 1949

Any study of Lu Xun's relationship with Russian literature has to start, as Fadeyev's tribute indicates, with the general humanitarian appeal in the Russian convention that captured the attention of Lu Xun, notably the depiction of the underdog and the unheroic, and a concern for literature as an instrument for social reform. Writing in 1920, Lu Xun explained how, failing to find works in the Chinese heritage that would transform the national spirit,[12] he extended his search to foreign literature. He had read many books by "writers from Russia, Poland, and the Balkan States..." and absorbed the monitory and insurgent content of these works.[13] Russian literature, as Lu Xun pointed out years later, acted as an impetus, and a form of solace to many May Fourth men of letters, who were conscious of being oppressed: "from it we can see the kindly soul of the oppressed, their sufferings and struggles. Hope blazed up in our hearts when we read the works of the forties, and sorrow flooded

---

[11] Fajieyefu (Fadeyev), "Guanyu Lu Xun—jinian Lu Xun shishi shisan zhou-nian", *WYB*, 3 (1949.10), p. 4.

[12] Lu Xun, for example, refers to literature of the past as one of concealment and deceit. See his "Lun zhengleyan kan" (1925), *LXQJ*, Vol. 1, p. 240.

[13] *SW*, Vol. 3, p. 262. See Hanan's study of Lu Xun's literary relationship with these countries, as n. 2.

our souls when we read those of the sixties. . . ."[14]

Lu Xun's concern for the plight of the little man and the down-trodden in Russian literature is further evidenced in his translations and testimonies. Zhou Zuoren mentioned that in his student days in Japan (1902–1909), Lu Xun liked the works of Garshin, Korolenko, and above all, Gogol and Andreyev. In particular, Gogol's "Diary of a Madman", "How Ivan Ivanovich Quarrelled with Ivan Nikoforvich", and his comedy *The Inspector* impressed Lu Xun.[15] This is a valuable piece of information. As there is no dearth of studies on Lu Xun's relationship with Gogol,[16] suffice it to say here that Gogol's main appeal for Lu Xun lies in his comic vision—his celebrated device of "tears through laughter", and his ability to satirize. Lu Xun stated as early as 1909 that Gogol "revitalized his countrymen with his invisible tears".[17] The appeal of Garshin and Korolenko is understandably their benign attitude towards humanity, and their faith in a better future. Garshin's "Four Days", which Lu Xun translated in 1909,[18] expresses a detestation of the horrors of war; it depicts with sympathy and psychological insight the suffering of the helpless hero, a wounded soldier who

[14] "Zhu ZhongE wenzi zhi jiao", *SW*, Vol. 3, p. 210, translated under the title "The Ties between Chinese and Russian Literature". Lu Xun did not read Russian. Most of his translations of Russian literary works were rendered from German and Japanese translations. For Lu Xun's early educational experience, see Lee, as n. 3.

[15] Zhou Zuoren, "Guangyu Lu Xun zhier", in *Yuzhou feng*, 30 (1936.12), pp. 305–306. Zhou's testimony remains to date the most useful for understanding the early Lu Xun, as the brothers shared practically the same views on literature and worked very closely together until their relations cooled off in 1923.

[16] Hanan argued that Lu Xun was primarily drawn to the ironic technique of Gogol. Fokkema attributed Lu Xun's use of the underdog as the spokesman of truth to the influence of Gogol, see Fokkema, "Lu Xun: The Impact of Russian Literature", in Goldman (ed.), *MCL*. I would argue that it is the celebrated Gogolian technique of the "poshlost" that Lu Xun is most attracted to. See "Lu Xun yu Eluosi wenxue", *Dousou*, 22 (1977.7), pp. 1–13.

[17] *LXQJ*, Vol. 1, p. 64.

[18] *LXQJ* (1938), Vol. 11, pp. 215–231. Lu Xun also translated "A Very Short Tale" by Garshin, collected in *Lu Xun yiwenji*, Vol. 10. This translation first appeared in *Funü zazhi*, 1922.2. V. Garshin (1855–1888), Russian writer of stories. Obsessed by the evil and suffering of the world and consumed by pity, he wrote a few fine stories, often allegorical, before melancholy drove him to suicide. Particularly remarkable are "Chetyre Dyna" (Four Days, 1877) and "Krasnyy tsvetok" (Red Flower, 1883).

remained four days on the battlefield unable to move, lying next to the putrefying corpse of a dead Turk, his supposed enemy. His "Red Flower", another story that Lu Xun loved, is about a madman in an asylum who sees it as his mission to root out the evils of society—the prevalence of sin and wickedness, the oppression of the weak by the strong—and to restore his fellows to a state of purity and innocence.[19] This deep concern for the unfortunate has prompted Mirsky to call Garshin "the 'genius' for pity and compassion".[20] Sympathy and faith in human goodness permeated Korolenko's fundamentally optimistic world. His story "Makar's Dream", a favourite of Lu Xun,[21] deals with an old Yakut who is freezing to death and dreams of disputing in Heaven with the Lord about the hardships and injustices of earthly existence. Korolenko holds that man is good by nature, only the evil conditions created by despotism and the brutal selfishness of capitalism have made him what he is—a poor, helpless, absurd, pitiful and irritating creature. Lu Xun's concern for Russian humanitarianism is further embodied in his appreciation of Andreyev's *Red Laugh*, a novel about the horrors of war and the bestiality in men which allows them to wage war, and his *The Seven Who Were Hanged*, a novel which protests vehemently against the inhumanity of capital punishment.

While Lu Xun's regard for Russian humanitarianism persisted, it is important to point out that his emphasis in the 1920s shifted from the Russian underdog to the battered intellectual hero, as his

[19] Zhou Zuoren refers to the similarity between Garshin's "Red Flower" and Lu Xun's "Changmingdeng" (The Lamp That Was Kept Alight) in *Lu Xun xiaoshuo li de renwu*, p. 179. Hanan, however maintains that the similarity is confined to a single thematic device. Although Lu Xun may have learned much from Garshin's formal technique, the influence is not apparent in this particular story. As n. 2, pp. 72–73.

[20] Mirsky, *A History of Russian Literature*, p. 335.

[21] See Zhou Zuoren, as n. 15. "Makar's Dream" was translated by Zhou and published in *XQN*, 1920.10.1. Vladimir G. Korolenko (1853–1921), Russian short story writer. Of mixed Ukrainian and Polish origin he was educated in St. Petersburg and Moscow, and known for his populist sympathies. His stories are memorable for their profound humanity and affectionate humour. Apart from "Son Makara" (Makar's Dream, 1885) and other stories, Korolenko's finest work is his unfinished autobiography *Istoriya moyego sovremennika* (The Story of My Contemporary, 1909–1922).

translations of the period testify. Permeating these translations—
"Into the Dark Distance" and "The Book" by Andreyev, "The
Doctor" and "Shevyrev" by Artzybashev, and Chirikov's "Provincial
Town"[22]—is the theme of the frustrated intellectual hero, who
finds himself misunderstood, tormented, isolated and even hounded
to death in his struggle to reform society.

In the epilogue to his translation of Andreyev's "Into the Dark
Distance", Lu Xun declared that in many of Andreyev's short stories
and plays is depicted "the boredom and gloom of the Russians
towards the end of the nineteenth century".[23] This could be taken
to apply as much to all the Russian works he translated, as to
Andreyev's works in particular. All the stories of Andreyev that
Lu Xun rendered into Chinese interestingly dwell on the theme of
the failure to communicate, and all have intellectuals as their
protagonists. Though a lapse of twelve years divides Lu Xun's first
translations of "The Lie" and "The Silence" (1909), and "Into the
Dark Distance" and "The Book" (1921),[24] the close proximity of
the theme of these stories underlines his concern for the intellectual
typology in Andreyev's works. "Silence" delineates the punishment
of the penitent priest, whose pride prevents him from communicating
with his daughter, and subsequently causes her suicide. "Into the
Dark Distance" depicts a family whose son, Nikolai, presumably
rebelling against the restricted life of the older generation, leaves
home for some mysterious other existence. His unexplained return
home seven years later brings no joy to the family and they are
oppressed by his presence. The alienated existence of the awakened
intellectual, felt as a threat by the secure conventional world, is
brought to the fore when Nikolai returns at the end of the story
to "the dark menacing distance from which he came". Human
deception is the theme of "The Lie", expressed in the student's

[22] *LXQJ* (1938), Vol. 11, pp. 277–301. Little is known of Eugene Chirikov
(1864–1937), except that he was of noble descent, and the author of social plays
and light, sentimental novels about youth. He emigrated after 1917 and died in
exile in Prague. The story "Shenghui" (Provincial Town) has no English translation.
Lu Xun presumably rendered it from the German.

[23] *LXQJ* (1938), Vol. 11, p. 259. This is not a translation of Andreyev's "In
Fog", as Hanan mistakenly asserted in his study.

[24] All these translations are contained in Vol. 11 of *LXQJ* (1938). Lu Xun also
began, but never completed, a translation of *Red Laugh*. See *LXQJ*, Vol. 7, p. 123.

inability to tell whether the girl he loves is lying when she says she loves him. The student kills the girl, only to realize that he has "immortalized the lie". "The Book" portrays the tragic fate of a dying writer, who consumes all his energy in the completion of his novel *For the Unfortunate*. All he receives in return is the protest of the printing workers, the cynicism of the supposed "unfortunates" whom he is championing. Lu Xun was deeply struck by the stark reality and cynicism of the story, commenting that it is "seemingly as funny as the gloomy colour of lead".[25]

The plight of the solitary reformer and his lack of communication with a hostile world figure even more explicitly in Artzybashev's "The Doctor" and "Shevyrev", both translated by Lu Xun in 1921. "The Doctor" describes the Czar's pogrom of the Jews at the turn of the century. Caught up in the conflict between duty and hate—should he cure the merciless commissioner of police or not?—scenes of the atrocities for which the Commissioner was responsible flare up in the doctor's mind, and he gallantly defies the police, risking his own life. Lu Xun commented: "this story lucidly portrays [the author's] resistance to the principle of non-resistance, and the conflicts between love and hate. The author rejects the principle of non-resistance because hate is necessary to human nature, and this hate is rooted in a greater love."[26] Opposition to the principle of non-resistance is taken to an extreme by Shevyrev in a story of the same title. Shevyrev's life can be epitomized in the word "resistance"—from resisting despotism and reforming society, to taking revenge on human society in his utter disillusionment. Lu Xun's response to the story is worth noting. While admiring Shevyrev's endeavour "to die for the common cause", and sympathizing with his plight in being practically persecuted to death, Lu Xun took issue with the nihilistic revenge of Shevyrev, who "took revenge on everybody, destroyed everything".[27]

Chirikov's "Provincial Town" differs from the blandness of Artzybashev's stories, and lacks the chilliness of Andreyev's tone.

---

[25] *LXQJ*, Vol. 10, p. 187. The irony of this remark can be understood in the light of the fact that Lu Xun's major preoccupation at the time was the torment of the awakened reformer caused by the ignorant and unsympathetic masses.

[26] Ibid., pp. 176–177.

[27] *LXQJ*, Vol. 3, p. 357.

The theme of the solitary revolutionary is filtered through the lyrical reminiscences of the I-hero, who returns to his native place after many years of absence. His sense of superfluousness is highlighted by his realization that the good old world is lost, while the present situation is still oppressive. Upon seeing an old acquaintance selling out his former principles, and feeling his inability to render any help, the I-hero leaves full of a sense of uncertainty and helplessness.

It could be safely deduced at this juncture, that the appeal these works hold for Lu Xun, given their thematic consistency, coupled with his own testimony, was principally thematic—the typology of the intellectual hero in his various manifestations. It is revealing to see that in Lu Xun's own stories of this period, he deals with a strikingly similar phenomenon—the plight of the awakened intellectual. Certain thematic and typological affinities can be discovered between his own works and those of his Russian precursors.

III. The Awakened Intellectual

Passer-by: ". . . I must go on. If I go back, there's not a place without celebrities, not a place without landlords, not a place without expulsion and cages, not a place without sham smiles and hypocritical tears. I hate them. I am not going back."[28]

"The Passer-by" in *Wild Grass*

And forward trudges the passer-by, with his feet gashed and spirit drained, knowing neither repose nor destination.

Such is the fate awaiting Lu Xun's awakened intellectual hero. Having appointed himself to work for the betterment of his fellows, his hero has no other option but to soldier on, burdened with his never-ending frustration, or to relapse into passive despair.

Before actually delineating the typology of Lu Xun's awakened intellectual, let us examine the implications of a talk he gave at the Beiping Women's Normal College on December 26, 1923, which is a revealing guide to his fiction of the period. This talk, entitled "Nala zouhou zenyang" (What Happens After Nora Leaves Home?) takes over where Ibsen leaves off in *A Doll's House*. Assuming that Nora

[28] *Wild Grass*, in *SW*, Vol. 1, p. 338.

has not been starved to death, Lu Xun suggests that only two alternatives lie ahead of her: to go to the bad or return to her husband. Lu Xun compares Nora's fate to that of a caged bird: "Of course there is no freedom in the cage, but if it leaves the cage there are hawks, cats, and other hazards outside; while if imprisonment has atrophied its wings, or if it has forgotten how to fly, there certainly is nowhere it can go."[29] On this sombre note, Lu Xun takes up his pathetic theme that the most painful thing in life is to wake up from a dream and find no way out. For Lu Xun, "dreamers are fortunate people. If no way out can be seen, the important thing is not to awaken the sleepers."[30] But for those awakened, like Nora and her kind, it is hard to return to the dream world. They are doomed to suffer, whipped and lashed along the path to their defective vision of the future, "made more sensitive to the intensity of their misery, [they] are awakened in spirit to see their own putrid corpses".[31] It is precisely these frustrations and this dejectedness of the awakened intellectual in his chosen path that Lu Xun typifies in some of the most pathetic stories of this period.

"A Story of Hair" (Toufa de gushi) written in 1920 provides an appropriate introduction to the consideration of Lu Xun's awakened intellectuals. As the first story of its kind, it contains all the elements that are to be re-echoed in Lu Xun's more mature typologies. A story cast in the form of a reminiscence, "A Story of Hair" is topic-centred—with very few changes it could be cast as an essay. The I-narrator, who listens nonchalantly to his friend N's memories of the 1911 Revolution and its aftermath, is scarcely more than a listening ear (and he is already bored, like the later models). As an early zealot for social reform, N suffered untold miseries after he cut off his queue when he went abroad to study—"laughter and taunts followed me wherever I went". His comrades, however, suffered even more intensely:

[29] Ibid., *SW*, Vol. 2, p. 86.

[30] Ibid., Lu Xun confided to Xu Guangping in March 23, 1925, his pessimism upon seeing people awakening from their dreams: "In a word, once men got out of their paralyzed state, they would only add to their suffering and be rendered speechless. 'Hopes for the future' is but a way of consoling or even deceiving oneself." *LXQJ*, Vol. 11, p. 25.

[31] *LXQJ*, Vol. 1, p. 160. Lu Xun has borrowed these two lines from Artzybashev's "Shevyrev", a point I will go into later in this chapter.

... some young men, after years of toil and struggle, were quietly dispatched with bullets; others who had escaped the first blow were imprisoned and thrown into the torture chamber for months; some with their lofty ideals simply disappeared without trace ... scorn, vilification, persecution and betrayal were their lot when they lived; now their tombs, neglected and forgotten, are gradually being levelled by time....[32]

As for N, lacking the gallantry and endurance of his fellow revolutionaries, he opts for forgetfulness and oblivion, and retreats into a solitary existence. This explains his cynicism, believing it would only cause "senseless suffering" when the so-called visionaries advocated bobbed hair for women in 1920. For him, the real "blessing is to forget"—both the past and the present.

Can N really find "blessing" in "forgetting"? We are not told. What we know is that his Nietzsche-like remark towards the end of the story: "You people have no poison fangs in your mouths; why must you put the label 'poisonous vipers' on your foreheads to invite destruction by the beggar snake-catchers"[33] is complicated by a feeling of helplessness. Only a few years before, he was one of those who labelled himself a "poisonous viper". While N's typology remains sketchy, his helplessness and downward slide represent the prevailing path of Lu Xun's awakened intellectuals in *Wandering*—Lü Weifu, Juansheng, and Wei Lienshu.

Lü Weifu in "In the Tavern" (Zai jiulou shang)

Sometimes I think: "If my old friends were to see me now, probably they would no longer acknowledge me as a friend. But this is what I am like now." (*SW*, p. 195)

Lü Weifu

The above remark, wrung from the once enthusiastic and sentimental Lü Weifu, reveals a woeful situation. The story (1924) takes the shape of the I-narrator's recollection of his encounter with his old friend Lü Weifu in the town of S, near his native place, where both of them had taught. The futility of the lives of both

---

[32] Ibid., pp. 461–462. "A Story of Hair", translated by Chi-chen Wang, in *Ah Q and Others: Selected Stories of Lusin*, p. 60. Cited here with minor adaptations.
[33] *Ah Q and Others*, p. 64.

characters is underlined in the course of their gloomy and desultory conversation.

In his younger days, Lü Weifu was full of noble sentiments; and sought to define his mission in life as the betterment of his country. Along with many iconoclastic young men of his time (the I-narrator is one of them), he scathingly attacked superstition, believing this to be one of the major obstacles to the country's progress. As he recalls:

> . . . I still remember the time when we went together to the tutelary god's temple to pull off the idols' beards, and how for days on end we used to discuss methods of reforming China until we even came to blows. (p. 195)

His degeneration since those heroic days is shown by his stony stare and pallid hue, and his slow movements, in stark contrast to his piercing looks and vigorous gestures of the past. The mystery of his sluggishness is unveiled when he discloses that he had been doing "just futile work, amounting to nothing at all" (p. 192) in these intervening years. Even his return this time, as he reveals to the I-hero, is "for something quite futile"—to move the grave of his brother, and at the same time, to send some artificial flowers to A Shun, the daughter of his former neighbour. Why should these tasks be futile? We have to approach them in the light of Lü Weifu's past.

First, his present act of moving the grave of his younger brother would undoubtedly have been treated with derision by his former iconoclastic self, as something perpetuating superstition. The "futility" of the whole affair is heightened, when finding that "not even a trace of hair remained" (pp. 179–180), Lü nevertheless buries the clay where his brother's body had been in a new coffin beside the grave of his father, so as to deceive his mother. This incident poignantly exposes how much one who once fervently championed the destruction of idols and of the family has deteriorated. For this Lü Weifu sighs in dismay, revealing his helplessness: "This is how I am now, willing to let things slide and to compromise." (p. 195)

The futility of his second task is to be interpreted in a different light. It lies not in the act of presenting artificial flowers to A Shun, which is perfectly honourable, but in the effect of that act which torments him. Not knowing that A Shun is already dead, Lü arrives with goodwill and enthusiasm, only to be greeted as an unwelcome intruder. The impact of that cold reception on Lü Weifu is striking. He immediately retreats into himself and becomes extremely despondent: "I dithered, then walked away. Nowadays I just let things slide . . . Because I know what a nuisance I am, I am even sick of myself; so knowing this, why inflict myself on others." (p. 198) The present "self" that he dislikes is in sombre contrast to his past self. He comes to recognize that such noble feelings as hoping the world would change for the better for A Shun's sake "were only the residue of my old dreams" (p. 197).

The unrelieved sense of remorse is frankly disclosed in his revelation that he is now teaching the Confucian classics. The following conversation is worth quoting in full:

> "When I have muddled through New Year I shall go back to teaching the Confucian classics."
>
> "Is that what you've been teaching?" I asked in astonishment.
>
> "Of course. Did you think I was teaching English? First I had two pupils, one studying the *Book of Songs*, the other *Mencius*. Recently I have got another, a girl, who is studying the *Canon for Girls*. I don't even teach mathematics; not that I wouldn't teach it, but they don't want it taught."
>
> "I could really never have guessed that you would be teaching such books."
>
> "Their father wants them to study these. I'm an outsider, it's all the same to me. Who cares about such futile affairs anyway? There's no need to take them seriously. . . ." (p. 200)

One hardly need elaborate on the touching ridiculousness of the situation, where a former campaigner against the "cannibalistic traditions" is teaching the *Canon for Girls*, a work enshrining the feudal standards of behaviour for girls and the virtues they should cultivate.

By the sharp contrasts of Lü Weifu's past with his present, Lu Xun depicts the dejection of his hero with understanding and sympathy. Lü Weifu may have betrayed the world-weariness that many take on with the years, but his fate is much more pathetic than that. After he has woken from the dream world, and taken his first strides forward, Lü has reached a point of no return. In seeking refuge from the disappointment of life in daydreams and oblivion, deep down in his heart Lü is plagued by an intense desolation. His solitary existence synchronizes his dual sense of remorse and helplessness.

Juansheng in "Regrets for the Past"

"Regrets for the Past" (1925) begins with the hero Juansheng's remorse for the death of his former lover Zijun. The hero then reverts in flashback to their courtship, cohabitation, and eventual parting. As an awakened intellectual of the May Fourth period, Juansheng manages to persuade the innocent Zijun to share his belief in individualism and freedom. Inspired by him, she breaks with her family and sets up house with him as a matter of principle. Their bold action, however, meets with the censure of society, and Juansheng loses his job as a result. With their worsening financial situation, their estrangement, which had already begun, grows greater. Dissatisfied with Zijun's growing domestication, and the fading of her fearlessness, Juansheng begins to think that she has "forgotten all she had ever learned" (p. 258), and feels that she "ought to make a clean break". The break comes after he reveals that he no longer loves her, and she eventually leaves. The hero repents of his heartless action. In his solitude, he refuses to face the reality of his experience and retreats into forgetfulness, prepared to accept illusions which he recognizes for what they are.

Contrary to the assertion that Juansheng is a character of courage and stamina, and that his final recognition heralds a new life,[34] I believe that he is essentially a self-centred person, and his final decision is no more meaningful or "heroic" than that of Lü Weifu

---

[34] For example, Xu Qingwen in "Panghuang" fenxi simply states that Lu Xun put much hope on the character of Juansheng. His most admirable quality lies in his vigour and persistence in striving on irrespective of the many obstacles (p. 84). Wang Xiyan in Lun A Q he tade beiju goes a step further and attempts an explanation of the paradoxical ending of the story. He holds that Juansheng's path towards "falsehood" and "oblivion" is meant to be ironical. The sentimentalism and sorrow pervading the story are to him an expression of the author's agitation and anger, rather than pessimism and desperation. I find both explanations far-fetched.

before him.[35] His discourses on the tyranny of home life, the need to break with tradition, and the equality of men and women, inspiring as they are, do not offer practical solutions. Zijun's fearless break with her family is largely a response to his call: "I am my own mistress. None of them has any right to interfere with me." (p. 251) Like a young flower that requires sunshine and watering, her strivings need to be buttressed by the hero's care, understanding, and above all, love. But this is what seems to be lacking. The fact that her housekeeping "left her no time even to chat, much less to read or go for walks" (p. 255) may indeed be a cause for concern, but on the other hand, a relationship built on visionary dreams and on the intellect, without any practical sense of understanding and sympathy, is little more than a house built on sand. While he picks on Zijun's worrying over trifles, the hero's own impatience, and his over-reaction to the care she devotes to the household animals, reveal exactly how persistent trivialities are. What dominates him once their relationship has gone sour is his own desire to "soar anew through the boundless sky before it is too late" (p. 258). Zijun, who was a source of strength in his life, has become, in the course of just a few months, a yoke too burdensome for him to bear. Only after Zijun's departure, when he is oppressed by a sense of loneliness, does the hero begin to see her view of things. Her ashen face and childlike eyes haunt him, together with the adamant sternness of her father, the unsympathetic gaze of bystanders, and the thought that at the end there will not even be a tombstone for her grave. The recognition of his selfishness and heartlessness fills him with a remorse which is intensified when the news of Zijun's death reaches him. He repents his own folly and pride. Silence and emptiness haunt him. There seems to be no individual regeneration open to the penitent hero, who is resigned to advancing silently, led along towards "oblivion and falsehood" (p. 271).

Surely then Juansheng is essentially a self-centred intellectual.

---

[35] Though in a recent article, Li Xifan sees Juansheng as a self-centred intellectual, his interpretation of the ending at the story, that Juansheng has awakened from his dream and trod forward onto his new path, left unexplained the hero's reference to "falsehood" and "oblivion", in *"Nahan" "Panghuang" de sixiang yu yishu*, pp. 200–201.

His self-centredness makes him blind to the hardships and aspirations of Zijun, who yearns for a tender and loving family life after she has broken away from the cold and strict family of her father. On a deeper level, Juansheng's intellectual pride induces him to seek what he thinks is intellectually honest and satisfying. From this springs his disappointment at Zijun's increasing domesticity, symbolizing, to the intellectual hero, that she has "forgotten what she has learnt". Ideals, visions of the future, the honouring of one's ego and one's principles overshadow his craving for care, tenderness and sympathy. For intellect, he sacrifices sensitivity, his heart for his head. Zijun's romantic notion of a happy home life is shattered by his intellectual scrutiny. She becomes first a willing captive to his intellectual discourses, and then the victim of his pride, which operates under the guise of truthfulness.

Where does this intellectual integrity lead him? Nowhere. In a philistine and hostile society, he is doomed to fail. His refusal to compromise precipitates his personal tragedy, and occasions the death of Zijun. His remorse means much more than just regret for her passing away. The bell tolls also for him, for the burial of his principles, something he values more than he values his lover. In his disillusionment is therefore intricately interwoven the loss of his beloved, of his ideals, and above all, of his own self. One almost sees him joining forces with Lü Weifu and N in sticking to his solitary path, and eating his heart out in perpetual lethargy and remorse.

Wei Lienshu in "The Isolate"

If the typologies of both Lü Weifu and Juansheng are characterized by their lapse into forgetfulness, that of Wei Lienshu is coloured by his ugly course towards revenge. He is unmistakably one of the strangest and most pathetic of Lu Xun's intellectual heroes. His strangeness is shown by his inconsistencies—as a zoology graduate, he teaches history in school; while treating others in a cavalier fashion, he likes to concern himself with their affairs; and while maintaining that the family system should be abolished, he remits his salary to his grandmother the same day he draws it.

His habitual reserve and surface coldness conceal an ardent heart.

Two incidents show his noble and tender feelings. The wolflike howl during his grandmother's funeral, in which anger, sorrow and agony are mingled, highlights his indignation at those around him, his intense feeling for the passing of his grandmother who tasted the bitterness of the loneliness she created for herself, and above all, his agony for the "many other people like that" (p. 238). This sorrow at his powerlessness to champion the cause of the oppressed is relieved temporarily by his tenderness towards the children of his landlord. The mere sight of them would "dispel Wei's customary coldness" (p. 230). Believing that China's only hope lies in children, one can therefore imagine his mortification when he recounts later that a mere toddler he once met pointed at him with a reed, and shouted "kill".

His liberal ideas and daring arguments about society and the family alienate him from his colleagues. Anonymous attacks in the "less reputable papers" culminate in his dismissal from his teaching post. His distress is further reinforced by the desertion of his landlord's children, who "don't even want to eat anything I give them" (p. 235). In this dry mockery is cloaked his loss of hope, not only for these children but for the future of the country in general. However, he still soldiers on with great tenacity. As he writes to the I-narrator:

> "Would there be anything for me there? Even copying work, at twenty to thirty dollars a month, would do, I . . ." I was surprised. I had not thought he would consider anything so low, and did not know how to answer. "I . . . I have to live a little longer. . . ." (p. 239)

"What for?" is the immediate reaction of the narrator, as much as it is ours. Having lost out on all counts, and with his hope for the future vanquished, what is the purpose of such persistence?

Wei himself provides the answer, and, moreover, the reasons for his dramatic change, in his pathetic letter to the narrator. According to him, what sustains him through his days of decline is not his own self, but his principles. With the death of this "other self", which is "trapped and killed by the enemy" (p. 241), he finds no further cause to live for. He goes against his former principles by taking the post as counsellor to the Warlord General Du. Thereupon he wins new ways of bribing and flattering, but also a new haughtiness and contempt, a new sleeplessness and vomiting of blood. By becoming a wilful agent of the insidious power of the established order, Wei is in fact tormenting himself through his "delights", destroying himself in his conquests.

His growing dejection is most acutely manifested in the retribution he exacts from the landlord's children. While he still buys them presents, he would "make them bark like dogs and make a thumping kowtow" (p. 246). What a contrast to the former Wei Lienshu who became so worried when one of these children was said to have measles that his already dark face took on an even darker hue. Through his active cooperation with the devil, one sees clearly that Wei is literally courting his own death. His fate is not much different from that of the "opium addicts" Lü Weifu and Juansheng in the twilight world of dreams. The point where these destinies finally meet and merge is, sadly, extinction in its different guises.

To sum up, Lu Xun delineates succinctly, in his solitary heroes, the tragedies of many awakened intellectuals. Lured by the vision of a golden future, these people who are noble, generous, single-minded, contemplative and "advanced" in thinking try to realize their ideals in their self-appointed tasks of achieving the betterment of society. In daring to commit themselves, they discover that they have unwillingly but inevitably been swamped by the sinister forces surrounding them. Their winning generosity and singleminded ideals prove to be pathetically vulnerable. We witness their wings being clipped, their body and soul crushed. Their downward slide reveals the "dialectics" of change in these harbingers of reform. In the typologies of these solitary heroes, Lu Xun not only reiterates the belief that the forces of truthfulness and deception, freedom and authority, progress and conservatism are by definition antithetical, but also that those of conscience and aspiration, commitment and scruples, nobility of mind and tenacity of purpose are seemingly incompatible. The picture he projects in his stories is thus disturbingly pessimistic.[36] It is interesting to compare this picture with the Russian stories that Lu Xun translated.

---

[36] Though written in 1902, Lu Xun's poem "Zi ti xiaoxiang", encapsulating his personal vision of a lone martyr, is still relevant to his thought in the 1920s.

IV. The Russian Connection

All the Russian stories that Lu Xun translated in this period deal with the theme of the solitariness of the intellectual hero—his anxiety to communicate, his desire for a future golden age, and his agony upon recognizing his own powerlessness. Some collapse, like Andreyev's hero in "Silence" and "The Lie"; some dwindle away, like Chirikov's heroes in "Provincial Town"; and some avenge themselves, like Shevyrev in Artzybashev's story of the same title. It is interesting to observe the many thematic and typological affinities permeating Lu Xun's own stories of the period of translation, and to study his indebtedness to the Russian precursors. The two major sources of influence are Artzybashev and Chirikov.

Artzybashev's "Shevyrev"

In 1926, Lu Xun again talked to the students of the Beiping Women's Normal College (we remember that he talked in the College on "Nora" in 1923). Again he dwelt on his favourite topic—the plight of the reformers. Again he highlighted Artzybashev's "Shevyrev". He gave the background and his reasons for translating this book in 1921. During World War One, he was sent by the Ministry of Education to confiscate a number of books held by German nationals in Beijing. Artzybashev's "Shevyrev" (in German translation) was among the many German books confiscated. He chose to translate it because he thought that "before the Republic and after its establishment, the plight of many of our reformers was remarkably similar to Shevyrev's". In 1926, he reiterated his belief that "not only now, but in the immediate future, and even decades later, the suppression of reformers, the sufferings of representatives, and the plight of many more reformers to come, will resemble Shevyrev's".[37] This constituted his reason for reprinting the translation in that year. Two aspects of the work struck him forcibly, namely, Shevyrev's arguments about the "golden future", and the image of the reformer-avenger. Both find their way into Lu Xun's works, notably in "Regrets for the Past" and "The Isolate".

---

[37] *LXQJ*, Vol. 3, pp. 356–357.

a. The future golden world

Lu Xun's translation of "Shevyrev" appeared in October 1920, but he had already referred to the story in the previous year, in his "A Story of Hair" (his translation of Artzybashev's "Happiness" was published in the same month). In it the protagonist N borrowed Shevyrev's argument to drive home his point about forgetting and being forgotten: "Let me put to you the question raised by Artzybashev: 'You promise their descendents a golden world, but what are you giving them themselves?'"[38] This is, as far as one can trace, the first time Lu Xun ever used the concept of the future "golden world" in this sense.[39] From then on, at least up to 1926, this remained his major preoccupation and became a leitmotiv in his essays, letters, prose poems, and above all, short stories. Lu Xun clearly owed this concept to Artzybashev's "Shevyrev".

The section from which Lu Xun drew his idea appeared in Chapter Nine of the work. Shevyrev, the frustrated revolutionary, overhears a conversation between his neighbour Olenka (a seamstress) and Aladiev (a university student). By providing Olenka with books to read, Aladiev has inculcated in her a romantic as well as an idealistic vision of life and the world. She falls in love with him. Living in abject poverty, she is, however, forced to marry Vasily, a hawker whose vulgarity she detests. She comes to Aladiev for help. When the latter offers nothing but words of solace, Shevyrev lashes out at him:

> She came to you because she loves you, . . . because she has a pure and innocent soul. You have awakened her . . . Now, she is on the path of degeneration. She came to you looking for the right thing—for the love you taught her. What can you say to her? Nothing . . . you dreamer, you idealist, you must understand how you have instilled in her the craving for the future world. Aren't you afraid that in her nuptial bed, pressed by the fierce and lustful flesh, she will curse you who talked endlessly about the golden dreams of a happy life. . . .
>
> The awful thing is to make the corpse stand up and see its putrid state . . . to implant some innocent valuable things in the human soul, thus

---

[38] *Ah Q and Others*, p. 100.

[39] I have come to this conclusion after studying Lu Xun's published works— essays, fiction, letters and diaries—prior to October 1919.

making it more sensitive to its sorrow, and his suffering and anxiety more acute. . . .

You who dream ceaselessly of man's future happiness . . . Don't you know and don't you understand that in order to reach this future world, you will have to pass through a number of bloodbaths . . . You are cheating these people. You are telling them to dream of the things which they will never experience . . . don't you know how many unfortunate people were cheated by you. They are not dead, and they don't kill. They only cry to God, waiting for something. Because there are no other arbiters, there is no more justice. . . .[40]

I have quoted Shevyrev's argument at length here because the gist of it re-appeared in Lu Xun's "Nora" essay. The set phrases like "the future golden world", "awakening her to stand up to see its putrid corpse", "making one more sensitive to one's sorrow and suffering" were reproduced almost word for word in Lu Xun's essay. While Lu Xun inherited from Ibsen the problem of Nora, he took the answers from Artzybashev. Lu Xun did carry the argument a step further with the bitter proposal that one ought never to awaken the sleepers.

The impact of Shevyrev's arguments on Lu Xun was tremendous. In addition to "Nora Leaving Home" and "A Story of Hair", he revitalized this argument in many of his major writings of the period. In a letter to Sun Fuyuan in 1923, he remarked that the twenty or so essays (collected mostly in *Refeng* [Hot Wind] and *Fen* [Tomb]) he had written thus far were specifically designed to "waken the so-called reformers from their dreams of the golden world".[41] This was also one of his main themes in his letters to Xu Guangping, especially in the early months of 1925. For instance, he quoted the example of Shevyrev in his letter of March 18, and repeated the Russian hero's point that those idealists who talked of the golden world are either nostalgic about their "past", or hoping for the "future"; as to the problem of the "present", they have handed in

[40] *LXQJ* (1938), Vol. 11, pp. 686–688. I have here used Lu Xun's translation of Artzybashev's story. Pinkerton's English translation is not as accurate as Lu Xun's Chinese translation, though the latter has been re-translated from the German. Also, Lu Xun's own translation offers valuable grounds for comparison with his own works.

[41] *LXQJ*, Vol. 11, p. 416.

a blank paper.[42] Five days later, he reiterated Shevyrev's argument in another letter: whenever men came out of their paralysis, they would inflict more suffering on themselves. Circumscribed, their so-called "hope for the future" is but a self-consolation, or even a self-deception.[43] He concluded that in China's present situation, people had best be intoxicated to the extent of not knowing the present or the future. Such arguments were also repeated in *Wild Grass*, his collection of prose poems. For example, in "Autumn Night", Lu Xun has, like Shevyrev, taken a step back, and watches with a discerning eye how the fate of the "awakened" youths was sealed.[44] However, the influence of "Shevyrev" is most keenly felt in "Regrets for the Past".

I mentioned elsewhere that "Regrets" has a special quality in its being Lu Xun's attempt to explore imaginatively the problem posed in the "Nora" essay.[45] I go further here and say that Lu Xun is restaging in "Regrets" the parting scene of Aladiev and Olenka in "Shevyrev", at the same time expanding it to incorporate his own thoughts on the whole problem of the awakened intellectual. The similarities between the two stories are extensive. These include the circumstances leading to the parting of the central characters, and the special effect of the parting on the hero. Just as Olenka is awakened by Aladiev, so is Zijun by Juansheng. As Juansheng recalled: "I was unspeakably happy to know that Chinese women were not as hopeless as the pessimists made out, and that we should see them in the not too distant future as the splendour of dawn." (p. 251) The catalysts of the awakening of the female characters are also similar. Olenka was given the books of Chekhov to read by Aladiev, and Zijun those of Ibsen, Byron and Shelley. Even some minute details correspond to each other. In Aladiev's room hung the portrait of his mentor Tolstoy, in Juansheng's, that of Shelley. In the end, Olenka's love was rejected by Aladiev, and she went

[42] Ibid., p. 20.

[43] Ibid., p. 25.

[44] For an analysis of Lu Xun's different levels of consciousness in *Wild Grass*, see my article "To Awaken or Not to Awaken—Symbols of Anxiety in *Wild Grass*", *Renditions*, No. 26 (Autumn 1986), pp. 151–164.

[45] See my article "Lu Xun and Russian Literature" in *The Journal of The Institute of Chinese Studies*, Vol. 13 (1982), pp. 252–285.

broken-hearted to face the stern reality of marrying somebody she detested. Zijun likewise had her love rejected by Juansheng, and went back to face the icy coldness of her father. The love and hope of both heroines were thus fostered by the hero and shattered by the hero.

It is however in the anti-climax of both stories that their likeness is most noticeable. Olenka revealed that she was about to marry Vasily, hoping Aladiev would act. He came up with a non-committal reply: ". . . Well, this is good for you. . . . I wish you happiness . . ." (p. 682). This reply sounded like a death knell for the heroine. On hearing the words, Olenka is described as moving unconsciously, wanting to say something, but incapable of doing so. Her lips trembled, and she breathed with acute difficulty. Her face "turned ashy pale, like a corpse. Olenka was silent, at one moment she raised her head, and Aladiev encountered her big, searching, reproaching and beseeching eyes. For a moment they gazed at each other, horror was clearly expressed in the girl's eyes." (pp. 682–683) Juansheng was equally cool when he revealed to Zijun that they should part: "this makes it much better for you, because it'll be easier for you to go ahead without any regret . . ." (p. 364). Like Artzybashev, Lu Xun also depicts the face, eyes, silence and horror of Zijun upon their parting. This is how Lu Xun describes it: "I was expecting a scene, but all that followed was silence. Her face turned ashen pale, as pale as death, but in a moment her colour came back and that childlike look darted from her eyes. She gazed around like a hungry or thirsty child searching for its kindly mother. But she only stared into space, fearfully she avoided my eyes." (ibid.) After Olenka took her leave, Aladiev knew that she was gone forever. Standing in the centre of the room, he was oppressed by an indescribable feeling. He understood that Olenka came to him with the pain of one approaching death. He regretted his heartless action and hoped that Olenka would come back. Likewise, after Zijun left, Juansheng was oppressed by his surroundings and the beseeching eyes of Zijun. He also regretted his heartless action. Both came to the recognition of their past "follies" in awakening the heroine, though in Aladiev's case, his recognition was accentuated by the heckling of Shevyrev, and in Juansheng's, by his own haunting self-awareness.

The psychotic state of both heroes further serves to emphasise their common lineage. Aladiev seemed to have heard a low moaning and a desperate cry of woe, penetrating the enshrouding silence like the blade of a sharp knife. This cry of woe represented unbearable suffering, unspeakable sorrow, and unattainable hope. Aladiev understood that this was the cry of woe of Olenka. He "could distinguish that there is not only one voice, but two ... three, twelve, a thousand voices. The surrounding darkness seemed to have joined in and cried together." (p. 689) The voices haunted Aladiev like the heavy and painful knelling of the death bell. In the same vein, Juansheng was haunted by the darkness: "Around me was a great void and deathly silence. I seemed to see the darkness before the eyes of those, each one in turn, who die unloved; to hear all their bitter, despairing cries as they struggled." (p. 269) When finally Aladiev was alone in the room, he was in a state of paralysis. He looked round his room—the desk full of books and paper, the painting hanging on the wall—and was suddenly plagued by a sickness: the sickness of an unspeakable detestation, which made him tremble from head to foot. He hated his intellect, his work, and the future days. A thought came to him. He wished a pair of powerful hands would clench this whole world, shake it from above, so that every house, human being, thought and endeavour would be blown away in the thin air like dust. He closed his eyes amidst this void and darkness. But a "distinctive image, with a pair of big and beseeching eyes filled with tears floated in front of him. With it was a peculiar animal laughter, and the vanishing of the bright and comforting dream of life." Likewise, Juansheng was also plagued by a sense of emptiness. Like Aladiev, his thought also revolved round his dwelling—the same dilapidated house, the same bed, the same half-rotten wistaria tree—but what had made him happy, to love and hope and to live, was gone. The image of Zijun—alone bearing the burden of emptiness, walking on a grey path—also came back to haunt him. With his regrets, he also wanted to forget, to forget his promises, his idea of truth, and take forgetfulness and falsehood as his guide.

From the manner in which Juansheng's regret is depicted, it is clear Lu Xun drew upon the example of Artzybashev's Aladiev for his own remorseful hero. Artzybashev's influence, however, did not just end here. It also permeates the typology of Wei Lienshu, Lu

Xun's most eccentric reformer-avenger. The source of influence is the image of Shevyrev.

b. The image of the reformer-avenger

Shevyrev, we have seen in the previous chapter, suffered the loss of his family, wife and comrades for the cause. Hunted by his pursuers and those he had vowed to help, he took revenge by firing at them in utter desperation. While Shevyrev became a model for Ba Jin's Du Daxin, his influence on Lu Xun's thinking and works, though less well-defined, is also far-reaching. Let us broach the subject from Lu Xun's afterword to his translation of the novelette:

> Life is of prime importance to the human being. In their championship of the cause of the deprived, many reformers "sacrificed the most precious thing in their life", and "died for the common cause". Shevyrev [in the story] is the single surviving soul. Even then, he can only try to avoid the hunters pursuing him for his life, enveloped by forces of destruction. Not only is his suffering incommunicable to the fortunate, it is also incommunicable to the so-called "unfortunate". These unfortunates, on the contrary, help the pursuers to persecute, and take satisfaction in his death. They ruin their lives as much as the fortunate. (p. 591)

The significance of this passage lies as much in Lu Xun's concern for the fate of the reformers as in the depth of feeling with which he expressed it. His admiration, as he confides to Xu Guangping, is for the courageous man who risked his life for the people, was persecuted by them in turn, and ended up a loner before meeting his own destruction. He reacts with understanding and sympathy to Shevyrev's frustrated anger and his final path of revenge. From Lu Xun's many writings of the time, we know that he toyed with the thought of taking revenge on the oppressors—though he disapproved of the way taken by Shevyrev.[46] He finds horrifying his final action of "taking revenge for the sake of revenge, destroying for the sake of destruction". He warned that this type of avenger "has not appeared in China yet, and is not likely to appear. I don't want him to appear."[47]

[46] See his letters to Xu Guangping in March 11, 23 and 31. *LXQJ*, Vol. 11, pp. 11–16, 25–26, 30–33.
[47] *LXQJ*, Vol. 3, p. 357.

"The Isolate" is his answer to "Shevyrev". Through the example of Wei Lienshu, Lu Xun tries to put forward imaginatively his thinking on the kind of revenge, which, in his tormented state of mind at this time, he thinks will suit the Chinese environment. In the image of Lu Xun's reformer-avenger, we see clearly both the extent and the limits of Artzybashev's influence on him.

Let us first look at the parallels which run through both stories. Both Artzybashev and Lu Xun depict, in their respective loner-reformer, someone who has taken on a surface coldness because of his shattered ideals.[48] Both authors make it clear that underneath the cold and forbidding look of their heroes is concealed an ardent heart. Thus, both were depicted as exceptionally gentle and sympathetic to the less fortunate. Both began life in the story as well-intentioned reformers, who came to be frustrated by the people they wanted to help. The life cycle of both heroes thus follows a similar pattern of progression: from love to hate, from an aspiration towards a better future to utter nihilism, from non-resistance to evil to vengeance on the oppressors.

Two situational parallels between the stories are worthy of discussion. Both centre on the discourse on love and hate, and both underline the metamorphosis of the central character. First, in Chapter One of Artzybashev's story, Shevyrev and Aladiev engage in a discussion about human nature. Aladiev holds that human beings are good by nature. With a healthy rational faculty and a sound judgement in their possession, there would not be any evil people. It is the environment which prevents people from becoming good. Shevyrev counters that human beings are by nature evil. But it is precisely the adverse environment which created one or two good people. After a heated argument, during which neither is convinced by the other, Shevyrev again shows his coldness, which, according to Aladiev, betrays his inner worries and feeling for revenge. A discussion on human nature is also held in *The Isolate*— between Wei Lienshu and the I-narrator. The I-narrator assumes the position of Shevyrev. Wei holds that human nature is good; he loves children for their innocence. He further contends that "If

---

[48] Xu Qingwen was the first to note a possible similarity between the two characters, though he did not elaborate, as n. 34, pp. 72–73.

they turn out badly later . . . it is because they have been moulded by their environment" (p. 231). The I-narrator disagrees: "Without the root of evil, how could they bear evil fruit in later life?" (ibid.) Their conversation ends with Wei's annoyance and his reverting to his customary cold silence. His encounter later with a toddler pointing a reed at him and shouting "kill" thus highlights the irony of the situation. He eventually comes to accept the fact that human nature is evil.

The second thematic parallel occurs in the climactic scene. It comes in the form of inner conflicts between the protagonist's present and former self. In Chapter Ten of "Shevyrev", the protagonist's former self, which embodies the principle of non-resistance, comes back to haunt him, exhorting him to love and sacrifice: "You cannot do anything without sacrifice . . . and the greater the sacrifice, the purer and holier the meaning . . ." (p. 702). His present self, the cold-blooded avenger, fights back: "Why should I love people? Because they devour each other like pigs . . . I don't love them. I hate them . . . They have taken away from me all those I loved and all that I believed . . . I want to take revenge . . . you understand! . . . I cannot live any longer . . . I want to instruct you, there is an authority which is stronger than love, and that is to hate with all of one's unquestioning might . . . and that is enough . . ." (p. 700). In the end, the present self wants to take revenge on those who "drink our blood, sport with our suffering, make fun of us", and drive away his former self. The battle between Wei's former and present self is, unlike the struggles of Shevyrev, disclosed in his letter to the I-narrator. Wei discloses that his former self, who was willing to "beg for the cause, to go cold and hungry for it, to suffer hardship for it", is now being "trapped and killed". His present self now wants "to live to spite those who wished me dead" (p. 241). In the form their revenge takes, however, is revealed the marked typological difference between the two heroes. Shevyrev takes his revenge on his pursuers and the indifferent masses: "without taking aim, [he] fired straight at the sea of calm, unconscious spectators" (p. 746), "with cold-blooded brutal joy, it avenged the insults, the sufferings, or the ruined lives of which he knew so much" (p. 747). Wei's revenge, however, is essentially a self-immolation. He is doing precisely what Shevyrev condemned in his former self—drinking his own blood and playing with his own suffering: "I am now giving up all I formerly believed in and upheld. I have really failed—but I have won." (ibid.) The observation of the I-narrator at Wei's funeral: "there seemed to be an ironical smile on his lips, mocking the ridiculous corpse" is echoed in what Shevyrev told Aladiev: "for the sake of this hope [of the golden future] . . . people are awakened in spirit to see their own putrid corpses." While marking the above similarities, one should be careful to note that "Shevyrev" and *The Isolate* differ in plot, tone and mode of narration. However, before studying Lu Xun's fictional art in the next section, I would like to examine another source of influence on Lu Xun—Chirikov's "Provincial Town".

Chirikov's "Provincial Town"

The similarities between Lu Xun's "In the Tavern" and Chirikov's "Provincial Town" are many. They cover both plot, theme and typology. Structurally, both stories relate the I-narrator's recollections of his visit to his native place, a provincial town, after a long absence. Each meets an old acquaintance who was a comrade-in-arms in their younger days, and discovers that this acquaintance has since abandoned his former principles. Both stories end with the I-narrator's disillusionment and uncertainty as to his future. Thematically, they both underline the sense of futility of the protagonists, in particular their inner conflict between trying to achieve a better society, their awareness of their impotence to change things, and the realization that their own revolutionary fervour is draining away. Both stories are heavily tinted with the sombre and desolate mood of the solitary hero. The sense of futility of the I-narrator is immediately captured through the interplay of the past and present in his memory. In "Provincial Town", the sight of the familiar vegetation and the unfamiliar changes induce in the I-narrator a psychological malaise—through the contrast between his happy adolescence and his present unhappiness, his sweet first love and his present listlessness, his former feeling for the place and his present rootlessness. Haunted by his *Wanderlust*, he says: "to whose family should I go? I don't know. I will not go to anyone's family. O you sordid provincial town, which has witnessed my young days,

I've come to you, should we not at heart know each other?" (p. 278) Similarly, the I-narrator in "In the Tavern" is tormented by his homelessness—his friends have gone, the school he had taught at has changed its name and looks different. He finds that "the north was certainly not my home, yet when I came south, I could only count as a stranger" (*SW*, p. 190).

The sense of strangeness felt by both narrators is not simply the result of their long absence. It epitomizes their sorrow in recognizing their failure in life's struggle. Revolutionaries in their younger days, both have witnessed the waning of their passion. Chirikov's I-hero comes to admit that his own existence is futile. Like a ship without a rudder, he "no longer believes in propaganda sheets, and my hands are no longer stained with the blue ink of the rubber prints . . ." (p. 296). He is insignificant, futile, more so now because his "aspiration to witness the coming of a happy motherland has evaporated" (p. 296). This sense of futility is further enhanced upon his encountering an old acquaintance in the police station, who has since become the deputy commissioner. His friend talks with great enthusiasm about his former revolutionary fervour, of how in his undergraduate days he "slapped the mouth of the executive". His facial expression, as the I-narrator observes, has lost all trace of the police officer when he talks about these past enthusiasms. The narrator's futile question—'Why has he joined the police force when he should be in their custody instead?"—is countered with an even more futile answer: "Don't look at me like that. I am just wearing this uniform. Things are helpless, please let them slide. . . ." (p. 299) Oppressed by his friend's surrender of his former principles, the narrator recognizes the powerlessness of human beings, and in resignation of mind, he reasons that "maybe like me, grey haired, he has lost his bloom along the lengthy road of life" (p. 301).

Similarly, the I-narrator of Lu Xun's story also meets his old friend. As we have already seen, Lü Weifu has also been purged of his former revolutionary ideals and has taken up teaching the classics, including the *Canon for Girls*. He concludes "who cares about such futile affairs anyway? There's no need to take them seriously." (p. 200) Like Chirikov's hero, he is also "willing to let things slide and to compromise" (p. 195). The I-narrator also leaves his friend in resignation of mind: "I saw that the sky, already dark, had interwoven with the houses and streets in the white, shifting web of thick snow." (p. 201)

We can see from the above examples that the similarities between the two stories are manifold: the interaction of the I-narrator and his old acquaintance, the place where they meet (the police station is the only place which Chirikov's hero finds unchanged, likewise the tavern in Lu Xun's story), and the situations of their friends— both have compromised their principles, and are doing things that formerly they campaigned vigorously against. Both now have the same attitude towards life—let things slide. Each realizes his friend's uselessness, each understands that the other's life duplicates his own—Chirikov's hero: "he is like me", Lu Xun's narrator: "I too have simply flown in a small circle"—enhances their feeling of superfluousness. Moreover, the beginning and end of both stories are also similar. Chirikov's begins with the I-narrator's travels, featuring his "indolence and nostalgia", and his "wanderer's *Wanderlust*". Both stories end poetically. The sense of uncertainty and inconsistency in Chirikov's story is symbolized in his thoughts about the fading of the flower of life, whereas the *Weltschmerz* of Lu Xun's I-narrator is relieved by his contemplation of the "thick web of shifting snow"—rendering the world featureless. Given the above similarities, coupled with Lu Xun's appreciation of the "candid, vivid, fresh and psychological depiction" of Chirikov,[49] one can safely talk of Lu Xun taking Chirikov's story as a model for his own, though the two stories differ in subtleties of thought, a point I will have to return to later.

Andreyev's "The Lie" and "Silence"

I should like to mention in passing two thematic devices employed by Andreyev which may have some bearing on Lu Xun's "Regrets". Zhou Zouren suggested that the ambiguity of the story is partly a result of the "Andreyevan" diction that Lu Xun used.[50] By "Andreyevan" diction, Zhou presumably meant Lu Xun's somewhat lurid descriptions of Juansheng's state of mind after the departure of Zijun. Such descriptions, as I have established, have their main

---

[49] *LXQJ*, Vol. 10, p. 188.
[50] Zhou Zuoren, *Zhitang huixianglu*, pp. 126–127.

source in Artzybashev. But given Lu Xun's fondness for Andreyev, the example of his stories may have also contributed to the lurid description of Juansheng's psychotic state. The two "Andreyevan" devices are: the puzzlement over the ambiguity of truth in "The Lie", and his use of silence as a form of punishment for the penitent hero in "Silence"—both stories, we remember, were rendered into Chinese by Lu Xun. The protagonist in "The Lie" kills the heroine in the name of truth, because he is unable to tell whether the heroine he loves is lying when she says she loves him. The irony is that he comes to realize that in his excessively egoistic action he has "immortalized the lie". The ambiguity between truth and deception also emerges as a major theme in the latter part of "Regrets". Juansheng seeks to break away from Zijun in the name of truth. With Zijun's death, of which the hero's egoism operating under the cloak of truth is the prime cause, Juansheng comes to realize that he has made a mockery of truth, believing that he should "forever dedicate to her my lies". He reasons that if truth is to be treasured, it should not be for her such a futile burden. In the end he is resigned to advancing silently, taking forgetfulness and deception as his guides. The lie in both stories thus symbolizes grief as a basic lack of understanding and confidence between people.

As to the affinities between "Silence" and "Regrets", both stories depict the relationship of a proud and stubborn hero with an acquiescent though determined heroine. In the case of "Silence", the relationship is between Father Ignaty and his daughter Vera. Father Ignaty is adamant that Vera should abide by his moral code: "Am I responsible for her being born hard-hearted? Did I not teach her of God, of humility, and of love?"[51] His daughter Vera's defiance therefore poses a strong challenge to the core of his very existence—his pride, and results in his disappointment and anger. Juansheng in "Regrets" is also tainted by pride and self-centredness. He aims at moulding Zijun according to his own moral principles: "the shabby room would gradually be filled with the sound of my pronouncements on the tyranny of the family, the need to break with tradition, the equality of men and women . . ." (*SW*, p. 250).

---

[51] "Silence" in *Silence and Other Stories*, translated into English by W. H. Howe, p. 89.

His disillusionment grows from the heroine's failure to live up to his principles.

In their different ways, the demand of both heroes for "truth" leads to the death of the heroine. Both heroes commit the mistake of honouring intellect and reason more than love and understanding. Both become penitent, and are drowned in the silence that engulfs them. Both are haunted by the eyes of the innocent heroine. For Father Ignaty, the beautiful black eyes of the heroine's portrait are as though enclosed in black mourning frames, "and wherever Fr. Ignaty placed the portrait, the eyes continually followed him, not speaking, but silent" (p. 86). In "Regrets", we have seen how Zijun's childlike and beseeching eyes tormented the hero in the gloom after her departure. In their regret for the heroines' deaths, both heroes are depicted as enclosed in a state of emptiness, in an impenetrable silence. For Fr. Ignaty, "the silence choked him: it kept rolling backwards and forwards through his head in icy waves, and stirred his hair: it broke against his bosom, which groaned beneath the shocks . . ." (p. 97). For Juansheng, "around was a great void and deathlike silence". Crouching in this great void, he can only "allow this deathlike silence to eat away his soul" (p. 269). Both heroes mourn the death of the heroine, begging for her forgiveness and pity. Fr. Ignaty goes out to Vera's tomb, hoping that by speaking to her, Vera will rise from her grave, and "that not only would she rise; but all the dead who could be felt, so awesome in their solemn cold silence, would rise too" (p. 96). Likewise, "Regrets" ends with the hero's yearning for forgiveness from the heroine. Zijun's funeral springs to the mind of Juansheng, and he wishes that there really was a hell, so that he could, no matter how the subterranean wind roars, "seek out Zijun to tell her of my remorse and grief, to beg her forgiveness" (p. 270). In both cases, the proud hero can find no sympathy or forgiveness. Their afflicted hearts are left immured behind a wall of silence.

While we cannot deduce from these parallels that there is actually an "Andreyevan" influence, we can say that the employment of such devices endows Lu Xun's work with a chilliness which is characteristic of Andreyev. Such a chilliness, as Lu Xun remarked, pervaded the ending of his story "Medicine", and is attributable to the Russian writer.[52] Maybe the appropriate question to ask at this juncture, having studied the assorted examples of affinities and parallelism is, how are we to put into perspective the whole question of literary influence, particularly Russian influence, on Lu Xun's fictional works? Do the extensive borrowings or adaptations affect Lu Xun's stature as an original and innovative artist?

V. Adaptation and Innovation

In 1935, Lu Xun wrote that after "Medicine" (1919), which showed traces of Andreyev's sombre chill, he escaped from the influence of foreign writers. At the same time, as his technique matured, his depictions also became slightly more subtle. This remark appears to run counter to what I have been asserting in this chapter. While we should not take Lu Xun's remark about foreign influence at its face value, as he has elsewhere made other equally strong remarks acknowledging his indebtedness to foreign writers, particularly to the Russian, the real problem is to see how he tackled foreign material as his technique matured. The fact that his borrowings and adaptations pervade such stories as "In the Tavern", "Regrets for the Past", and to a lesser extent, "The Isolate", and that they are not readily distinguishable is worth remarking upon. The "Artzybashevan", "Chirikovian" or "Andreyevan" elements formed an integral as well as integrated part of these stories, making the task of unravelling them exceptionally tricky. The difficulty reflects the depth and control of Lu Xun as a writer of fiction, as he succeeds in swallowing, digesting and making effective use of these elements. By assessing the exact degree of foreign influence, seeing how far its limits extend, we can obtain fresh insights into his fictional art.

It is beyond doubt that Lu Xun borrowed the Aladiev-Olenka parting scene from Artzybashev for his own in "Regrets". It is also true that Artzybashev's depiction of the psychotic state of the

---

[52] Such chilliness is also found in Lu Xun's *Yecao*. One can in fact establish a close link between Andreyev's "Ben Tobit", which was translated into Chinese by Zhou Zuoren in 1919, with Lu Xun's "Fuchou, zhier".

remorseful hero—his employing such devices as the heroine's beseeching eyes, the surrounding emptiness and the thematic silence—is repeated in "Regrets". Can we conclude from this that Lu Xun's work lacked originality? The answer is clearly "no". While adaptation is nothing new in literary creation—Shakespeare, for example, borrowed extensively from Holingshed for the plots of his plays; the issue at stake is to see what actually happened, and, more importantly, *how* the process of homogenization takes shape. This merits a study of the adaptation from a wider perspective, to include aspects such as the organization of the story, the overriding mood, and the voice of the narrative—in other words, the whole technique.

Let me illustrate my point from "Regrets". First, despite Lu Xun's preoccupation with Artzybashev's concept of the golden future, when he used it in connection with Zijun and Juansheng, he produced a story which is distinctly Chinese, immensely topical and understandably popular during the May Fourth period. He also dwelt on an elemental human situation—the conflict of intellect and feeling, pride and understanding between the central characters. Epitomized in the story are the current thinking and modes of behaviour or would-be behaviour of many "awakened" May Fourth intellectuals. These "modes" were delineated with insight and poetry, and solidly related to the story's background. As in his other stories, Lu Xun was able, by resorting to a few words or motifs, to capture the feel of his time, thus bringing out the "nativeness" of his story. This technique, as we can see, is used with great effect in "The True Story of A Q." By setting the story of "Regrets" in a *huiguan* (a hostel for patrons from their native province or prefecture who have become dwellers in Beijing or in the big cities), Lu Xun also succeeded in endowing his work with a particular flavour. He seized upon one particular episode in modern China when young intellectuals flooded the cities from provincial towns, seeking work, higher education, or just a taste of city life. The *huiguan* motif was developed to attain further effect. The shabby room tucked away in a forgotten corner of the hostel, the broken window with the half-dead locust tree and old wistaria outside, and the square table, the mouldering wall and wooden bed inside—convey an air of dilapidation, and offer a glimpse into the quality of life of the young "awakened" intellectuals, whether it is that of the protagonist or his real life counterparts. The *huiguan* motif later becomes, in Juansheng's consciousness, a powerful symbol of his regretted past. They are the only things which remained unchanged, and it was in this shabby room that his drama with Zijun began to unfold. By adopting this technique of the familiar, Lu Xun succeeds in "making believe", arousing the readers' awareness of a common situation, common values and expectations. Taken in general, this technique also has a moderating effect, rendering the foreign interventions less obvious.

In line with this "familiarizing" technique is the superb control of the author. Juansheng's narrative, told in flashback in the first person, is a concise and remorseful recalling of his former happy days and a reflection on his present wretched state. It is a story well told, beginning from the beginning, leading to their happy moments together, the cooling off of their relationship, the climactic parting scene, and the anti-climax about the hero's torments. In each part of the story there is a severe visual economy, concentrating on what is essential to the central scheme. The effect is achieved through the author's use of perspectives. First, everything is seen from the viewpoint of the I-narrator. The author (or implied author) keeps at a distinct distance, resolutely silent, unobtrusive. This authorial distance results in a consistency of point of view—Juansheng's remorse is conveyed entirely through his own eyes and experience. The voice is consistently his own—that of an inexperienced young man who acquired stature as he tasted the cup of bitterness he prepared for himself. The narrative is therefore restricted to, and inferred from, the focal position of the I-narrator. When it comes to incorporating foreign elements into the narrative, this strict consistency comes as a key strength. Because of its internal unity—in the story line, the attitude and voice of the I-narrator— Lu Xun is able, once he has suited the borrowed segments to the central scheme, effectively to absorb them into his own story.

Furthermore, one sees Lu Xun's efforts, whether intentional or otherwise, to indigenize these foreign elements from the beginning. We have seen that the foreign transplants—the beseeching eye symbol, the enshrouding emptiness and the thematic silence—were emphasized in the latter part of "Regrets". To facilitate their transition into the story proper, Lu Xun skilfully paved the way for their entry into the narrative at an early stage. For example, the reader is made aware of the childlike eyes of Zijun when she first appears. Her eye-movements continue to be noted in the narrative; it comes to the fore whenever there is a change or crisis in their relationship. Lu Xun also prepares his readers for the enshrouding silence. In fact, up to the verge of the breakdown of their relationship, silence is not something to be dreaded. The silence of Juansheng's room in the hostel actually conjures up in his mind the vision of a peaceful life. He sees in his "silence" with Zijun the growth of a new hope. Silence is therefore given a twist of meaning in the anti-climax, as a powerful irony which mocks ruthlessly the heartless action of the hero. Lu Xun's well executed and strictly controlled narrative thus acquires an internal strength and balance which effectively absorbs and transforms any foreign elements, such as those from Artzybashev's "Shevyrev".

Another strength lies in Lu Xun's use of the language. One characteristic of Lu Xun's short stories is the use of opacity, especially in language. In "Regrets", the language takes the form of short and fragmented phrases or sentences, much of the time in the passive. Take for example the opening paragraph of the story: "If I can, I want to write down my remorse and sorrow, for Zijun, for myself. This shabby room, tucked away in a forgotten corner of the *huiguan*, is so quiet and empty. Time flies. I love Zijun. A whole year has elapsed since I, through her, escaped from this silence and emptiness."[53] In his specially constructed language, which becomes more obvious as the story unfolds, is disclosed the fragmented and unfocussed consciousness of the central hero. In fact, "Regrets" has a special quality, when compared to stories such as "In the Tavern", in that it is the most "internalized" of Lu Xun's fictional writing. The narrator effaces himself to allow the protagonist express the special nature of his mental process. Added to this internal focalization is the somewhat oblique and grey kind of tone of the author, conveyed through the opaque and sometimes awkward use of the vernacular. In it is the consumed passion of

---

[53] I have departed from Yang's translation, hoping to bring out more adequately the syntactic structure of Lu Xun's language.

a concerned onlooker, who finds communication difficult. This, as we shall see later, is the underlying tone of all of Lu Xun's mature works. This deliberate use of vagueness necessarily distances, even estranges the reader from the narrative, constituting what Zhou Zuoren called the "ambiguity" of "Regrets". Such estrangement however adds depth to Lu Xun's work. On a rudimentary level, it helps to keep the movement of the story on an even keel, and maintain his narrative at a measured pace, thus avoiding sensationalism.[54] Also, the distancing of the observer from the central character makes possible the emergence of a multi-focal structure, exemplified in such stories as "The Isolate" and "In the Tavern".

This brings us to the point of Lu Xun's originality. Though the course of development of "The Isolate" was inspired by Shevyrev, the similarities between the two stories lie rather in generalities, in the attitude, conflicts and torments of the intellectual heroes. Even here, the heroes follow their own ways in solving their problems, and finally end their lives. The tone and mode of narration of the stories also differ. Artzybashev's story is a straight third-person narration, adopting mainly an external perspective. The writer carefully conceals his own omniscience, releasing information about the characters in a slow process of revelation. This is shown in the mysteries enshrouding the central character which culminate in the final dramatic blood-letting scene. Hence the shocking effect of the story.

Lu Xun's story, on the contrary, is both subdued and ironic. Through the morbid self-revenge of the hero and the helpless observation of the I-narrator, we see an awareness of the author's own impotence to change anything.

This growth in stature of the I-narrator (also in "In the Tavern") is important, both typologically and structurally. While the I-figure in earlier stories such as "A Small Incident", "My Old Home" or "A Story of Hair" sometimes doubts his moral or intellectual adequacy, he invariably finds courage to move on; in "The Isolate" (and in "New Year's Sacrifice" and "In the Tavern"), he is seen as

---

[54] The above points are developed in my recent article, "Cong 'Shangshi' yu 'Gongren Suihuilüefu' bijiao kan Lu Xun xiaoshuo jiqiao de jiejian he chuangxin", in *Lu Xun yanjiu dongtai*, 1986.11, pp. 22–31.

infinitely more ineffective and superfluous.[55] He plays the roles of witness, analyst and commentator. In his show of surprise at the action of the focal hero—Wei Lienshu's strange howl during the funeral, his "naïve" belief in the goodness of human nature, his hopeless continuation of the struggle after defeat, and his morbid way of selling himself out—the author achieves the effect of "estrangement", as the I-narrator is supposed to be the only person who understands Wei. This act of incomprehension renders "obtuse" Wei's different acts, and heightens his solitariness and tragedy.

Moreover, the incapacity of the I-figure also reveals his own moral as well as intellectual inadequacy. Despite his morbid self-immolation, Wei's persistence wins one's sympathy. But as to the I-figure, he opts for compromise instead of Wei's howls in the wilderness, relieving his anxiety in the contemplation of nature: "It had been snowing all day, and the snow had not stopped by evening. Outside it was so still, you could almost hear the sound of the stillness. I closed my eyes and sat there in the dim lamplight, doing nothing, imagining the snow-flakes falling to fill the boundless drifts of snow . . ." (pp. 227–228). This unconcerned mood is only slightly disturbed by Wei's dramatic letter of "betrayal". Aware that "at least his livelihood was secure, and I need not worry any more at any rate, I could do nothing more" (p. 231), he immediately lapses into his customary silence, and forgets about Wei. The recognition of his own failure of compassion explains his reaction upon seeing Wei's corpse. Compelled by the feeling that Wei mocked himself to death, he feels that "some heavy barrier" lies ahead of him that is impossible to break through. However, his sense of compunction is relieved when a voice like "the howl of a wounded wolf" sounds in his ears. This sense of release can best be seen as a result of his shedding of his conscience—when he reasons that his friend's sorrow is over, and that he does not need to worry about him any more.[56]

---

[55] I find it difficult to agree with Ding Ergang's assertion that taken as a whole, the "I-narrator" in Lu Xun's fiction is a revolutionary intellectual with an unmistakable sympathy towards the working people, and he is forever fighting the dark forces of society. See his article, "Lu Xun sixiang fazhan de xianming guiji—lun Lu Xun xiaoshuo zhong 'wo' de yishu xingxiang", *Zhongguo xiandai wenxue yanjiu congkan*, 1980.1, p. 158.

[56] The ending of the story is obscure. Hanan remarks that the story seems to him inarticulate: "the narrator bids his emotions, of affection, or helpless guilt, or whatever they may be, and the cry of grief with which he greets his friend's

In the doubts and actions of the I-narrator is revealed somebody whose apprehensiveness ("sometimes even fearing I might be considered as stirring up trouble when cigarette smoke escaped from my window", p. 239) has incapacitated him for action. His is the subdued voice of one torn by world-weariness. He is resigned, oppressed by his own powerlessness, and in his sombre detachment he has lost even the ability to feel guilty, as I-narrators in *Outcry* did. In the critical eyes of the author, the I-narrator is but another character to be pitied. Herein lies the oppressiveness and irony of the story.

The close alliance between the I-narrator and the focal hero in "In the Tavern", which involves an affective, and moral as well as intellectual relationship marks the complexity of this short and apparently simple narrative.[57] While Lu Xun has taken the framework of Chirikov's "Provincial Town" as a model for "In the Tavern", his story has outgrown its predecessor by virtue of its obliqueness and irony. Lu Xun in fact considered that Chirikov's stories "in general lack subtlety of thought" (p. 275). A comparison of the treatment of the two stories will clearly show the point.

Chirikov's "Provincial Town" represents a straightforward chronicle of the I-narrator's emotional changes, observations, and sense of oppression, mainly through the interplay of the past and present in his mind. Everything is seen and described through the eyes of the narrator; even in the climactic scene, the interchange between the I-narrator and his friend is filtered through the feelings of the former. The emotional charge of the story is thus primarily restricted to that of one single viewpoint. Lu Xun's story shows a basic difference. While following a similar framework, Lu Xun doubles the emotional charge of his story by allotting the centre of action to a fictional hero. The I-narrator immediately retreats

---

death is inexplicable unless the reader brings to the story a full interpretation", as n. 2, p. 94.

[57] Li Changzhi in his *Lu Xun pipan* considers "In the Tavern" one of the failures among Lu Xun's short stories. Li argues that the monologue form of the story is monotonous. Lu Xun's efforts to bring in lyrical elements fail to break the monotone, and they also have the adverse effect of breaking its unity. I believe this is a misreading of Lu Xun's rather contrived efforts—the idea of distancing, the solitary mood extended through various contrasts; moreover, the story is expressed essentially in dialogue form, not monologue.

into the background with the appearance of Lü Weifu, playing the concerned yet helpless observer. In his pathetic sensitivity to the mood of the protagonist, Lü Weifu, his own superfluousness is revealed. Twice in their conversation Lü refers to the past in terms of "we"—we went to the tutelary god's temple to pull off the idols' beard and discuss possibilities of reforming China; has anything of all we planned in the past turned out as we hoped?—providing a glimpse of the past history of the I-narrator, adding more pathos to his reply to "Couldn't you have flown a little further?" "That's difficult to say. Probably I too have simply described a small circle" (p. 192). His inadequacy is further shown by the fact that he can only listen with a passive receptiveness to the pitiable "sell out" of his friend, and is totally incapable of rendering any help. After a show of surprise: "I could really never have guessed you would be teaching such books" (p. 200), he lapses back into his submissive silence, aware of his own powerlessness. After they have parted company he feels self-pity, as much as pity for his friend. Heaving a sigh, and with mingled gloom and anxiety, he steps into the "white, shifting web of thick snow", interwoven with the houses and streets.

   In the antithesis between the focal hero's degeneration and the extreme delicacy of feeling of the I-narrator and the omniscient author, who is capable of seeing through the futility of the entire situation, the narrative succeeds in engaging the reader on three levels. The action passes at will from the consciousness of the focal hero to that of the I-narrator, and in turn to that of the narrator. To quote Genette, this triple narrative method unifies the apparent contradiction of being inside and outside at the same time.[58] Discounting Lu Xun's acute observations and analysis of typical events in his stories, the technique of multiple focalization is the main reason for the depth and subtlety of his story. It is the hallmark of Lu Xun's mature works, and marks out the major difference between his technique and that of Chirikov.

The Limits of Influence

Such comparisons reveal both the extent and the limits of influence of foreign works on Lu Xun and enable us to single out a special

---

[58] Gerard Genette, *Narrative Discourse: An Essay in Method*, p. 210.

quality of Lu Xun's fictional works, defining his strength as a writer. As he himself tells us, many of his stories have resulted from "what I have been unable to erase from my memory". Many stories in *Outcry* are simply flashbacks to the past. According to Zhou Zuoren, most of Lu Xun's fictional characters have models in the author's friends, relatives and acquaintances, e.g. Runtu in "My Old Home", N in "A Story of Hair", Chen Shicheng in "White Light".[59] Likewise, many first person narrations in *Outcry* are no more than reflections of events in his past. Lu Xun's fictional world is therefore not only "Chinese", but also "private". Things happen and evolve essentially around his native village, the nearby town, familiar *hutong* (back alley) or hostel. The action centres on his own life, his family, his friends or the neighbours. Lu Xun documents these past events with a depth of feeling, which provides his story with much lyricism, poetry and realism.

This pattern of creation prevails in the more mature works in *Wandering*, albeit taking a slightly different form. To quote Zhou Zuoren again, quite unlike the other stories there are no traceable protoypes in the characters of Lü Weifu, Wei Lienshu and Juansheng. While Juansheng's typology is an imaginary construction corresponding to Shevyrev's argument, those of Lü Weifu and Wei Lienshu point to a different source. The two incidents in "In the Tavern"—Lü Weifu's "futile" affair of moving the grave, and the tragic death of A Shun his neighbour—according to Zhou Zuoren are "references to his (Lu Xun's) own life, though the elements of poetry and reality are not the same".[60] The strangeness of Wei Lienshu's being a zoology graduate teaching history stems from Lu Xun's own past history. Wei's wolflike howl during his grandmother's funeral, Zhou writes, "is wholly the author's own". Zhou Zuoren states that "though there is no dearth of autobiographical elements in the author's prose and fiction, it seems that nowhere else is there as truthfully and realistically depicted an episode as here. Moreover, this affair is scarcely known to people."[61] Zhou's comments shed some valuable light on the art of Lu Xun's fiction. By transferring to the fictional hero the events and sufferings of his

[59] See Zhou Zuoren, as n. 19.
[60] Ibid., p. 163.
[61] Ibid., p. 187.

own life, and at the same time allowing the I-narrator helplessly
to watch and describe them, Lu Xun succeeds in engaging the
emotions of his readers on different levels—the dejection of the
fictional hero, the helplessness of the narrator, and above all, the
presence of the author as an onlooker, who, delicate in emotion
and heightened in consciousness, looks with concern upon the
failings and agonies of his protagonists, which are no other than
his own. This technique of distancing, of dividing and doubling the
emotional charge, adds much subtlety and pathos to the story, and
involves the readers more with the author's feeling of guilt and
remorse.

This personal manner of narration, together with the sense of
ambiguity that pervades these works, accentuated by the feeling
of uncertainty covering the endings of such stories as "My Old
Home", "New Year's Sacrifice", "In the Tavern" and "The Isolate",
endows Lu Xun's work with a particular character. The ambiguity
crystallizes the author's inner conflicts. His is a wandering soul, as
he writes in "The Shadow's Leave-taking" (Ying de gaobie) in *Wild
Grass*, "wandering between light and shade, uncertain whether it
is dusk or dawn".[62] He confides to Xu Guangping in March 1925
that as much as he wants to battle against cannibalistic traditions
and autocracy, his meticulous and scrupulous character and his
wariness of bloodshed prevent him from taking action, except by
relieving his anger in his writings.[63] However, this ambiguity adds
to rather than harms his stories. Lu Xun has a strong sense of
proportion and control as a writer of fiction. Instead of being carried
away by his personal affairs, he typifies and generalizes. His creative
writings, as a critic put it recently, "reflect his persistent exploring
of a kind of collective consciousness to which he could relate his
personal experience".[64] Lu Xun describes his creative method in
"How I Came to Write Stories" (Wo zenmo zuoqi xiaoshuo lai)
singling out the harmonizing of these two elements: "the happenings
I described generally arose from something I had seen or heard, but
I never relied entirely on facts. I just took one occurrence and
modified or expanded it till it expressed what I had in mind. The

[62] *SW*, Vol. 1, p. 320.
[63] *LXQJ*, Vol. 11, pp. 31–32.
[64] Leo Lee, as n. 3, p. 188.

same was true of the models of characters—I did not pick on specific individuals. My characters were often a mixture of a mouth from Zhejiang, a face from Beijing and clothes from Shanxi."[65] His awakened intellectuals—N, Lü Weifu, Wei Lienshu and Juansheng, or the omniscient inadequate I-narrator, epitomize the conflicts tormenting many an intellectual of his time, as much as they do those of Lu Xun himself. Through his techniques of familiarization and estrangement, Lu Xun succeeds in depicting with psychological realism and much foreboding a vitally human situation. In attempting both to individualize and depersonalize these "sickly symptoms", as he termed them, of Chinese society, Lu Xun roots his work firmly in Chinese soil.

Furthermore, the author's communicative use of his language, achieved largely through his distancing devices, allows the reader to reconstruct an image of the author's voice, and of the other voices contained in the multi-focal structure of his stories. In its ability to arouse the reader to comprehend the shared values, experiences and expectations, Lu Xun's fictional work achieved a high degree of interpersonality, and consequently a wide-ranging appeal. The ambiguity inherent in his art, which represents the marriage of the past and present, of sympathy and indifference, of privateness and typicality, and of a deliberate blurring and a sharpness of vision, constitutes therefore the special yet human quality of his work, and as such, his creativeness and innovative power in modern Chinese fiction.

Whilst there is little doubt that Lu Xun's reading and translating of certain Russian works gave him a starting point for several of his stories, the use he made of them clearly reveals his own individual strength. In trying to choose an artistic mode to depict his awakened intellectuals, Lu Xun has drawn on the Russian stories he liked and translated, which either portray a similar phenomenon, provide a workable framework, or both. However, enthusiastic as he was about Russian literature, the strength of Lu Xun as a writer of fiction is more patently shown, perhaps paradoxically, in the limits of the influence of these writings on his own. In the strange combination of sympathy and cynicism towards his heroes, the acute blending

[65] *SW*, Vol. 3, p. 264.

of the qualities of ambiguity and psychological realism, and of familiarity and estrangement, Lu Xun endows his stories with much insight, subtlety and pathos, and thus, a greater degree of universality. Lu Xun indeed learnt and even adapted much from his Russian precursors, and became, as a result, all the better as a writer and an artist.

Part III: In Search of a New Hero

8 Conclusion

I. The Infantile Idealist

Before the May Fourth era the Chinese fiction writer had never been so seriously caught up in his own ethical and intellectual predicament. The intensity of the writer's (and his hero's) desire to gratify his intellect, his endless fights with his inner self about whether or not to devote himself to a cause, a person, or his own belief, and his debilitating sense of nihilism after committing himself to a fruitless task, especially after the Northern Expedition in 1927—have no parallels in past writings. At the root of his work is the discordance between the writer's (and his hero's) pride in his individual talents and potential to do the task he thinks history has assigned to him, and his experience of the appalling environment and all-enveloping suffering from which he has no escape. The conflicts between thought and action, ideal and reality, feeling and intellect burden such celebrated fictional heroes as Lü Weifu, Juansheng, Zhang Qiuliu, Wong Zhongzhao, Du Daxin, Wu Renmin, Yu Dafu's I-narrator, just as they haunt their authors. Herein are contained some of the most remarkable features of May Fourth fiction: remarkable in that the writer pours into his writings the very soul of the time; in that his work can be read as the most poignant chronicle of the intellectual predicament of the May Fourth era; remarkable also in the emergence and subsequent preeminence of the new and "unheroic" hero, whose negative qualities—half-heartedness, loquacity and supineness—are overridden by his troubled conscience, and his concern for the problems of his country and its people. The negative traits of this hero become positive ones, and expose to us his naked self. The individual exists in these works not only as part of the social whole, but as a representative of the hero's awareness of himself as a solitary being, battered about in his groping for fulfilment in life. He is unique precisely in his "unheroism". Whatever guises he takes—whether awakened, estranged or defeated—his selfhood and ultimate fate remain the same. He is the prisoner of his own moral and intellectual sensitivity.

The May Fourth era provided a unique historical environment for the prevalence of the intellectual hero. The 1917 Literary Revolution and the 1919 Movement aroused in many young people a romantic vision of the Chinese nation rising phoenix-like from the ashes of her past. Awakened, many drifted to the urban centres, particularly Beijing and Shanghai, believing that life in the seats of new learning would enlighten them and quench their thirst for great achievements. They were attracted both by the intellectual freshness and the romanticism of their pursuits. This is how Ai Wu, who later became a major writer, summarized his experience: Born in a village in 1901. Went to village school, and later to teacher training college. Dismissed because of his radical ideas in the times of the May Fourth Movement. Went to urban Nanjing, found work as a clerk in a school. Studied English in his spare time and enrolled as a student in a modern school. Unemployed upon graduation. Began writing poetry. Went to Beijing, became an associate student in the University there. Secured a job as a copywriter with the help of a professor. Attended lectures on literature. Here he describes his life in Beijing University: "There was no lack of people in my situation in the four-storeyed building of Beijing University. They were mostly poor people, with no money to pay tuition fees or to buy books. With empty stomachs, ragged clothes, and their dishevelled hair . . . they were forever saying that Marx was like this, Kropotkin was like that, how marvellous Rousseau's political ideas were, how grandiose the poems of Byron was, and how strange Freud's psychoanalysis appeared. By borrowing a few big names and their ideas, they indulged in deceiving themselves, escaping from reality, and forgetting about their immediate suffering. Poverty-stricken, too poor to buy oil for their lamps for months on end, they went to bed early in the evening, and lay there dreaming about nihilism, communism and anarchism. . . ."[1] For the speaker and young "romantics" of his kind, the journey to the wonderful world of enlightenment was both a means and an end. They were, in short, men of the future (like Lu Xun's Juansheng or Ba Jin's Du Daxin). The grindstones of reality (as many May Fourth writers were fond of saying)—the Northern Expedition and its aftermath—crushed to pieces their optimism and future dreams. Finding their faceless existence in the cities, notably Shanghai, lonesome and oppressive, many developed a divided personality, torn between mind and heart. Choosing to forget themselves in theatres, dance-halls, teahouses and brothels, they nevertheless admitted that underneath their escapism was an aching heart.[2] This widespread sense of superfluousness and nihilism provided ample subject-matter for the May Fourth writer. Many, in fact, poured into their works their thwarted desires, or related their own feelings in stories about those around them. Mao Dun's observation that works of the early 1920s invariably dealt with the life of the young intellectual and his surroundings can be extended to include an entire corpus of works which stretched into the mid-1930s.[3] The writers felt their way into the real-life models, and this accounts for the strongly biographical or autobiographical nature of May Fourth fiction and the sense of circumscription of its writers. Yu Dafu, for example, was the protagonist of his own works, whereas the characters of Lu Xun, Mao Dun, Ba Jin and the like were patched together from fragments of their own lives, or of those of their friends or acquaintances. This craving for real-life models sprang from the writers' desire to relate and dramatize the actual and

[1] Ai Wu, "Moshuiping guazi jingzishang xiezuo de", *WYWX*, pp. 69–70.

[2] Yi Ka, "Qingnian de kumen", *Xuesheng zazhi*, 17.5 (1930.5), p. 3; see also his other article "Ershinian laide Zhongguo xuesheng" published in the same magazine in January 1931.

[3] See Mao Dun's essays published in this period, included in *MWZJ*, Vol. 1, pp. 34–176.

topical. To them, this was the proof of good and realistic art. Fictional works were perceived as the microcosm of life which was or had been lived. The central figure of their fictional works, the infantile idealist or the superfluous man, which arose from the free flow of the author's feeling about his own life or about the lives around them, infused these works with an electrifying power. A consequence was that these writings were often interspersed with the sentimental and romantic outbursts of the naïve hero (Lu Xun's work is an exception).

This predilection for the "intellectual" is conducive to the widespread popularity of May Fourth fiction. These works are written mainly by intellectuals for and about intellectuals—high school and college students, teachers, journalists, petty officials, and the many drifters and layabouts who haunt the city centres. Words like free love, individuality, intellect, destruction, revolution, anarchism and nihilism fill the pages. Many of the fictional heroes, let it be said, mouthed such words because it was "modern" to do so; they were quite often unaware of their exact meaning and implications. However, the persistent appearance of such words means that they have acquired an extra dimension of meaning. Irrespective of whether or not the speakers understand words like revolution or nihilism, they use such words and adopt the mentality that goes with them as the accepted, or even required social norm for the "modern" city-dwelling intellectual. Conventions build on existing conventions. Many young people, in fact, go to literature, not life, for instruction; and many writers instruct by laying bare their minds and hearts. The result is the popularity of the divided intellectual type, and the almost complete wiping away of boundaries between the writer and his hero (Lu Xun is again a sober exception), and between the writer/hero and his reader. Not only does the somewhat naïve writer (and his hero) assume the unlikely role of speaker for many readers, his works also effectively, perhaps quite unpremeditatedly at the time, led, regulated, conditioned, reinforced or even transformed the tastes, modes of behaviour, and views of life of his young readers, as many testimonies from the readers themselves reveal. However, no matter how extensively May Fourth fiction is drawn from life, the intellectual typology of a good number of the major works, especially those in the 1920s, owes a lot to their authors' reading of Russian literature.

Because of the May Fourth writers' utopian ideals and romantic notions of revolution, which often resulted from their reading of Russian thinkers like Kropotkin, Bakunin or Herzen, and because of their intellectual scruples, the characters to whom they reacted most favourably in Russian literature were the "revolutionary Hamlets", the accursed hero-type. The reflective works of Turgenev (*Rudin, Fathers and Sons, Virgin Soil*), Andreyev (*Red Laugh, To the Stars, The Life of Man*), Artzybashev (*Sanin and* "Shevyrev"), Ropshin (*The Pale Horse*) and the short stories of Chirikov won the hearts and minds of many. The protagonist in these works is invariably an intellectual who is at odds with his environment—either incapable of acting, defeated in his attempts, or driven to suicidal despair. To the Chinese readers and writers, such works dealt with a situation similar to that of China, thus providing them with a relevant message. The Russian hero's intense concern for the affairs of his country especially appealed to them. He quickly became a figure for identification or emulation. The appearance of the Chinese Rudins, Shevyrevs, Sanins and Georges is an eloquent testimony to the powerful sway that these works held over the May Fourth reading public.[4] The central position they occupied in the fictional works of the 1920s and early 1930s came as a result of the author's self-portrayal, or his portrayal of the recurrent types in Chinese society, or a combination of both factors. This easy susceptibility to the Russian intellectual type denotes not only the lack of a strong native tradition in the 1920s and early 1930s, it also underscores the cosmopolitan outlook of May Fourth writers, as well as the craving for models with ideological and political relevance. This last factor did much to confine the influence of Tolstoy and Dostoevsky in China. It is true that *Poor Folks* and *Resurrection* became well known in the 1920s. Their popularity, however, was due almost entirely to a narrowly defined idea of social revolution and ideological regeneration. Even Devushkin (in

---

[4] See the testimonies of Zheng Zhenduo, Mao Dun, Cao Juren and Gao Changhong quoted in the previous chapters.

Poor Folks) and Nekhlyudov (in *Resurrection*) who have been mentioned earlier, did not fit their notion of the "intellectual" type. They were welcomed as representational images of the insulted and the repentant nobleman, but as a type for emulation in their creative activity they had little impact. None of the more mature types of both authors—Prince Andrei and Anna Karenina, Ivan Karamazov and Prince Myshkin—aroused any interest. May Fourth readers indeed paid tribute to the "greatness" of both, but there was little or no attempt on their part to appreciate the epic dimensions and multifarious form of Tolstoy's works, or the spiritual world and "dialogic" structure of Dostoevsky's novels,[5] from which they derive their greatness. What is more, both writers, in fact, were ridiculed by leftist critics in the late 1920s and 1930s because of their so-called conservatism and reactionary stand.[6]

This superficial reception of Russian literature points as much to the limited vision of the May Fourth writers as to the character of their thought. There is every justification, from our present day viewpoint, for saying that many writers of this period lacked profundity, and that many of their works bordered on the sentimental. But it is equally important to emphasize that their responsiveness to foreign, especially Russian, ideas brought about a most fruitful period of intellectual and literary cross-fertilization. Like their Russian exemplars, May Fourth writers are mostly reflective in nature, and represent in artistic colours the life of a generation of young intellectuals in distress. In his intense concern for their situation and in his sympathetic delineation of the liberal predicament of the intellectuals, the May Fourth writer provides evidence of his humanity. Flawed and unheroic as the Chinese "Hamlet" may be, he nevertheless represents the author's efforts to humanize a whole spectrum of values: social, political, philo-

[5] See Mikhail Bakhtin's thesis on Dostoevsky's polyphonic novel, especially his chapter on Dostoevsky's discourse in *Problems of Dostoevsky's Poetics*, pp. 181–269.

[6] Tolstoy, for example, was denounced as an "ugly preacher" by Feng Naichao in "Yishu yu shehui shenghuo", in *Wenhua pipan*, 1 (1928), pp. 3–13. While Chinese leftwing writers began to dissociate themselves from the Tolstoyan or Dostoevskian brand of humanitarianism towards the close of the 1920s, they were, however, never slow to emphasize the Russians' esteem of the common people. See nn. 28, 32 of Chapter Three.

sophical and aesthetic. Just as the intellectual tradition remained in the mainstream of Russian fiction, it was also a mainstay of Chinese fiction up to 1949, even though with the increasing radicalism of writers in the 1930s in the wake of the Japanese invasion, "Hamletism" became a matter of growing concern, and subsequently the object of ridicule. With the formation in 1930 of the League of Leftist Writers under the leadership of the underground party in Shanghai, many Chinese writers were beginning, either consciously or under the direction of the Communist Party, to adumbrate a different literary type—the "Liberated Don Quixote", after the title of a play by Lunacharsky, the Commissar of Education in the Soviet Union.[7] The pallid complexions of the divided intellectuals were given a rosy hue; and their place was gradually taken by the strong-willed, straightforward, and healthy heroes. Thus began the odyssey to the socialist new world.

II. "To Moscow"

In his novelette "To Moscow" written shortly before his execution by the Guomindang in 1931, Hu Yepin showed his protagonist, a petty-bourgeois intellectual, shaking off her bourgeois habits and making her way to Moscow where, she believed, the future is bright.[8] This work, and a host of others, like Jiang Guangci's *Lisha de aiyuan* (The Sorrow of Lisa, 1929) and Ding Ling's "Shui" (Water, 1931), constituted what was known as the first wave of proletarian literature in China. While the literary currents in the late 1920s and 1930s and their interaction with the socio-political scene are too complicated to describe here, the impact of the Soviet literary experience on the Chinese is too obvious to be put aside. Young revolutionary writers and critics like Qian Xingcun and Jiang Guangci were busy in the late 1920s promoting "proletarian realism"

---

[7] Lunacharsky's work was published in 1922. Lu Xun translated Act One of the play for *Bei Dou*, which published it in November 1931. The translation work was later taken over and completed by Qu Qiubai. Lu Xun expressed his appreciation for the work which showed that the October Revolution led the Russians to a new life, *LXQJ*, Vol. 7, p. 400.

[8] *Hu Yepin xuanji*, Vol. 2, pp. 685–767.

as expounded by A. Zonin, the leading theoretician of RAPP (Association of Proletarian Writers).[9] While they echoed Zonin's proposal for a "dialectical-materialist" method in literature, and like RAPP, waged war on those they considered to be "fellow-travelling" writers, they ignored the Russian position as summed up in the latter's famous slogans, "for the living man" and "tear off all masks". In fact, both Lu Xun and Mao Dun, targets of attack from the young revolutionary writers, were closer to RAPP in their clear stand for psychological realism and for a form of literature comprehensible to the masses.[10] Lu Xun's dissatisfaction with the "false witness" of the revolutionary writers provoked him to delve more deeply into Soviet literature. The result was his translation of Lunacharsky's and Plekhanov's works on art and literature in 1929 and 1930 respectively, which opened a new chapter of his literary activities.

Lu Xun's interest in Soviet literature is important. It set the trend for those who looked upon him as their mentor. Their fascination with the October Revolution prompted them to assume that works depicting how the socialist new men would swiftly take the place of classical Russian literature. Consequently, a total of 103 titles by 41 writers were included in a list of Soviet fictional works translated into Chinese up to 1930.[11] The list enumerates translations from writers of different Soviet schools: those who were already well known before the October Revolution, like Issac Babel, Ehrenburg, A. Tolstoy, and Sholokov; "fellow-travellers" like Pilniak, Ivanov, Fedin, Yakovlev, Zoshchenko, Romanov and Lunts; and important proletarian writers such as Gladkov, Fadeyev, Libedinsky, Fur-

---

[9] See Gálik's detailed study of Qian Xingcun's theory of proletarian realism and "literature of power" in *The Genesis of Modern Chinese Literary Criticism (1917–1930)*, pp. 166–190. Xia Yan also recalled that when drafting the general guidelines of the League of Leftist Writers, the committee members took those of RAPP in Japan as a basis. See Xia Yan, *Zuolian huiyilu*, Vol. 1, p. 41.

[10] Mao Dun's views were expressed most clearly in his articles "Cong Guling dao Dongjing" and "Du *Ni Huanzhi*". He reiterated his theme against the shallowness of the Chinese revolutionary writers in another article entitled "Zhongguo Suweiai geming yu puluo wenxue zhi jianshe" in *MWZJ*, Vol. 1, pp. 324–329. Lu Xun's views are most succinctly summed up in his article "Shanghai wenyi zhi yipie", *LXQJ*, Vol. 4, pp. 291–307.

[11] Pu Shao, "Zhong yi SuE xiaoshuo bianmu", *ZXCS*, Vol. 2, pp. 280–289. See also Chapter One, n. 30 for the translation of Gorky's works.

manov, Semonov and Serafimovich.[12] It is interesting to observe that in their initial response, the Chinese writers and translators essentially took what was available to them, often through Japanese mediation. When they were not involved in polemics, their concern about the allegiances of the individual writers they tried to introduce was not particularly noticeable. Lu Xun, for example, translated the works of "fellow-travellers" like Yakovlev, Fedin, Lunts, and above all Zamyatin, the spokesman of the "Serapion Brothers". But his best known translation of a Soviet work is undoubtedly Fadeyev's novel *The Rout*. Jiang Guangci translated works by "fellow-traveller" Romanov as well as the well-known proletarian novel, *A Week*, by Libedinsky, an active member of RAPP. Cao Jinghua's list of translations includes works by Ehrenburg, Seifullina, Ivanov (all "fellow-travellers") and *The Iron Torrent* by Serafimovich, the well-known proletarian classic. In the end, it was the works of the proletarians—Fadeyev, Furmanov, Gladkov and Serafimovich which reached eminence in China.

This period of spontaneous response was short-lived. In 1932, when the Union of Writers of the USSR was founded, the stage was set in the Soviet Union for the total regimentation of the writers under the Party banner. Two years later, Zhdanov, in his principal speech to the First Writers' Congress, promulgated "socialist realism" as the basic method of literary creation, and this formally brought Soviet literature under Party control. Zhdanov's speech extolled the representation of reality "in its revolutionary development". Artistic portrayal had to combine a "truthfulness and historical concreteness" with "the ideological remoulding and education of the toiling people in the spirit of socialism".[13] This Stalinist dogma had a far-reaching effect in China. Chinese left-wing and later communist literature, from the mid-1930s till the Sino-Soviet split in 1960, never deviated from it.

Briefly, two concepts stand out in the doctrine of "socialist realism": "partiynost" (party-mindedness) and "narodnost" (devotion to the common people combined with patriotism). "Partiy-

---

[12] See Edward Brown's *Russian Literature since the Revolution* for a discussion of the Soviet literary scene in the 1920s and 1930s.

[13] A. A. Zhdanov, "Soviet Literature—the Richest in Ideas, the Most Advanced Literature", in *Soviet Writers' Congress, 1934*, p. 21.

nost" requires the writer to write in conformity with the current party-line, as party-sponsored truth is the only truth. As for "narodnost", works are to be written in simple, comprehensible language devoid of any "modernist" tendencies. This elevation of the common man also dictates the depiction of the "socialist hero", who, as a "typical character", is healthy, strong, self-confident and party-conscious. Works such as Gorky's *Mother* (1907), Furmanov's *Chapaev* (1923), Gladkov's *Cement* (1925), Fadeyev's *The Rout* (1927), Ivanov's *Armoured Train No. 14-69* (1922), and Serafimovich's *Iron Torrent* (1924) were exalted in the 1930s as socialist exemplars. Later models include Azhayev's *Far Away from Moscow* (1948), Fadeyev's *The Young Guard* (1946, 1951), Katayev's *Time Forward* (1932), Ostrovsky's *How the Steel Was Tempered* (1932-1934), Panferov's *Brusski* (1930-1937), Polevoy's *A Story about a Real Man* (1946), Sholokov's *And Quiet Flows the Don* (1928-1940) and *Virgin Soil Upturned* (1931-1960). In addition, Simonov's play *The Russian People*, Leonov's *Invasion* and Korneichuk's *The Front* also became models for emulation.[14] These autobiographical or biographical works all underlined Marxist-Leninist historiography and revolutionary lore. The proletarian positive hero has, since he made his debut in the early 1920s, continued to dominate Soviet fiction to the present day.

May Fourth readers were kept up to date with the contemporary Soviet literary scene through the articles and translations of Lu Xun, Jiang Guangci, Qu Qiubai and party functionaries like Xia Yan and Zhou Yang. The latter's article "On Socialist Realism and Revolutionary Romanticism" gave them the first sample of this new literary doctrine.[15] It was, however, the Soviet models which exerted more influence. For example, Fadeyev's *The Rout*

[14] For an official short list of the Soviet model novels, see Katerina Clark, *The Soviet Novel, History as Ritual*, pp. 261–263.

[15] This article was published in *Xiandai*, 4.1 (1933.4), pp. 21–31. Of the thirty-five or so leftwing magazines published between 1928 and 1937, almost every single one of them carried translations of or introductions to Soviet literature. For example, Fadeyev's *The Rout* was translated and serialized in *Mengya* from January 1930 onwards, Libiedinsky's *A Week* appeared in *Hai feng zhoubao* in January 1929. A good number of essays by Xia Yan, Zhou Yang and others on the Soviet literary scene were also published. See Ma Liangchun and Zhang Daming (eds.), *Sanshi niandai zuoyi wenyi zhiliao xuanbian*, pp. 223–576, for the Soviet works published in these magazines.

was translated by Lu Xun in 1931 and hailed by him as a work which showed the way to a new birth.[16] It attained instant popularity, partly because Lu Xun's name was attached to it. Gorky's *Mother* was most avidly read from the time Xia Yan translated it into Chinese in 1929. Banned as subversive by the Guomindang in 1931, when it had already gone through several reprints, this novel was one of the "clandestine" books most sought after by intellectuals at the time.[17] The same was true of *Iron Torrent*. The translation, which went "underground" immediately after its publication in 1931, was ever popular with its readers. It was said that those who took part in the legendary Long March in 1934–1935 had all read this novel. Some even viewed the heroic deeds of the Chinese Red Army as China's "Iron Torrent".[18] *Cement* and *Armoured Train*, translated several times, were also popular with their Chinese readers.[19] As for Furmanov's *Chapaev*, it became well known to the Chinese through the film version, which was shown in Shanghai in 1936. Favourably impressed by the film, Yao Ke, later a well-known playwright, read the book and was struck by its greatness.[20] In addition, biographical data and literary reminiscences of Soviet officially sanctioned writers like Gorky, Fadeyev, Gladkov, Libedinsky, Ivanov, Serafimovich and Sholokov appeared regularly in the left-wing magazines in the late 1920s and 1930s, providing food for thought for many readers. It would, indeed, be difficult to find a single issue of these publications without any mention of Gorky after his well-publicized return to the Soviet Union in 1931.[21]

During the Sino-Japanese War years, the translation of Soviet literature continued almost without interruption. Many pieces were published in *Soviet Literature*, which came out in Japanese-occupied Shanghai in 1942 and lasted until 1949.[22] Soviet "defensive"

---

[16] *LXQJ*, Vol. 10, p. 336.

[17] See Xia Yan, "Muqin zai Zhongguo de mingyun", *Xia Yan lun chuangzuo*, pp. 85–87.

[18] Cao Jinghua, *Fei hua ji*, pp. 153–168.

[19] As n. 11.

[20] Yao Ke, "Du *Quepaiyefu* yihou", *Yeying*, 1.4 (1936.6), p. 310.

[21] See *Sanshi niandai zuoyi wenyi zhiliao xuanbian*, pp. 223–576.

[22] Altogether 37 issues of *Soviet Literature* were published between 1942 to 1949.

literature, produced in the wake of the German invasion of the
Soviet Union in 1941, won popular approval in China. This included
novels by Grossman (*People Are Immortal*), Pavlenko (*The Fire
of Revenge*), Gorbatov (*The Unvanquished*), Fadeyev (*The Young
Guard*), Simonov (*Days and Nights*), Sholokov (*They Fought for
Their Country*), Wasilevskaya (*The Rainbow*), and the three well-
known plays: Simonov's *The Russian People*, Leonov's *Invasion*,
Korneichuk's *The Front*.[23] These works, according to critics,
showed Chinese readers the way to victory at a time of invasion,
and also the truth that had propelled history forward.[24]

The practice of learning everything from Soviet literature was
blessed by Mao Zedong himself. He officially announced the policy
of following the Russian high road in 1940.[25] Two years later, in
his famous "Yan'an Talks on Literature and Art", he emphasized
the point that Soviet literature could instruct the Chinese how to
build their new literature. He also extolled Soviet fiction with its
optimistic tone and its positive hero as a model for the Chinese.
Soviet literature thus became, first in Yan'an and in the 1950s in
the whole of the People's Republic, the model for Chinese writers.
The extent of the Soviet impact can be seen from the strong presence
of Russian works in Chinese translation. The number of Russian
literary works translated rose steadily from 37 in 1949 to 277 in
1956. The breakdown of relations with the Soviet Union and a severe
paper shortage brought the number down to 62 in 1960.[26] The
figures are more significant when compared first, with the number
of such translations of foreign literature published, and second, with
the number of Chinese literary works published. The first set totalled
52 in 1949, 480 in 1956 and 119 in 1960; while the second included
21 in 1949, 2,657 in 1956 and 1,408 in 1960. Russian translations
represented in 1949 an astounding 50.7% of all translations and

[23] In his article, "Waida weiguo zhanzheng zhong de Sulian wenxue", Ge
Baoquan included a list of the Soviet defensive works translated into Chinese.
See his article in *WYFX*, 3.3 (1947.5), pp. 349–359.
[24] See Mao Dun, "Jinnian lai jieshao de waiguo wenxue", in *MWZJ*, Vol. 2, pp.
1055–1063; A Ying, "Eluosi he Sulian wenxue zai Zhongguo", in *A Ying wenji*,
Vol. 2, pp. 656–659.
[25] Mao Zedong, "Xin minzhu zhuyi lun", in *Mao Zedong xuanji*, Vol. 2, p. 661.
[26] These figures are included in Wolfgang Bauer's study, *Western Literature and
Translation Work in Communist China*, pp. 16–20.

original works published. They were still an impressive 8.8% in 1956 and declined to a low of 4.1% in 1960. In the field of literary works in translation alone, the Russian figure is even more impressive: 71.2% in 1949, 57.7% in 1956, and 52.1% in 1960. While the exact strength of the Russian literary impact awaits further study, the strong presence of the Soviet model in Chinese literary life in the 1950s is beyond question.

Although Mao gave the general direction, it was Zhou Yang, the guardian of Chinese literary policy until his downfall in the mid-1960s, who gave detailed instructions on how Soviet literature was to be received. In his article entitled "Socialist Realism—the Road for Chinese Literature", written for *Pravda* (1952.12) and printed in *Xinhua yuebao* in 1953, Zhou Yang paid lavish tribute to Soviet literature. He proclaimed that Stalin's directives as well as Zhdanov's lectures on literature and art, had provided "the most correct and most important guidance" for China. According to Zhou, China had moved into an epoch of socialist construction and witnessed the emergence of the socialist "new man". Since workers had taken their place as leaders of the country, peasants were busy setting up collectives and intellectuals had been educated in the Marxist outlook, the time had come for the development of socialist realism in literature. However, Chinese writers were still inexperienced in portraying these new people. Their characters tended to be stereotypes, and their works written according to a formula. Zhou Yang believed that the Soviet positive heroes, who epitomized "the high morality and quality of communism", were models for the Chinese readers and writers.[27] He singled out Soviet models from which the Chinese could learn: *Iron Torrent, The Rout, And Quiet Flows the Don, Virgin Soil Upturned , How the Steel Was Tempered , The Young Guard, Days and Nights, The Russian People* and *The Front*. This thesis was repeated again in his speech in the Second Congress of the Soviet Writers' Union in 1955. As to the examples of the Soviet hero, he mentioned, apart from the protagonists of *How the Steel Was Tempered* and *The Young Guard*, those in Polevoy's *The Story of a Real Man*, Pavlenko's

---

[27] Zhou Yang, "Shehuizhuyi xianshizhuyi—Zhongguo wenxue qianjin de daolu", in ZWCZ, Vol. 3, pp. 204–211.

Happiness (1947), Nikolayeva's *Harvest* (1951) and Azhayev's *Far Away from Moscow*.[28]

It is significant that all the above works are official models of the Stalinist era. The Chinese were, as Zhou Yang's 1952 article attested, staunch supporters and defenders of the Stalinist policy. Their adhesion to the Stalinist line was even more obvious after Stalin's death in 1953. The de-Stalinization campaign saw the first "thaw" in Soviet literature, after the title of Ehrenburg's novel, and the appearance of anti-bureaucratic works like Dudintsev's *Not by Bread Alone*.[29] The Chinese reaction to this "thaw" can best be described as cold. Dudintsev's work was indeed translated, but restricted to internal circulation.[30] In a Special Issue on Soviet literature in 1957, the editors of *Yi wen* (Translations) chose works of the following writers for translation: Bednyi, Blok, Ehrenburg, Fadeyev, Fedin, Gorky, Lavrenyov, Leonov, Malyshkin, Maya-kovsky, Privshvin, Serafimovich, Surkov, A. Tolstoy, Tvardovsky, and Yesenin.[31] What is remarkable about this list is that they are all "reliable" writers who had established their names before the Revolution or as early as the 1920s. Moreover, as Fokkema pointed out in his study, the young writers who made their name in China, like Katsis, Chukovsky and Zakbrutkin were all known for their conservative views.[32]

With his advocacy of a "fusion of revolutionary realism and revolutionary romanticism" in literature in 1958, Mao Zedong

---

[28] *Sulian renmin de wenxue*, Vol. 1, p. 203.

[29] Dudintsev's work, which appeared in 1956, was about the conflict between an individual who has a vital idea and a Soviet collective dominated by men whose chief interest is in protecting their own preserves and furthering their own careers. The author was criticized for presenting careerists and opportunists as creatures of the Soviet power system. See Deming Brown, *Soviet Russian Literature since Stalin*, pp. 299–300.

[30] Fokkema holds the opinion that Wang Meng's story "Zuzhibu laile ge nianqingren", which appeared in September 1956, has many similarities with Ehrenburg's *The Thaw*, although no evidence has been found that Wang Meng knew Ehrenburg's work. But judging from the extensive borrowings of his protagonists from Soviet letters and Russian culture, Wang Meng, as Fokkema rightly points out, seemingly at that time approved of the superiority of Soviet and Russian culture over the indigenous Chinese. See Fokkema's work, *Literary Doctrine in China and Soviet Influence, 1956–1960*, pp. 99–101.

[31] Ibid., p. 187.

[32] Ibid., pp. 223–224.

turned Chinese literature away from the Soviet model.[33] Mao's doctrine, which stipulated that literature should concentrate on depicting a visionary communist society to be brought about by the revolution, without being bogged down by excessive details, was foreign to Soviet writings of that time. Seen from such a background, Zhou Yang's condemnation of Grigorev Baklanov's work *The Foothold* is no coincidence. This work, and a body of novels of the war which began to appear in 1956, tried to analyse the psychology of soldiers in the trenches, showing men under the cruel conditions of war but without dwelling on war's horrors. The writers were keenly interested in moral problems, often placing their protagonists in situations where they were alone with their consciences and where their conduct depended on the strength of their conviction and sense of duty. The appearance and popularity of these works reflected a more "liberal" attitude to literature in the Khrushchev era. Although Zhou Yang only mentioned his disapproval of the vignettes of the private life of the soldiers: their thoughts and fears, loves and hates, courage and cowardice, there is no doubt as to his concern about a larger problem—the alarming trend in Soviet literature towards humanist values.[34] The Chinese campaign against "humanism" in literature in 1958 was their protest against the Soviet "big brother".[35] In 1960, Zhou Yang threw away all pretence and lashed out at "the recent Soviet revisionists' vicious attacks on socialist realism". This revisionist tide must be turned back, according to Zhou, by employing Mao's doctrine of the "fusion of revolutionary realism and revolutionary romanticism", so that "this heroic age and its heroes can be most truthfully and profoundly depicted".[36] Zhou again referred, as he had in 1952 and 1955, to the model novels: *Iron Torrent*, *The Rout*, *Chapaev*, *How the Steel Was Tempered*, *The Young Guard*, and *The Story of a Real Man*. For him, these were works which "truthfully depict the Soviet people's indestructible revolutionary will and their unceasing loyalty to the motherland and to Communism".[37] The

---

[33] Mao first mentioned this concept in his letter to Zhuang Kejia in 1958.
[34] Zhou Yang, *Woguo shehuizhuyi wenxue yishu de daolu*, pp. 57–58.
[35] Fokkema, as n. 30, pp. 231–255.
[36] Zhou Yang, as n. 34, pp. 42–43.
[37] Ibid., pp. 56–59.

Chinese continued to hold high the Stalinist banner.

With the Sino-Soviet split in the 1960s, the emulation of Soviet works abruptly came to an end. What followed was the already well-known story of the extreme Sino-centrism of the Cultural Revolution and the persecution of intellectuals. Soviet literature was branded as revisionist. For example, *Virgin Soil Upturned* was condemned as a "poisonous weed".[38] It is ironical that, among his many hats, Zhou Yang was given that of "a crony of Khrushchev",[39] and his article "On the Road of Socialist Literature and Art" (1960) was denounced as "the road to bourgeois literature and art".[40] Soviet literature ceased to be the guiding light of Chinese literature. Even after the downfall of the "Gang of Four" and the reappearance of Soviet classics, it never recovered its former glory. One may doubt whether it ever will.

III. The Positive Hero

While the influence of Soviet fiction on its Chinese counterpart remains a topic for study,[41] it is clear that the works produced in China were remarkably close to their Soviet precursors. This closeness was not merely the result of the Chinese taking the Soviet works as models, but was also due to the highly ritualized form and content of communist fiction in general. We see the same characters persistently appearing in Soviet as well as Chinese communist fiction. There is the strong, healthy, devoted, selfless and Party-conscious political hero; the heartless, cruel, faceless negative hero beyond the reach of pity and redemption; and the

[38] See *Ping Xiaoluohuofu de "Jingjing de Dunhe" he "Bei kaiken de chunüdi"*.

[39] See Qi Weihong, "Zhou Yang—Xialuxiaofu de yingshengchong", in *Chedi pipan Zhou Yang de fangeming xiuzhengzhuyi wenyi heixian*, pp. 45–50.

[40] Wu Jiwen, "Shehuizhuyi wenxue yishu daolu, haishi zhibenzhuyi wenxue yishu daolu", ibid., pp. 93–109.

[41] Cyril Birch mentioned Sholokov's *Virgin Soil Upturned* as an example for Zhou Libo's *Bao feng zhou yu*, "Fiction of the Yenan Period", *The China Quarterly*, 4 (1960), p. 9; Fokkema noted Wang Meng's indebtedness to Galina Nikolayeva's *The Director of the MTS and the Chief Agricultural Expert*, as n. 30; Ai Wu cited his learning from *The Rout*, *Iron Torrent*, *Cement* and *And Quiet Flows the Don*, in "Wo yu Sulian wenxue", *WYB*, 22 (1956), p. 17. All these are, however, passing comments which can be elaborated further.

immense and powerful masses of illiterate and essentially good-natured people in need of leadership. Whether these novels are about production, invention, war, revolution, the villain or spy, the guerilla or underground worker, about Western capitalism or history—the major themes of communist fiction—they follow the same dramatic designs. The protagonist of modest background, usually proletarian, sets out to accomplish the task he believes history has assigned to him. On his way, he comes to recognize the "bad elements" closing in on him, and this either causes him to waver in his singleminded resolve or to doubt the efficacy of his action. By subordinating his emotions to Party teaching, he is enlightened and faces his trials with renewed confidence and a greater consciousness. In the end he sees his tasks accomplished and becomes an example for others.[42] The life journey of the "positive hero" thus recapitulates symbolically the stages of historical progress as described in Marxist-Leninist theory. The consequence is that in communist fiction there can be only one kind of hero, performing one kind of task, with one kind of outcome, as Mathewson points out.[43] In fact, so depersonalized are the revolutionary deeds of these figures that they are almost completely reduced to being the functions of their roles, which are themselves ideologically determined.

It is precisely the protagonists' acting out the role assigned to them by the Zhdanov dogma (of looking into the future which is not a Utopia, but "being prepared for today by dint of conscious planned work"[44]) which accounts for the stock typology of Stalinist fiction. The same stock image can also be found in Stalinist-inspired Chinese works of the 1950s and 1960s. Looking at the galaxy of fictional heroes who enacted the communist drama in Chinese works since 1949, we find the portrait of a person whose selflessness and dedication in championing Party-sponsored truth has made him a model for emulation. He is invariably a worker, peasant, soldier or a revolutionary cadre with a definite purpose in life. Choices and decisions are made strictly according to Party principles.

[42] This "master plot" in Soviet fiction is summarized succinctly in Katerina Clark's book, as n. 14, pp. 255–260.
[43] Rufus Mathewson, *The Positive Hero in Russian Literature*, p. 228.
[44] Zhdanov, as n. 13, p. 22.

Internal conflicts often take the form of the protagonist's struggle
to perfect himself on his road to communism. It is sufficient to
quote the examples of Yang Zirong in Qu Bo's *Linhai xueyuan*
(Tracks in a Snowy Forest, 1956) and the underground workers in
Luo Guangbin's and Yang Yiyan's *Hongyan* (Red Crag, 1962), two
widely read works which sold by the million.[45]

Qu Bo's novel shows, among other things, the heroism of Yang
Zirong, a communist regiment scout of lower peasant background.
Yang demonstrates his fearlessness by killing a tiger by himself. He
further shows his skill and intelligence when, as a "mole" in their
camp, he outwits the Nationalist bandits. The most important thing
is that Yang owes his education and consciousness to the Party,
and his whole existence is geared to fulfilling the task that the Party
has assigned to him. No less heroic are the underground workers
like Sister Jiang and Xu Yunfeng in *Red Crag*. Imprisoned and
tortured by the Nationalist agents, these revolutionaries distinguished themselves by their extraordinary confidence in and
dedication to the Party. The source of their strength and their
superhuman qualities in enduring hardship is their belief that the
Party's cause will eventually triumph. For these people and for
communist positive heroes in general, suffering or even death for
the Party, when called for, is taken as a matter of course. Thus
the protagonist Ouyang Hai in *Ouyang Hai zhi ge* (The Song of
Ouyang Hai, 1966) is ready for his glorious end when he plunges
to his death to save the lives of his comrades and also state property.
The sanguine positive hero who leads the masses forward by his
example has never been allowed to relinquish the central position
in Chinese communist fiction.

In contrast, the urban intelligentsia, who dominated Chinese
fiction for half a century, have almost disappeared from the scene.
This has come as a result of the Party's suspicions about the
reliability of the urban intelligentsia. Chairman Mao stipulated in
his "Yan'an Talks" that literary works should specifically serve the
needs of the workers, peasants and soldiers. Writers with an
intellectual upbringing should reform their thoughts in order to

---

[45] For a study of the plot summaries of major Chinese communist novels, see
Joe Huang, *Heroes and Villains in Communist China*.

produce works which can truly reflect the revolutionary zeal of the proletariat. Behind his proclamation is the belief that the dry theorizing of the intellectuals is sterile, and that their concern for individuality is damaging to the revolution. The most potent and effective forces for bringing about positive change in agrarian China, the communist leader asserted, were to be found among the broad masses of illiterate peasants. It is within the ranks of the soldiers, peasants and workers that the most typical, significant and true hero in the communist sense of the word flourishes. The opposition between the country (the spontaneous, instinctive, uneducated peasant masses capable of popular uprising) and the city (the concerned, bureaucratized and Westernized intellectual elite seeking to direct the masses) has been made more acute because of the Party's distrust of the intellectuals.[46] Educating them to adopt a correct mass outlook has thus been one of the Party's most arduous tasks since its Yan'an days. Writers who were accustomed to depicting intellectual life, like Mao Dun, Ba Jin, Qian Zhongshu (author of *Wai cheng*, Besieged City), suddenly found themselves in a new milieu. This explains to a considerable extent why many writers of the May Fourth tradition who had initially welcomed the transition to socialism became so unproductive under the new regime. Ba Jin is a sombre example. Well known for his abundant output of "intellectual" novels, he later only produced some reportage about the bravery of the soldiers in the Korean front in 1953. As a result of his unfamiliarity with Party politics and army life, his work *Yingxiong de gushi* (The Tales of the Heroes) is little more than a repetition of revolutionary slogans.

Given such constraints, the only theme open to the writer who dares to depict the intellectual is the latter's transformation into a revolutionary hero. The portrayal of those who are opposed to the new age, or whose psychological make-up put them at odds with it, is simple. They are easily exposed as villains or class enemies. But presenting the intellectuals who have adjusted themselves or become revolutionized is more problematic. The tension between city and country, old and new, coupled with the Party's gnawing

[46] Clark refers to the conflict between spontaneity and consciousness in Soviet literature, as n. 14, pp. 15–24.

doubt about whether the intellectuals can actually disavow their petty-bourgeois class allegiance are all thorny issues which have to be thrashed out without deviating from current Party policy. The intensity of these problems is brought to the fore in the character types of such well-known works as Wen Cai in Ding Ling's *Taiyang zhao zai Sanggan he shang* (The Sun Shines Over Sanggan River, 1949), Liu Shiwu and Lin Zhen in Wang Meng's "Zuzhibu laile ge nianqingren" (A Young Newcomer to the Organization Department, 1956), and Lin Daojing in Yang Mo's *Qingchun zhi ge* (The Song of Youth, 1957).

Wen Cai, the first intellectual hero to appear in a major communist novel, embodies the conflict between city and country, consciousness and spontaneity. He belongs to the generation of urban intellectuals attracted to the communist cause who subsequently joined the Party, and went to the countryside hoping to enlighten the peasant masses. His May Fourth lineage is exhibited in his inclination towards self-expression, pomposity and pedantic theorizing. His alienation from the masses is shown in the way he bombards the peasants with six hours of indoctrination about the political situation of China, quoting Edgar Snow, Agnes Smedley and Wen Yiduo. Moreover, Wen Cai's distrust of the peasants not only sharpens the city-country opposition, but also disrupts his work as leader of the land reform team. The author's message is clear, when, at the end of novel, Wen Cai's mistake is rectified by the organization chief, Zhang Pin, a young cadre of peasant origin. Humbled and educated, Wen Cai carries out his task effectively.

Although Ding Ling, echoing Party policy, exposes Wen Cai's intellectualism in a negative light, this has not put his character beyond criticism. The crux of the matter lies with his "education". As critic Zhu Keyu points out, it is unrealistic that Wen Cai, lacking any positive qualities, should take on a positive image after reaching his so-called enlightenment. The thinking behind this dissenting view is that the transformation of the intellectuals, who have been moulded into an individual way of behaviour and an aloofness from the masses, is a difficult and tortuous task.[47] In her eagerness to

---

[47] Zhu Keyu, "Lun *Taiyang zhao zai Sanggan he shang*", included in Yuan Liangjun (ed.), *Ding Ling yanjiu zhiliao*, pp. 379–380.

show Wen Cai's regeneration, Ding Ling has allowed herself to fall into the trap of over-simplification.

Intellectual transformation is also the major concern in Wang Meng's story "A Young Newcomer to the Organization Department". This is crystallized in the conflict between Liu Shiwu and Lin Zhen. As a former student leader of Beijing University, Liu Shiwu has a taste for literature and likes the work of Turgenev and Sholokov. He is articulate and possesses an analytical mind, qualities which he puts to good use in his present work as Party district commissar of organization. As a revolutionary, Liu has the impeccable qualification of having been crippled by scoundrels when leading a procession against the Guomindang. Nonchalantly and with little enthusiasm, he now assumes his duty. His problem is simply that he has grown too complacent and inert, unwilling to deal with vital and sensitive issues. His reluctance to handle the case of Wang Qingquan, the incompetent manager of the gunny bag factory, brings the matter to a head and triggers the discontent of young Party member Lin Zhen, who has just been assigned as one of his assistants.

Lin Zhen represents the generation of intellectuals who have been nurtured by the Party since 1949. He has a strong orientation towards Russian literature and culture. The novels of Russian masters like Turgenev and Sholokov, and the music of Tchaikovsky provide spirtual food for him. He is especially inspired by Galina Nikolayeva's work, *The Director of the MTS and the Chief Agricultural Expert*, prescribed reading for the members of the Chinese Communist Youth League. It is the example of Nastya that Lin wants to emulate—a fervent yet inexperienced agricultural expert who singlehandedly challenges the stagnation of the cadres of the Machines and Tractor Station. His conflict with Liu Shiwu therefore signifies not only a difference in the style of work between the younger and older cadres, but shows the revolutionized intellectual cadres becoming sterile.

One might imagine that in so far as he shakes the Party bureaucracy into action, Lin Zhen would be a perfect fit for the label of "positive hero". He was not accepted as such. His character type, while liked by some, was vehemently disliked by others. One of the main criticisms levelled against him was his so-called one-sided and unhealthy feelings. According to this view, Lin Zhen is a young intellectual with little experience of life who attempts to solve complicated problems with bookish knowledge. Moreover, he makes his own individual choices and lacks a feeling for the collective.[48] While such views may be contested, the interesting thing is Wang Meng's readiness to admit his inadequacies, when he confessed that like his hero he also longed for a "simple and transparent" life, and that his tendency towards self-regard, sentimentality and melancholy was typical of the *petit-bourgeois* intellectual class. In the author's own words, not only was he unable to take issue with Lin Zhen's unhealthy feelings, he actually became their captive.[49]

Wang Meng's self-criticism reflects the difficulty in depicting the intellectual hero, who is by his very nature scrupulous, doubting, critical and easily given to discontent. Whereas the criticism of Wen Cai and Liu Shiwu is justifiable, that of Lin Zhen simply shows up the Party's distrust of the intellectuals. Whether these people are educated on the way and become socialized as a result or whether they have come of age with the Party is irrelevant. The case of Lin Daojing in *The Song of Youth*, a novel set in Guomindang China, is another example. Writing with caution, Yang Mo stressed that her theme was none other than the transformation of her heroine, a university student of wealthy background, from a *petit-bourgeois* intellectual into a revolutionary.[50] Through her education by the Party underground members, Lin had undoubtedly expurgated many of her *petit-bourgeois* sentiments, such as her romantic dreams about nature, love and revolution, as well as her melancholic temperament. Her year in prison further strengthened her and she was accepted into the Party. Again, one would assume that Lin possesses all the necessary qualities of a positive hero. If individualism can be charged against Lin Zhen, Lin Daojing is above such accusations by virtue of her compassion and generosity. The fact that she was still criticized for seeking an individual solution further underlines the perils of depicting intellectual transformation.

[48] See *Wang Meng zhuanji*, pp. 378–382.
[49] "Guanyu 'Zuzhibu laile ge nianqingren'", in ibid., p. 44.
[50] Yang Mo, "Tantan Lin Daojing de xingxiang", in *Chuangzuo jingyan mantan*, pp. 72–73.

Coming in to her defence, Mao Dun held that Lin's experience no doubt demonstrated the difficulty of the intellectual's road to greater consciousness, but that the work would have greater merit had the author allowed Lin Daojing a larger degree of integration with the workers and peasants. Such integration, Mao Dun reasoned, had become a reality at the time when Yang Mo penned her novel.[51]

The demand for the intellectual to effect a total integration with the workers, peasants and soldiers reached its zenith during the Cultural Revolution. At the time intellectuals were denounced as the scum of society. Fictional heroes were represented by Hao Ran's protagonist Gao Daquan (a name coined from the characters for loftiness, greatness and perfection) in *Jinguang dadao* (The Great Golden Road). The principle of "three prominences" (*san tuchu*), which focussed on the most revolutionary, heroic and positive aspects of the socialist new man, dominated literary creation for more than a decade. The intellectual hero, with his doubts and procrastination, was completely swept aside to make way for this positive hero of almost mythical stature.

Seen against this background, it is indeed remarkable that a work such as Dai Houying's *Ren ah, Ren!* (Man ah, Man!) ever got published at all.[52] It is true that the Party kept literature and art on a less tight rein in the immediate aftermath of the Cultural Revolution. This resulted in the mushrooming of a whole corpus of "scarred" literature which protested against the excesses and malpractices of the Cultural Revolution. While *Man*, published in 1980, is like these works in relating the traumatic experiences of its central characters in these lawless years, and gives the usual dose of anti-bureaucratism and anti-"Gang-of-Four-ism", it differs from the other writings in its principle. This is expressed, daringly, in the protagonist's lingering doubts about Marxism, or at least, a form

---

[51] Mao Dun, "Zenmo pingjia *Qingchun zhi ge*", in *Mao Dun pinglun wenji*, Vol. 1, p. 279.

[52] *Ren ah, Ren!* was published in November 1980, while her first work, *Shiren zhi si* was not published until two years later, presumably for some "internal reasons". The author wrote in her afterword to *Ren* that she recorded with infinite joy the resuscitation of humanity. She believes that Marxism and humanism are in mutual agreement, and that she is not afraid of "self-expression". She wants to express the relationship of this "self" with her times and its people, pp. 353–354.

of Marxism. This merits a more detailed study of the work and its underlying presuppositions.

IV. The Intellectual Predicament

The story line of *Man* is simple. It dwells on the life and thoughts of a group of intellectuals, mostly university teachers, who were reinstated in their former posts at C University after the trauma of the Cultural Revolution. The story begins with Zhao Zhenhuan, divorced from his childhood sweetheart Sun Yue during the Cultural Revolution, now finding a loveless life with his present wife difficult, and hoping to be reconciled with his former wife. Meantime, Sun Yue, who has become the Party Secretary of the Department of Chinese in C University, once again meets her former classmate He Jingfu, the protagonist of the novel. During the anti-rightist campaign in 1957 He had been severely criticized and was later classified as a rightist for daring to take the side of a classmate accused of having overseas connections. The attack on He abruptly put an end to the incipient relationship between him and Sun Yue. With his love thwarted and his political future in tatters, He left the university and became an underground man who went from place to place doing odd jobs to keep himself alive. While in his "underground" existence, He began research on the relationship between humanism and Marxism, and came to the conclusion that the state should treat its people as human beings, and respect their rights as individuals. He was against taking class struggle as an end and advocated instead more freedom, democracy and equality in a socialist society. As the story unfolded, Sun Yue fell in love with He again and the chances of He's manuscript, "On Marxism and Humanism", appearing in print looked good. Things seemed to be going well until he became once again the target of attack, this time for his "heretical" ideas on humanism. The Party authorities managed by devious means to halt the publication of the manuscript. The story ended with Sun Yue refusing Zhao's plea for reconciliation with him, and hinted that she would risk her future and stand by He in his efforts to obtain justice.

The above synopsis certainly does not do justice to a rather intricate plot, which is quite effectively executed through the internal monologues of the main characters and the author's experimentation with the device of showing the shifting viewpoints of her protagonists. This, however, is not my concern here. The real issue at stake is that, although Dai Houying, a former Shanghai Red Guard who personally persecuted well-known writers like the poet Wen Jie, may not have construed her work as a test of Party tolerance, that is exactly what the work has managed to become. Take the following conversation between the main characters:

> A colleague sighed: "Difficult as the situation is, as long as one has ideals, one will achieve peace of mind." "But the price is too high", Xu interrupted.
>
> "If we know what we are searching for, the price is all right", Sun Yue murmured, as if in a dream.
>
> He Jingfu looked at the others and said: "Isn't it amusing to look back on our student days. We were so excited then that when we talked of ideals, our faces glowed and our eyes were shining. Now look at us, we are so gloomy and introspective. Have our ideals become degraded, or have we?"
>
> To this Xu replied immediately: "Both!"[53]

What is worrying and even devastating is the cynicism which pervades the thinking of these intellectuals. It is no wonder that this work incurred the displeasure of the authorities, who banned it shortly after publication.

To do justice to Dai Houying, He Jingfu is less cynical than most of his contemporaries. When he refuses to give in to the high-handed action of the Party authorities in banning the publication of his manuscript, he once again puts his own life and future in jeopardy. In He's harrassments, the author portrayed sympathetically the lonely individual living out his life in a continual battle with adversity, constantly forging his identity as he struggles against hostile circumstances. The pathos of the whole situation is simply that he wishes to preserve the living seeds of existence as a human being. Seen in this perspective, the "small" way in which he manages to stay morally alive becomes heroic: the hero is spiritually

---

[53] Ibid., p. 198.

unbreakable, successful in his stance of opposition, true to his mission, an example to others.

Unlike Yang Zirong or Sister Jiang before him, He cannot be labelled a positive hero. The difference between the officially sanctioned hero and this battered survivor lies in their particular circumstances. The model hero lives and acts within the confines of an infallible doctrine promising certain success in the public domain, whatever the private cost. The survivor-hero generates his moral strength out of his own personal resources in conditions of solitude and continual adversity. Stretched to the limit of endurance, he develops and formulates ideas which he germinates out of experience. His personal "ideology" is a function of his character, not vice versa. Thus, the vitriolic attacks that he underwent during the anti-rightist campaign, his thwarted love affair with Sun Yue, and above all, his "underground" experience, serve to foster and strengthen his instinct for survival, mellow him into producing his treatise on "Marxism and Humanism", and immunize him against further harassments. As he says to Sun Yue: "In order to survive and search for the truth, one must learn to tolerate everything, including injustice and insult."[54] If in the world of fiction the model hero wins by exterminating evil whenever he finds it, the survivor triumphs precisely by defining it and holding it, at least temporarily, at bay.

In essence, He Jingfu is a communist new man: he is sure of himself, knows what he is after, and fights for it. But by honouring his own beliefs, which deviate from Party policy, he disqualifies himself from joining the family of the positive hero. In a different manner, his "Quixote-like" actions in redressing the wrongs of the Party bureaucracy also distinguish him from the ambivalent May Fourth intellectual tradition.

However, He Jingfu is not an entirely new type. His portrait provides a concrete example of the continuity and change in the delineation of character in modern Chinese fiction. Although immensely more heroic than his May Fourth predecessor, he has, nevertheless, an important affinity with him. Indeed, the experience of reading this novel is like that of revisiting a house one used to

[54] Ibid., pp. 309–310.

be familiar with after a lapse of many long years. The house may have been renovated, the old residents have left, but something of the past still hangs in the air. Like his many May Fourth predecessors, He is first and foremost a man of intellect, who seeks to define his existence through moral and intellectual convictions. It is partly because of his intellectual dissatisfaction with the official clichés about humanism that he sets out to redefine it in moral and intellectual terms. And his refusal to downgrade his intellect puts him at loggerheads with the Party authorities.

The May Fourth hero found himself in a similar predicament. The typical intellectual hero, often unheroic, self-conscious and hypersensitive, asserts himself less through his physical prowess and courageous deeds than through the superiority of his moral sensitivity and intellect. Individuals exist in these works not only as part of the social whole, but as representatives of the hero's awareness of himself as a solitary being, battered about as he gropes for fulfilment. The unavoidable clash between his social condition and consciousness predestines him to failure. Writers like Lu Xun, Yu Dafu, Mao Dun or Ba Jin are accompanied by their awakened yet estranged heroes in their odyssey across the troubled seas of the 1920s and 1930s. In their works is transmitted not only the "feel"of a national literature, but also the destiny of a nation. One sees in them forces seething and straining to break out but hemmed in, and unable to escape. In them the political, ethical and personal aspects of "la condition humaine" are explored, experienced, and dramatized with the utmost intensity.

It is this characteristic concern for the fate of the individual human being in a mass society that links Dai Houying's work with the mainstream of May Fourth writing. Writers in the finest May Fourth tradition, like their Russian predecessors, concerned themselves with the individual, with the problem of freedom and responsibility, with the relationship of each separate unit of humanity to the sum total: call it the broad masses, the collective, the organization, the group, or society. This theme, recurrent and inescapable in May Fourth writing, is pervasive in Dai Houying's *Man*, just as it is shunned in the officially sanctioned writings.

Shortly after this novel was published, it was criticized by the official channels for championing individualism and bourgeois humanism, for its abstract conception of life and for its attempt to throw mud at socialism. To the extent that the author challenges the status quo by exposing human suffering, or that she is concerned with the fate of individual human beings and expresses her respect for untrammelled thought, these criticisms of her work are justly directed. In the end the root of the problem rests with the philosophic conception of life and with the artistic representation of reality. On this we have only human experience as our final arbiter. In fact, the whole process of learning from the Russians, concentrated in the celebrated typologies of the superfluous and the positive hero, epitomized one chapter of human activity that is of the utmost importance in modern China. While the large-scale transplantation from Russian and Soviet literature is a historical phenomenon which may not be repeated, the experimentation with the two types and what they represent—exemplary political conduct and human fallibility—will hardly come to an end. The hero with a concern for a humanized relationship with society has indeed been given a new lease of life with the emergence of the "survivor" types.[55] The question remains as to how long these "survivors"—the writer and his protagonist—will be allowed to live out the night. In the end, the sort of soil these writers turn up will bear important witness not only to their artistic innovations, but, above all, to the quality of life in China in the years to come. . . .

The search for an answer goes on.

[55] The ambivalent and strongly existential I-figure in Zhao Zhenkai's *Bodong* (Waves), who has a strong taste for Western culture, is a remarkable example. See Bonnie S. McDougall, "Zhao Zhenkai's Fiction: A Study in Cultural Alienation", in *Modern Chinese Literature*, 1.2 (1985.5), pp. 103–127.

Glossary

A Shun	阿順
An Shouyi	安壽頤
Baixiang cipu	白香詞譜
Bao feng zhou yu	暴風驟雨
Baosu	抱素
Cai Yuanpei	蔡元培
caizi	才子
Cao Xie	曹謝
Chen Shicheng	陳仕誠
Cheng Fangwu	成仿吾
"Chuangzao"	創造
Chunguang shudian	春光書店
Daming	大溟
Donglin	東林
Du Daxin	杜大心
Du Fu	杜甫
Eguo qingshi	俄國情史
Ermei	二妹

Fan Zhongyan	范仲淹
Fang	方
Fen	墳
"Feng zeng Wei Zuocheng zhang ershier yun"	奉贈韋左丞丈二十二韻
Funü zazhi	婦女雜誌
Fusheng liuji	浮生六記
Fuyang	富陽
Gao Daquan	高大全
Gao Di	高地
Gao Juexin	高覺新
Gao Tao	高滔
Hangzhou	杭州
Hao Ran	浩然
He Daosheng	何道生
He Jingfu	何競夫
He Qiming	賀啓明
Heiyi jiaoshi	黑衣教士
Hong Lingfei	洪靈菲
Hong Zhijun	洪智君
Hongloumeng	紅樓夢
Hou Fangyu	侯方域
Hu Shi	胡適
Hua yue hen	花月痕
Huang Zhongze	黃仲則
Hui	惠
huiguan	會館
Ji Yihun	戢翼翬
[Sister] Jiang	江姐
Jiaxing	嘉興
Jiayin xiaozhuan	迦茵小傳
Jinbu	進步
Jing	靜
Jing Ping Mei	金瓶梅
Juansheng	涓生
juren	舉人
Kaiming shudian	開明書店

Lao Can	老殘
Lao Tongbao	老通寶
Li Baishi	李白時
Li Jingshu	李靜淑
Li Leng	李冷
Li Peizhu	李佩珠
Li Wai	李威
Li Yong	李邕
Lian	蓮
Lin Daojing	林道靜
Lin Zhen	林震
Lina	利娜
Lingnan yuyi nüshi	嶺南羽衣女士
Liu Man	劉曼
Liu Shiwu	劉世吾
Lu Yishi	路易士
Lu You	陸游
Lü Weifu	呂韋甫
Luo Guangbin	羅廣斌
Luo Guanzhong	羅貫中
Luo Pu	羅樸
Manghuji	猛虎集
Mei	梅
Mingdong	鳴東
mingshi	名士
Ouyang Hai	歐陽海
Pu Songling	蒲松齡
Putian zhongfen ji	普天衆憤集
Qian Zhongshu	錢鍾書
Qiang Weili	強惟力
Qiuju	秋菊
Qu Bo	曲波
Qu Yuan	屈原
Quanjun	荃君
Quanlin	荃麟
Refeng	熱風

Renjianshi	人間世
Ruan Ji	阮籍
"Semang"	色盲
Shanxi	山西
Shen Fu	沈復
Shi Naian	施耐庵
Shi Xun	史循
"Shi yu sanwen"	詩與散文
Sun Yue	孫悅
Tang Song shiwen chun	唐宋詩文醇
Tao Qian	陶潛
Taohua shan	桃花扇
Tian tao	天討
Wang Han	王翰
Wang Weigao	王維鎬
Wang Zhongzhao	王仲昭
Wei Lienshu	魏連殳
Wei Yu	韋玉
Wen Cai	文采
Wen Jei	聞捷
Wen Tianxiang	文天祥
Wen Zhu	文珠
Wenhua shenghuo congshu	文化生活叢書
Wenxue xunkan	文學旬刊
Wenying	文穎
Wu Renmin	吳仁民
Wu Shou	吳檮
Wu Sunfu	吳蓀甫
Wu Yue yishu	吳樾遺書
Wu Zhengzhi	吳敬梓
Xiandai	現代
Xihu jiahua	西湖佳話
Xin	新
Xinfan	新反
Xinhua yuebao	新華月報
Xinxiaoshuo huipian	新小說彙編
xiucai	秀才

Xixiang ji	西廂記
Xu	許
Xu Yunfeng	許云峰
Yan'an	延安
Yang Xiong	揚雄
Yang Yiyan	楊益言
Yenzi jian	燕子箋
"Yi Li Bai"	憶李白
Yin niukou	銀紐扣
Yixian	宜閑
Youhuan yusheng	憂患餘生
Yun	云
Yutian de shu	雨天的書
Yuzhou feng	宇宙風
Zhang Manqing	張曼青
Zhang Pin	章品
Zhang Ruolan	張若蘭
Zhang Weiqun	張爲羣
Zhao Zhenhuan	趙振環
Zhejiang	浙江
Zhou Dinghui	周定慧
Zhou Rushui	周如水
Zhuang Kejia	臧克家
Zijun	子君
Zizhi tongjian	資治通鑑
Zuihou yiye	最後一頁
"Zuzhibu laile ge nianqingren"	組織部來了個年青人

Bibliography

A Ying 亞英. See Qian Xingcun 錢杏邨.

Ai Wu 艾蕪. "Moshuiping guazai jingzishang xiezuo de" 墨水瓶掛在頸子上寫作的. In *WYWX*, pp. 65–73.

———. "Wo yu *Sulian wenyi*" 我與《蘇聯文藝》. *WYB*, 22 (1956), p. 17.

Ailuoxianke 愛羅先珂. "Zhishi jieji de shiming" 知識階級的使命. *DFZZ*, 19.4 (1922.2), pp. 107–112.

Andrew, Joe. *Russian Writers and Society in the Second Half of the Nineteenth Century*. London: Macmillan, 1982.

———. *Writers and Society during the Rise of Russian Realism*. London: Macmillan, 1980.

Andreyev, Leonid. *Plays by Leonid Andreyeff*, tr. Clarence Meader and F. N. Scott. London: Duckworth & Co., 1915.

———. *The Red Laugh, Fragments of a Discovered Manuscript*, tr. Alexandra Linden. London: T. Fisher Unwin, 1905.

———. *The Seven Who Were Hanged*, tr. Herman Bernstein. New York: Boni & Liveright, 1909.

———. *Silence and Other Stories*, tr. W. H. Lowe. New York: Knopf, 1906.

———. *To the Stars*, tr. Maurice Magnus. London, 1921.

Artzybashev, Michael. *Sanine*, tr. Percy Pinkerton. London: Martin Secker, 1921.

———. *Tales of the Revolution*, tr. Percy Pinkerton. London: Martin Secker, 1917.

Auerbach, Erich. *Mimesis: The Representation of Reality in Western Literature*, tr. Willard R. Trask. New Jersey: Princeton University Press, 1973.

Ba Jin 巴金 . "*Aiqing de sanbuqu* zongxu" 《愛情的三部曲》總序 . *BJZJ*, pp. 266–308.

———. "*Aiqing de sanbuqu* zuozhe de zibai" 《愛情的三部曲》作者的自白 . *BJZJ*, pp. 309–321.

———. *Ba Jin wenji* 巴金文集 , 14 vols. Beijing: Wenxue chubanshe 文學出版社, 1958–1962.

———. *Ba Jin xuanji* 巴金選集. Shanghai: Chunming shudian 春明書店 , 1936.

———. *Ba Jin xuanji* 巴金選集. Beijing: Wenxue chubanshe, 1956.

———. *Ba Jin zhuanji (1)*. 巴金專集(1). Jiangsu: Renmin chubanshe 人民出版社 , 1981.

———. *Ba Jin zizhuan* 巴金自傳 . Shanghai: Diyi chubanshe 第一出版社, 1934.

———. *Chenmo ji* 沉默集. Shanghai: Shenghuo shudian 生活書店, 1934.

———. *Chuangzuo huiyilu* 創作回憶錄 . Hong Kong: Sanlian shudian 三聯書店 , 1981.

———. *Chun* 春 . Shanghai: Kaiming shudian 開明書店, 1938.

———. *Dian* 電 . Shanghai: Liangyou gongsi 良友公司, 1934.

———. *Diandi* 點滴. Shanghai: Kaiming shudian, 1935.

———. "*Dianyi ji* daixu" 《電椅集》代序. In *Ba Jin wenji*, 7:3–11.

———. *Duanjian* 短簡. Shanghai: Liangyou gongsi, 1937.

———. "Guanyu wode duanpianxiaoshuo" 關於我的短篇小說. In *Ba Jin wenji*, 7:472–473.

———. *Hai di meng* 海底夢 . Shanghai: Xin Zhongguo tushu gongsi 新中國圖書公司, 1932.

———. "Heian shili de kaocha" 黑暗勢力的考察. In *Sheng zhi chanhui*, pp. 84–85.

———. *Jia* 家. Shanghai, 1937. English translation, New York: Anchor Books, 1972.

———. *Jiangjun* 將軍 . Shanghai: Wenhua shenghuo chubanshe 文化生活出版社, 1949.

———. *Lei* 雷. Shanghai: Kaiming shudian, 1933.

———. *Mabuji* 抹布集. In *Ba Jin wenji*, 8:3–31.

———. *Menkan* 門檻. Shanghai: Wenhua shenghuo chubanshe, 1936.

———. *Miewang* 滅亡. Shanghai: Kaiming shudian, 1929.

———. "*Miewang* zuozhe de zibai" 《滅亡》作者的自白 . In *Sheng zhi chanhui*, pp. 5–6.

———. "*Qianye* yiben xu" 《前夜》譯本序. In *Sheng zhi chanhui*, p. 126.

————. *Sheng zhi chanhui* 生之懺悔. Shanghai: Shangwu yinshuguan 商務印書館, 1936.

————. *Si qu de taiyang* 死去的太陽. Shanghai: Kaiming shudian, 1933.

————. *Suixiang lu* 隨想錄. Hong Kong: Sanlian shudian, 1982. English translation by Geremie Barmé, *Random Thoughts*. Hong Kong: Joint Publishing Co., 1984.

————. *Tansuo yu huiyi* 探索與回憶. Sichuan: Renmin chubanshe, 1982.

————. "Wode xin" 我的心. In *Sheng zhi chanhui*, pp. 3–4.

————. "Wode younian" 我的幼年. In *Duanjian*, pp. 7–8.

————. "*Wode zizhuan* yiben xu" 《我的自傳》譯本序. In *Sheng zhi chanhui*, p. 137.

————. *Wu* 霧. Shanghai: Xin Zhongguo tushu gongsi, 1931.

————. *Xinsheng* 新生. Shanghai: Kaiming shudian, 1932.

————. *Yi* 《憶》. Shanghai: Wenhua shenghuo chubanshe, 1936.

————. *Yu* 雨. Shanghai: Liangyou gongsi, 1932.

————. "Zai menkan shang" 在門檻上. In *Jiangjun*, pp. 120–147.

————, tr. *Yeweiyang* 夜未央 (*On the Eve* by Leopold Kampf). Shanghai: Wenhua shenghuo chubanshe, 1936. Pseud. Kangfu 康夫.

Ba Ren 巴人. "Cong du *Huanmie* suibi" 重讀《幻滅》隨筆. *WYB*, 21 (1956), pp. 6–8.

Bai Wei 白薇. "Wo zoudao wenxue quanli de chuzhong" 我走到文學圈裏的初衷. In *WYWX*, pp. 9–23.

Bakhtin, Mikhail. *Problems of Dostoevsky's Poetics*. Minneapolis: University of Minnesota Press, 1984.

Bao Tianxiao 包天笑. *Chuanyinglou huiyilu* 釧影樓回憶錄. Hong Kong: Dahua chubanshe 大華出版社, 1971.

Baring, Maurice. *Landmarks of Russian Literature*. London: Methuen & Co., 1910.

————. *An Outline of Russian Literature*. London: The London & Norwich Press, 1909.

Bauer, Wolfgang. *Western Literature and Translation Work in Communist China*. Frankfurt/Main: A. Metzner, 1964.

Bayley, John. *The Characters of Love: A Study in the Literature of Personality*. London: Constable, 1960.

————. *Pushkin: A Comparative Commentary*. Cambridge: Cambridge University Press, 1971.

————. *Tolstoy and the Novel*. London: Chatto and Windus, 1966.

————. *The Uses of Division and Disharmony in Literature*. London: Chatto and Windus, 1976.

Berlin, Isaiah. *Russian Thinkers*. London: Hogarth Press, 1978.

Bernal, Martin. *Chinese Socialism to 1907*. Ithaca: Cornell University

Press, 1976.

Berninghausen, John. "The Central Contradiction in Mao Dun's Earliest Fiction". In *MCL*, pp. 253–259.

Bi Xiushao 畢修勺, tr. *Yige fankangzhe de hua* 一個反抗者的話 (*Speeches of a Rebel* by Kropotkin). Shanghai: Pingming shudian 平明書店, 1948.

Bian Zhilin 卞之琳, *et al.* "Shinianlaide waiguo wenxue fanyi he yanjiu gongzuo" 十年來的外國文學翻譯和研究工作. *WXPL*, 1959.5, pp. 41–77.

Billington, J. H. *The Icon and the Áxè: An Interpretative History of Russian Culture*. New York: Vintage Books, 1970.

Birch, Cyril. "Chinese Communist Literature: The Persistence of Traditional Forms". *The China Quarterly*, 13 (January–March 1963), pp. 74–89.

———. "Fiction of the Yenan Period". *The China Quarterly*, 4 (October–December 1960), pp. 1–11.

———, ed. *Anthology of Chinese Literature*, London: Penguin, 1967.

———, ed. *Chinese Communist Literature*. New York: Prager, 1963.

Bloom, Harold. *The Anxiety of Influence: A Theory of Poetry*. London: Oxford University Press, 1973.

Bloomfield, Morton W., ed. *The Interpretation of Narrative: Theory and Practice*. Cambridge, Mass.: Harvard University Press, 1970.

Booth, Wayne C. *The Rhetoric of Fiction*. Chicago: University of Chicago Press, 1973.

Brandes, Georg. *Impressions of Russia*, tr. Samuel C. Eastman. London: Scott, 1889.

Brewster, Dorothy. *East-West Passage: A Study of Literary Relationships*. London: Allen & Unwin, 1954.

Brombert, Victor. *The Intellectual Hero: Studies in the French Novel, 1889–1955*. Chicago: University of Chicago Press, 1961.

Brown, Deming. *Soviet Russian Literature since Stalin*. Cambridge: Cambridge University Press, 1978.

Brown, Edward. *Russian Literature since the Revolution*. Cambridge, Mass.: Harvard University Press, 1982 (revised and enlarged edition).

Brusyanin, V. V. "The Symbolic Dramas of Andreyeff". In *Plays by Leonid Andreyeff*, pp. xi–xxvi.

Campbell, Joseph. *The Hero with a Thousand Faces*. London: Abacus, 1975.

Cao Jinghua 曹靖華. *Fei hua ji* 飛花集. Shanghai: Wenyi chubanshe 文藝出版社, 1978.

Cao Juren 曹聚仁. *Wo yu wode shijie* 我與我的世界. Hong Kong: Sanyu tushu wenju gongsi 三育圖書文具公司, 1972.

———. *Xiaoshuo xinyu* 小說新語. Hong Kong: Nanyuan shuwu 南苑書屋, 1964.

Capouya, E. and K. Tompkins, eds. *The Essential Kropotkin*. London: Macmillan, 1976.

Carlyle, Thomas. *On Heroes, Hero Worship and the Heroic in History*, 2 vols. London: Carlyle's House Memorial Trust, n.d. Chinese translation by Zeng Xubai 曾虛白, *Yingxiong yu yingxiong chongbai* 英雄與英雄崇拜. Shanghai: Shangwu yinshuguan, 1932.

Carr, Edward Hallett. *The Romantic Exiles: A Nineteenth-century Portrait Gallery*. London: Peregrine Books, 1968.

Chang Feng 常風. "Tuosituoyefusiji de *Baichi*" 陀思妥以夫斯基的《白癡》. *Wenxue zazhi* 文學雜誌, 2.1 (1947.6), pp. 203–208.

Chang Hao. *Liang Ch'i-ch'ao and Intellectual Transition in China, 1890–1907*. Cambridge, Mass.: Harvard University Press, 1971.

Charvet, P. E. *A Literary History of France*, Vols. 5 & 6. London: Ernest Benn, 1967.

Chen Duxiu 陳獨秀. *Duxiu wencun* 獨秀文存, 2 vols. Shanghai: Yadong tushuguan 亞東圖書館, 1934.

———. "Jing gao qingnian" 敬告青年. *XQN*, 1.1 (1915.9), pp. 1–6.

Chen Jialin 陳家麟 and Chen Dadeng 陳大鐙, tr. *Enuo xiaoshi* 婀娜小史 (*Anna Karenina*). Zhonghua shuju, 1917.

Chen Shuliang 陳叔諒. "Tuoersitai dansheng baizhounien jinian— Tuoweng de shengya yu tade sixiang yipie" 托爾斯泰誕生百週年紀念——托翁的生涯與他的思想一瞥. *DFZZ*, 25.19 (1928.9), pp.41–53.

Chen, Susan W. "The Personal Element in Mao Dun's Early Fiction". *HJAS*, 43 (1983), pp. 187–213.

Chen Xia 陳暇. "Bulanduisi" 布蘭兌司. *DFZZ*, 17.5 (1920.5), pp. 75–85.

Chen Yu-shih. "Mao Dun and the Use of Political Allegory in Fiction: A Case Study of His 'Autumn in Kuling'". In *MCL*, pp. 261–280.

Chen Zhejun 陳哲君. "Tongxin" 通信. *XSYB*, 13.12 (1922.12), pp. 2–3.

Cheng Ching-mao. "The Impact of Japanese Literary Trends on Modern Chinese Writers". In *MCL*, pp. 63–88.

Chernyshevsky, N. G. *What Is To Be Done?* Translated by Benjamin Tucker, expanded by Cathy Porter. London: Virago, 1982.

Chinnery, J. D. "The Influence of Western Literature on Lu Xun's 'Diary of a Madman'". *Bulletin of the School of Oriental and African Studies*, Vol. 23 (1960), pp. 309–322.

Chow Tse-tsung. *The May Fouth Movement: Intellectual Revolution in Modern China*. Cambridge, Mass.: Harvard University Press, 1960.

Churchward, L. G. *The Soviet Intelligentsia: An Essay on the Social Structure and Roles of the Soviet Intellectuals during the 1960s*. London: Routledge & Kegan Paul, 1973.

Clark, Katerina. *The Soviet Novel, History as Ritual*. Chicago: University of Chicago Press, 1981.

Dai Houying 戴厚英. *Ren ah, Ren!* 人啊，人! Guangdong: Renmin chuban-she 人民出版社, 1980.

―――. *Shiren zhi si* 詩人之死. Fujian: Renmin chubanshe, 1982.

Davie, Donald. *Russian Literature and Modern English Fiction*. Chicago: University of Chicago Press, 1965.

Debrecezeny, P. and Zeldin, J., tr. and eds. *Literature and National Identity: Nineteenth-Century Russian Critical Essays*. Lincoln: University of Nebraska Press, 1970.

Ding Ergang 丁爾綱. "Lu Xun sixiang fazhan de xianming guiji—lun Lu Xun xiaoshuo zhong 'wo' de yishu xingxiang" 魯迅思想發展的鮮明軌跡 ―論魯迅小說中「我」的藝術形象. *Zhongguo xiandai wenxue yanjiu congkan* 中國現代文學研究叢刊, 1980.1, pp. 156–169.

Ding Ling 丁玲. *Ding Ling wenji* 丁玲文集, 2 vols. Shanghai: Yiwen shudian 藝文書店, 1936.

―――. *Kuadao xinde shidai lai* 跨到新的時代來. Beijing: Renmin wenxue chubanshe, 1952.

―――. *Taiyang zhao zai Sanggan he shang* 太陽照在桑乾河上. Beijing: Xinhua shudian 新華書店, 1950.

Ding Yi 丁易, ed. *Yu Dafu xuanji* 郁達夫選集. Beijing: Renmin wenxue chubanshe, 1954.

Dobroliubov, N. A. "Gubernskie ocherki M. E. Saltykova-Shchedrina" (The Provincial Sketches of M. E. Saltykov-Shchedrin). *Sobraine sochinenii*, Vol. 2, pp. 126–127. Moscow, 1961–1964.

Doležalová, Anna. *Yu Ta-fu: Specific Traits of His Literary Creation*. London: C. Hurst & Co., 1971.

Donghai juewo 東海覺我 (pseud. of Xu Nianci 徐念慈). "Dingwei nian xiaoshuojie faxing shumu diaozhabiao" 丁未年小說界發行書目調查表. *Xiaoshuolin* 小說林, 9 (1907), pp. 1–10.

Dostoevsky, Fedor. *The Novels of Dostoevsky*, tr. Constance Garnett, 12 vols. London: Macmillan, 1913–1920.

Eastman, L. E. *The Abortive Revolution: China under Nationalist Rule, 1927–1937*. Cambridge, Mass.: Harvard University Press, 1974.

Egan Michael. "Yu Dafu and the Transition to Modern Chinese Literature". In *MCL*, pp. 309–324.

Fajieyefu 法捷耶夫 (Fadeyev). "Guangyu Lu Xun—jinian Lu Xun shishi shisan zhounian" 關於魯迅――紀念魯迅逝世十三週年. *WYB*, 3 (1949.10), pp. 4–5.

Fan Jun 樊駿. "Mao Dun de *Shi* he *Hong*" 茅盾的《蝕》和《虹》. In *Wenxue yanjiu jikan* 文學研究集刊, Vol. 4. Beijing, 1956.

Fanger, Donald. *Dostoevsky and Romantic Realism: A Study of*

Dostoevsky in Relation to Balzac, Dickens, and Gogol. Cambridge, Mass.: Harvard University Press, 1967.

Fanyi chuban waiguo wenxue zhuzuo mulu, 1949-1979 翻譯出版外國文學著作目錄，1949-1979. Beijing: Zhonghua shuju 中華書局, 1980.

Feng Naichao 馮乃超. "Yishu yu shehui shenghuo" 藝術與社會生活. *Wenhua pipan* 文化批判, 1 (1928), pp. 3-13.

Feng Xuefeng 馮雪峯. *Guolai de shidai. Lu Xun lun ji qita* 過來的時代·魯迅論及其他. Hong Kong: Xinzhi shudian 新知書店, 1948.

Fokkema, Douwe W. *Literary Doctrine in China and Soviet Influence, 1956-1960.* The Hague: Mouton & Co., 1965.

―――. "Lu Xun: The Impact of Russian Literature". In *MCL*, pp. 89-101.

Freeborn, Richard. *The Rise of the Russian Novel: Studies in the Russian Novel from "Eugene Onegin" to "War and Peace".* Cambridge: Cambridge University Press, 1973.

―――. *Turgenev, The Novelist's Novelist.* London: Oxford University Press, 1960.

―――, tr. *Rudin.* London: Penguin Books, 1975.

Freeborn, Richard, *et al.*, eds. *Russian Literary Attitudes from Pushkin to Solzhenitsyn.* London: Macmillan, 1976.

Fu Zhiying 伏志英, ed. *Mao Dun pingzhuan* 茅盾評傳. Hong Kong: Nandao chubanshe 南島出版社, 1968 (reprint).

Furst, Lilian. *The Contours of European Romanticism.* London: Macmillan, 1979.

―――. *Fictions of Romantic Irony in European Narrative.* London: Macmillan, 1984.

Furth, Charlotte, ed. *The Limits of Change: Essays on Conservative Alternatives in Republican China.* Cambridge, Mass.: Harvard University Press, 1976.

Gálik, Marián. *The Genesis of Modern Chinese Literary Criticism (1917-1930).* London: Curzon Press, 1980.

―――. *Mao Tun and Modern Chinese Literary Criticism.* Wisebaden: Franz Steiner Verlag GMBH, 1969.

―――. "Mayakovsky in China". *AAS*, 14 (1978), pp. 159-174.

―――. "The Names and Pseudonyms Used by Mao Tun". *AO*, 31 (1963), pp. 80-108.

―――. "Naturalism: A Changing Concept". *East and West*, 16:3-4 (1966), pp. 301-328.

―――. "On the Influence of Foreign Ideas on Chinese Literary Criticism, 1894-1904". *AAS*, 2 (1966), pp. 38-48.

Gao Changhong 高長虹. *Zoudao chubanjie* 走到出版界. Shanghai: Taidong shudian 泰東書店, 1929.

Garshin, V. *The Signal*, tr. R. Smith. London: Duckworth, 1915.

Gass, William H. *Fiction and the Figures of Life*. Boston: Nonpareil Books, 1971.

Ge Baoquan 戈寶權. "Gaoerji he Zhongguo" 高爾基和中國. *WXYJ*, 2 (1958.6), pp. 131–146.

———. "Gaoerji zuopin Zhongyiben bianmu" 高爾基作品中譯本編目. In *ZXCS*, 4(ii): 463–493.

———. "Lu Xun yu Ailuoxianke" 魯迅與愛羅先珂. *Guangming ribao* 光明日報, 1961.10.18.

———. "Puxijin he Zhongguo" 普希金和中國. *WXPL*, 4 (1959.8), pp. 1–16.

———. "Tugeniefu he Zhongguo wenxue" 屠格涅夫和中國文學. *Shijie wenxue* 世界文學, 1983.3, pp. 282–303.

———. "Tuoersitai he Zhongguo" 托爾斯泰和中國. In *Tuoersitai yanjiu lunwenji*, pp. 1–26.

———. "Weida weiguo zhanzheng zhong de Sulian wenxue" 偉大衞國戰爭中的蘇聯文學. *WYFX*, 3.3 (1947.5), pp. 349–359.

Genette, Gerard. *Narrative Discourse: An Essay in Method*, tr. Jane E. Lewin. Ithaca: Cornell University Press, 1980.

Geng Jizhi 耿濟之, tr. *Ren zhi yisheng* 人之一生 (*The Life of Man* by Andreyev). Shanghai: Shangwu yinshuguan, 1924.

———, tr. *Xunanshi ji qita* 巡按使及其他 (*The Inspector and Other Plays* by Gogol). Shanghai: Wenhua shenghuo chubanshe, 1941.

———, tr. *Yishu lun* 藝術論 (*What Is Art?* by Tolstoy). Shanghai: Shangwu yinshuguan, 1921.

Gettmann, R. A. *Turgenev in England and America*. Urbana: University of Illinois Press, 1941.

Gifford, Henry. *The Novel in Russia*. London: Hutchinson University Library, 1964.

Goethe, Johann Wolfgang. *The Sufferings of Young Werther*, tr. B. Q. Morgan. New York: F. Ungar, 1957.

Goldman, Merle, ed. *Modern Chinese Literature in the May Fourth Era*. Cambridge, Mass.: Harvard University Press, 1977.

Gorky, Maxim. *Reminiscences of Tolstoy, Chekhov and Andreev*, tr. Katherine Mansfield, S. S. Koteliansky and Leonard Woolf. London: The Hogarth Press, 1934.

———. "Wenxue yu xianzai de Eluosi" 文學與現代的俄羅斯, tr. Zheng Zhenduo 鄭振鐸. *XQN*, 8.2 (1920.10), pp. 1–9.

Guerney, B. G., ed. *A Treasury of Russian Literature*. New York: Vanguard Press, 1943.

Guillen, Claudio. *Literature as System: Essays Toward the Theory of Literary History*. New Jersey: Princeton University Press, 1970.

Guo Moruo 郭沫若. "Guhong—zhi Cheng Fangwu de yifengxin" 孤鴻——致成仿吾的一封信. In *Moruo wenji*, Vol. 10, pp. 286–301.

―――. *Moruo wenji* 沫若文集. 17 vols. Beijing: Renmin wenxue chubanshe, 1957–1963.

―――. "Zhong Su wenhua zhi jiaoliu" 中蘇文化之交流. In *Moruo wenji*, Vol. 12, pp. 21–26.

―――, tr. *Xinshidai* 新時代 (*Virgin Soil* by Turgenev). Shanghai: Shangwu yinshuguan, 1925. Pseud. Guo Dingtang 郭鼎堂.

Han Changjing 韓長經. *Lu Xun yu Eluosi gudian wenxue* 魯迅與俄羅斯古典文學. Shanghai: Wenyi chubanshe, 1981.

Hanan, Patrick. "The Technique of Lu Hsun's Fiction". *HJAS*, 34 (1974), pp. 53–96.

He Qifang 何其芳. *Xinghuo ji* 星火集. Shanghai: Qunyi chubanshe 群益出版社, 1949.

He Shaoxian 何少仙 (pseud. Shaoxian 少仙). "Xifeng chuilai de hua (1)" 西風吹來的話(1). *YS*, 5.27 (1929.9), pp. 49—51.

―――. "Xifeng chuilai de hua (2)". *YS*, 5.9 (1929.9), pp. 130–132.

He Yubo 賀玉波. *Xiandai Zhongguo zuojia lun* 現代中國作家論. Shanghai: Daguang shuju 大光書局, 1936.

Hemmings, F.W.J., ed. *The Age of Realism*. London: Penguin Books, 1974.

Herzen, Alexander. *My Past and Thoughts*, tr. Constance Garnett. Berkeley: University of California Press, 1973. Chinese translation by Ba Jin, *Wangshi yu suixiang* 往事與隨想. Shanghai: Yiwen chubanshe 譯文出版社, 1979.

Hingley, Ronald. *The Russian Mind*. New York: Scribner, 1977.

―――. *Russian Writers and Soviet Society, 1917–1978*. London: Weidenfeld and Nicolson, 1979.

Holzman, Donald. *Poetry and Politics: The Life and Works of Juan Chi, A.D. 210–263*. Cambridge: Cambridge University Press, 1978.

Howe, Irving. *Politics and the Novel*. New York: Fawcett World Library, 1967.

Hsia, C. T. *A History of Modern Chinese Fiction, 1917–1957*. New Haven: Yale University Press, 1961.

Hu Feng 胡風. "Lixiang zhuyizhe shidai de huigu" 理想主義者時代的回顧. *WYWX*, pp. 257–267.

Hu Lancheng 胡蘭成. "Lu Yishi" 路易士. In Yang Zhihua 楊之華 (ed.), *Wentan shiliao*, pp. 270–277.

Hu Yepin 胡也頻. *Hu Yepin xuanji* 胡也頻選集, 2 vols. Fujian: Renmin chubanshe, 1981.

Hu Yuzhi 胡愈之. "Jindai wenxueshang de xieshi zhuyi" 近代文學上的寫
實主義. *DFZZ*, 17.2 (1920.1), pp. 1–20.

———. "Tuosituoyifusiji de yisheng" 陀思妥以夫斯基的一生. *DFZZ*, 18.23
(1921.12), pp. 74–80. Pseud. Yuzhi 愈之.

———. "Women de shidai" 我們的時代. *Yiban* 一般, 1.11 (1926.11), pp.
324–331.

Huang, Joe. *Heroes and Villains in Communist China*. London:
Macmillan, 1973.

Hung, William. *Tu Fu, China's Greatest Poet*. Cambridge, Mass.: Harvard
University Press, 1952.

Issacs, Harold, ed. *Straw Sandals*. Cambridge, Mass.: Harvard University
Press, 1974.

Itō Toramaru 伊籐虎丸. "'Chinron' ron" 《沉淪》論. *Chugoku bungaku
kenkyu* 中國文學研究, 1 (1964.4), pp. 51–92.

Itō Toramaru, Innaba Shōji 稻葉昭二 and Suzuki Masao 鈴木正夫, eds.
Iku Tatsufu shiryō 郁達夫資料. Tokyo: University of Tokyo, Toyogaku
Bunken sentā sōkan 東洋文化研究所附屬東洋文獻センター, 1969.

Jarintzov, N. *The Russians and Their Language*. London: Oxford
University Press, 1916.

Jiang Guangci 蔣光慈. *Jiang Guangci xuanji* 蔣光慈選集. Hong Kong:
Gangqing chubanshe 港青出版社, 1979.

Jin Yi 斬以. *Jin Yi sanwen xiaoshuo ji* 斬以散文小說集. Hong Kong: Jianwen
shudian 建文書店, 1959.

Kagan-Kans, Eva. *Hamlet and Don Quixote: Turgenev's Ambivalent
Vision*. The Hague: Mouton, 1975.

Kai Ming 開明. "Tuoersitai de shiqing" 托爾斯泰的事情. *YS*, 14 (1925.5),
pp. 1–2.

Kampf, Leopold. *On the Eve*. New York: The International Library
Publishing Company, 1907.

Kaun, A. *Leonid Andreyev: A Critical Study*. New York: B. W. Huebsch
Inc., 1924.

Kropotkin, Peter. *Ethics: Origin and Development*, tr. Louis S. Friedland
and Joseph R. Piroshinikoff. New York, 1924. Chinese translation by
Ba Jin, *Rensheng zhexue: qi qiyuan ji qi fazhan* 人生哲學：其起源及
其發展. Shanghai: Ziyou shudian 自由書店, 1929.

———. *Ideals and Realities in Russian Literature*. New York: Alfred A.
Knopf, 1915. Chinese translation by Han Shiheng 韓侍桁, *Eguo
wenxueshi* 俄國文學史. Shanghai: Beixin shudian 北新書店, 1930.

Lampert, E. "Modernism in Russia, 1893–1917". In M. Bradbury and J.

McFarlane (eds.), *Modernism, 1890–1930*. London: Penguin Books, 1976.

Lang, Olga. *Pa Chin and His Writings: Chinese Youth between the Two Revolutions*. Cambridge, Mass.: Harvard University Press, 1967.

Larkin, Maurice. *Man and Society in Nineteenth-century Realism*. London: Macmillan, 1977.

Lechowska, T. "In Search of a New Ideal: The Metamorphoses of Pa Chin's Model Heroes". *AO*, 42 (1974), pp. 310–322.

Lee, Leo Ou-fan. "Genesis of a Writer: Notes on Lu Xun's Educational Experience, 1881–1909". In *MCL*, pp. 161–188.

―――. *The Romantic Generation of Modern Chinese Writers*. Cambridge, Mass.: Harvard University Press, 1973.

Leng 冷 (pseud of Chen Jinghan 陳景韓), tr. "Sharen gongsi" 殺人公司. *Yueyue xiaoshuo* 月月小說, 17 (1908), pp. 1–6.

Lenin, V. I. *On Literature and Art*. Moscow: Progress Publishers, 1967.

Levin, H. *The Gates of Horn*. New York: Oxford University Press, 1966.

Li Changzhi 李長之. *Lu Xun pipan* 魯迅批判. Shanghai: Beixin shudian, 1936.

Li Dichen 李笛晨. "*Du Wang xing zhong*" 讀《往星中》. *MY*, 1.11 (1926), pp. 519–520.

Li Guangtian 李廣田. "Shuo Guogeli de *Waitao*" 說果戈理的《外套》. *Wenyi chunqiu* 文藝春秋, 6.3 (1948.3), pp. 15–22.

Li Helin 李何林. *Jin ershinian Zhongguo wenyi shichao lun* 近二十年中國文藝思潮論. Shanghai: Shenghuo shudian, 1939.

Li Jiye 李霽野. "Xu *Hei jiamianren*" 序《黑假面人》. *MY*, 2.1 (1926), pp. 38–42.

Li Xifan 李希凡. "*Nahan*" "*Panghuang*" *de sixiang yu yishu* 《吶喊》《彷徨》的思想與藝術. Shanghai: Wenyi shudian 文藝書店, 1981.

Li Zhichang 李之常. "Ziranzhuyi de Zhongguo wenxue lun" 自然主義的中國文學論. In Sun Nanggong 孫俍工 (ed.), *Xinwenyi pinglun* 新文藝評論, pp. 27–38. Shanghai: Shangwu yinshuguan, 1930.

Liang Qichao 梁啓超. "Xinzheng zhaoshu gongba" 新政詔書恭跋. In *Wuxu zhengbianji* 戊戌政變記. Taiwan: Zhonghua shuju, 1959 (reprint).

Liang Yuchun 梁遇春. *Lei yu xiao* 淚與笑. Shanghai: Kaiming shudian, 1944.

Liang Zhen 梁鎮, tr. *Eluosi wenxue* 俄羅斯文學 (*An Outline of Russian Literature* by Maurice Baring). Shanghai: Shangwu yinshuguan, 1931.

Lin Ling 林陵. "Zai diwei pohaixia jianchide *Sulian wenyi*" 在敵偽迫害下堅持的《蘇聯文藝》. *WYB*, 22 (1956), pp. 15–16.

Lin Yüsheng. *The Crisis of Chinese Consciousness: Radical Anti-*

traditionism in the May Fourth Era. Madison: The University of Wisconsin Press, 1979.

Link, Perry. *Mandarin Ducks and Butterflies: Popular Fiction in Early Twentieth-century Chinese Cities*. Berkeley: University of California Press, 1981.

Liu Chun-jo. "The Heroes and Heroines of Modern Chinese Fiction: From Ah Q to Wu Tzu-hsu". *Journal of Asian Studies*, 16.2 (1957.2), pp. 201–211.

Liu E 劉鶚. *Lao Can youji* 老殘遊記. Shanghai: Dada tushu gongyingshe 大達圖書供應社, 1934.

Liu Shousong 劉綬松. "Lun Mao Dun de *Shi* yu *Hong*" 論茅盾的《蝕》與《虹》. *WXPL*, 2 (1963), pp. 23–41.

Liu Wu-Chi. *Su Man-shu*. New York: Twayne, 1972.

Lord, Robert, *Dostoevsky, Essays and Perspectives*. London: Chatto & Windus, 1970.

Lovejoy, Arthur O. *The Great Chain of Being: A Study of the History of an Idea*. Cambridge, Mass.: Harvard University Press, 1936.

Lu Xun 魯迅. "Andande yanaili" 黯澹的烟靄裏. *LXQJ* (1938), 11:235–260.

———. "Cao Jinhua yi *Sulian zuojia qirenji* xu" 曹靖華譯《蘇聯作家七人集》序. *LXQJ*, 6:552–555.

———. "Changmingdeng" 長明燈. *LXQJ*, 2:56–67.

———. "Fuchou (1 and 2)" 復讎(之一、二). *LXQJ*, 2:172–176.

———. "Gongren Suihuilüefu" 工人綏惠略夫. *LXQJ*, 11:595–748.

———. "Guangyu *Hongdexiao*" 關於《紅的笑》. *LXQJ*, 7:123–128.

———. "Guduzhe" 孤獨者. *LXQJ*, 2:86–109.

———. "Guoke" 過客. *LXQJ*, 2:188–194.

———. "*Huimie* dierbu yizhisanzhang yizhe fuji" 《毀滅》第二部一至三章譯者附記. *LXQJ*, 10:335–337.

———. *Huimie* houji" 《毀滅》後記. *LXQJ*, 10:325–334.

———. "Ji tanhua" 記談話. *LXQJ*, 3:355–360.

———. "Liangdishu, diyiji" 兩地書·第一集. *LXQJ*, 11:3–102.

———. "Lianqiao" 連翹. *LXQJ* (1938), 11:270–276.

———. "'Lianqiao' yizhe fuji" 《連翹》譯者附記. *LXQJ*, 10:188–189.

———. *Lu Xun quanji* 魯迅全集, 20 vols. Shanghai: *Lu Xun quanji* chubanshe 魯迅全集出版社, 1938.

———. *Lu Xun quanji*, 16 vols. Beijing: Renmin wenxue chubanshe, 1981.

———. *Lu Xun yiwenji* 魯迅譯文集, 10 vols. Beijing: Renmin wenxue chubanshe, 1959.

———. "Lun zhengleyan kan" 論睜了眼看. *LXQJ*, 1:237–242.

———. "Man" 謾. *LXQJ* (1938), 11:191–201.

———. "Mo" 默. *LXQJ* (1938), 11:202–214.

————. "Moluo shili shuo" 摩羅詩力說. *LXQJ*, 1:63–115.
————. "*Nahan* zixu"《吶喊》自序. *LXQJ*, 1:415–420.
————. "Nala zouhou zenyang" 娜拉走後怎樣. *LXQJ*, 1:158–165.
————. "Qiongren xiaoyin"《窮人》小引. *LXQJ*, 7:103–108.
————. *Selected Works of Lu Xun*, 4 vols. Translated by Yang Hsienyi and Gladys Yang. Beijing: Foreign Languages Press, 1980.
————. "Shanghai wenyi zhi yipie" 上海文藝之一瞥. *LXQJ*, 4:291–307.
————. "Shangshi" 傷逝. *LXQJ*, 2:110–131.
————. "Shenghui" 省會. *LXQJ* (1938), 11:277–301.
————. "Shuji" 書籍. *LXQJ* (1938), 11:261–269.
————. "'Shuji' yizhe fuji"《書籍》譯者附記. *LXQJ*, 10:184.
————. "'Shuqin' qianji"《豎琴》前記. *LXQJ*, 4:432–436.
————. "Siri" 四日. *LXQJ* (1938), 11:215–231.
————. "Toufa de gushi" 頭髮的故事. *LXQJ*, 1:461–466.
————. "Tuosituofusiji de shi" 陀思妥夫斯基的事. *LXQJ*, 6:411–413.
————. "Wei Eguo gequtuan" 爲俄國歌劇團. *LXQJ*, 1:382–384.
————. "Wenhua pianzhi lun" 文化偏至論. *LXQJ*, 1:44–62.
————. "Xie zai *Fen* de houmian" 寫在《墳》的後面. *LXQJ*, 1:282–288.
————. "Yile 'Gongren Suihuilüefu' zhihou" 譯了《工人綏惠略夫》之後. *LXQJ*, 10:165–171.
————. "Yingde gaobie" 影的告別. *LXQJ*, 2:165–166.
————. "'Yipian henduande zhuanqi' yizhe fuji"《一篇很短的傳奇》譯者附記. *LXQJ*, 10:456–457.
————. "'Yipian henduande zhuanqi' yizhe fujier"《一篇很短的傳奇》譯者附記二. *LXQJ*, 10:458–459.
————. "'Yisheng' yizhe fuji"《醫生》譯者附記. *LXQJ*, 10:176–177.
————. "Yuwai xiaoshuoji xu"《域外小說集》序. *LXQJ*, 10:161–164.
————. "Zai jiulou shang" 在酒樓上. *LXQJ*, 2:56–57.
————. "Zhi Sun Fuyuan" 致孫伏園. *LXQJ*, 11:416–417.
————. "Zhongguo xinwenxue daxi, xiaoshuo erji xu"《中國新文學大系·小說二集》序. *LXQJ*, 6:238–265.
————. "Zhu ZhongE wenzi zhi jiao" 祝中俄文字之交. *LXQJ*, 4:459–465.
————. "Zhufu" 祝福. *LXQJ*, 2:5–23.
————. "Zixuanji zixu" 自選集自序. *LXQJ*, 4:455–458.
Lukács, Georg. *The Historical Novel*. London: Merlin Press, 1962.
————. *The Meaning of Contemporary Realism*. London: Merlin Press, 1963.
————. *Studies in European Realism: A Sociological Survey of the Writings of Balzac, Stendhal, Zola, Tolstoy, Gorki and Others*. London: Merlin Press, 1972.
Lunacharsky, Anatoly. *On Literature and Art*. Moscow: Progress

Publishers, 1973.

Luo Guofu 羅果夫 (V. N. Rogov), ed. *Lu Xun lun Eluosi wenxue* 魯迅論俄羅斯文學. Shanghai: Shidai chubanshe 時代出版社, 1949.

———. "Lu Xun yu Eluosi wenxue" 魯迅與俄羅斯文學. *WYB*, 1.4 (1949.11), pp. 8–9.

Luo Jialun 羅家倫. "Bu Hu Xianxiao jun de Zhongguo wenxue gailiang lun" 駁胡先嘯君的中國文學改良論. *Xinchao* 新潮, 1.5 (1919.5), pp. 761–784.

Lyell, William A., Jr. *Lu Hsun's Vision of Reality*. Berkeley: University of California Press, 1976.

Lyon, D. W. "The Past Decade in Chinese Literature". *Journal of the North China Branch of the Royal Asiatic Society*, Vol. LXV (1934), pp. 62–72.

Ma Junwu 馬君武, tr. *Xinyu* 心獄 (*Resurrection*). Shanghai: Zhonghua shuju, 1913.

Ma Liangchun 馬良春 and Zhang Daming 張大明, eds. *Sanshi niandai zuoyi wenyi zhiliao xuanbian* 三十年代左翼文藝資料選編. Chengdu: Renmin chubanshe, 1980.

Mao Dun 茅盾 (pseud. of Shen Yanbing 沈雁冰). "Andeliefu" 安德列夫. *DFZZ*, 17.10 (1920.5), pp. 60–68. Pseud. Yanbing 雁冰.

———. "Andeliefu sihao" 安德列夫死耗. *XSYB*, 11.1 (1920.1), p. 4.

———. "Chuangzuo de qiantu" 創作的前途. *MWZJ*, 1:52–55.

———. "Cong Guling dao Dongjing" 從牯嶺到東京. *XSYB*, 19:10 (1928.10), pp. 1138–1146.

———. "Da zhuanbian shiqi he shi laine?" 大轉變時期何時來呢？*MWZJ*, 1:158–160.

———. "Daoyan" 導言. In *Zhongguo xinwenxue daxi, xiaoshuo yiji* 中國新文學大系·小說一集, pp. 1–32. 1935.

———. *Dongyao* 動搖. Shanghai: Kaiming shudian, 1930.

———. "Du Ni Huanzhi" 讀《倪煥之》. *MWZJ*, 1:277–294.

———. "Eguo jindai wenxue zatan, shang" 俄國近代文學雜談，上. *XSYB*, 11.1 (1920.1), pp. 1–5. Pseud. Bing 冰.

———. "Eguo jindai wenxue zatan, xia" 俄國近代文學雜談，下. *XSYB*, 11.2 (1920.2), pp. 1–4. Pseud. Yanbing.

———. *Hong* 虹. Shanghai: Kaiming shudian, 1930.

———. *Huanmie* 幻滅. Shanghai: Kaiming shudian, 1930.

———. "Huanying *Taiyang*" 歡迎《太陽》. *MWZJ*, 1:261–264.

———. "*Huisema* xu" 《灰色馬》序. In Zheng Zhenduo (tr.), *Huisema*, pp. 1–8.

———. "Jinnian lai jieshaode waiguo wenxue" 近年來介紹的外國文學. *MWZJ*, 2:1051–1076.

———. "Lanshalesi" 藍沙勒斯. *DFZZ*, 17.10 (1920.5), pp. 91–111. Pseud.

Mingxin 明心, note by Yanbing.

———. "Leguan de wenxue" 樂觀的文學. *MWZJ*, 1:135–136.

———. *Lu* 路. Shanghai: Kaiming shudian, 1935 (reprint).

———. "Lun wuchan jieji yishu" 論無產階級藝術. *MWZJ*, 1:182–199.

———. *Mao Dun lun chuangzuo* 茅盾論創作. Shanghai: Wenyi chubanshe, 1980.

———. *Mao Dun pinglun wenji* 茅盾評論文集, 2 vols. Beijing: Renmin wenxue chubanshe 人民文學出版社, 1978.

———. *Mao Dun wenji* 茅盾文集, 10 vols. Beijing: Renmin wenxue chubanshe, 1958–1961.

———. *Mao Dun wenxuan* 茅盾文選. Shanghai: Qingchun chubanshe 青春出版社, 1946.

———. *Mao Dun wenyi zalunji* 茅盾文藝雜論集. Shanghai: Wenyi chubanshe, 1981.

———. *Mao Dun zixuanji* 茅盾自選集. Shanghai: Kaiming shudian, 1934.

———. "Ouzhou dazhan yu wenxue" 歐洲大戰與文學. *XSYB*, 15.8 (1924.8), pp. 1–41.

———. "Qingnian de pijuan" 青年的疲倦. *XSYB*, 13.8 (1922.8), pp. 1–2.

———. "Renwu de yanjiu" 人物的研究. *XSYB*, 16.3 (1925.3), pp. 1–20.

———. *Shanrenxing* 三人行. Shanghai: Kaiming shudian, 1931.

———. "Shehui beijing yu chuangzuo" 社會背景與創作. *MWZJ*, 1:48–51.

———. "Shemo shi wenxue—Wo duiyu xianwentan de ganxiang" 甚麼是文學——我對於現文壇的感想. *MWZJ*, 1:147–154.

———. "Tongxin—fanyi wenxueshu de taolun" 通信——翻譯文學書的討論. *XSYB*, 12.2 (1921.2), p. 2.

———. "Tongxin—ziranzhuyi de lun zhan" 通信——自然主義的論戰. *XSYB*, 13.5 (1922.5), pp. 1–3.

———. "Tuoersitai de wenxue" 托爾斯泰的文學. *Jiefang yu gaizao* 解放與改造, 3.4 (1920.12), pp. 95–98.

———. "Tuosituoyifusiji de sixiang" 陀思妥以夫斯基的思想. *XSYB*, 13.1 (1922.1), pp. 2–13. Pseud. Shen Bing.

———. "Tuosituoyifusiji zai Eguo wenxueshi shang de diwei" 陀思妥以夫斯基在俄國文學史上的地位. *XSYB*, 13.1 (1922.1), pp. 19–22. Pseud. Lang Sun 郎損.

———. "Wei xinwenxue yanjiuzhe jin yijie" 為新文學研究者進一解. *Jiefang yu gaizao*, 3.1 (1920.9), pp. 99–102. Pseud. Yanbing.

———. "Weilaipai wenxue zhi xianshi" 未來派文學之現勢. *XSYB*, 13.10 (1922.10), pp. 1–5. Pseud. Bing.

———. "Wenxue he ren de guanxi ji Zhongguo gulai duiyu wenxuezhe shenfen de wuren" 文學和人的關係及中國古來對於文學者身份的誤認. *MWZJ*, 1:22–26.

————. "Wenxue shangde gudianzhuyi, langmanzhuyi he xieshizhuyi" 文學上的古典主義、浪漫主義和寫實主義. *XSYB*, 11.9 (1920.9), pp. 1–19. Pseud. Yanbing.

————. "Wenxue yu rensheng" 文學與人生. *MWZJ*, 1:110–114.

————. "Wenxue yu zhengzhi shehui" 文學與政治社會. *MWZJ*, 1:115–117.

————. Wenxuezhe de xinshiming" 文學者的新使命. *MWZJ*, 1:217–219.

————. *Wo zhouguode daolu* 我走過的道路. Vol. 1, 1981; Vol. 2, 1984. Hong Kong: Sanlian shudian.

————. "Xiandai wenxuejia de zeren shi shenmo?" 現代文學家的責任是甚麼？ *MWZJ*, 1:3–5.

————. "Xiaoshuo xinchaolan xuanyan". *MWZJ*, 1:6–11.

————. "Xiezai *Yeqiangwei* de qianmien" 寫在《野薔薇》的前面. In *Mao Dun lun chuangzuo*, pp. 51–52.

————. "Ximengnuofu fangwenji" 西蒙諾夫訪問記. *WYFX*, 3.16 (1948.8), pp. 649–653.

————. "Xinwenxue yanjiuzhe de zeren yu nuli" 新文學研究者的責任與努力. *XSYB*, 12.2 (1921.2), pp. 2–5. Pseud. Lang Sun.

————. *Xiyang wenxue tonglun* 西洋文學通論. Shanghai: Kaiming shudian, 1933. Pseud. Fang Bi 方璧.

————. "Yinianlai de ganxiang yu mingnian de jihua" 一年來的感想與明年的計劃. *MWZJ*, 1:65–70.

————. "Zenmo pingjia *Qingchun zhi ge*" 怎麼評價《青春之歌》. In *Mao Dun pinglun wenji*, 1:273–282.

————. "Zhongguo Suweiai geming yu puluo wenxue zhi jianshe" 中國蘇維埃革命與普羅文學之建設. *MWZJ*, 1:324–329.

————. *Zhuiqiu* 追求. Shanghai: Kaiming shudian, 1930.

————. "Ziranzhuyi yu Zhongguo xiandai xiaoshuo" 自然主義與中國現代小說. *MWZJ*, 1:83–99.

————. *Ziye* 子夜. Shanghai: Kaiming shudian, 1933.

————. "Zuihou yiye" 最後一頁. *XSYB*, 20.5 (1929.5), p. 901.

Mao Dun, Hu Yuzhi, Shen Zemin 沈澤民. *Jindai Eguo wenxuejia lun* 近代俄國文學家論. Shanghai: Shangwu yinshuguan, 1923.

Mao Zedong 毛澤東. *Mao Zedong xuanji* 毛澤東選集. Beijing, 1953.

Maquire, Robert A. *Red Virgin Soil: Soviet Literature in the 1920's*. New Jersey: Princeton University Press, 1968.

————, ed. *Gogol from the Twentieth Century, Eleven Essays*. New Jersey: Princeton University Press, 1976.

Masaryk, T. G. *The Spirit of Russia: Studies in History, Literature and Philosophy*. Vols. 1 and 2. London: Allen & Unwin/Macmillan, 1955 (2nd edition); Vol. 3, London: Allen & Unwin, 1967.

Mathewson, Rufus W., Jr. *The Positive Hero in Russian Literature*, 2nd edition. Stanford, California: Stanford University Press, 1975.

Matlaw, Ralph E., ed. *Belinsky, Chernyshevsky and Dobrolyubov: Selected Criticism*. New York: Dutton, 1962.

McDougall, Bonnie S. "The Impact of Western Literary Trends". In *MCL*, pp. 37–61.

————. *The Introduction of Western Literary Theories into Modern China, 1919–1925*. Tokyo: The Centre for East Asian Cultural Studies, 1971.

————. "Zhao Zhenkai's Fiction: A Study in Cultural Alienation". *Modern Chinese Literature*, 1.2 (1985.5), pp. 103–127.

————, ed. *Popular Chinese Literature and Performing Arts in the People's Republic of China, 1949–1979*. Berkeley: University of California Press, 1984.

Mei Chuan 梅川. "*Hongdexiao* yinyan" 《紅的笑》引言. *YS*, 5.15 (1929.6), pp. 63–68.

Meisner, Maurice. "Cultural Iconoclasm, Nationalism, and Internationalism in the May Fourth Movement". In Benjamin Schwartz (ed.), *Reflections on the May Fourth Movement: A Symposium*, pp. 14–22.

Meng Shihuan 孟十還. "Dazhan qian Eguo wenxue shang de teshu sixiang" 大戰前俄國文學上的特殊思想. In Zheng Zhenduo and Fu Donghua (eds.), *Wenxue baiti*, pp. 192–198.

Ming Xingli 明興禮 (Jean Monsterleet). *Ba Jin de shenghuo he zhuzuo* 巴金的生活和著作, tr. Wang Jiwen 王繼文. Shanghai: Wenfeng chubanshe 文風出版社, 1950.

Mirsky, D. S. *A History of Russian Literature*. London: Routledge and Kegan Paul, 1968.

Muchnic, Helen. *Dostoevsky's English Reputation*. Smith College Studies in Modern Language, Vol. 20 (April and July, 1939). Mass.: Northampton.

Nabokov, Vladimir. *Lectures on Russian Literature*. London: Picador, 1981.

————. *Nikolai Gogol*. London: Editions Poetry, 1947.

Nakamura Mitsuo. *Contemporary Japanese Fiction, 1926–1968*. Tokyo: Kokusai Bunka Shinkokai, 1969.

————. *Modern Japanese Fiction, 1868–1926*. Tokyo: Kokusai Bunka Shinkokai, 1968.

Newcombe, Josephine M. *Leonid Andreyev*. Hertfordshire, England: Bradda Books Ltd., 1972.

Ng Mau-sang 吳茂生. "Ba Jin and Russian Literature". *Chinese Literature: Essays, Articles, Reviews*, 3.1 (1981.1), pp. 67–92.

————. "Cong 'Shangshi' yu 'Gongren Suihuilüefu' bijiao kan Lu Xun xiaoshuo jiqiao de jiejian he chuangxin" 從《傷逝》與《工人綏惠略夫》比較看魯迅小說技巧的借鑒和創新. *Lu Xun yanjiu dongtai* 魯迅研究動態, 1986.11, pp. 22–31. Beijing: Lu Xun Museum.

————. "Juewang yu xiwang de paihuai—tantao *Yecao* de qingnian zhuti yu zhongxin sixiang" 絕望與希望的徘徊——探討《野草》的青年主題與中心思想. *Lu Xun yanjiu* (forthcoming).

————. "Langman zhuyi yingxiong? Lun Yu Dafu xiaoshuoli de lingyuzhe" 浪漫主義英雄？論郁達夫小說裏的零餘者. *Zhongguo xiandai wenxue yanjiu congkan* 中國現代文學研究叢刊, 4 (1982), pp. 133–158.

————. "Lu Xun and Russian Literature: A Study of the Typological Affinities between Lu Xun's Awakened Hero and His Russian Precursors". *The Journal of The Institute of Chinese Studies of The Chinese University of Hong Kong*, 13 (1982.12), pp. 251–285.

————. "Lu Xun yu Eluosi wenxue" 魯迅與俄羅斯文學. *Dousou* 抖擻, 22 (1977.7), pp. 1–13.

————. "To Awaken or Not to Awaken—Symbols of Anxiety in *Wild Grass*". *Renditions*, 26 (1986), pp. 151–164.

Olgin, M. J. *A Guide to Russian Literature*. New York: Harcourt, Brace and Howe, Inc., 1920.

Oveharenko, A. *Socialist Realism and the Modern Literary Process*. Moscow: Progress Publishers, 1978.

Pascal, Roy. *The German Sturm and Drang*. Manchester: Manchester University Press, 1953.

Petrov, V. V. *Lu Sin (Lu Xun)*. Moscow, 1960.

Phelps, W. L. *Essays on Russian Novelists*. New York: Macmillan, 1911.

Pickowicz, Paul. *Marxist Literary Thought in China: The Influence of Ch'ü Ch'iu-pai*. Berkeley: University of California Press, 1981.

Ping Xiaoluohuofu de "Jingjing de Dunhe" yu "Bei kaiken de chunüdi" 評蕭洛霍夫的《靜靜的頓河》與《被開墾的處女地》. Hong Kong: Sanlian shudian, 1967.

Pipes, Richard, ed. *The Russian Intelligentsia*. New York: Columbia University Press, 1961.

Plaks, Andrew H., ed. *Chinese Narrative, Critical and Theoretical Essays*. New Jersey: Princeton University Press, 1977.

Plekhanov, G. *Unaddressed Letters—Art and Social Life*. Moscow: Progress Publishers, 1957.

Pollard, David E. *A Chinese Look at Literature: The Literary Values of Chou Tso-jen in Relation to the Tradition*. London: C. Hurst & Co., 1973.

Price, Don C. *Russia and the Roots of the Chinese Revolution*,

1896–1911. Cambridge, Mass.: Harvard University Press, 1974.

Průšek, Jaroslav. "A Confrontation of Traditional Oriental Literature with Modern European Literature in the Context of the Chinese Literary Revolution". *AO*, 32 (1964), pp. 365–375.

———. "Lu Hsun's 'Huai Chiu', a Precursor of Modern Chinese Literature". *HJAS*, 29 (1969), pp. 169–176.

———. "Subjectivism and Individualism in Modern Chinese Literature". *AO*, 25.2 (1957), pp. 261–286.

———. *Three Sketches of Chinese Literature*. Prague: Oriental Institute, 1969.

———. "Ye Sheng-t'ao and Anton Chekhov". *AO*, 38 (1970), pp. 437–452.

———, ed. *Studies in Modern Chinese Literature*. Berlin: Akademie-Verlag, 1964.

Pushao. See Xu Diaofu.

Qi Weihong 齊衛紅. "Zhou Yang—Heluxiaofu de yingshengchong" 周揚—赫魯曉夫的應聲蟲. In *Chedi pipan Zhou Yang de fangeming xiuzheng-zhuyi wenyi heixian* 徹底批判周揚的反革命修正主義文藝黑線, pp. 45–50. Guangdong: Renmin chubanshe, 1970.

Qian Xingcun 錢杏邨 (pseud. A Ying 阿英). *A Ying wenji* 阿英文集, 2 vols. Hong Kong: Sanlian shudian, 1979.

———. *Anteliefu pingzhuan* 安特列夫評傳. Shanghai: Wenyi shuju 文藝書局, 1931.

———. "Cengjing wei ren de dongwu—wei Gaoerji chuangzuo sanshi-wu zhounian jinian zuo" 曾經爲人的動物——爲高爾基創作三十五週年紀念作. *XSYB*, 19.6 (1928.6), pp. 764–773.

———. "Eluosi wenxue manping" 俄羅斯文學漫評. *XSYB*, 19.1 (1928.1), pp. 189–196.

———. *Lide wenyi* 力的文藝. Shanghai: Taidong tushudian, 1929.

———. *Wan Qing wenyi baokan shuliie* 晚清文藝報刊述略. Shanghai: Gudian wenxue chubanshe 古典文學出版社, 1958.

———. *Wan Qing xiaoshuo shi* 晚清小說史. Hong Kong: Taiping shuju 太平書局, 1966.

———. *Xiandai Zhongguo wenxue zuojia* 現代中國文學作家, 2 vols. Shanghai: Taidong tushudian, 1928.

———. *Xiaoshuo sitan* 小說四談. Shanghai: Guji chubanshe 古籍出版社, 1980.

———. "'Xuehen'—Azhibashuifu de duanpian xiaoshuo ping"《血痕》—阿志巴綏夫的短篇小說評. *XSYB*, 19.11 (1928.11), pp. 1352–1356.

———, ed. *Wan Qing wenxue congchao, Eluosi wenxue yiwen juan* 晚清文學叢鈔·俄羅斯文學譯文卷, 2 vols. Beijing: Zhonghua shuju, 1961.

————, ed. *Wan Qing wenxue congchao, xiaoshuo xiqu yanjiu juan* 晚清文學叢鈔·小說戲曲研究卷. Beijing: Zhonghua shuju, 1960.

Qu Qiubai 瞿秋白. *"Eluosi mingjia duanpian xiaoshuo ji xu"* 《俄羅斯名家短篇小說集》序. *QQWJ*, 2:543–546.

————. *"Guogeli: Puyushi"* 果戈理:《僕御使》. *QQWJ*, 5:1304–1305.

————. *"Huisema yu Eguo shehui yundong"* 《灰色馬》與俄國社會運動. *XSYB*, 14.11 (1923.11), pp. 1–10.

————. *"Lun Puxijin de Bianerjin xiaoshuo ji"* 論普希金的《弁爾金小說集》. *QQWJ*, 2:541–543.

————. *Qu Qiubai wenji* 瞿秋白文集, 4 vols. Beijing: Renmin wenxue chubanshe, 1954.

————. *"Shijimo de beiai"* 世紀末的悲哀. *QQWJ*, 2:255–256.

————. *"Tantan Sanrenxing"* 談談《三人行》. *QQWJ*, 2:334–342.

————. *"Zhongguo de duoyu de ren"* 中國的「多餘的人」. *QQWJ*, 1:169–172.

Raeff, Marc, ed. *Russian Intellectual History: An Anthology*. New York: Harcourt, Brace and World, 1966.

Raglan, F.R.S. *The Hero: A Study in Tradition, Myth and Drama*. London: Methuen and Co., 1936.

Reed, T. J. *Thomas Mann: The Uses of Tradition*. London: Oxford University Press, 1976.

Ripp, Victor. *Turgenev's Russia. From "Notes of a Hunter" to "Fathers and Sons"*. Ithaca: Cornell University Press, 1980.

Robertson, J.G. *A History of German Literature*. Edinburgh and London: William Blackwood, 1970 (6th edition).

Ropshin, V. (Savinkov, Boris). *The Pale Horse*, tr. Z. Vengerova. Dublin and London: Mannsel and Co., 1971.

Roy, David Tod. *Ko Mo-jo: The Early Years*. Cambridge, Mass.: Harvard University Press, 1971.

Ryan, Marleigh Grayer. *Japan's First Modern Novel, "Ukigumo" of Futabatei Shimei*. New York: Columbia University Press, 1967.

Rzhevsky, Nicholas. *Russian Literature and Ideology: Herzen, Dostoevsky, Leontiev, Tolstoy, Fadeyev*. Urbana/Chicago/London: University of Illinois Press, 1983.

Scalapino, Robert A. and George T. Yu. *The Chinese Anarchist Movement*. Berkeley: University of California Press, 1961.

Schenk, H. G. *The Mind of the European Romantics: An Essay in Cultural History*. London: Constable, 1966.

Schwartz, Benjamin. "The Chinese Perception of World Order, Past and Present". In John K. Fairbank (ed.), *The Chinese World Order*, pp. 276–288. Cambridge, Mass.: Harvard University Press, 1968.

————. *In Search of Wealth and Power, Yen Fu and the West*. Cambridge, Mass.: Harvard University Press, 1964.

————. "The Intelligentsia in Communist China: A Tentative Comparison". In Richard Pipes (ed.), *The Russian Intelligentsia*, pp. 164–181.

————, ed. *Reflections on the May Fourth Movement: A Symposium*. Cambridge, Mass.: Harvard University Press, 1972.

Semenov, V. I. *Lu Xun and His Predecessors*, tr. Charles Alber. New York: M. E. Sharpe, 1980.

————. "Teoriya prozy v Kitae na rubezhe XIX-XX vekov" (Chinese Fictional Theory at the End of the Nineteenth Century and the Beginning of the Twentieth Century). In *Problemy teorii literatury i estetiki v stranakh vostoka* (The Problems of the Theory of Literature and Aesthetics in Oriental Studies), pp. 161–206. Moscow, 1960.

Shen Pengnian 沈鵬年. *Lu Xun yanjiu ziliao bianmu* 魯迅研究資料編目. Shanghai: Wenyi chubanshe, 1958.

Shen Yanbing 沈雁冰. See Mao Dun 茅盾.

Shen Ying 沈穎, tr. *Qianye* 前夜 (*On the Eve* by Turgenev). Shanghai: Shangwu yinshuguan, 1921.

Shi Chenhai 石沉海. "Youren Majun de yishu" 友人馬君的遺書. *YS*, 5.12 (1929.5), pp. 629–647.

Shils, Edward. *Tradition*. Chicago: University of Chicago Press, 1981.

Shneider, M. E. *Russkaya klassika v Kitae* (Russian Classics in China). Moscow, 1977.

Shu Xincheng 舒新城. *Jindai Zhongguo liuxueshi* 近代中國留學史. Shanghai: Zhonghua shuju, 1933.

Sibley, William F. "Naturalism in Japanese Literature". *HJAS*, 28 (1968), pp. 157–169.

Slominsky, Alexander. "The Technique of the Comic in Gogol". In Robert A. Maquire (ed.), *Gogol from the Twentieth Century*, pp. 323–376.

Slonim, Marc. *The Epic of Russian Literature: From Its Origins through Tolstoy*. London: Oxford University Press, 1969.

————. *From Chekhov to the Revolution: Russian Literature 1900–1917*. London: Oxford University Press, 1972.

————. *Soviet Russian Literature: Writers and Problems, 1917–1977*. Revised edition. London: Oxford University Press, 1977.

Snow, Edgar, ed. *Living China: Modern Chinese Short Stories*. London: George G. Harrap and Co., 1936.

Sōkichi Tsuda. *An Enquiry into the Japanese Mind as Mirrored in Literature—The Flowering Period of Common People Literature*, tr. Fukamatsu Matsuda. Tokyo, 1970.

Solovev, Vladimir. "Tri rechi v pamiat Dostoevskoyo" (In Memory of Dostoevsky). In Debrecezeny (ed.), *Literature and National Identity*, pp. 169–179.

Solzhenitsyn, Alekandr. *The Nobel Lecture on Literature*, tr. Thomas P. Whitney. London: Harper and Row, 1972.

Strakhov, Nikolai. "Tolstoy's *War and Peace*". In *Literature and National Identity*, pp. 119–167.

Strich, Fritz. *Goethe and World Literature*. London: Routledge and Kegan Paul, 1949.

Su Manshu 蘇曼殊. *Duanhong lingyan ji* 斷紅零雁記. Hong Kong: Yuanye shuwu 原野書屋, 1956.

Sulian renmin de wenxue 蘇聯人民的文學, 2 vols. Beijing: Renmin wenxue chubanshe, 1955.

Sulian wenyi 蘇聯文藝. Shanghai: Shidai chubanshe, 1942–1949.

Sun Fuyuan 孫伏園. "Lu Xun xiansheng de xiaoshuo" 魯迅先生的小說. *Yuzhou feng* 宇宙風, 30 (1936.12), pp. 308–310.

Sun Zhongtian 孫中田, Zha Guohua 查國華, eds. *Mao Dun yanjiu ziliao* 茅盾研究資料, 3 vols. Beijing: Zhongguo shehui kexue chubanshe, 1983.

Taine, H. *History of English Literature*, tr. H. van Laun, 4 vols. London: Chatto and Windus, 1890.

Tang Tao 唐弢, *et al.*, eds. *Zhongguo xiandai wenxueshi* 中國現代文學史, 3 vols. Beijing: Renmin wenxue chubanshe, 1982.

Thorlby, Anthony, ed. *European Literature*. The Penguin Companion to Literature (2). London: Penguin Books, 1969.

Tian Han 田漢, Zhong Baihua 宗白華, and Guo Moruo. *Sanye ji* 三葉集. Shanghai: Yadong tushuguan, 1920.

Tolstoy, L. N. *The Centenary Edition of Tolstoy*, tr. Louise and Aylmer Maude, 21 vols. London: Oxford University Press, 1928–1937.

Tonghua 桐華. "Zhongguoren de daiyu you yize" 中國人的待遇又一則. *YS*, 5.12 (1929.5), p. 668.

Treadgold, Donald W. *The West in Russia and China: Religious and Secular Thought in Modern Times*. Vol. 2: *China 1582–1949*. Cambridge: Cambridge University Press, 1973.

Trilling, Lionel, *Sincerity and Authenticity*. Cambridge, Mass.: Harvard University Press, 1971.

Tuoersitai yanjiu lunwenji 托爾斯泰研究論文集. Shanghai: Wenyi chubanshe, 1983.

Turgenev, Ivan. *The Diary of a Superfluous Man*, tr. Constance Garnett. In *The Novels of Ivan Turgenev*, Vol. 13. London: Heineman, 1894–1899.

——. *Fathers and Sons*, tr. Rosemary Edmunds. London: Penguin Books, 1965.

————. *First Love*, tr. Constance Garnett. In *The Novels of Ivan Turgenev*, Vol. 11.

————. *Home of the Gentry*, tr. Richard Freeborn. London: Penguin Books, 1970.

————. *On the Eve*, tr. Gilbert Gardiner. London: Penguin Books, 1950.

————. *Sketches from a Hunter's Album*, tr. Richard Freeborn. London: Penguin Books, 1967.

————. *Virgin Soil*, tr. R. S. Townsend. London: J. M. Dent and Sons Ltd., 1948.

Ulam, Adam Bruno. *Ideologies and Illusions: Revolutionary Thought from Herzen to Solzhenitsyn*. Cambridge, Mass.: Harvard University Press, 1976.

Venturi, Franco. *Roots of Revolution*, tr. F.J.H. Haskell. London, 1960.

Wang Chi-chen, tr. *Ah Q and Others: Selected Stories of Lusin*. Westport, Conn.: Greenwood Press, 1971.

Wang Duqing 王獨清. *Duqing wenyi lunji* 獨清文藝論集. Shanghai: Guanghua shudian 光華書店, 1932.

Wang Furen 王富仁. *Lun Xun qianqi xiaoshuo yu Eluosi wenxue* 魯迅前期小說與俄羅斯文學. Shaanxi: Renwen chubanshe, 1983.

Wang Meng 王蒙. *Wang Meng xiaoshuo baogao wenxue xuan* 王蒙小說報告文學選, Beijing: Beijing chubanshe, 1981.

————. *Wang Meng zhuanji* 王蒙專集. Guizhou: Renmin chubanshe, 1984.

Wang Dezhao 王德昭. *Qingdai keju zhidu yanjiu* 清代科舉制度研究. Hong Kong: The Chinese University Press, 1982.

Wang Xiyan 王西彥. *Lianyu zhong de shenghuo* 煉獄中的聖火. Beijing: Renmin wenxue chubanshe, 1982.

————. *Lun A Q he tade beiju* 論阿Q和他的悲劇. Shanghai: Xinwenyi chubanshe 新文藝出版社, 1957.

————. *Shu yu shenghuo* 書與生活. Guangzhou: Huacheng chubanshe 花城出版社, 1981.

Wang Yao 王瑤. "Lun Ba Jin de xiaoshuo" 論巴金的小說. *WXYJ*, 4 (1954.12), pp. 124–154.

————. *Zhongguo xinwenxue shi gao* 中國新文學史稿. Shanghai: Xinwenyi chubanshe, 1953.

Watt, Ian Pierre. *The Rise of the Novel: Studies in Defoe, Richardson and Fielding*. London: Chatto and Windus, 1957.

Wei Congwu 韋叢蕪. "*Tuosituofusiji quanji* zongxu" 《陀思妥夫斯基全集》總序. In *Qiongren ji qita* 《窮人》及其他 (*Poor Folks and Others* translated by Wei Congwu), pp. 1–2. Shanghai, 1947.

————, tr. *Zui yu fa* 罪與罰 (*Crime and Punishment* by Dostoevsky). Shanghai, 1931.

Wei Gu 韋愨, ed. *Pushigeng shishi baizhounian jinianji* 普式庚逝世百週年紀念集. Shanghai: Shangwu yinshuguan, 1937.

Wei Suyuan 韋素園. "*Waitao* de xu"《外套》的序. *MY*, 1.16 (1926), pp. 645–651.

———. "Xu *Wang xing zhong*"序《往星中》. *MY*, 1.10 (1926), pp. 406–411.

Weisstein, Ulrich. *Comparative Literature and Literary Theory.* Bloomington: Indiana University Press, 1973.

Wellek, René. *Concepts of Criticism.* New Haven: Yale University Press, 1969.

Wilson, Colin. *The Outsider.* London: Victor Gollancz, 1956.

Woodcock, George. *Anarchism: A History of Libertarian Ideas and Movements.* London: Pelican Books, 1975.

Woodward, James B. *Leonid Andreyev: A Study.* London: Oxford University Press, 1969.

Wu Benxing 吳奔星. *Mao Dun xiaoshuo jianghua* 茅盾小說講話. Shanghai: Nitu she 泥土社, 1953.

Wu Jiwen 伍集文. "Shehuizhuyi wenxue yishu daolu, haishi zhibenzhuyi wenxue yishu daolu" 社會主義文學藝術道路，還是資本主義文學藝術道路. In *Chedi pipan Zhou Yang de fangeming xiuzhengzhuyi wenyi heixian*, pp. 93–109.

Wusi shiqi qikan jieshao 五四時期期刊介紹, 6 vols. Shenyang: Renmin chubanshe, 1979.

Xia Yan 夏衍 (pseud. of Shen Duanxian 沈端先). "*Muqin* zai Zhongguo de mingyun"《母親》在中國的命運. In *Xia Yan lun chuangzuo* 夏衍論創作, pp. 85–87. Shanghai: Wenyi chubanshe, 1982.

———. "Tugeniefu" 屠格涅夫. *Xiandai* 現代, 3.6 (1932.10), pp. 836–831.

———. "Wo maole yici daxian—gaibian *Fuhuo* houji" 我冒了一次大險——改編《復活》後記. In *Xia Yan lun chuangzuo*, pp. 56–57.

Xiao Hang 小航. "Tuosituoyifusiji zhuanlüe" 陀思妥以夫斯基傳略. *XSYB*, 13.1 (1922.1), pp. 13–18.

Xie Liuyi 謝六逸. "Eguo zhi minzhong xiaoshuo jia" 俄國之民衆小說家. *XSYB*, 11.8 (1920.8), pp. 1–8.

———. "*Lieren riji* yanjiu"《獵人日記》研究. *XSYB*, 13.3 (1922.3), pp. 7–15.

———. "Tugeniefu zhuanlüe" 屠格涅夫傳略. *XSYB*, 13.3 (1922.3), pp. 1–7.

Xin Di 辛笛. *Yedu ouji* 夜讀偶記. Shanghai: Shanghai chuban gongsi 上海出版公司, 1948.

Xin Yi 辛夷. "*Zhuiqiu* zhong de Zhang Qiuliu"《追求》中的章秋柳. In Fu Zhiying (ed.), *Mao Dun pingzhuan*, pp. 85–104.

Xu Diaofu 徐調孚 (pseud. Pu Shao 蒲梢). "Chuqi xinwenyi chubanwu

bianmu" 初期新文藝出版物編目. In *ZXCS*, 1:107–121.

———. "Fandui zhanzheng de wenxue" 反對戰爭的文學. *XSYB*, 15.8 (1924.8), pp. 1–9.

———. "Han yi dongxiyang wenxue zuopin bianmu" 漢譯東西洋文學作品編目. In *ZXCS*, 1:271–323.

———. "Zhongyi SuE xiaoshuo bianmu" 中譯蘇俄小說編目. In *ZXCS*, 2:280–289.

Xu Jie 許傑. "Ni bishang nidi yanjing ba!" 你閉上你的眼睛吧！*WYFX*, 2.3(1947.5), pp. 281–282.

Xu Qinwen 許欽文. "*Nahan*" *fenxi* 《吶喊》分析. Beijing: Zhongguo qingnian chubanshe 中國青年出版社, 1956.

———. "*Panghuang*" *fenxi* 《徬徨》分析. Hong Kong: Wencai chubanshe 文采出版社, 1970.

Xu Zhimo 徐志摩. "Manshufeier" 曼殊菲兒. *XSYB*, 14.5 (1923.5), pp. 1–12.

———. *Xu Zhimo quanji* 徐志摩全集, 6 vols. Taibei: Zhuanji wenxue 傳記文學, 1970.

Yachnin, Rissa and Stam, David T. *Turgenev in English: A Checklist of Works by and about Him*. New York, 1962.

Yan Fu 嚴復. *Tian yan lun* 天演論. Shanghai: Shangwu yinshuguan, 1931.

———. *Yan Fu shiwen xuan* 嚴復詩文選. See Zhou Zhenfu 周振甫.

Yang Hsien-yi and Gladys Yang, tr. *Selected Works of Lu Hsun*, 4 vols. Beijing: Foreign Languages Press, 1980.

Yang Mo 楊沫. *Qingchun zhi ge* 青春之歌. Hong Kong: Sanlian shudian, 1960.

———. "Tantan Lin Daojing de xingxiang" 談談林道靜的形象. In *Chuangzuo jingyan mantan* 創作經驗漫談, pp. 63–74. Beijing: Renmin wenxue chubanshe, 1979.

Yang Sao 楊騷. "Zuichu he waiguo wenxue jiechu shi zai Riben" 最初和外國文學接觸是在日本. In *WYWX*, pp. 138–143.

Yang Zhihua 楊之華, ed. *Wentan shiliao* 文壇史料. Shanghai: Zhonghua ribao she 中華日報社, 1944.

Yao Ke 姚克. "Dule *Quepaiyefu* yihou" 讀了《却派也夫》以後. *Yeying* 夜鶯, 1.4 (1936.6.15), pp. 308–310.

Ye Daosheng 葉道生 (I. Genähr) and Mai Meisheng 麥梅生, tr. *Tuosi zhongjiao xiaoshuo* 托氏宗教小說. Hong Kong: Rhenish Missionary Society, 1907.

Ye Shengtao 葉聖陶. *Ye Shengtao wenji* 葉聖陶文集, 3 vols. Beijing: Renmin wenxue chubanshe, 1958.

Ye Ziming 葉子銘. *Lun Mao Dun sishinian de wenxue daolu* 論茅盾四十年的文學道路. Shanghai: Wenyi chubanshe, 1959.

Yi Ka 伊卡. "Ershinian laide Zhongguo xuesheng" 二十年來的中國學生. *Xuesheng zazhi* 學生雜誌, 18.1 (1931.1), pp. 6–12.

———. "Qingnian de kumen" 青年的苦悶. *Xuesheng zazhi*, 17.5 (1930.5), pp. 1–9.

Yi Qiubai 憶秋白. Beijing: Renmin wenxue chubanshe, 1981.

Yiming 佚名. "*Ye weiyang* xuyan"《夜未央》序言. In Qian Xingcun (ed.), *Wan Qing wenxue congchao, xiaoshuo xiqu yanjiu juan*, p. 306.

Yu Dafu 郁達夫. "Beiguo de weiyin" 北國的微音. *YDWJ*, 3:91–95.

———. "Bingxian riji" 病閒日記. *YDWJ*, 9:24–33.

———. "Bodian" 薄奠. *YDWJ*, 2:288–299.

———. "Cai shi ji" 采石磯. *YDWJ*, 1:194–212.

———. "Chanyu dubai" 懺餘獨白. *YDWJ*, 7:249–252.

———. "Chenlun" 沉淪. *YDWJ*, 1:16–53.

———. "*Chuangzao yuekan* juantou yu"《創造月刊》卷頭語. *YDWJ*, 2:290–291.

———. "Chunfeng chenzui de wanshang" 春風沉醉的晚上. *YDWJ*, 1:237–251.

———. "Cunju riji" 村居日記. *YDWJ*, 9:34–62.

———. "Dafengquan wai (zizhuan zhi qi)" 大風圈外（自傳之七）. *YDWJ*, 3:433–439.

———. *Dafu quanji* 達夫全集, 7 vols. Shanghai, 1927–1933.

———. "*Dafu zixuanji* xu"《達夫自選集》序. *YDWJ*, 7:254–256.

———. "Fengling" 風鈴. In *Dafu quanji*, Vol. 3, *Guoqu ji* 過去集.

———. "Haigu milianzhe de duyu" 骸骨迷戀者的獨語. *YDWJ*, 3:122–124.

———. "Haishang tongxin" 海上通信. *YDWJ*, 3:71–77.

———. "He Ercan" 赫爾慘. *YDWJ*, 5:164–168.

———. "Jiguo weidade zuojia yizhe xuyan" 幾個偉大的作家譯者序言. *YDWJ*, 7:245–248.

———. "Jizhong yu *Huangmianzhi* de renwu" 集中於《黃面誌》的人物. *YDWJ*, 5:169–188.

———. "Laosheng riji" 勞生日記. *YDWJ*, 9:8–23.

———. "Lingyuzhe" 零餘者. *YDWJ*, 3:84–90.

———. "Lusao de sixiang yu tade chuangzuo" 盧騷的思想與他的創作. *YDWJ*, 6:19–35.

———. "Lusao zhuan" 盧騷傳. *YDWJ*, 6:1–18.

———. "Mangmangye" 茫茫夜. *YDWJ*, 1:116–146.

———. "Niaoluo xing" 蔦蘿行. *YDWJ*, 1:213–228.

———. "Renyao" 人妖. *YDWJ*, 1:281–287.

———. "Riji wenxue" 日記文學. *YDWJ*, 5:261–267.

———. "Shenme jiao shijimo wenxuesichao" 甚麼叫世紀末文學思潮. *YDWJ*, 6:287–289.

———. "Shidumu" 施篤姆. *YDWJ*, 5:107–116.

———. "Shisanye" 十三夜. *YDWJ*, 2:155–169.

———. "Shiyiyue chusan" 十一月初三. *YDWJ*, 1:338–353.

———. "Tugeniefu de *Luoting* wenshi yiqian" 屠格涅夫的《羅亭》問世以前. *YDWJ*, 6:176–185.

———. "Weibing" 胃病. *YDWJ*, 1:110–115.

———. "Wenxue gaishuo" 文學概說. *YDWJ*, 5:65–100.

———. "Wenxue shang de jiejidouzheng" 文學上的階級鬥爭. *YDWJ*, 5:134–140.

———. "Wuliu nian lai chuangzuo shenghuo de huigu" 五六年來創作生活的回顧. *YDWJ*, 7:176–181.

———. "Xiaoshuo lun" 小說論. *YDWJ*, 5:1–36.

———. "Yinhuise zhi si" 銀灰色之死. *YDWJ*, 1:1–15.

———. "Yishu yu guojia" 藝術與國家. *YDWJ*, 5:149–154.

———. *Yu Dafu wenji* 郁達夫文集, 12 vols. Hong Kong: Sanlian shudian, 1982–1985.

———. "Zai hanfeng li danxingben xu" 在《寒風裏》單行本序. *YDWJ*, 7:229–230.

———. "Zaping Manshu de zuopin" 雜評曼殊的作品. *YDWJ*, 5:255–260.

———. "Zhongguo xinwenxue daxi, sanwen erji daoyan" 《中國新文學大系·散文二集》導言. *YDWJ*, 6:256–278.

———. "Ziwokuang zhe Xudeerne" 自我狂者須的兒納. *YDWJ*, 5:141–148.

Yu Jiuhong 俞久洪. "Lin Shu fanyi zuopin kaosuo" 林紓翻譯作品考索. In Xue Suizhi 薛綏之, et al. (eds.), *Lin Shu yanjiu zhiliao* 林紓研究資料, pp. 403–427.

Yu Pingbo 俞平伯. "Ba *Huisema* yiben" 跋《灰色馬》譯本. *XSYB*, 14.10 (1923.10), pp. 1–8.

Yuan Liangjun 袁良駿, ed. *Dingling yanjiu zhiliao* 丁玲研究資料. Tianjin: Renmin chubanshe, 1982.

Yue Ying 岳煐, tr. *Gongnü Ma Delan* 工女馬德蘭 (*Les Mauvais Bergers* by Octave Mireau). Shanghai: Kaiming shudian, 1928.

Zemin 澤民. "Acaibaxifu yu Shaning" 阿采巴希甫與沙寧. *DFZZ*, 17.21 (1920.10), pp. 65–74.

Zeng Pu 曾樸. *Nie hai hua* 孽海花. Shanghai: Zhenshanmei shudian 真善美書店, 1947.

Zhang Jinglu 張靜廬. *Zhongguo chuban shiliao bubian* 中國出版史料補編. Beijing: Zhonghua shuju, 1957.

———. *Zhongguo jindai chuban shiliao* 中國近代出版史料, 2 vols. Beijing: Zhonghua shuju, 1957.

———. *Zhongguo xiandai chuban shiliao* 中國現代出版史料, 4 vols. Beijing: Zhonghua shuju, 1954–1959.

Zhang Mianyue 張眠月. "*Huanmie* de shidai miaoxie" 《幻滅》的時代描寫. In *Mao Dun pingzhuan*, pp. 69–79.

Zhang Yiping 章衣萍 (pseud. Yiping 衣萍). "Dongcheng jiulü" 東城舊侶. *YS*, 45 (1925.9), pp. 372–374.

———. "E yi *A Lian* zixu ji wode zixuzhuan lüe" 俄譯《亞蓮》自序及我的自敍傳略. *YS*, 4.1 (1928.4), pp. 123–134.

Zhang Yunhou 張允侯, *et al.*, eds: *Wusi shiqi shetuan* 五四時期社團. Beijing: Shenghuo, Dushu, Xinzhi Sanlian shudian 生活，讀書，新知，三聯書店, 1979.

Zhao Zhenkai 趙振開. *Bodong* 波動. Hong Kong: The Chinese University Press, 1985.

Zhdanov, A. A. "Soviet Literature—The Richest in Ideas, the Most Advanced Literature". In *Soviet Writers' Congress, 1934, The Debate of Socialist Realism and Modernism*, pp. 15–24. London: Lawrence and Wishart, 1977.

Zheng Zhenduo 鄭振鐸 (pseud. Xiti 西諦). "Azhibashuifu yu *Shaning*—*Shaning* de yiben xu" 阿志巴綏夫與《沙寧》——《沙寧》的譯本序. *XSYB*, 15.5 (1924.5), pp. 1–12.

———. "Daoyan" 導言. In *Zhongguo xinwenxue daxi, wenxue lunzhengji* 中國新文學大系·文學論爭集, pp. 1–22.

———. "Eguo wenxue fada de yuanyin ji jingxiang" 俄國文學發達的原因及影響. *Gaizao*, 3.4 (1920.12), pp. 83–94.

———. *Eguo wenxueshi lüe* 俄國文學史略. Shanghai: Shangwu yinshuguan, 1924.

———. "Guanyu Eguo wenxue yanjiu de zhongyao shuji jieshao" 關於俄國文學研究的重要書籍介紹. *XSYB*, 14.8 (1923.8), pp. 1–12.

———. "*Huisema* yizhe yinyan" 《灰色馬》譯者引言. *XSYB*, 13.7 (1922.7), pp. 1–5.

———. *Zheng Zhenduo wenji* 鄭振鐸文集, 3 vols. Beijing: Renmin wenxue chubanshe 1983.

———, ed. *Eguo duanpian xiaoshuo yicong* 俄國短篇小說譯叢. Shanghai, 1936.

———, tr. *Huisema* 灰色馬 (*The Pale Horse* by Ropshin). Shanghai: Shangwu yinshuguan, 1931 (3rd edition).

Zheng Zhenduo and Fu Donghua 傅東華, eds. *Wenxue baiti* 文學百題. Shanghai: Shenghuo shudian, 1934.

———, eds. *Wo yu wenxue* 我與文學. Shanghai: Shenghuo shudian, 1934.

Zhongguo xiandai wenxueshi cankao zhiliao 中國現代文學史參考資料, 4 vols. Beijing: Gaodeng jiaoyu chubanshe 高等教育出版社, 1959.

Zhongguo xiandai zuojia tan chuangzuo jingyan 中國現代作家談創作經驗, 2 vols. Jinan: Shandong Renmin chubanshe 山東人民出版社, 1980.

Zhongguo xinwenxue daxi 中國新文學大系, 10 vols. Shanghai: Liangyou tushu gongsi, 1935–1936.

Zhou Weiqun 周爲羣. "Qingniande yizhong fanmen" 青年的一種煩悶. *Yiban* 一般, 1.12 (1926.12), pp. 522–531.

Zhou Xiao 鄒嘯, ed. *Yu Dafu lun* 郁達夫論. Shanghai: Beixin shudian, 1933.

Zhou Yang 周揚. "Jianshe shehuizhuyi wenxue de renwu" 建設社會主義文學的任務. In *ZWCZ*, 3:143–183.

———. "Shehuizhuyi xianshizhuyi—Zhongguo wenxue qianjin de daolu" 社會主義現實主義——中國文學前進的道路. In *ZWCZ*, 3:203–210.

———. *Woguo shehuizhuyi wenxue yishu de daolu* 我國社會主義文學藝術的道路. Beijing: Renmin chubanshe, 1960.

———, et al. *Wenyi zhanxianshang de yichang dabianlun* 文藝戰綫上的一場大辯論. Beijing: Zuojia chubanshe, 1958.

Zhou Zhenfu 周振甫, ed. *Yan Fu shiwen xuan* 嚴復詩文選. Beijing: Renmin wenxue chubanshe, 1959.

Zhou Zuoren 周作人. "Chen lun" 沉淪. *Chen Bao fujuan* 晨報副鐫, 1922.3.16.

———. "Guanyu Lu Xun zhier" 關於魯迅之二. *Yuzhou feng*, 30 (1936.12), pp. 303–307.

———. *Lu Xun xiaoshuo li de renwu* 魯迅小說裏的人物. Shanghai: Shanghai chuban gongsi, 1954. Pseud. Zhou Xiashou 周遐壽.

———. *Lun Lu Xun de qingnian shidai* 論魯迅的青年時代. Beijing: Zhongguo qingnian chubanshe, 1957. Pseud. Zhou Qiming 周啓明.

———. "Sixiang geming" 思想革命. In *ZXD*, 1:226–227.

———. "Wenxue shang de Eguo yu Zhongguo" 文學上的俄國與中國. *XQN*, 8.5 (1921.1), pp. 1–7.

———. "Xincun de jingshen" 新村的精神. *XQN*, 7.2 (1920.2), pp. 129–139.

———. *Yishu yu shenghuo* 藝術與生活. Beijing: Zhonghua shuju, 1926.

———. *Zhitang huixianglu* 知堂回想錄, 2 vols. Hong Kong: Sanyu tushu wenju gongsi, 1971.

———. *Zhongguo xinwenxue de yuanliu* 中國新文學的源流. Beiping: Renmin shudian 人民書店, 1932.

———, tr. "Chitong" 齒痛 ("Ben Tobit" by Andreyev). *XQN*, 7.1 (1919.12), pp. 65–73.

———, tr. "Majiaer de meng" 馬加爾的夢 ("Magi's Dream" by Korolenko). *XQN*, 8.2 (1920.10), pp. 1–30.

Zhu Keyu 竹可羽. "Lun *Taiyang zhao zai Sanggan he shang*" 論《太陽照在桑乾河上》. In Yuan Liangjun (ed.), *Ding Ling yanjiu zhiliao*, pp. 361–398.

Zhu Xizu 朱希祖, tr. "Wenyi de jinhua" 文藝的進化 (by Kuriyagawa Hakuson). *XQN*, 6.6 (1919.11), pp. 581–584.

Zuolian huiyilu 左聯回憶錄, 2 vols. Beijing: Zhongguo shehui kexue chubanshe 中國社會科學出版社, 1982.

Index